KT-167-636

Scots
cooking

Also by Sue Lawrence

Entertaining at Home in Scotland
Cooking for Pleasure
Food with Flair
Feasting on Herbs
On Baking
The Sunday Times Cookbook
On Salads

Scots
cooking

The best traditional
and contemporary
Scottish recipes

SUE LAWRENCE

In memory of my dear friend Fiona

Copyright © 2000 Sue Lawrence

The right of Sue Lawrence to be identified
as the Author of this Work has been
asserted by her in accordance with the
Copyright, Designs and Patents Act 1988.

First published in 2000
by HEADLINE BOOK PUBLISHING

10 9 8 7 6 5 4 3 2 1

All rights reserved. No part of this
publication may be reproduced, stored in a
retrieval system, or transmitted, in any
form or by any means without the prior
written permission of the publisher, nor be
otherwise circulated in any form of binding
or cover other than that in which it is
published and without a similar condition
being imposed on the subsequent
purchaser.

British Library Cataloguing in
Publication Data

Lawrence, Sue, 1955–
    Scots cooking
    1. Cookery, Scottish
    I. Title
    641.5'9411

ISBN 0 7472 7125 9

Edited by Jane Middleton
Art directed by Ellen Wheeler
Designed by Town
Photography by Marie-Louise Avery
Food styling by Jacqueline Clarke

Printed and bound in Italy by
Canale and C.S.p.A

HEADLINE BOOK PUBLISHING
A division of the Hodder Headline Group
338 Euston Road
London NW1 3BH

www.headline.co.uk
www.hodderheadline.com

Acknowledgements

I should like to thank my parents for delving into the past to recall what they ate some 60 or 70 years ago. Also, my sister Carol for her invaluable help researching Arbroath recipes; and my dear aunts, Muriel and Bette, for remembrance of things past – and for my grandmother's recipe book.

As ever, I am eternally grateful to my family's tastebuds: thank you, Pat, Euan, Faith and Jessica for being (occasionally unwilling!) guinea pigs.

Special thanks to Catherine Brown for the inspiration I have received from her splendid books. And to Clarissa Dickson Wright and Joanna Blythman for their unfailing support, encouragement and friendship.

And to the following people for helping to make it happen

Kenny Adamson, baker, Pittenweem

Robin Adamson, University of Dundee

Catherine and Roddy Aflin, Stornoway, Isle of Lewis

Gavin Borthwick and Christine McFarlane at
    George Armstrong, fishmonger, Edinburgh

Lady Buccleuch, Drumlanrig Castle

Clark Brothers, fishmongers, Musselburgh

Joan Bunting, Gosforth, Newcastle

Herbert Cox, The Seafield Hotel, Cullen

David Craig, Robertson's Butcher, Broughty Ferry

Guy Craig, Udny Arms, Aberdeenshire

Audrey Dyer and Alec Smith at George Bower,
    Butcher, Edinburgh

David Goodfellow, Goodfellow & Steven, Dundee
    and Broughty Ferry

Alison and Ian Gray, Edinburgh

Sue and Frank Hadden, Edinburgh

Simon Hopkinson, London

Margaret Horn, The But 'n' Ben, Auchmithie

Caroline Keith, Scottish Tourist Board

Anthony Laing, Shortbread House of Edinburgh

Fred and Moira MacAulay, Perth

Dods Macfarlane, Isle of Lewis

Aggie MacKenzie, Rothiemurchus

Mackie family, Mackie's Ice-cream, Aberdeenshire

Iain Macleod, butcher, Stornoway, Isle of Lewis

Rhoda Macleod, Isle of Harris

Jo, Kate and John Macsween, Edinburgh

Arthur McDonald, of the Crofting Township
    Development Scheme

Angela McKenzie, pastry chef, Peebles Hydro

Alan McPherson, The Seafield Bakery, Cullen

Effie Morrison, Isle of Harris

Grace Mulligan, North Humberside

Ramsay of Carluke, Lanarkshire

Tom Rodger, Aberfeldy Water Mill

Rosemary Shrager, Amhuinnsuidhe, Isle of Harris

Alec Smith, Arbroath

Hamish Taylor, Isle of Harris

Carol and Jim Tollerton, Arbroath

Beverley Tricker, Aberdeen and Grampian Tourist Board

Georgia Wishart, Shetland

Martin Wishart, Restaurant Martin Wishart,
    Edinburgh

Linda Wood, Tarbert

John Young, Breadalbane Bakery, Aberfeldy

Contents

Introduction

'We don't always eat chips. Sometimes we leave them overnight and eat them cold next day – and that's what in Scotland we call a salad.'

This riposte on Radio 4's 'News Quiz' by Scottish comedian Fred MacAulay certainly made everyone laugh. But, sad to say, there is more than a hint of truth in it. The words 'healthy diet' and 'Scotland' have not often been uttered in the same breath. And with one of the worst records for heart disease in the world, it was not before time when health boards recently began to look critically at Scotland's diet. And what a lot of chips they found.

But it was not always thus. Chips only came to Scotland at the turn of the century. Indeed, many of the traditional dishes that have been saved from extinction are exceedingly healthy, provided they are not supplemented by commercial cakes or pappy white bread. And provided everything is not deep-fried in batter.

Consider the mainstays of the Scots diet over the centuries: oatcakes, porridge, Scotch broth and herring. Oats are one of those super-healthy foods that we are advised to eat more of because of their good soluble fibre, iron, zinc and vitamins. Broths bulging with barley and vegetables retain many health-giving minerals and vitamins, instead of being boiled away to nothing or, worse, tipped down the sink in the vegetable-boiling water. And herring and other oily fish such as salmon are well known for their health-giving properties because of their omega-3 fatty acids, which can help prevent both cancer and heart disease.

If, therefore, we went 'back to basics' instead of embracing every new processed or takeaway food on offer, we would be an exceedingly healthy nation indeed. And since there are those in Scotland who wish to 'rise and be a nation again', why not start by returning to the old – and undoubtedly healthier – diet?

As I looked through old books while researching recipes, I was interested – and, I must say, surprised – by the variety of foods on offer throughout the centuries. Sadly, much of this variety was confined to the big houses, to the aristocratic and grand families who could afford servants to bleed their hares and pluck their pheasants. Theirs was a diet that included copious breakfasts of porridge, oat or barley bannocks, conserves and cured fish. Lunch ('dinner') was soup, such as barley broth, partan bree or cock-a-leekie, followed by some sort of meat or fowl, boiled or roasted or served in a pie. Until Victorian times, when *service à la russe* (individual courses) became popular, puddings and sweets were served with the second course, beside the roasts. So you might have a lemon 'hatted-kit' (junket) or 'sillie bub' served at the same time as the roast kid or hare ragout. Supper was similar, with perhaps some lighter dishes such as eggs or fish.

But for poorer people, the diet was less diverse. And although it was plain, possibly mundane, there was nothing wrong with it, for it was honest, simple fare that sustained men and women for centuries, whatever their lot. My parents ate mince and tatties several times a week during their childhood, with little except broth and porridge at other meals. But they did not complain, for it was good and wholesome. Nothing fancy. Fancy food, such as cloutie dumpling or black bun, was for special occasions like birthdays and Hogmanay.

In previous centuries, breakfast for the average unprivileged person would have been porridge or brose, followed by broth for dinner (fish based if they were near the sea) and an evening meal of root vegetables such as turnips or potatoes and kail with oatcakes or bannocks – with milk if they had cattle. In less fertile areas and in times of shortage, the proportion of dairy food would have been higher. Martin Martin, writing in 1703 in *A Description of the Western Islands of Scotland*, tells of the people of Skye's 'ordinary diet': there was butter, milk, cheese, potatoes and brochan (oatmeal boiled with water). For poor Highlanders and Lowlanders, meat was a luxury that was seldom enjoyed, except at special festivities. Or, if there were 'casualties' among the herds of cows, sheep or goats, people would use the entire animal to make black puddings, white puddings, sheep's head broth, goat hams and pickled mutton, which would last for months. Shetland's famous reestit (reested) mutton is still very much in demand before Christmas, the traditional time for killing and preserving the beasts.

Those poorer people who lived near the sea would eat shellfish that we now think of as a luxury. Oysters, crabs and lobsters were everyday fare. Salmon was so plentiful that farm workers used to stipulate that they did not want to eat it more than twice a week. There is a lovely tale of a Highland gentleman visiting London in the early 1800s and ordering beef steak for himself and salmon for his servant, since in Scotland the fish was so cheap. He was surprised to discover that his own meal cost mere pence and his servant's several shillings. Seaweed was also used – and indeed still is by people living beside the sea – in soups and stews. One such person is Margaret Horn from Auchmithie, who was brought up on plain fare such as grilled dulse, Scotch broth and boiled lobster before the latter became a luxury.

In all the references to Scots meals and food throughout literature, whether it is the critical Samuel Johnson commenting on the pre-breakfast dram in 1773, the more cheerful Dorothy Wordsworth writing in 1803 about oat bread and blue-milk cheese for breakfast, or Tom Steel describing the St Kildans' pre-evacuation life in 1930 with their fulmar brose and puffin-flavoured porridge, there is one overriding sentiment noted by all visitors, and that is hospitality. For however we may enjoy the 'You'll have had your tea' jokes, there is little doubt that Scots are renowned for their hospitality. Whether with a dram and a piece of 'shortie' or a cup of tea and a scone, visitors are always welcomed to the home. Offering food and drink plays an integral part.

While this warmth and conviviality have – hopefully – not altered over the centuries, our eating habits have. Perhaps instead of resorting to pre-packed processed meals laden with preservatives and

unnecessary additives we could return to the honest ingredients raised and grown on our soil and treat them with the respect they were accorded in days of dire poverty. Then perhaps we would realise that true Scots cooking is good. It is simple and healthy, unintimidating and unpretentious, accessible to everyone, rich and poor. Even non-Scots can understand the sentiment, if not all the words, in this verse from Burns' famous poem about egalitarianism, 'A Man's a Man for a' That', written in 1795, shortly after the French Revolution (with which Burns sympathised):

'What though on hamely fare we dine
Wear hoddin grey and a' that
Gie fools their silks and knaves their wine
A Man's a Man for a' that.'

There has never been anything wrong with homely fare. Let us revisit our roots, return to natural ingredients, eschew unhealthy processed foods and remember that Scots cooking means simple, honest – and, most importantly – good food.

Sue Lawrence

breakfast and preserves

'Not long after the dram, may be expected the breakfast, a meal in which the Scots, whether of the Lowlands or mountains, must be confessed to excel us. The tea and coffee are accompanied not only with butter, but with honey, conserves and marmalades. If an epicure could remove by a wish, in quest of sensual gratifications, wherever he had supped he would breakfast in Scotland.'

Thus spake Dr Samuel Johnson during his voyage around Scotland with James Boswell in 1773. Praise indeed from a man who disparaged much of the country's diet throughout the tour, particularly the Scots' staple, oats. But apart from the tea, coffee, honey, conserves and porridge, let us not forget the black pudding, Lorne sausage, Ayrshire bacon and eggs. Or ham 'n' haddie, hot-buttered Arbroath smokie or grilled finnan haddock – with barley or oat bannocks, oatcakes, butteries and baps on the side.

I have to agree with Dr Johnson about Scotland being the perfect place for breakfast, provided it is proper porridge (made slowly with salt and water, never milk) and local ingredients judiciously cooked to provide that essential first meal of the day, which we now know should be wholesome, sustaining and hearty. I also find myself concurring with his opinion about an old-fashioned dish offered to him in the Hebrides. James Boswell tells the lady of the house he does not think the Doctor will accept sheep's head for breakfast, but she offers it anyway:

'"Do you choose any cold sheep's-head, sir?"

"No, madam," said he with a tone of surprise and anger.

"It is here, sir," said she, supposing he had refused it to save the trouble of bringing it in.

They thus went on at cross purposes, till he confirmed his refusal in a manner not to be misunderstood; while I sat quietly by and enjoyed my success.'

I wonder what he would have thought about the rice crispies and soggy white toast on offer in many establishments providing so-called Scottish breakfasts today. I think even he might opt for sheep's head instead.

Breakfast Pancakes

My cousin Frank is hardly ever in the kitchen, so busy is his working day. But Sunday morning is sacred, for this is when he cooks the family pancakes for breakfast. He follows a tight routine, which alters little from one week to the next. First he gets up half an hour before everyone else and begins to prepare the batter. Once the first pancake is cooking, it is time to separate the Sunday papers into 'reading' and 'bin'. Then, once the rest of the family has been called – and Frank's younger son, Scott, has devoured at least six pancakes – Frank allows himself the last two, with melted butter, golden syrup, lime juice and brown sugar. The only other essential accompaniment is the sports supplement of the paper. The rest has in all probability landed in the bin.

Makes 12–15
300g/10½oz flour (either plain or self-raising; use whatever you have to hand)
2 large free-range eggs, beaten
500ml/18fl oz semi-skimmed milk
a pinch of salt
1 tablespoon melted butter, plus extra to serve
golden syrup, lime juice and soft brown sugar, to serve

Sift the flour into a bowl and mix in the eggs with a fork. Add the milk and, using a hand-held electric mixer, beat until the batter is smooth. Add the salt and a third of the melted butter, folding them in to combine.

Heat a pancake pan (a regular 20cm/8in crêpe pan) and lightly smear the base with some of the remaining melted butter, using a wad of kitchen paper. Leave to heat up for a couple of minutes, then pour in a small ladleful – or 1½ tablespoons – of the batter and swirl it around the base. Cook over a medium heat for about 40 seconds, until it no longer looks raw, then flip it over. (Frank tosses each pancake ceilingwards unless he has a hangover.) Cook the other side, which should take no more than 30 seconds. (It is time to begin sorting out the Sunday papers.)

Remove the pancake, smear the pan lightly with more butter and cook the remaining pancakes. Depending on the reliability of the pan, you might not need to smear it every time. The pancakes can be piled up on a plate to keep warm while you make the rest. Serve with melted butter, golden syrup, lime juice and soft brown sugar.

Porridge

'Halesome parritch, chief o' Scotia's food,' wrote Burns, Scotland's great bard. And surely Burns, with his keen sense of irony, would have found it exceedingly amusing to discover that, over 200 years later, Scotland's humblest dish was the height of fashion. London's latest eating places cannot make enough porridge to satisfy their eager customers. The white chocolate, banana and cinnamon toppings might have offended the purist in him but he was, after all, known for his liberal views.

Ever since polenta – north Italy's peasant maize porridge – became hugely fashionable during the 1990s, our own oatmeal porridge has been long overdue for a comeback. Not that it ever went away for most Scots. When I was a child, porridge was cooked for breakfast every single day, summer and winter. My sister and I took our porridge in the Sassenach way, with brown sugar and top of the milk drizzled over it – or rather, the milk was poured around the sides, moat-like. But when my parents were children, they ate it in the traditional Scottish way: hot porridge was ladled into bowls (usually wooden) and a smaller bowl containing milk placed alongside. Then, with your spoon (usually horn), you took a spoonful of porridge, dipped it into the milk bowl and ate it. This meant the porridge stayed hot and the milk cold longer. It was only embellished with salt, never sugar. Porridge was, interestingly, always referred to as 'they' – and 'they' were traditionally eaten standing up, never seated.

F. Marian McNeill's recipe for porridge is one that many people still use. Instead of soaking the oatmeal overnight and cooking it the next day, she recommended that it should be slowly released through the fingers of a clenched fist while stirring madly with the spurtle (also called a theevil) – the long wooden stick used specifically for porridge. Polenta is, of course, made in the same way and the *bastone* – polenta-stirrer – is also a long wooden stick.

And just as polenta is cooked, cooled then fried or grilled, so is porridge: porridge would be ladled into the drawer of a kitchen dresser (called a kist in the north-east of Scotland) and left to cool. Once solid, it was cut and taken into the hills as sustenance for a hard day's work. In the evening, slices (called calders) were cut off to be fried and served with eggs or fish.

But it is at breakfast that porridge has always been the star attraction, whether you adhere rigidly to the salt-only dogma or top with brown sugar and cream. It is recorded that on the now uninhabited island of St Kilda, 'breakfast normally consisted of porridge and milk, with a puffin boiled in with the oats to give flavour'. Each to their own.

To Dr Samuel Johnson's remark that oats were a 'grain, which in England is generally given to horses but in Scotland supports the people' came the marvellous riposte by a Scot, Lord Elibank: 'And where will you get such men and such horses?' A bowl of porridge is indeed the most healthy and delicious breakfast possible. Enjoy them!

Traditionally oatmeal is used for porridge. If you are using rolled or porridge oats (which have far less flavour than oatmeal as they are already steamed or part-cooked), you will need 1 cup of oats to about 2½ cups of water and you can reduce the cooking time below to 3–4 minutes. Medium oatmeal is the most commonly used but I prefer coarse. Pinhead makes a nice change, with its pronounced nubbly texture.

Serves 3–4

1 cup of medium, coarse or pinhead oatmeal
about 3 cups of cold water
a good pinch of salt

Put the oatmeal in a pan with the water and leave to soak overnight. Next day, add the salt and bring slowly to the boil. Stirring frequently – preferably with a spurtle – cook for about 10 minutes (about 15 minutes for pinhead oatmeal) over a medium to low heat, until thick and creamy. Serve at once.

Brose

Brose is an acquired taste. Having been brought up on porridge, I found it difficult to enjoy brose at first, especially since butter is added with the salt, but then I remembered that butter was stirred into the oat, barley and rice porridges I enjoyed in Finland during the year I spent there. The addition of butter seemed to make the oatmeal even smoother. If you don't like the butter, just dip spoonfuls of the brose into milk or cream, or even douse it with sugar, syrup or treacle if you prefer. But do not do this anywhere near a 'brosie' person, which is old Scots dialect for 'fed with brose'.

One such person is Ian Gray, an Aberdonian now living in Edinburgh, who has eaten brose almost every day of his life. He likes the texture to be smooth, although some prefer it 'knotty' – with lumps, the insides of which should contain raw oatmeal. Ian's father, from Buchan, not only likes knotty brose, he also adds pepper to his morning bowlful. And Evelyn Stevens from Caithness recommends brose for poor stomachs. As a child, as well as her daily oatmeal brose she also had peasemeal brose, made of milled roasted dried peas, which is typical in certain areas, particularly the north-east.

Flavourings such as honey, sugar or dried fruit can be added to brose. But the St Kildan habit of pouring the stock from a boiled fulmar over oatmeal to make a simple breakfast brose is unique; the St Kildans believed it to be good for the stomach. There is a Hebridean recipe for brose made with cream, not water, in which the cream is mixed directly with the dry oatmeal. Boiling beef stock or buttermilk is also sometimes used instead of boiling water.

Brochan, a thin oatmeal gruel, is taken instead of brose in certain areas. And sowens, another type of brose or porridge, is an alternative. It is made by soaking the mealy husks of the ground oats in a tub of water for several days until they begin to ferment, then this is sieved and boiled with water and salt to produce a thin porridge similar in texture to brochan. According to F. Marian McNeill, sowens cooked with butter was a traditional Hallowe'en dish; a ring was placed in it and whoever got the ring would be the first to marry.

She also describes in detail the method of making brose: 'Put into a bowl two handfuls of oatmeal. Add salt and a piece of butter. Pour in boiling water to cover the oatmeal and stir it up roughly with the shank of a horn spoon, allowing it to form knots. Sup with soor dook [buttermilk] or sweet milk, and you have a dish that has been the backbone of many a sturdy Scotsman.'

It was, however, only certain sturdy Scotsmen and women who would take brose in the mornings – primarily single men living in bothies (rough huts used as living accommodation for unmarried farm workers) and also cottars who lived in the farmer's tied cottages. Since they were often paid in kind with farm produce such as oatmeal, it made sense to cook and eat it. The staple diet of these farm workers would have been primarily milk, tatties and meal, with brose eaten at least twice a day. It was surely one of the earliest forms of fast food. And because the oatmeal was uncooked, it did not swell as much as porridge, so a person was capable of consuming an inordinate amount in one dish – anything up to 350g/12oz, which would have made 8–10 bowls of porridge! It is little wonder that traditionally men stood to eat breakfast; sitting down might have proved painful. Nowadays it is only in certain north-eastern and Hebridean areas and parts of Fife that the brose habit persists, unlike porridge which is popular throughout Scotland.

Serves 1
2 tablespoons medium oatmeal
a pinch of salt
a small knob of butter

Warm a bowl slightly (I place it in a low oven for 10 minutes or so as I pad about the kitchen, coming to in the morning with the first of many mugs of tea). Place the oatmeal in the bowl with the salt and butter. Pour over enough boiling water to form a fairly stiff, yet soft consistency – anything from 7–10 tablespoons. Stir well, then continue stirring until smooth. Eat dipped into milk.

Lorne Sausage and Egg

Lorne sausage is a square sausage made of beef. Although there can be some decidedly grim offerings that are far too greasy, a well-made Lorne sausage is sublime. David Craig of Robertson's Butcher's in Broughty Ferry prepares his with a minimum of 75 per cent beef. It makes a wonderfully satisfying breakfast – especially if you do as many Scots do and cram the sausage into a soft morning roll, with or without an egg. You are unlikely to encounter this joyful gastronomic treat in luxury hotel dining rooms but go on any of the Caledonian Macbrain ferries (Calmac to the passengers) to the islands and this – preceded by a mighty bowl of porridge – will greet you on the morning runs. Come rain, hail or shine.

Serves 1
2 slices of Lorne sausage (if you slice it yourself, cut it fairly thickly)
1 large free-range egg

Heat a reliable heavy frying pan until very hot, then add the Lorne sausage (without fat) and fry for 2–3 minutes before checking to see if a good crust has formed underneath. If so, turn over and continue to fry for 2–3 minutes, until cooked through. Meanwhile, fry the egg in the fat that has come out of the sausage. If you feel you need more fat, add a drop or two of oil.

To serve, eat as it is or place the sausage and egg in a large morning roll (lightly buttered) and devour with a mug of tea all by yourself, so that no one need comment on the juices and egg yolk dripping down your chin.

Black Pudding with Ayrshire Bacon

There are many variations on black pudding throughout Scotland but only one traditional Ayrshire bacon. Like Wiltshire bacon, it is brine-cured, but whereas Wiltshire bacon sides are cured with the rind on and bones in, the Ayrshire sides have the rind off and bones out. Ayrshire bacon became a by-product of dairy farming (the whey being fed to pigs) many centuries ago. Ramsay of Carluke is probably the only butcher's that cures its meat by hand in the traditional way from start to finish. The pigs are skinned, then boned, trimmed, cured, matured, rolled and either smoked or left green. The typical breakfast cut is Ayrshire middle, which Andrew Ramsay calls frying bacon. The fat on his bacon is firm and white and the flesh bright; the taste is good old-fashioned real food.

As for the black pudding, every butcher seems to have a different recipe. I am particularly fond of one from the Isle of Lewis. Iain Macleod of Charles Macleod's Butchers (known locally as Charley Barley's) in Stornoway sells a wonderful pudding made primarily of sheep's blood and oatmeal. It has a lovely crumbly, moist texture and a true, mutton-like flavour. He has never divulged the exact recipe to me but it is similar to those puddings still made at home in the Hebrides. Lewis-born Rhoda Macleod let me into the secret of her recipe for *marag dubh* (Gaelic for black pudding) which is simply 2 cups of oatmeal, 1 of flour, 2 of suet, 2 of onions and enough sheep's blood to give a dropping consistency.

At John Henderson's butcher's in Kircaldy, black pudding is made from lamb's blood, pork fat, cloves and nutmeg. He describes this as Scottish black pudding, as it has finely shredded pork fat throughout, instead of the larger chunks of fat typical of most English puddings and French *boudins*.

Serve this wonderfully simple breakfast dish with a fried egg, grilled tomatoes and plenty of hot buttered toast.

Serves 2
6 slices of Ayrshire middle bacon
4 thick slices of black pudding

Cook the bacon for 2–3 minutes in a hot frying pan (without extra fat), then turn it over and push to one side. You should now have enough bacon fat in the pan to fry your black pudding. If not, add a tiny knob of butter. Add the black pudding slices and cook for 4–5 minutes (depending on thickness), turning once, or until crisp on each side and cooked through. Serve at once on warm plates.

Butteries

It was half-past midnight as I strolled down the road to The Seafield Bakery in Cullen. It was still almost light – midsummer night – and there was a chill wind blowing in from the sea; this was the north coast of Aberdeenshire, after all. I had come to see butteries, also known as Aberdeen rowies, being made in the traditional way in a small bakery and it would surely be worth losing several hours' precious sleep.

Once he began his night's work, Alan McPherson reminded me of a juggler trying to keep all his balls in the air. After mixing a 'softie' dough, a brown bread dough, an oatmeal one and a pan bread, he finally began the butterie dough. The first stage had been prepared earlier – mixing some soft flour with white fat and lard. Despite the name, butter is never used because it makes them hard; they are called butteries because they are always eaten buttered. The bread dough was then mixed and kneaded with a large bread hook in one of the four mixers Alan was running around checking, filling and emptying. Then the dough was left to rest for half an hour before being folded neatly into a rectangle on the huge kneading table. By this stage there were five other doughs resting, all neatly tucked up and looking agonisingly like pillows. I, too, wanted to rest.

But I'd come to see the butterie from start to finish, so it was on to the next stage – folding and chopping the fat mixture into the bread dough. Then the mixture was cut into large rounds and each round into 30 pieces. Each of these was squashed into the classic butterie shape by hand on a baking sheet and left to rest again in a steam press or prover. It was now 2.30am, but once the rolls were baked in Alan's ancient Scotch oven (built between 1800 and 1830) I had to admit it had been worth staying up and being covered in fine clouds of flour for a taste of a warm butterie straight from the oven. Why eat croissants when you can have butteries?

Makes 16
450g/1lb strong white flour
20g/¾oz fresh yeast
20g/¾oz granulated sugar
about 300ml/10fl oz tepid water

For the fat dough:
250g/9oz white shortening
75g/3oz lard
20g/¾oz salt
50g/2oz plain flour

First prepare the fat dough by mixing all the ingredients together. Leave at room temperature so it is soft enough to work with.

Next make the bread dough. Place the flour in a bowl and make a well in the centre. Mix the yeast and sugar together, then mix into the water. Combine with the flour and knead by hand or with a dough hook until smooth; this will take about 10 minutes by hand. Place in a bowl, cover and leave for 30–45 minutes, until well risen. Then knock back the dough and roll it out into a long rectangle on a floured work surface.

Divide the fat dough into three and spread a third of it over the bread dough. Fold down the top third of the rectangle, then fold over again. Roll out to a rectangle once more and spread over another portion of fat dough. Fold and roll as before. Repeat this once more to use up the remaining fat dough. Then fold over. (Instead of rolling out the dough, Alan 'chops' the fat dough into it using a Scotch scraper, like a large spatula.) The dough should be slightly sticky and rough. Keep flouring your hands and the worksurface.

Cut the dough into 16 pieces and place these on a baking sheet. Shape them by pressing the front part of your floured hand – fingers only – on to each, so they are flattened and dimpled with fingerprints with one stroke. Then cover with a sheet of oiled clingfilm and leave to prove somewhere warm for 30 minutes. Preheat the oven to 220°C/425°F/Gas 7.

Bake the butteries for 25–30 minutes, until crisp and golden. Transfer to a wire rack to cool.

Ham and Haddie

Ham means bacon in Scotland and so this most comforting of breakfast dishes is quite simply smoked haddock (haddie) and bacon. It is traditionally made from finnan haddock (whole haddock with the head removed and the bone left in, then split – so the bone lies to one side – brined and cold-smoked), which is named after the village of Findon, south of Aberdeen, where the cure was perfected. For the ham, I suggest using dry-cure bacon but Parma ham is also excellent: grill or fry it for only a minute or two, until crisp.

This makes a delicious breakfast dish but is also good for tea. If you are serving it at teatime, a welcome addition is a little chopped parsley or lovage stirred into the cream sauce at the last minute.

Serves 1

1 finnan haddock
100ml/3½fl oz full-fat milk
40g/1½oz butter
2–3 rashers of dry-cure back bacon
2 tablespoons double cream

Place the finnan haddock in a saucepan with the milk and half the butter. Bring slowly to the boil, then cover and cook gently for 3–4 minutes until just done. Using 1 large or 2 medium spatulas, carefully transfer the fish to a serving plate and keep warm. Reserve the liquor in the pan.

Dry-fry or grill the bacon until crisp. Meanwhile, melt the remaining butter in another pan, stir in the cream and 2 tablespoons of the poaching liquid and let it bubble away for a minute or two until slightly thickened. Taste and add salt and pepper if necessary.

To serve, pour the sauce over the fish and top with the bacon. (A poached egg on top makes this wonderful breakfast dish sublime.)

Oatcakes

Although oatcakes are traditionally made on a girdle, I have given the oven method first, since most cooks are more familiar with baking trays than girdles. The classic way to make them is to cook one side on the girdle, then toast them on a special toasting stone in front of the fire. They are not turned over on the girdle to finish the cooking since this would make them tough. Once cool, the oatcakes are traditionally stored in a girnel (oatmeal chest) to keep them crisp. I bury mine in the large Tupperware box I keep porridge oats in.

The finished texture of the oatcakes will depend on the type of oatmeal you use: I like a base of medium oatmeal with either pinhead or fine added for a rough or smooth texture respectively. There are also regional variations on the thickness of the oatcake, from thin and crisp to thick and rough.

Oatcakes have long been part of the Scots' staple diet, with references to Scottish soldiers packing in their bag some oatmeal and a broad metal plate on which to cook oatcakes. It is recorded that Bonnie Prince Charlie's patriotic Highland soldiers set up roadside stalls to provide fresh oatmeal bannocks. The word bannock is interchangeable with oatcake in the west of Scotland, whereas in the east and north-east a bannock contains a proportion of wheat flour with the oatmeal to soften it. My recipe here is for crisp, not soft cakes.

Traditionally eaten for breakfast, oatcakes were also used to make sandwiches ('pieces') instead of bread. I can highly recommend them buttered, topped with a mature farmhouse Cheddar such as Isle of Mull or a blue cheese such as Lanark Blue or Dunsyre Blue, and sandwiched with another oatcake on top. This is messy but memorable picnic food.

Makes 8
175g/6oz medium oatmeal
50g/2oz fine or pinhead oatmeal
½ teaspoon salt
¼ teaspoon baking powder
25g/1oz butter, melted
about 50–75ml/2–3fl oz boiling water

Preheat the oven to 170°C/325°F/Gas 3. Place all the dry ingredients in a bowl and stir. Pour in the melted butter and enough boiling water to form a fairly stiff dough.

Sprinkle some fine or medium oatmeal over a board and gently roll out the mixture into a thin circle, about 23–25.5cm/9–10in diameter. Cut into 8 wedges and transfer carefully to a buttered baking tray. Bake in the oven for about 20 minutes, until just firm. Carefully transfer to a wire rack to cool.

Girdle method

Bake the oatcakes, 4 at a time, on a lightly buttered girdle over a moderate heat for 4–5 minutes on one side only. Once they are light brown underneath, transfer to a wire rack. Place this on a baking tray and set in a low oven (140°C/275°F/Gas 1) for about 25 minutes or until they have completely dried out. Leave to cool.

Barley Bannocks

There are many types of barley bannock but this recipe is from Shetland, where beremeal (barley flour) gruel or porridge is also eaten. These thick, hearty bannocks would be just the thing to warm you up – with a cup of tea or bowl of broth – before battling out against the bracing Shetland wind. The treacle is an optional extra but I like the rich colour and deep, sweet flavour it imparts.

As a general rule, a bannock is thicker and softer than an oatcake. Samuel Johnson wrote in his 1773 journal: 'Their native bread is made of oats or barley. Of oatmeal they spread very thin cakes, coarse and hard ... their barley cakes are thicker and softer: I began to eat them without unwillingness, the blackness of their colour raises some dislike but the taste is not disagreeable.'

Some bannocks, however, are as thin and pliable as chapatis, and indeed those I have seen in the Hebrides and Orkney (not Shetland) are thinnish and smaller – about 15cm/6in diameter. They are spread with butter then rolled up before being eaten.

Makes 4 thick bannocks
150g/5oz plain flour, sifted
200g/7oz barley flour (beremeal)
25g/1oz butter
1 dessertspoon black treacle
1 level teaspoon bicarbonate of soda
1½ teaspoons cream of tartar
250ml/9fl oz buttermilk or sour milk
(to sour milk, add 1 teaspoon lemon juice and leave for 5 minutes)

Mix the flours together in a bowl and make a well in the centre. Melt the butter and treacle together and pour them into the well. Add the bicarbonate of soda and cream of tartar to the milk, stir well, then tip into the bowl. Combine everything gently but thoroughly. Using floured hands, turn out on to a lightly floured board and knead very gently to a thick round, about 25.5cm/10in diameter. Cut into quarters.

Heat a girdle over a medium heat, then grease very lightly, using a wad of kitchen paper. The heat should not be too high or the bannocks will burn before the insides are cooked. Place the bannocks on the girdle and leave for 4–5 minutes, until lightly coloured underneath, then turn. Leave for another 6–7 minutes, until cooked through. If necessary, tear the end off one to check that it is done inside. Transfer to a wire rack, then eat warm, split and spread with butter.

Baps

When I was a child, breakfast in bed, should I be so lucky, was a fried egg tucked neatly inside a soft, floury bap. This was impractical to eat in bed, as the minute you bit into it the yolk dripped down your chin and most probably on to the sheets. It was, however, sheer bliss.

Baps – or morning rolls as they are often called – are perfect for breakfast since they are soft, floury and unchallenging as the first food of the day. In Aberdeenshire they are called softies if they have no flour on them and floury baps if they do. Just as we picture every French household sending someone to fetch the morning baguette, so the Scottish family used to send a minion (usually the youngest member) to the baker's for morning rolls before breakfast on certain days – not every day, as porridge and toast were daily staples. Now most families have morning rolls on a Sunday, bought from the local newsagent with the Sunday papers. Split and spread with butter they are then eaten with bacon, egg, sausage or, my favourite, black pudding and tomato.

If you want to eat these freshly baked for breakfast, leave the dough in the fridge overnight for the first rising, then knock it back the next morning and continue with the recipe.

Makes 12
600g/1¼lb strong white flour,
plus extra for dusting
1 heaped teaspoon salt
7g packet of easy-blend/fast-action
dried yeast
25g/1oz butter, diced
about 350ml/12fl oz warm (hand-hot)
milk and water, mixed,
plus extra milk for brushing

Sift the flour and salt into a bowl and stir in the yeast. Rub in the butter, then make a well in the centre. Gradually pour in enough of the warm liquid to form a stiffish dough, bringing it together with lightly floured hands. Turn this out on to a lightly floured board and knead for about 10 minutes or until you feel it change from rough and nubbly to smooth and elastic. Place in a lightly oiled bowl and cover. Leave somewhere vaguely warm (I use my airing cupboard) for 1½–2 hours or until well risen.

Knock back the dough and divide into 12 pieces. Shape each into a round by rolling, then tucking any joins underneath so that the top is perfectly convex. Place well spaced apart on a lightly oiled baking sheet and cover loosely. Leave for about 30 minutes – again in a vaguely warm place.

Preheat the oven to 220°C/425°F/Gas 7. Using the heel of your hand, press down lightly on each bap to flatten it slightly. Brush the tops with milk and dust lightly with flour. Bake for about 15 minutes or until puffed up and golden brown. Eat warm.

Scrambled Eggs with Smoked Venison

Cold-smoked venison is not only good with eggs for breakfast. Try it as a starter with wedges of melon or figs, as you might serve Parma ham.

Be sure to serve these scrambled eggs shortly after stirring in the venison: you are not cooking the meat, just heating it through in the eggs. Accompany it with thick wholemeal toast.

Serves 1
3 medium free-range eggs
1 tbsp milk (or single or double cream)
25g /1oz butter
25g /1oz cold-smoked venison, slivered

Beat the eggs in a bowl with some salt and pepper and the milk or cream. Slowly melt the butter in a saucepan, then increase the heat to medium (not high) and add the egg mixture. Stirring frequently, cook for a maximum of 3-4 minutes, until it is just beginning to firm up. Remove from the heat, add the venison. Stir and serve at once.

Dundee Marmalade

This is fellow Dundonian and food writer Grace Mulligan's recipe for Seville marmalade, from her book, *Dundee Kitchen*. Grace recommends freezing Seville oranges during their short season in January and February. When using frozen fruit, you will need to add 2–3 extra oranges to the marmalade as the pectin content diminishes with freezing, reducing the ability to set.

The word marmalade comes from the Portuguese word for quinces, *marmelos*, and 'marmelada', a sugary, solid mass of quinces, was first mentioned in Britain's port records at the end of the fifteenth century. According to many accounts it was an enterprising young grocer, James Keiller, who first sold orange marmalade as we know it today, after his wife, Janet, used a consignment of bitter oranges (bought cheaply because they were inedible raw) to make it. This was apparently in the early 1700s, then by 1797 descendants of the Keillers opened their famous marmalade factory.

However, W. M. Mathew, in his book *Keiller's of Dundee*, declared this to be complete nonsense. The James who gave his name to the company was the son of Janet, not the husband, and he was only 22 and unmarried in 1797. What we know to be a fact, however, is that the Keillers were mainly confectioners, and did not specialise in marmalade until the 1800s, when they became the first firm to produce Scottish 'chip' marmalade. They did not invent the principles of marmalade making, as there was already a Scottish recipe for marmalade made from Seville sours in 1760 and an English recipe written by Sir Hugh Plat in 1605. James Boswell's wife Margaret sent home-made orange marmalade from Edinburgh to Samuel Johnson in London in 1777. What the Keillers did, however, was produce a specific and marketable product from Dundee, which soon became world famous.

The other fetching anecdote concerns Mary, Queen of Scots. As quinces were regarded at that time as a healing fruit, she took some with her on her voyage from France to Scotland in 1561. In order to alleviate her sea-sickness, the call was heard from her ladies, *'Marmalade pour Marie malade.'* Nice story, if you believe it!

Makes about 10 x 450g/1lb jars
1.3kg/3lb Seville oranges, scrubbed
2 lemons, scrubbed
3.5 litres/6 pints water
2.7kg/6lb granulated sugar
a knob of butter

Pour enough boiling water over the oranges and lemons to cover them. Leave until cool enough to handle, then cut the lemons in half and squeeze out the juice. Put the juice into a preserving pan or a large heavy-based pan and discard the skins. Cut the oranges in half and squeeze out most of the juice, then pour it into the pan. Put all the pips in a bowl. Cut each empty orange half into 3. Now, in 2 or 3 batches, place the orange peel in a food processor and process until it is chunky, watching to avoid overprocessing. Tip the chopped peel into the pan and add the water. Tie up the pips in a piece of muslin or fine nylon curtain and add to the pan. Cover and leave for about 6 hours or overnight to soften the peel.

Bring the contents of the pan to the boil, turn down the heat and simmer, uncovered, so the liquid will evaporate. Cook until it is a thick mush – this can take anything up to 2 hours – stirring often to prevent sticking.

Meanwhile, warm the sugar in a low oven. Add it to the fruit, stirring until dissolved, then turn up the heat and boil the marmalade for 15–20 minutes or until it reaches setting point (it may take longer). To test for setting point, put a teaspoon of marmalade on a cold saucer and refrigerate. After 1 minute, push the marmalade sideways; if it forms a skin the marmalade is ready. Lift the pan carefully on to a board and stir in the butter to disperse the foam. Pot the marmalade in warm sterilised jars (see below) and cover with a wax disc (or screw on metal lids). Cover with cellophane when cool (if using wax discs). Store in a cool, dark, dry place.

Note
To sterilise jam jars, wash them well in hot soapy water and then dry in a low oven. Alternatively, if you have a dishwasher you can put them through it and then microwave on High for 1½ minutes.

Sassermaet

Sassermaet (sassermeat) is Shetland's sausagemeat – with a difference. Made primarily by butchers, it is still occasionally prepared at home and is basically raw salted beef mixed with fat, pepper, allspice, cinnamon, cloves and sometimes ginger or nutmeg. This is formed into a square or round mound and then sliced to order. It is fried (without fat, as it is fairly fatty) and served with either fried onion, egg or plain boiled potatoes. I like it with an egg fried in the fat from the pan. Delicious.

Serves 4
8 slices of sassermaet
1 large onion, peeled and sliced,
or 4 free-range eggs

Heat a dry frying pan and add the sassermaet. Cook for 2–3 minutes on each side, then remove from the pan and keep warm. Fry the onion or eggs in the fat and serve with the sassermaet.

Blackcurrant Jam

Apart from her famous raspberry jam, my mother made blackcurrant jam and jelly with fruit from our own blackcurrant bushes. She always employed my Great-Auntie Maggie's test for setting point: after boiling the jam for the requisite time, hold the wooden spoon high above the pan. Once most of the liquid has dropped off, run the nail of your forefinger along the back of the spoon. If it leaves a discernible line that is fairly solid, then it is ready.

Nowadays I go to my local pick-your-own farm with the children and pick strawberries and raspberries, but I buy the blackcurrants at the farm shop as the children don't enjoy eating them raw – and that is one of the greatest (illicit) pleasures of picking fruit straight from the field.

In Marion Lochhead's account of a Scots household in the eighteenth century, she writes, 'One of the noblest of conserves, blackcurrant jam, used to be kept as the most pleasant of remedies for colds and sore throats; a truly Scots touch.' A classic case of: it not only tastes good, it does you good, too!

Makes about 10 x 450g/1lb jars
1.8kg/4lb blackcurrants
1.75 litres/3 pints cold water
3kg/6½lb granulated sugar
a knob of butter (optional)

Place the blackcurrants in a preserving pan or a large deep saucepan with the water. Simmer gently for about 45 minutes, skimming off any scum from the surface, until the fruit is really soft. It is important that the skins are very soft before you add the sugar.

Add the sugar and stir until dissolved, then increase the heat. You can add the butter if you like, to help disperse the scum. Bring to the boil and boil rapidly for about 10 minutes or until setting point is reached. Test by my mother's method (above) or by dripping a little of the mixture on to a cold saucer: after a minute or two you should be able to run your forefinger through it, leaving a trail. Even when it is ready to pot, the mixture will look extremely runny. Don't panic; it will firm up nicely on cooling. This is not a stiff, solid jam, but rather a soft, spreadable one.

Pot immediately in warm sterilised jars (see page 19) and cover either at once or when completely cold. Label and store in a cool, dark, dry place.

Blackcurrant jam and butteries
(see page 10)

Raspberry Jam

This was the one jam my mother always had in stock because we had so many raspberries at the bottom of our garden. Her blackcurrant and apple jellies would often run out by early spring but raspberry lasted all year. I vividly remember the sweet, heady aromas of jam wafting out through the kitchen door, luring me into the house from playing in the garden in those long, halcyon days of childhood summers.

I like to add Drambuie to my raspberry jam to enhance the flavour. The recipe for this whisky-based liqueur was allegedly given by Bonnie Prince Charlie to Captain John MacKinnon, one of the Prince's most loyal Jacobite followers, in 1746. Many years later, in 1906, the MacKinnon descendants began its commercial production. I like to add splashes to any raspberry pudding and to many chocolate and ice-cream recipes.

Makes 3 x 450g/1lb jars
1kg/2¼lb fresh raspberries
1kg/2¼lb preserving sugar
(granulated will also do)
a knob of unsalted butter
1–2 tablespoons Drambuie (optional)

Place the raspberries in a preserving pan or a large, deep saucepan and simmer very gently for about 20 minutes, until they release their juices. Add the sugar and heat gently until dissolved, stirring constantly. Add the butter, then bring to the boil and boil rapidly for about 25 minutes or until setting point is reached. During this time, it will splatter – but don't be tempted to reduce the heat. I'm afraid you'll just have to wipe up after! Setting point is determined by placing a few drips of jam on a cold saucer and allowing it to cool quickly. Push it with your finger and if it wrinkles it is ready.

If using the Drambuie, add it now. Pot the jam in warm sterilised jars (see page 19) and seal either immediately or when completely cold. Label and store in a cool, dark, dry place.

Lemon Curd

I confess I always make my lemon curd in the microwave, as it is far quicker. This recipe is absolutely foolproof, presuming you follow the instructions and whisk or beat madly every minute; otherwise you will have sweet lemon scrambled eggs.

Although lemon curd cannot be claimed as as an exclusively Scottish recipe, it has been used extensively in Scotland for many years. I have seen versions made with heather honey instead of sugar, which might – or might not – add to its authenticity.

Use this at breakfast time to spread on toast, oatcakes or butteries. Since it is only worth preparing a decent-sized batch, use the rest to make luscious puddings (such as bread and butter pudding made with fruit loaf or Selkirk bannock), to fill rich, dark chocolate cake or to dollop on to pancakes or waffles.

Makes 3 x 450g/1lb jars
225g/8oz unsalted butter
450g/1lb granulated sugar
grated zest of 6 large unwaxed lemons
350ml/12fl oz freshly squeezed lemon juice
6 free-range eggs

Place the butter and sugar in a large, microwave-proof bowl with the lemon zest and juice. Cook, uncovered, on High, for 4–5 minutes, stirring every minute, until the butter has melted and the sugar dissolved. Remove and leave to cool for a couple of minutes.

Beat the eggs together and strain them through a sieve. Whisk them into the bowl, then return it to the microwave. Cook for 6–8 minutes, removing and whisking madly every minute.

When the curd has thickened to the consistency of lightly whipped cream (it will firm up more on cooling) pour it at once into warm sterilised jars (see page 19). Tap to level the surface and remove any air bubbles, then wipe the jars. Label and seal only when completely cold. Store in the refrigerator for up to 6 weeks.

2

soups

S oup is something we do well in Scotland. Always have
done. Since the first kail-pot was hung over a peat fire, we
have chopped and stirred, simmered and supped. Local produce –
mutton, lamb or beef bones, barley, root vegetables and kail –
have been thrown into the pot with water and cooked to
nourishing perfection.

Well-known soups such as Scotch broth, cock-a-leekie and
Cullen skink need little preface. But allow me to introduce you to
crab- and rice-based partan bree, Shetland's memorable reestit
(reested) mutton soup and my great-grandmother's magnificent
hare soup, known in Scotland as bawd bree. All these can be meals
in themselves, served in large bowls with bread, bannocks or
oatcakes on the side. Or they can be served in shallow soup plates
as a starter, which is how I ate soup every day as a child, come rain,
hail or shine. Yes, even in the heatwaves of nostalgic childhood
summers, there was always hot soup to come home to. It was part
of growing up in Scotland.

And when we were ill, a mug of soup was always first on the
invalid's menu. It is surely no coincidence that when we are unwell
or just a little under the weather, our bodies crave soup. Hearty
vegetable soup, wholesome lentil soup or perhaps a light chicken
broth – they all slip down gently while nourishing the body and
soothing the soul. In my opinion you can forget bangers and mash
or jam roly-poly in the comfort-food stakes. Give me a good bowl
of soup any day (with steamed treacle pudding and custard
afterwards . . . assuming my infliction was not life-threatening).

Some references suggest that the Scots' soup-making skills should
be attributed to the French and the Auld Alliance. Whereas certain
soups and pottages seem to be directly linked, it is a fact that long
before the claret trade began with Leith and before Mary, Queen of
Scots sailed from France to reside in Edinburgh, we were ladling out
delicious soups. They were undoubtedly not grand, complicated or
sophisticated but rather homely, hearty and nourishing. Which is my
idea of perfection in a soup bowl, whether I am feeling well or – as
we say in Scotland – awfy no' weel.

Kail Brose

Many broths made with oatmeal are known as brose. This one is typical of several regions of Scotland, where kail or curly kale used to be widely grown throughout the winter; the vegetable suits the Scottish climate admirably because of its ability to withstand frost. It also provided an essential intake of vitamins and minerals throughout the cold, bleak winter months. The kail-yard was the common term for the kitchen garden, where vegetables were grown. So essential was this hardy vegetable to the diet that in parts of Lowland and north-east Scotland, kail was also the name given to the midday meal. The iron kail-pot and iron girdle were the two most basic pieces of cooking equipment found in crofts and cottages. Besides being made into broths and soups, it was also served on its own, with butter and milk added when available. Dr Samuel Johnson remarked in his *Journey to the Western Islands of Scotland* that 'when they [the Scots] had not kail, they probably had nothing'.

Ena Baxter in her *Scottish Cookbook* describes kail brose as one of her least favourite childhood meals. The way it was eaten was similar to the porridge ritual, with milk and porridge in separate bowls. She describes how oatmeal was placed in each bowl with a pinch of salt, then a ladleful of boiling hot beef broth stirred in and the purèed kail served separately. A spoonful of kail was dipped into the broth and the two eaten together, swilled down with a glass of milk. At the onset of spring, nettles would often be substituted for kail but in this case a lighter chicken stock was likely to be used to suit the more delicate flavour of nettles.

Instead of using ready-made stock, it is more authentic to boil up a piece of ox head, cow heel or marrowbone with water first to make some good fatty stock, which is best for this recipe. So if you get your hands on a heel or a head, boil away!

Serves 4
300g/10½oz kail (curly kale), well washed, stalks removed
1.2 litres/2 pints hot beef stock
50g/2oz medium oatmeal
1 heaped teaspoon salt
thick oatcakes and butter, to serve

Place the kail in a large saucepan with the hot stock and bring to the boil. Then cook, uncovered, over a medium heat for 10–15 minutes, until tender. Meanwhile, place the oatmeal on a sheet of foil and toast under a hot grill for 3–4 minutes, until golden brown, shaking often so it does not burn.

Using a slotted spoon, transfer the kail to a blender and purée with a ladle or so of the stock, then return it to the pan. Add the salt and plenty of freshly milled pepper. Gradually add most of the toasted oatmeal and, stirring constantly to avoid lumps, cook for 4–5 minutes, until thickened. Check the seasoning and ladle the soup into warmed bowls. Sprinkle over the remaining oatmeal and serve with buttered oatcakes.

Partan Bree

This is a rich, creamy crab soup: partan means crab, bree is liquid or gravy. If you are using a live crab as your base, boil it for 15–20 minutes, then remove the creamy brown body meat and place in a bowl; put the sweet white (claw and leg) meat in another. Discard the feathery 'dead men's fingers' as you work. You can buy cooked crab from a fishmonger but avoid dressed ones, as these sometimes have other ingredients added to them such as breadcrumbs.

Popular in many seaside areas of Scotland, this recipe has, of course, variations. Lady Clark of Tillypronie suggested adding some anchovy (presumably anchovy essence); I also rather like a shake or two of Worcestershire sauce. I have included a blade of mace for extra flavour.

Serves 4–6
75g/3oz long-grain rice
600ml/1 pint full-fat milk
a blade of mace
the meat of 1 large crab or about
300g/10½oz fresh or defrosted frozen
crabmeat (about 200g/7oz brown meat
and 100g/3½oz white meat)
600ml/1 pint hot fish stock
150ml/5fl oz double cream (optional)
anchovy essence

Put the rice, milk and mace in a pan, bring to the boil and simmer for about 15–20 minutes, until the rice is tender. Discard the mace and tip the rice and milk into a liquidiser or food processor with the brown crabmeat. Process until combined, then pour back into the pan and add the hot stock. Place over a medium heat until just below boiling point, then add the white crabmeat and the cream, if using. Heat gently for a couple of minutes, then add salt, pepper and anchovy essence to taste. Serve in warm bowls and add an extra dash of anchovy essence – and extra cream – to each portion if you like.

Arbroath Fishermen's Soup

My brother-in-law Jim's friend, Alec Smith, has been a fisherman in Arbroath for over a quarter of a century. He goes to sea in the family boat to catch mainly haddock and whiting. During the four or five days they are at sea, there is plenty of fish on board. And so this old family recipe comes into its own. The soup is prepared one day, then reheated the next. The quantities are large but it is more main meal than first course. Once it has fed the entire crew – or just your family – it will keep in the fridge for a couple of days.

   The addition of evaporated milk might seem rather bizarre but that is what the fishermen take to sea instead of fresh milk to put in their tea. If you do not approve, use double cream instead.

Serves 10

2 large onions, peeled and chopped

6 medium potatoes, peeled and cut into large chunks

2 heaped tablespoons medium oatmeal

1 level tablespoon salt

6 thick haddock fillets (about 1.5kg/3lb 5oz in total), each cut into about 8 large chunks

300ml/10fl oz evaporated milk, or 150ml/5fl oz double cream

chopped parsley and thick oatcakes, to serve

Place the onions, potatoes and oatmeal in a very large saucepan with 2.25 litres/4 pints of cold water. Add the salt and plenty of freshly ground pepper. Bring to the boil, skimming off any scum. Once it is bubbling, add the fish, then cover the pan and reduce the heat to a simmer. Cook for 10 minutes, just until the potatoes are tender. (If you are cooking it the day before, as the fishermen do, remove from the heat at this stage and leave to cool completely before refrigerating or keeping somewhere cold. The next day, reheat gently until piping hot.) Stir in the evaporated milk or cream and check the seasoning. Ladle into warmed bowls, sprinkle over some parsley, crumble over some oatcakes and serve at once.

Cullen Skink

There are many different recipes for Cullen skink. The one I ate at the Seaforth Hotel in Cullen, made by chef Gareth Eddy, was flavoured with leeks, thyme, mustard and even garlic – delicious, although not exactly traditional. The classic one is made with whole finnan haddock (finnan haddie) but you can use smoked haddock fillets instead – make sure they are undyed. Jerusalem artichokes are also wonderful in this soup instead of potatoes.

Serves 6
2 finnan haddock or 500g/18oz undyed smoked haddock fillets
2 onions, peeled and finely chopped
2 large potatoes (about 600g/1¼lb), peeled and finely diced
450ml/16fl oz full-fat milk
25g/1oz unsalted butter
double cream and chopped chives, to garnish

Put the haddock in a large pan with 300ml/10fl oz cold water. Bring to the boil and simmer for 5–10 minutes, until the fish is just cooked (finnan haddock will need a little longer than fillets). Remove the fish with a slotted spoon and flake into large chunks (discard the bones if using finnan haddock), then set aside.

Add the onions and potatoes to the pan with plenty of pepper. Pour in some of the milk if the water doesn't cover the vegetables, then cover the pan and cook over a moderate heat for 12–15 minutes, until tender. Remove the pan from the heat and, using a potato masher, roughly mash the contents, keeping some of the texture. Add the milk and butter and bring to the boil, then simmer for a couple of minutes. Add the fish and reheat gently for 2–3 minutes. Season to taste, then serve in warm bowls with a swirl of cream and some chopped chives.

Cock-a-Leekie

This is hailed by many to be Scotland's other national soup, and it never ceases to amaze me how such a delicious soup can be made from so few ingredients. I like to serve the broth in bowls and the chicken on a separate ashet (platter) to be carved at table, then the pieces dropped into the soup as required. Alternatively, the cook can chop the meat in the kitchen and reheat it in the soup just before serving. The main thing is to avoid overcooking the chicken, otherwise it will be tough. Traditional recipes recommend simmering it for 4 hours (in those days, an old boiling fowl would probably have been used), then serving at once. I like to cook the chicken only for 20 minutes or so, leave it to cool in the stock, then reheat the bird either whole or in pieces. I also discard the rather slimy green part of the leeks and replace them with the white part, which is cooked until just done.

In Scott's *The Fortunes of Nigel*, the king (James VI and I) says, 'My lords and lieges, let us all to dinner for the cockie-leekie is a-coolin' – which reminds us that this is a very old dish. Interestingly some recipes exclude the prunes, but I think they are essential for their contrasting sweetness.

Serves 6

1 free-range chicken, weighing about 1.1–1.3kg/2½–3lb

6 long, thick leeks (choose ones with plenty of green and white)

10–12 black peppercorns

12–16 stoned prunes

1 tablespoon chopped parsley

Place the chicken in a large saucepan. Halve the leeks lengthways, wash them well, then cut off the green parts. Chop these roughly and add to the pan with the peppercorns and enough water just to cover: about 2 litres/3½ pints. Bring slowly to the boil, then cover and simmer for about 20 minutes. Remove from the heat, cover tightly and leave for about an hour.

Then take out the chicken and use a slotted spoon to remove the leeks, which can be discarded. Chop the white part of the leeks, add to the pan with the prunes and bring to the boil again. Simmer for about 10 minutes, until the leeks are just done.

If you are serving the chicken whole, return it to the pan for the last 3–5 minutes or so to warm through. Otherwise, remove the chicken flesh from the bones, chop it into pieces and add these to the soup. Add plenty of salt and pepper to taste and serve with the chopped parsley on top.

Tattie Soup

Although this is traditionally made with mutton stock, my recipe uses chicken stock, which I reckon more people are likely to have at home. It must be good quality, however, preferably from a free-range or organic chicken.

If you make this in late spring or early summer, you could add a handful of chopped young nettle leaves a couple of minutes before serving.

Serves 6–8

1.2 litres/2 pints good chicken stock
(I use about 850ml/1½ pints jellied stock
mixed with 300ml/10fl oz water.)
1kg/2¼lb potatoes, peeled and diced
1 large onion, peeled and diced
3–4 carrots, peeled and diced
chopped chives, parsley or young
nettle leaves

Bring the stock to the boil in a large saucepan. Add the vegetables and some salt and pepper, then cover and cook over a medium heat for 25–30 minutes, until all the vegetables are tender. Taste and check the seasoning.

If using nettle leaves, stir them in and heat through for 2 minutes. If using chives or parsley, sprinkle each portion with some after ladling the soup into bowls.

Dulse Soup

Margaret Horn is a highly respected Scottish cook who has not wandered far from her roots. Born and brought up in Auchmithie, a tiny village nestling on the cliffs three miles north of Arbroath, she and her husband have owned The But 'n' Ben since 1977. Because seaweed was part of her childhood diet, she has incorporated it into some dishes served at the restaurant. Dulse and tangles (kelp) are two of her favourite seaweeds and not only does she cook with them, she also nibbles on them as she picks the seaweed whenever the tide is out. She uses tangles (*Laminaria digitata*) to wrap up haddock for steaming. The dulse (*Palmaria (Rhodymenia) palmata*) is made into a simple soup, particularly in the winter months when it is tougher and less suitable for grilling. It is surprising how flavoursome this soup is, for no stock is used, but the pure flavour of the sea comes through in a pleasingly distinctive yet not overpowering way.

When picking wild seaweed, ensure it is from clean water and that there is not a sewage plant lurking just around the bay! Dried dulse can be substituted for fresh. For this recipe use a minimum of 50g/2oz dried dulse and soak it in water for 5–10 minutes first.

Serves 6

about 200g/7oz freshly picked dulse,
well washed
4 large potatoes, peeled and chopped
2 onions, peeled and chopped

Place all the ingredients in a large saucepan and add enough water to cover. Bring to the boil, then simmer for about 10 minutes or until the potatoes are tender. Purèe in a blender, then reheat gently, adding salt and pepper to taste. Serve as it is or garnished with some grilled dulse (see page 110).

Reested Mutton Soup

It was at the opening of Edinburgh's latest restaurant, Restaurant Martin Wishart – which has become one the city's best – that I met Georgia Wishart, Martin's mother. She and I talked, not of the foie gras millefeuille nor the heavenly chocolate délice on our plates, but of reested mutton, brunnies and krappin. For Georgia was born and brought up in a remote part of Shetland, the westerly hamlet of Garderhouse. As a child she ate porridge (oatmeal or beremeal), boiled 'piltak' (two-year-old saithe), which her father would catch with a fishing line from the rowing boat he built himself, brunnies (wholemeal girdle scones), beremeal bannocks and tattie soup flavoured with reested mutton. Some weeks later, Georgia cooked her soup for me and I was charmed by its flavour.

Reested (reestit) mutton is cured mutton that has been salted for at least 10 days, then hung up on hooks to dry (preferably over a peat fire) for as long as it takes to be eaten up. After some time it looks rather like salt cod, with an ivory hue and a stiff, cardboard feel. Some people have it hanging there for so long that they wrap newspapers around it to prevent the dust settling. The mutton is then sliced as thinly as Parma ham and fried with onions, or, best of all, made into soup. Georgia's soup had both the smell and taste of mutton and was thick and chunky with vegetables. After just one bowl of it, I was hooked – the flavour is so distinctive. It is well worth the long trek north to Shetland any day.

Reested mutton was traditionally eaten during the winter months, when there was little fresh meat available, and it can still be found in butcher's shops in the run-up to Christmas.

Serves 6–8
450g/1lb reested mutton
1 onion
4–5 large carrots
1 medium turnip (called swede in England)
6–8 floury potatoes

Place the mutton in a large pan and cover with cold water. Bring to the boil and simmer for about 30 minutes. Peel all the vegetables and chop them into good-size chunks, then add them to the soup. Return to the boil and cook, covered, until everything is tender – about 20 minutes. Remove the meat from the pan, cut off slices and put them on a plate. Serve the soup piping hot, with the plate of sliced meat on the side.

Scotch Broth

'This is the comfortable *pot au feu* of Scotland,' wrote Meg Dods about Scotland's national soup. Most people enjoying a bowl of broth as a starter might not see the similarities but, served (as it was and often still is) in two parts – as a soup course, then with the meat and freshly boiled vegetables to follow – it is closer to France's famous *pot au feu* than any other dish. Often tiny whole potatoes, turnips or carrots would be added with the other vegetables and cooked until tender, then removed to an ashet (platter) and arranged around the meat.

As I grew up, there was always a pot of soup sitting on the cooker, whatever the weather, and broth was the favourite. When my mother and father were children in Dundee, there was broth to start every dinnertime. Like so many things that were good for you, it was seldom talked about, just eaten, but what a health-giving soup it is, packed full of freshly cooked vegetables and meat stock. Meg Dods also described it as 'the bland, balsamic barley-broth of Scotland'. And whereas bland I would disagree with, the word balsamic (before its connotations of fashionable vinegars arose) describes it aptly. For after a plate of broth, all seems well with the world. It is soothing and comforting, invigorating and restorative. It is the Scots' panacea, our very own Jewish chicken soup. The critical Dr Samuel Johnson, however, ate several platefuls of broth, and had his own opinion. 'You never ate it before?' inquired James Boswell, his travelling companion in their 1773 tour of the Highlands. 'No sir, but I don't care how soon I eat it again.'

Finally, I should warn you that my recipe might produce a soup that is too thick and hearty for some people's tastes. If that is the case, simply add more boiling water after the initial cooking. Bear in mind that my idea of good broth is summed up in the opening lines of Robert Crawford's poem 'Scotch Broth': 'A soup so thick you could shake its hand and stroll with it before dinner.'

Serves 6
a piece of boiling beef
(runner, thin rib or flank), or
neck of mutton or shoulder of lamb,
weighing about 700g/1½lb
150g/5oz dried marrowfat peas,
soaked overnight and then drained
75g/3oz pearl barley,
soaked overnight and then drained
25g/1oz parsley (including the stalks)
200g/7oz carrots, peeled and finely diced
150g/5oz kail (curly kale),
washed and finely chopped
200g/7oz turnip (called swede in England),
peeled and finely diced
1 large onion, peeled and finely chopped

Place the meat in a large pan with the soaked peas and barley and the parsley stalks. Cover with cold water – about 2.25 litres/4 pints – and bring slowly to the boil. Then skim off any scum and reduce to a simmer. Cover and cook for at least 1 hour or until the peas are tender. Remove the parsley stalks if possible (don't worry if some remain) and add all the vegetables. Bring to the boil again and cook for about 20 minutes, until the vegetables are tender. Chop the parsley and add most of it to the soup, with salt and pepper to taste.

To serve, remove the meat from the pan and cut it into pieces. Add these to the soup and serve sprinkled with the remaining parsley. You could, if you like, serve the vegetable broth first, then the beef as a main course, in which case add a few tiny whole vegetables with the diced ones to serve with the meat.

Mussel Brose

This is a delicious soup for a bitterly cold winter's day. The mussels are cooked lightly, then their liquor reheated with some milk and fish stock and thickened with oatmeal – hence the name brose. The mussels are returned to the pan towards the end and it is served in warm bowls with a scattering of chives. Perhaps the etymology of brose goes back to the Ancient Greek and Latin ambrosia – food of the gods.

Serves 4
1kg/2¼lb mussels
300ml/10fl oz milk
300ml/10fl oz fish stock
75g/3oz fine oatmeal, toasted
chopped chives, to garnish
a little cream, to serve (optional)

Scrub the mussels thoroughly, discarding any open ones that don't close when tapped on a work surface. Place in a pan with 600ml/1 pint of cold water. Cover tightly and bring slowly to the boil, shaking the pan a couple of times. Boil for about 1 minute or until the mussels have opened, then remove from the heat and strain over a large jug.

Heat together the milk, fish stock and 600ml/1 pint of the mussel liquor. Bring slowly to the boil, then reduce the heat to medium. Put the oatmeal in a bowl. Remove a ladleful of the liquid from the pan and add it to the oatmeal, stirring until smooth. Add this mixture gradually to the pan, whisking or stirring well until smooth (if it is still rather 'knotty', tip into a blender and whiz until smooth). Cook gently for a couple of minutes.

Remove the mussels from their shells and return them to the pan. Reheat gently for a minute or so, then season to taste. Serve in warm bowls with some chopped chives and a swirl of cream, if you like.

Hare Soup

Every year my father and his brother and sisters used to go to their grandmother's home in Dundee for the family Christmas meal, hare soup (bawd bree in Scots). Since she had been in service in one of the big estates in Angus, my great-grandmother was an expert in dealing with game. My aunts can still remember the tiny chunks of hare throughout the soup and its rich, gamy taste. My father simply remembers that it was not his favourite; that's because it was not mince and tatties.

A dollop of cranberry sauce or redcurrant jelly stirred into the soup just before serving is by no means authentic but it does contrast beautifully with the rich flavour.

Serves 6

1 hare, skinned, cleaned and cut into pieces
40g/1½oz flour, seasoned with salt and pepper
60g/2½oz butter
2 large onions, peeled and chopped
75g/3oz unsmoked streaky bacon, chopped
3–4 carrots, peeled and chopped
2 celery sticks, chopped
2–3 sprigs of parsley
2–3 sprigs of thyme
1.5 litres/2½ pints hot beef stock
50ml/2fl oz port

My butcher advises washing the hare pieces in salt before cooking: just put them in the sink and rub with salt, then rinse under cold running water before patting thoroughly dry.

Dip the hare in the seasoned flour and brown all over in 40g/1½oz of the butter in a large heavy pan (you will need to do this in batches). Remove the meat from the pan. Add the remaining butter and gently fry the onions and bacon in it for about 10 minutes. Add the carrots and celery and cook for about 5 minutes, then return the meat to the pan with the herbs, hot stock and some salt and pepper. Bring to the boil, skim if necessary, then cover and simmer gently for about 2 hours (an older, tougher hare will need about 3 hours).

Remove the hare pieces from the pan and leave until cool enough to handle, then tear the meat into small pieces. Purée the soup in a blender and return it to the pan with the meat. Stir in the port, reheat gently, then add salt and pepper to taste. Once it is hot, check if it needs any extra port – a final splash would not go amiss.

3

fresh and smoked fish

Turn the clock back a couple of decades and take a look in a Scottish fishmonger's window. There would be little other than haddock, sole and herring. And some of the haddock was totally unrecognisable, dressed as it was in a hideous orange robe called ruskoline. Fast-forward to the present day and there is an increasing interest in fish, resulting in fishmonger's slabs covered with snapper, tuna, orange roughy and hoki, mostly air-freighted in from the other side of the world. All well and good, we must expand our palate, but not to the detriment of our own produce.

There has been an increasing interest in fish from our own shores, too, although a slightly unfortunate result of this is the establishment of so many salmon farms, which have not always proved beneficial to either the environment or the fish industry. Fishmongers are happy to offer alternatives to traditional fish, say, ling instead of haddock for fish pie, or mackerel instead of herring to be fried in oatmeal for tea. And with more piscine awareness from customers, there is a general feeling that fish is *the* food for the turn of the century, as it is light, versatile and exceedingly healthy.

Although, sadly, the reduction of cod and haddock quotas because of over-fishing means that fishmongers and chip shops might have to alter their range, there are still other fish in the sea. And, of course, in our rivers. Cured fish, particularly smoked fish, have been an important part of Scotland's heritage for centuries. Arbroath smokies, finnan haddock and oak-smoked salmon are well known worldwide and are now more easily available in good fishmonger's and by mail order.

Some of the fish dishes in this chapter are classics — herring in oatmeal, Tweed kettle and potted salmon, for example. But others may baffle you with their intriguing titles. Crappit heid, hairy tatties and cabbie-claw might not be the first thing you think of for a simple Friday fish supper *à deux* but do give them a try. Like so many old Scottish recipes, they may not win prizes for their looks but, my, how they taste good.

Tatties and Herring

This is a ridiculously simple dish but tastes absolutely delicious when made with good salt herring. One of the oldest references to curing herring is in Martin Martin's book on the Western Islands, written in 1703. In his day, herrings were cured by hanging them up in the smoky rafters to dry. But in spite of prohibitive salt duties, pickling or salting the herring in barrels soon took over from air-drying and eventually became the customary method of preserving them. By the mid-nineteenth century, salted herring formed a crucial part of the crofters' winter diet in the Western Isles.

In Ena Baxter's *Scottish Cookbook*, she writes that the herring industry became established around the Caithness coast in the 1790s, which meant that during the nineteenth century, tatties and herring was the staple diet of most Caithness people. Until relatively recently, most Caithness cottages had a 'firkin' (a small wooden barrel for salting fish) at their door to last them throughout the winter. The herrings were packed in these barrels over layers of salt, head to tail alternately.

In *Growing Up in Scotland*, there are some lovely recollections from an Aberdeenshire man from 1910: 'My brother would collect fish that had dropped while they were unloading the boats and loading up the carts. He would put one on each finger through the gills to carry them. He went round the doors with them and got tuppence a dozen for his herrin' and that was all profit since he hadn't had to pay for them. Everybody had a barrel of salt herrin' for the winter.'

The usual way to eat salt herring is to soak them in water (milk in Shetland) and either boil the herring and potatoes separately (as they do in the Hebrides) or layer them in a pot and cook them together. Whichever way you choose, it is important to use unpeeled potatoes. And it is customary to eat the herrings with your fingers, to tackle the bones more easily.

I buy salt herring from my fishmonger but if yours does not sell them they are easy to prepare yourself. My fishmonger removes the gills and gently pulls out the long gut, leaving the head. (The fish is not slit for normal gutting as the 'melts' – soft roe – are left in.) They are then cleaned and packed in dry salt for about six weeks. Traditionally they are eaten on Hogmanay (Auld Year's Night) because they cleanse the body after Christmas excess. They also arouse a great thirst . . .

Serves 6
6 salt herring
12–18 potatoes, scrubbed

First soak the salt herring for 24 hours, changing the water a couple of times.

Method 1

Fill a heavy-based pot with scrubbed unpeeled potatoes and add enough water to come half way up the potatoes. Rinse the soaked herring and place them on top. Cover tightly, bring to the boil and simmer until the potatoes are tender.

Method 2

I prefer this method, as the fish cannot overcook and more salt is removed. Place the soaked herring in a pan of cold water, bring to the boil and then carefully tip out the water. Refill with cold water and bring to the boil again. Remove from the heat, cover and allow to cool, by which time the herrings will be cooked. Meanwhile, boil the potatoes in their jackets in another pan.

To serve, dish the fish and potatoes out on to each plate straight from the pan. Milk is the traditional drink.

Salmon with Lemon Thyme Butter

In Mistress Dods' *Cook and Housewife's Manual of 1829,* her instructions for baking salmon or trout include a sprig of lemon thyme in the vinegar mixture to pickle the fish once cooked. I have developed this idea to make a lemon thyme butter for serving with simply seared salmon. Boiled new potatoes and a green vegetable are good with this dish.

Serves 4

4 middle-cut salmon fillets, weighing about 200g/7oz each, pin-bones removed, skinned

olive oil

For the lemon thyme butter:

75g/3oz unsalted butter, softened

2 heaped tablespoons finely chopped lemon thyme leaves

To make the lemon thyme butter, beat the butter until smooth, then beat in the thyme and some salt and pepper. Spoon on to a sheet of foil and mould into a sausage shape, then roll up in the foil and chill until solid.

Put the salmon on a plate, rub all over with olive oil and set aside for 30 minutes. Heat a heavy-based frying pan or griddle pan until very hot – this can take up to 10 minutes. Smear the base with oil, using a wad of kitchen paper, then, once it is very hot again, add the salmon. Season with salt and pepper and turn after 2 minutes, by which time a good crust should have formed. Continue cooking until just done – 2–4 minutes depending on thickness.

Cut off discs of the lemon thyme butter. Serve the fish on warm plates with a couple of discs of butter on top.

Potted Salmon

This is ideal to make after you have cooked Tweed Kettle (see page 47) or whenever you have some cooked salmon left over. Serve with lemon wedges and brown toast or oatcakes.

Serves 6–8

400g/14oz cooked salmon, in chunks

100g/3½oz unsalted butter, softened

6 anchovy fillets, snipped

scant ¼ teaspoon ground mace

a good pinch of cayenne pepper

Put all the ingredients in a bowl and pound together with a wooden spoon until combined. Alternatively process in a food processor, using the pulse button – it should have some texture, rather than being a homogeneous paste. Season to taste with salt and pepper and pile into small dishes. Chill well before eating, spread thickly on toast or oatcakes.

Cabbie-Claw

I'll admit that I was not keen on the idea of this dish initially – salted cod with a parsley and egg sauce. But then I remembered the divine brandade of Provence, which is basically salt cod beaten with milk and oil, and the delicious Caribbean saltfish cakes made with salt cod and potatoes. My Scottish recipe had parsley, horseradish and cayenne to zap it up, so it was definitely worth a go.

In Shetland the dialect word for codling is kabbilow, which is very similar to the name of this dish. However, some historians believe the possible etymological link is from the French for cod, *cabillaud*. But perhaps a more likely theory – because of all the trade between Scotland and Holland – is that it derives from the Dutch for cod, *kabeljauw*.

Cabbie-claw is a very old dish, dating back to the times when preserving fish did not mean slinging it in a freezer. Instead it was salted, wind-dried, then stored for use throughout the year, usually to be cooked and served with mashed potatoes. The introduction of an egg and parsley sauce was obviously a later, more sophisticated idea, and I include it here because it does enhance the dish. Which, incidentally, despite my misgivings, I found absolutely delicious.

You could also serve the salted cod without the egg sauce, dunked into a caper-heavy salsa verde – inauthentic but surprisingly good.

Serves 6
1 very fresh young codling, weighing about 1.1kg/2½lb
salt (my fishmonger uses fine powdered salt; I recommend regular table salt)
a handful of parsley stalks (use the leaves for the sauce)
1 tablespoon horseradish sauce

For the egg sauce:
40g/1½oz butter
40g/1½oz plain flour
200ml/7fl oz milk
3 large free-range eggs, hard-boiled and chopped
a handful of chopped parsley leaves
cayenne pepper

Ask your fishmonger to remove the head of the fish, leaving the lugs on (the lugs are the hard bones connecting the head to the undergill). The guts should then be removed and the fish should be thoroughly cleaned by scrubbing. Then it should be split on one side, so that the bone remains to one side, leaving a flat fish. Wipe well.

Sprinkle a good 1cm/½in layer of salt into a large plastic or china container, then place the fish on top. Cover it with another thick layer of salt. Cover and leave somewhere cool (a larder, not a fridge) for 24 hours. The next day, the fish will be sitting in a puddle of thick brine. Remove it and hang it up to dry. To do this, insert a knitting needle or a skewer through the lugs and hang it up with a hook (I hang it from a large pair of steps or an upturned stool and place a bowl underneath for excess brine to drip into). Ideally it should be placed somewhere cool and breezy, preferably in the fresh air in a strong wind. But unless you want all the neighbourhood cats around, just place it somewhere draughty with cool air circulating. Leave for 24–36 hours, depending on the outside temperature, then rinse thoroughly under a running tap, removing all salt adhering to the outsides.

Place the fish in a large saucepan of cold water. Bring slowly to the boil, then, when you see bubbles, pour away all the water. Cover again with cold water, add the parsley stalks and the horseradish and bring slowly to the boil. Do not actually allow it to boil: this makes it hard. Cover, and simmer gently for 15 minutes, then carefully lift the fish out and drain the liquid into a jug. Once the fish is cool, remove the skin and bones, break the flesh into large chunks and place in a dish. Keep warm while you make the sauce.

Melt the butter in a pan, stir in the flour and cook for a minute or two, then gradually add 300ml/10fl oz of the hot fish cooking liquid and the milk, whisking until smooth. Simmer for 10–15 minutes, then taste and add pepper if necessary – no salt. Stir in the chopped eggs and parsley and pour the sauce over the fish. Dust lightly with cayenne pepper to serve.

Tweed Kettle

Basically a poached salmon dish (originally using fish from the River Tweed), Tweed kettle is extremely versatile as it can be served warm or cold, or used to make Potted Salmon (see page 44). When poaching salmon, it is essential never to add salt to the poaching liquid, as this can stiffen the flesh of the fish.

Serves 8
A large bunch of dill
12 black peppercorns
3 fresh bay leaves
1.8kg/4lb tail-end piece of salmon, cleaned
300ml/10fl oz white wine

Place the dill, peppercorns and bay leaves along the rack of a fish kettle. Put the fish on top and pour over the wine, then pour over enough cold water just to cover the fish. Bring slowly to the boil; this will take a good 15–20 minutes. Once the liquid is boiling, allow to bubble for 3 minutes, then switch off the heat, cover tightly with the lid and leave until completely cold, which can take up to 4 hours. If you want to serve the salmon warm, remove after 3 hours.

Lift out the rack, shake dry, place a serving dish on top and invert: the uppermost side of the salmon should now have a dill and peppercorn pattern. Serve with new potatoes, green vegetables and mayonnaise.

Potted Herring

Potted (or soused) herring is a typical teatime dish, eaten with salad and potatoes or brown bread and butter. Lady Clark of Tillypronie recommends serving it for breakfast and also suggests cooking sea trout in the same way.

My fishmonger advises using smaller herring to make this, as they are the sweetest and so no sugar is required in the sousing. Also, the vinegar and water solution will dissolve the tiny featherbones easily in small fish; larger ones have harder bones, which take longer to dissolve.

I have occasionally wrapped the herring in sheets of nori (dried Japanese seaweed) for a change, but you must skin the herring before wrapping. If using nori, smear a little wasabi (Japanese horseradish) over the fillets first.

Serves 4–6

6–8 boned herring (about 75–100g/3–3½oz each, after boning)
1 medium onion, peeled and sliced
150ml/5fl oz white wine vinegar
150ml/5fl oz water
10–12 black peppercorns
a blade of mace
2 fresh bay leaves

Preheat the oven to 180°C/350°F/Gas 4. Season the herring inside with salt and pepper. Scatter half the onion slices over the base of an ovenproof dish. Roll up the herring from the tail end, with the skin side out, and place them on top of the onion, packing them tightly together to keep them rolled up. (Don't worry that the fins are still on – they will come away easily once cooked. Trying to remove them before cooking will only result in a large hole in the back.) Scatter over the remaining onion slices.

Put the vinegar, water, peppercorns, mace and bay leaves in a saucepan, bring to the boil, then pour it over the herring: the liquid should almost cover the fish. Cover tightly and bake in the oven for 25 minutes, then remove and leave, still covered, until cold.

Herring (or Trout) in Oatmeal

Another traditional dish I remember from my childhood. This is wonderful teatime fare but can also be served for breakfast. My mother remembers going to the meal shop in Dundee before her mother fried herring for tea. This was where most Dundonians would buy their oatmeal in different grades (medium, pinhead, coarse, fine) for dishes varying from porridge to fried herring. It also sold dried pulses.

Because herring is best between early June and September in Scotland, fried herring is often served with boiled new potatoes – preferably dug straight from the garden – for a true taste of summer.

You can use pinhead or medium oatmeal: pinhead gives a crunchier texture but medium coats more evenly.

Serves 2

50–65g/2–2½oz medium or pinhead oatmeal

4 boned herrings (about 100g/3½oz each, after boning)

or 2 trout fillets

25–40g/1–1½oz butter

Spread the oatmeal out on a large plate and season with salt and pepper, then press the fish into it, turning to coat both sides. If the fish has been freshly filleted for you, the oatmeal should stick well, but if it has been done earlier in the day, swish it briefly under a cold tap and shake dry before coating it in the meal. Heat the butter in a frying pan, then add the fish, flesh-side down. After about 3 minutes, turn it over and fry for another 3 minutes or until cooked through. Serve with new potatoes and lemon wedges or mustard.

Kipper Pâté

Although the kipper originated in the north-east of England, Scotland is also famous for its kippers. Most of the best ones are cured along the west coast – Loch Fyne, Achiltibuie or Mallaig – where plump herring have been fished for many years. Good ones are also available in the north-east of Scotland, where a fishmonger from Buckie, called Edward Mair (whose shop is called Eat Mair Fish), told me that Scottish kippers are incomparable in flavour because they are smoked over oak shavings from whisky barrels. It is this, he says, that makes Scottish kippers unique. His most certainly are.

Serves 6–8

2 large kippers

75g/3oz unsalted butter, softened

1 tablespoon Worcestershire sauce

juice of 1 lemon

a pinch of cayenne pepper (optional)

Place the kippers in a bowl, cover with boiling water and leave for 1 hour, then drain and pat dry. Peel away the skin and place the flesh in a food processor, discarding the bones. Add the butter, Worcestershire sauce and lemon juice and process until blended (the mixture does not have to be too smooth – a little texture is always welcome in potted fish or meat). Add the cayenne, if using, and some salt and pepper to taste. Pack into a small bowl and chill.

To serve, spread on hot toasted muffins or oat bannocks.

Crappit Heid

Crappit heid means stuffed head, and food writer F. Marian McNeill described it as a 'piscatorial haggis'. It was Rhoda Macleod, who now lives on Harris but was brought up on Lewis, who told me all about crappit heid, which she knows by the Gaelic name, *ceann cropaig*. She explained that first you need a very fresh fish. You must clean the liver thoroughly, then mash it with oatmeal with your hands before stuffing it into the head and boiling. She also sometimes steams the liver mixture in a bowl and discards the head, or makes *marag iasg* (fish pudding) from the mashed-up liver (no oatmeal) by packing it into the cleaned fish gullet and boiling it like a black or white pudding.

Rhoda also makes sheep's head broth (*ceann caorach*) by singeing the head, removing the eyes and splitting the head in half. After soaking in salt water overnight, it is rinsed, the brains are smeared all over it (to remove the taste of singeing) and then it is boiled to make a fine broth with turnips, carrots, onion and barley. None of this is for the faint-hearted.

Another Hebridean, Hamish Taylor of east Harris, told me he makes small fishcakes from the liver but he prefers to use coley rather than cod, since there are fewer worms. After washing the fish liver well, he mashes equal quantities of liver and wholemeal flour (again with the hands – their heat helps release the fish oil, which binds the mixture) and drops little cakes of the mixture into simmering water to poach.

Regional variations of crappit heid include stappit heidies in Caithness, Banff and Aberdeenshire, and krappin in Shetland. The latter is the mixture that is stuffed into a fish head or sometimes into a fish stomach (a 'muggie') to become krappit muggie. There is reference to fishermen taking fish-liver oatcake sandwiches to sea as their 'piece'. Who needs pastrami on rye anyway ...?

Although this dish would not win in the beauty stakes, it is truly delicious and well worth the rather arduous preparation. And you have all that lovely poaching broth to convert into fish soup afterwards.

Serves 6
1 cod's head, about 2kg/4½lb
(cleaned weight)
1 cod's liver, about 600g/1¼lb
(cleaned weight)
medium oatmeal
parsley or watercress, to garnish (optional)

First you have to clean the cod's head, which I ask my fishmonger to do for me. Remove the gills, then all the innards come out easily. Leave the lugs on (see Cabbie-claw on page 46), as these make ideal flaps to close over the stuffing. The eyes should be removed through the back, to give you perfect sockets; if you cut them out from the front, there will be tendons left in. Now wash it all out and dry well.

Now tackle the liver. Cod's liver invariably has lots of tiny worms in it, so these should be removed. The easiest way is just to snip away with a sharp knife – or use your fingers. The worms are creamy white little rings. They are easier to remove than you might think, as they are all on the surface so most come away as you pull at the outer skin. Once all the worms are out, wash the liver thoroughly and pat dry.

Place the liver in a large bowl with an equal weight of oatmeal and season well. The fun begins now, as you must get in with your hands and squish everything together until it is thoroughly mixed. Then stuff the head: I find it easiest to position the head in the large pan you are to cook it in, then push in the stuffing, remembering to lift the lugs and tuck some in beside the cheeks. You can pack it quite tightly. Close over the flaps to cover but don't worry if the stuffing is not all enclosed. Pour over about 1.8 litres/3 pints of cold water (which will come most of the way up the head) and bring slowly to the boil. Then skim off any scum, cover and cook gently for 30 minutes. Take off the heat, remove any scum and allow to cool in the liquid, still covered, until warm, not hot.

Transfer the head carefully to an ashet (platter) and, if you like, decorate with some greenery such as parsley or watercress. My fishmonger suggests (tongue in cheek) inserting a couple of large kalamata olives into the eye sockets! The broth can be used as the base for a simple fish soup. When you serve, ensure everyone has a bit of the delicacies – tongue and cheek – as well as some stuffing.

Hairy Tatties

Hairy tatties – a mixture of mashed potatoes and salt fish – are a speciality of Aberdeenshire, where they are eaten with oatcakes and cold milk. There is another Scots dish called freckled tatties – baked sliced potatoes layered with fried onions, milk and ground pepper – which can be served, like the French *gratin dauphinois*, with roasts or steaks. Leftover hairy tatties can be shaped into fishballs or cakes, dipped in egg and breadcrumbs or oatmeal and fried until golden brown.

Serves 4–6
600–700g/1¼–1½lb salt cod
1.5kg/3lb 5oz floury potatoes, peeled and cut into chunks
100g/3½oz butter
200ml/7fl oz hot full-fat milk
2 heaped teaspoons Dijon mustard
2 tablespoons chopped parsley
2 free-range eggs, hard-boiled and sliced

Soak the cod in cold water for 24 hours, changing the water 2 or 3 times (more often if you know it is a heavy salt cure).

Put the cod in a pan, cover with fresh cold water and bring slowly to the boil. Reduce to a simmer, cover the pan and cook slowly for 5 minutes, then remove the fish and drain well. Leave until cool enough to handle, then flake the flesh into chunks, carefully removing skin and bones.

Boil the potatoes until tender, then drain well. Mash with the butter and milk and stir in the mustard and some pepper to taste (no salt). Fold in the flaked fish, then top with the parsley and slices of hard-boiled egg just before serving.

Hot-buttered Arbroath Smokies

The Arbroath smokie was first recorded in Arbroath Abbey's land register in 1178, as a gift from King William to the monks, though it is probable that it dates back even further. They were originally made in Auchmithie, three miles north of Arbroath, and it was only when fishermen from Auchmithie were enticed to migrate to Arbroath and its new harbour in the 1880s that the fisherfolk moved, taking with them the secret of their unique hot-smoked haddock.

To make Arbroath smokies, the haddock are gutted, beheaded, lightly brined and then hot-smoked in pairs, tied together by their tails, until just cooked. The smoking used to be done in barrels sunk into the ground. The haddock were hung from wooden poles over beech or oak chips, then damp hessian bags were placed over the top. Depending on the size of the fish, they would need only 30–45 minutes' smoking before emerging a gorgeous bronzed, tarry colour with soft, succulent, delicately flavoured flesh. These days, the smoking is done in more or less the same way but by commercial companies, on a larger scale.

My parents remember the Arbroath and Auchmithie fishwives, in their distinctive navy blue flannel skirts ('coats') and plaid shawls, coming to Dundee to sell fish from willow creels – mainly smokies but also Finnan haddie. My brother-in-law's grandmother, Isabella (Ise) Smith, was one of Arbroath's last fishwives to do this. Once a week, she travelled all the way from Arbroath to Perthshire to sell fish to the 'big houses' there. She was away for the entire day, most of which was spent travelling, by train to Perth, then bus. Amazingly she continued until she was nearly 70 years old, which was in the late 1960s – not so long ago.

This recipe is for the simplest way to enjoy a smokie. But they can, of course, be eaten cold in salads (because they are hot-smoked, they are completely cooked), whizzed into pâtés or mousses, or made into quiches or soufflés.

Serves 2
1 pair of Arbroath smokies
40g/1½oz butter, softened

Preheat the oven to 180°C/350°F/Gas 4. Remove the bone from each smokie. The easiest way to do this is to place the fish on a board, skin-side down, then press with your thumb along the length of the bone to release it. Gently pull and the whole bone should come away.

Place the boned smokies side by side on a large sheet of foil. Dice the butter and smear it over the insides. Close up and wrap the fish in the foil and bake for 15–20 minutes or until piping hot.

Place each smokie on a warm plate and pour over the buttery juices. Serve with either a baked potato or some rough country bread to soak up the juices. A salad on the side would be nice but, of course, is not traditional.

Arbroath Smokie Pancakes

This is one of many easy dishes you can make with the versatile smokie. When Margaret Horn cooks this in Auchmithie's But 'n' Ben, she makes a delicious soup with the skin and bones (remember, most of the flavour from the smoking is in the skin), boiling them up with water and flavourings such as onion, bay and peppercorns. After half an hour or so, this is strained and leeks, potatoes and other vegetables are simmered in it to make a soup. Towards the end of cooking, I like to add a good handful of lovage, which complements the smokie flavour well.

The easiest way to remove the flesh from smokies is to heat them briefly either in a low oven for 10 minutes or in a microwave for 2–3 minutes.

Serves 4
300ml/10fl oz double cream
3 medium smokies
(or 2 small pairs, i.e. 4 small smokies)

For the pancakes:
225g/8oz plain flour, sifted
3 medium free-range eggs
350ml/12fl oz full-fat milk
a little butter for frying

First make the pancake batter: place the flour, eggs and milk in a food mixer or processor and process until smooth. Or beat together by hand until smooth. Pour into a wide jug and chill for an hour or so. To make the pancakes, smear the base of a crêpe pan with a little butter, then, once hot, add 2 tablespoons of the batter and swirl it around to cover the base of the pan. Once the underside is done, flip over and cook the other side (2–3 minutes altogether). Stack the pancakes in a pile. This amount should make 12.

For the filling, bring the cream slowly to the boil in a saucepan and cook over a medium heat for a couple of minutes until slightly thickened. Season well with pepper. Remove the flesh from the smokies and, ensuring it is bone-free, add it to the pan. Stir for a minute or so, then remove from the heat. Place a spoonful of the mixture in each pancake and roll up. If the pancakes are still hot, serve at once; otherwise tuck them into an ovenproof dish, side by side, and cover with foil. Heat gently in an oven preheated to 180°C/350°F/Gas 4 for about 15 minutes or until piping hot.

Cullen Skink Tart

The idea for this tart came from my visit to Alan McPherson's bakery in Cullen to see how butteries are made. As Alan was kneading and shaping the butteries, Derek the pie man poured a thick cullen skink mixture into dinky little pastry cases for his cullen skink pies. Here is my version – a thinner tart, made with a polenta or oatmeal pastry. I serve it warm with salad.

Serves 6–8

1 small onion, peeled and chopped
1 medium potato, peeled and diced
25g/1oz butter
400g/14oz undyed smoked haddock fillets
300ml/10fl oz full-fat milk
3 medium free-range eggs
2 tablespoons chopped parsley or lovage

For the pastry:

200g/7oz plain flour, sifted
25g/1oz fine oatmeal or polenta
125g/4½oz butter, diced
1 large free-range egg
1 teaspoon olive oil

For the pastry, place the flour, oatmeal or polenta and butter in a food processor, then add the egg and oil and process briefly. (Alternatively, put the dry ingredients in a bowl, rub in the butter, then mix to a dough with the egg and oil.) Wrap in clingfilm and chill for an hour or so. Roll out and use to line a buttered 28cm/11in loose-bottomed flan tin. Prick all over with a fork and chill again. Preheat the oven to 190°C/375°F/Gas 5.

Line the pastry case with foil, fill with baking beans and bake for 15 minutes. Remove the foil and beans and bake for a further 5 minutes, then leave to cool.

Sauté the onion and potato in the butter until tender, then set aside. Poach the fish in the milk for 3–4 minutes, then strain over a jug and break the fish into chunks. Beat the strained milk with the eggs, herbs and some seasoning. Place the onion, potato and fish in the pastry case. Pour in the liquid and bake for 30–35 minutes or until golden brown. Serve warm.

shellfish and crustaceans

4

It is extraordinary to think that until relatively recently, the consumption of shellfish went hand in hand with poverty. Oysters were eaten daily by the poor. It is recorded that in early-nineteenth-century Edinburgh (a much smaller city than today) some 100,000 oysters were consumed every single day. Lobster and crab were so cheap that they were daily fare in coastal villages and were eaten particularly in times of scarcity. Other molluscs, such as mussels, which we nowadays make into glorious stews and soups, were used only as bait.

How times have changed. Apart from mussels, which are still fairly inexpensive, most shellfish are now regarded as a luxury item. This is partly because industrial pollution spoiled shellfish beds in the shallow waters, resulting in fishermen going further afield; also, at long last we Scots — and, it seems, the rest of the British Isles — have woken up to the fact that shellfish are absolutely delicious.

The recipes in this chapter are incredibly simple, as befits some of the finest ingredients in the world. So Hebridean clamcakes are simply scallops (often called clams in the Hebrides) coated in oatmeal and fried. Stewed oysters are those fabulous molluscs sautéed very lightly in butter and served on thick slices of toast. Mussels in a bag are mussels cooked in foil parcels over a peat fire or, for those sultry summer days, a barbecue.

Two lobster recipes show how versatile that beast is. The more sophisticated one includes an adaptation of Lady Clark of Tillypronie's mayonnaise sauce for lobster. The other is Margaret Horn's chew and spit lobster, which is just that: boiled lobster attacked with lobster picks and fingers, the meat chewed, then any pieces of shell spat out. Just as sublime as Lady Clark's dish but definitely more 'hands-on' — perhaps more suited to kitchen supper than dining-room dinner.

If you are nervous about preparing shellfish yourself, do not overlook these recipes, for your fishmonger is there to help. If no help is forthcoming, change shops and go to the one down the road.

Mussel and Onion Stew

The garlic in this delicious and simple stew is not authentic but I think it enhances the whole dish. Serve this with plenty of crusty bread to dunk into the juices.

Serves 4
1kg/2¼lb mussels
2–3 sprigs of thyme
400ml/14fl oz dry white wine
40g/1½oz butter
2 onions, peeled and chopped
2 large garlic cloves, peeled and chopped
40g/1½oz parsley, chopped

Scrub the mussels thoroughly, discarding any open ones that don't close when tapped on a work surface. Place them in a large pan with the thyme sprigs and white wine, cover tightly and bring slowly to the boil. Boil for about 1 minute, until the shells have opened, then remove from the heat and strain over a jug. Discard any mussels that have not opened.

Heat the butter in the pan in which the mussels were cooked and gently fry the onions and garlic in it for about 10 minutes, until softened. Increase the heat and add the mussel liquor. Bring to the boil and bubble away for 4–5 minutes to reduce a little, then taste and season accordingly. Return the mussels to the pan in their shells. Stir gently and warm through over a low heat for a minute or so, then scatter over the parsley. Ladle into warm bowls and serve immediately.

Chew and Spit Lobster

When Margaret Horn was growing up in the tiny coastal village of Auchmithie in Angus, chew and spit lobster and crab were everyday summer fare. She was a child during the Second World War, when the lobster pots set down in the harbour were full most days. But because the lobsters could not easily be sent to the country's smart restaurants, many were consumed locally. Margaret remembers shortly after the war being taken to dinner in Edinburgh by her husband-to-be and ordering lobster. It was only when she saw his face – and later the bill – that she realised that lobster was a luxury everywhere else.

The whole family would sit down to a tray in the middle of the table bearing freshly boiled lobsters and crabs, accompanied only by some bread and butter (no lemon wedges in those days), then proceed to tuck in with their hands. There were no forks used – and absolutely no finesse, which is why Margaret's family called it chew and spit lobster. The meat was prodded and poked out with the ends of teaspoons, then the claws and legs sucked dry of their juices, and any tiny pieces of shell were spat out.

When you eat lobster in this manner, with only some bread and a glass of chilled white wine (milk or water when Margaret was a child) you begin to appreciate that the best things in life are often the simplest. No adornments of mayonnaise or the complication of thermidor are required. Just plenty of time and patience. And finger bowls if you absolutely must.

Serves 2
1 live lobster, weighing
600–700g/1¼–1½lb
lemon wedges (optional)

Place the lobster in the freezer for a couple of hours to chill it into unconsciousness before boiling, as recommended by the RSPCA. Then bring a large pan of salted water to the boil, plunge the lobster in head first and, using tongs, keep it immersed for at least 2 minutes, then allow the water to return to the boil. Counting from when the water returns to a full boil, cook for 15 minutes. Lobsters over 700g/1½lb will require 20 minutes; ones over 1.1kg/2½lb, will need 25 minutes. Remove the lobster, place on a board and leave to cool.

Once it is cool enough to handle (it is easier to extract the flesh if the lobster is still a little warm), twist off the main claws and remove the rubber bands binding them. Lay the lobster on a board, shell uppermost, pull back the tail to extend the body and, with a sharp knife, cut down the middle, all along the length of the lobster. You might need to give it a few sharp taps as you go. Remove and discard the inedible stomach sac (which looks like crumpled clingfilm), the dark intestinal thread running down the tail and the greyish, feathery gills.

And now everything you see is edible. Squeeze over some lemon juice, if you like. If it is a hen lobster, you have the bonus of eating the coral. Bash the claws to open them, or simply poke at them with a lobster pick or skewer to remove the meat. Then remove the main tail meat in one piece. Continue by sucking at the legs to extract every last morsel of meat. Nibble on some brown bread and butter and slurp a chilled glass of fine white burgundy or champagne. Your hands will now be covered in lobster bits and pieces and reek of crustacea. But then so are your dinner partner's. And besides, when you are indulging in one of life's sweetest pleasures, table manners go by the board.

Potted Crab

This recipe is versatile: it can be chilled and served in little ramekins or served hot, straight from the pan. The latter is one of Clarissa Dickson Wright's great party dishes. Both ways are delicious, provided you use the best ingredients. Only freshly cooked crabmeat should be used, never tinned.

Serves 4
75g/3oz unsalted butter
250g/9oz freshly boiled crabmeat
(white and brown)
scant ½ teaspoon ground mace
juice of ½ lemon
a pinch of cayenne pepper

Melt the butter in a saucepan then add the crabmeat, mace, lemon juice and cayenne. Heat gently for 8–10 minutes, then taste and add salt and pepper accordingly.

Either serve warm from the pan or pour into 4 ramekins and chill until set – preferably overnight. Eat with warm toast or oatcakes.

Scallops with Mash

This is not a traditional recipe but it is the type of dish chefs are serving up more and more: local produce cooked in a straightforward way. Delicious, yet very simple.

The scallops are also wonderful served with a pea mash made by puréeing 250g/9oz fresh or frozen peas – just cooked – with half the butter and them mixing them with the potatoes. Add some chopped fresh mint to make it even more special.

The reason you should separate the scallop muscle from the coral before cooking is that the coral requires less cooking and it tends to burst and splutter in a very hot pan if cooked for too long. Smaller scallops can be left whole.

Serves 4

12 plump, fresh scallops,
(ensure they have not been frozen)

olive oil

1kg/2¼lb floury potatoes
(e.g. Maris Piper, Desiree, King Edward),
peeled and chopped

100g/3½oz butter

100ml/3½fl oz hot full-fat milk

Separate the scallop muscle (which is white) from the coral (which is orange). Marinate both muscle and coral in a little olive oil, turning until well covered. Leave for 20 minutes or so.

Meanwhile, cook the potatoes in boiling salted water until tender, then drain well. Mash with the butter and milk and season well with salt and pepper. For the scallops, heat a good solid frying pan until very hot, then add the scallop muscles (which because of their marinade require no further oil). Season with salt and pepper, cook for 1 minute and then turn Add the scallop corals and cook for 1–2 minutes, until both muscle and coral are cooked – just.

To serve, place a mound of mash in the centre of each plate and top with the scallops and the coral.

Hebridean Clamcakes

These are not clams but scallops, which are known as clams on some Hebridean islands. They are simply coated in oatmeal and fried until crunchy outside, soft and tender inside. Delicious.

This recipe uses only the scallop muscle. Instead of discarding the corals, I like to poach them gently in a little fish stock (about a cupful for the 6 corals), then whizz them up in a blender with seasoning and serve with the clamcakes.

Serves 2 as a starter

6 plump, fresh scallops, trimmed, corals carefully cut off

1 medium free-range egg, beaten

75g/3oz medium oatmeal

25g/1oz butter

Dip the scallops in the beaten egg, then coat in the oatmeal. Chill for an hour or so, then dip in egg again and re-coat in oatmeal. Chill again. Bring the scallops to room temperature for 15–20 minutes before cooking.

Heat the butter in a frying pan until medium-hot, then fry the scallops for 2–3 minutes on each side, until just done. Serve piping hot.

Stewed Oysters

'I ate some excellent oysters at the table of this learned man [a Doctor in Prestonpans, east of Edinburgh] as was not to be wondered at, seeing that I was in the place where the most famous oysters are taken in abundance; the rocks at the surface of the sea around the coast are covered with them. They are large, plump and of an exquisite taste; and are held in such estimation, that they are exported to the principal cities of England and Holland.' Thus wrote B. Faujas de Saint-Fond in *A Journey Through England and Scotland to the Hebrides in 1784*. For, up until the twentieth century, oysters were not only plentiful, they were cheap. In the 1880s some 1,200 million oysters a year were eaten in Britain, according to *The Story of Loch Fyne Oysters* by Christina Noble. She describes how in Edinburgh's elegant New Town, the Oyster Lassies from Newhaven went around calling, 'Wha'l o caller ou?' ('Who'll have fresh oysters?') Their dress – rather like the Arbroath and Auchmithie fish wives – was distinctive, with dark blue jacket, striped petticoats and a basket creel full of oysters on their back.

There are several old recipes for cooked oysters and one that often crops up is oyster loaves – stewed oysters served in a hot bread roll or small loaf. The following recipe can be served in this way, or – my favourite – on thick slices of hot buttered toast.

Loch Fyne is probably the most famous place in the country for oysters these days. Pacific or rock oysters (*Crassostrea gigas*) have been farmed in this sea loch for some years now. Available all year, they have a superb flavour and are also relatively cheap. If, however, you can get your hands on native oysters (*Ostrea edulis*), these are the ones to savour raw (it would be a sacrilege to cook them; besides they are expensive) – with a pile of fresh brown bread and butter, a wedge or two of lemon and a glass of champagne, chilled white wine or Guinness. The latter is not exactly Scottish, I know, but the combination is truly perfect. And as for those scaremongers who insist that whisky, brandy or any spirits should never be drunk with oysters . . . There is no reason why a glass of peaty malt whisky should not accompany oysters if you wish. I personally like claret with this dish; Leith (famous for the centuries-old claret trade) is, after all, the next port along the coast from Newhaven.

Serves 2
a dozen oysters in their shells
40g/1½oz butter
a little white wine
thick toast or hot rolls, to serve

First shuck the oysters: wrap your left hand in a tea towel (assuming you are right handed) and place an oyster, cup-side down, hinge towards you, in your palm. Insert an oyster knife or small sharp knife into the hinge. Push and twist simultaneously, passing the knife under the top shell to cut the muscle and sliding it along the length to open fully. Remove the oyster from its shell, retaining all the juices.

Melt the butter in a large frying pan and toss in the oysters and any juices with plenty of black pepper (you don't need salt). Sauté them very briefly – for about 2 minutes – just until they are warm, then add a splash of wine and remove from the heat.

Serve on thick slices of hot buttered toast or in individual hot rolls (top sliced off, insides scooped out, and heated in a hot oven for 5 minutes). Eat at once – perhaps with an improbable-sounding glass of claret, in true Edinburgh style!

Dods Macfarlane's Mussels in a Bag

Dods Macfarlane has lived in the port of Ness on the Butt of Lewis all his life. For most of the year he sells fresh and salt herring, mackerel, smoked haddock, cod and ling. Every summer, however, he and nine other men of Ness make a voyage to a remote rock in the Atlantic, Sula Sgeir, some 40 miles north of Lewis, to harvest guga, as part of a legacy that has existed for some four centuries.

Gugas are plump young gannets, 2,000 of which are harvested every year. Although they are protected birds, a statutory order inserted into the 1954 Protection of Birds Act allows Nessmen to continue the tradition of hunting them. Once the men arrive on the tiny island they set up camp, then spend 14 days catching the birds, which involves remarkable rock-climbing skills, usually amid the most adverse weather conditions. After being killed, the birds are decapitated, plucked, singed, dewinged and split. They are then salted and piled in a mound (a 'pickling stack') with a wheel formation. When the men return home to Ness with their harvest, they are met on the quay by a queue of locals, all eager to buy a pair of gugas, which will be desalinated, boiled and eaten with potatoes. It is one of Dods' favourite dishes – the taste often described as neither fish nor fowl, but somewhere between steak and kipper. Last year Dods took a barbecue to Sula Sgeir, amid much teasing from his fellow hunters. In the morning he marinated some guga in HP sauce before barbecuing them that night. He insists it was absolutely delicious.

And an equally delicious – but more accessible – Dods dish is mussels wrapped in foil and thrown on to a peat fire. He adds no flavours as he says that there are enough juices in the mussels. Since few of us have peat fires, I recommend cooking the mussels on a barbecue. And I also suggest some supplementary flavourings. Sorry Dods.

Serves 4
24–28 large mussels
a little oil

Optional flavourings:
3–4 spring onions, chopped
2 teaspoons grated fresh root ginger
2 garlic cloves, peeled and chopped
2 tablespoons white wine
2 tablespoons olive oil

Scrub the mussels well, discarding any open ones that don't close when tapped on a work surface. Cut 4 pieces of foil about 30cm/12in square and place on a work surface. Lightly oil them, then place the spring onions, ginger and garlic, if using, on each one. Top with the mussels, then divide the wine and oil between them, if using. Crimp the edges of the foil together to seal, then place the parcels either on a peat fire or on the hottest part of your barbecue for about 10 minutes, until the mussels have opened. Eat straight from the bag.

Grilled Lobster

with Lady Clark's Mayonnaise Sauce

Lady Clark of Tillypronie was an inveterate recipe collector, with an unusual (for that time) curiosity about food. She would ask cooks in the houses she dined in for recipes then have her own cooks prepare them in her home in north-east Scotland. After she died, a cookbook was compiled from her collection as a memorial, requested by her husband. Her mayonnaise sauce recipe for lobster, crab or crayfish is enlivened with mustard, gherkins and capers. She also stirred in some thick cream at the end. I prefer adding yoghurt to thin it down slightly and sharpen the flavour, although it is wonderful served as it is – thick and glossy, without any embellishment.

It is worth heeding Lady Clark's advice about mayonnaise: 'To be well made this requires much care.' Mayonnaise is hard work by hand, as you have to whisk continually while drizzling in the oil, but for such a small quantity I find it is not worth dirtying the food processor. If you feel safer using a machine, however, you should probably double the quantities, as this amount is too small for most food processors.

Serves 2
1 live lobster, weighing 600–700g/1¼–1½lb

For the mayonnaise:
1 medium free-range egg yolk
½ teaspoon Dijon mustard
150ml/5fl oz oil (I use half olive, half sunflower)
1 tablespoon chopped mixed capers and gherkins
1 tablespoon Greek yoghurt (optional)

First make the mayonnaise: put the egg yolk and mustard into a bowl and place it on a damp cloth to stop it slipping. Whisk until combined. Now add the oil – literally drop by drop at first – whisking all the time until it thickens. After you have added about a third of the oil, add the rest in a very thin stream, whisking continuously. Once all the oil has been added, stir in the capers and gherkins, and the yoghurt if using. Season to taste with salt and pepper.

Now prepare the lobster in the same way as for Chew and Spit Lobster (see page 60), but boil (once the water has returned to a full boil) for only 5 minutes. Cool, split in half, remove the stomach sac and dark intestinal tract. Don't worry if you see green slime – it is the liver (called the tomalley) which is edible. If it is a female lobster, remove the coral and add it to the mayonnaise. (If you prefer, you could grill the lobster without par-boiling: cut it in half when you remove it from the freezer by pushing a sharp knife through the well-defined cross on the back of the head and quickly splitting it in half lengthwise down the back. Remove the stomach and intestinal tract.) Twist off the claws (removing the rubber bands), brush them with oil and cook for about 5 minutes over a medium barbecue or under a grill.

Brush oil all over the body section, then place the halves, shell-side down on a barbecue or under a grill, shell-side up for 8–10 minutes. Turn and cook, flesh-side down on a barbecue, flesh-side up – towards the heat – under a grill for about 2–3 minutes or until just done. You will need 15–20 minutes altogether (an extra 5 minutes) if the lobster has not been par-boiled.

Serve the warm lobster with the mayonnaise sauce.

5

meat and poultry

'Some hae meat and canna eat
And some wad eat that want it
But we hae meat and we can eat
Sae let the Lord be thankit.'

Robert Burns' famous Selkirk Grace sums it up really. Meat has always been of prime importance in Scotland. Whether eaten on high days and holidays or as everyday fare, it has always been revered – until the introduction of intensive farming. Gradually many people began to eat less meat, because of the resulting inferior quality and because of the concomitant food scares and welfare issues. I believe red meat is a valuable addition to the diet, with its high iron content and vitamins. Ironically, though, many consumers gave up red meat and opted for white meat such as chicken, which although also good for you, is the meat most likely to have been inhumanely reared in cramped conditions.

But it was not always thus. And thankfully meat eaters in Scotland and elsewhere are welcoming the return of extensive, often organic, farming, not only on welfare grounds but also because the meat tastes better. Some old-fashioned dishes such as stoved howtowdie simply would not work with battery chicken, with its flabby, wet flesh. It requires a sturdy, firm chicken, whose life has involved plenty of activity.

Scottish beef and lamb are some of the finest in the world (you will notice that pork does not come into the equation, as we Scots have always harboured an innate aversion to pork, apart from bacon and ham). And when you see great, lumbering Aberdeen Angus standing proud in a field of lush green grass in Aberdeenshire, or Cheviot sheep nibbling their way along a dry-stane dyke in the Borders, you begin to appreciate that Scottish meat is inherently free-range in the true sense of the word.

A joint of Scottish beef – from a reliable butcher who not only hangs his meat well but also assures you it is from traditionally reared, grass-fed cattle – is a memorable feast. A leg of Borders, Shetland or Hebridean lamb, simply roasted, is another sublime dish. In this chapter, there are, of course, some embellishments to basic roasts, stews and mince but, provided you have top-quality meat, I like to do as Escoffier advised and 'Faites simple' – keep it simple.

Mince and Tatties

'Yes, but can she cook mince?' A young Scotsman extolling the beauty and talents of his intended bride to his family was invariably asked this question. Mince is such an important dish in Scotland that it is virtually written into the wedding contract. My mother reckons she ate it at least three days a week when she was a child. And with the mince it was always tatties. Occasionally, if you were very lucky, there might be a green vegetable, too, but more likely it was a tin of peas or beans. We Scots did not acquire our anti-vegetable reputation for nothing. In Aberdeenshire, a white (mealie) pudding is placed over the mince for the last 15–20 minutes or so of cooking and is called mince and mealies. If you do this, don't worry if the pudding bursts as this only enhances the flavour of the mince.

My mother's basic recipe is to brown the mince in a little dripping, add chopped onion and water then simmer until cooked, thickening at the end with Bisto. Instead of Bisto I either crumble in some stock cube or add a little Marmite for a good savoury flavour. A shake of Worcestershire sauce is not traditional but my family likes it. You could also add mushroom ketchup if you can find it.

The good flavour comes from using only the best-quality mince, preferably steak minced in front of you at the butcher's. If you know it is not terribly lean, then do not use any fat to brown it; just place it in a very hot pan on its own. As for the texture, it should be soft enough to dribble seductively over your mound of mash but thick enough to make a decent forkful. The derogatory Scottish expression, 'thick as mince', did not arrive on the linguistic scene by chance.

Serves 4
a knob of dripping or butter
500g/18oz best beef mince
1 medium or ½ large onion, peeled and finely chopped
½ beef stock cube or
1 teaspoon Marmite
Worcestershire sauce or mushroom ketchup (optional)
Champit Tatties (see page 112), to serve

Heat the dripping or butter in a solid, reliable pan, then add the mince and brown over a high heat, stirring around to break it up. This should take about 5 minutes. Add the onion, crumble in the stock cube or stir in the Marmite and season with some salt and pepper. Add 3–4 tablespoons of boiling water, stir well, then cover and cook over a medium heat for about 20 minutes. Add a good shake of Worcestershire sauce or mushroom ketchup if required, then check the seasoning again. Serve piping hot with the tatties and some freshly cooked peas or stir-fried cabbage.

Potted Hough

Similar to English brawn, which is made with pork, potted hough is a traditional dish that uses up cheaper cuts of beef. The word 'hough' (pronounced hoch, as in loch) means shin and it is this meat that is boiled up for hours until tender and gelatinous. It is then potted and served with salad or bread, although in my mother's family it was eaten in the summer with new potatoes and a vegetable such as cabbage or turnips, the warmth of the hot potatoes melting the jelly on top of the meat.

This version is based on my Auntie Bette's recipe. She only used salt and white pepper as seasoning, never spices, but I give these here as an optional extra. Auntie Bette also used to pot it in teacups to make individual servings.

Serves 6–8
900g/2lb hough (shin of beef)
1 knap (fore-nap) bone or knuckle, washed
½ teaspoon mace blade (optional)
½ teaspoon peppercorns (optional)
½ teaspoon whole allspice (optional)

Wipe the meat all over and place it in a large soup pot with the bone and cold water to cover – about 2.25 litres/4 pints. If using the mace, peppercorns and allspice, tie them in a piece of muslin and add to the pan. Cover tightly and simmer over a very low heat for about 5–6 hours, until the meat is very tender. Remove the bone and place the meat on a board. Strain the stock, remove the spice bag and add salt and pepper to the stock to taste.

Shred or finely chop the meat and return it to the stock pan. Bring back to the boil and boil for about 5 minutes, then remove. Pour the mixture into wetted moulds or bowls (rinsed in cold water) and leave until completely cold.

Meatroll

Meatroll (or meatloaf) recipes vary from region to region, and also in shape and size. My mother's was always round, made in a pottery meatroll 'jar'. In the north-east it is called Aberdeenshire sausage or roll and was often made in a round coffee tin.

My recipe is based on that of Mrs Doig, the minister's wife. My dear friend Isabelle Doig and I would always play together at the manse after school and I was usually asked to stay for tea. I always agreed, and especially enjoyed it if it was Mrs Doig's famous meatloaf. After tea, realising the time, I had to run home – arriving a little late – and sit down to a second tea. Sadly my appetite has not diminished much over the years.

Serves 6–8

450g/1lb lean minced beef

250g/9oz lean minced pork

75g/3oz fresh breadcrumbs

1 medium free-range egg

½ large onion, peeled and finely chopped

1 tablespoon Worcestershire sauce or mushroom ketchup

1 tablespoon chopped parsley

Preheat the oven to 150°C/200°F/Gas 2. Mix everything together and season generously with salt and pepper. Spoon into a lightly buttered 900g/2lb loaf tin, pressing down well. Cover loosely with foil and bake for 1¾–2 hours. Leave to cool in the tin for at least 20 minutes, then carefully drain off any liquid and turn out on to a plate. Cut into thick slices and serve warm with a fresh tomato sauce and new potatoes or tagliatelle, or cold with salad and good crusty bread.

Stornoway Black Pudding and Potato Stack

The idea for this comes from Roddy Aflin, chef-proprietor at the Park Guest House in Stornoway, who uses butcher Iain Macleod's wonderful black pudding. He serves it as a starter with a red wine reduction flavoured with oil and vinegar, but I like to serve it with a simple balsamic vinegar and olive oil dressing. It is also divine without the dressing. Roddy uses sweet potato, which looks good, but it tastes superb with ordinary potato, too.

Serves 4

16 x 1cm/½in slices of black pudding (preferably Stornoway pudding), skinned

16 x 5mm/¼in slices of potato or sweet potato

melted butter for brushing

2 tablespoons extra virgin olive oil

1 tablespoon balsamic vinegar

Place the black pudding and potato slices on a sheet of foil and brush with melted butter, then season with salt and pepper. Place under a preheated grill for 3 minutes, then turn the potatoes over. Remove the black pudding after 2 minutes (so they are cooked for 5 minutes altogether) and keep warm – and continue to cook the potato slices until done – about 7–8 minutes altogether.

To assemble, stack up alternative slices of black pudding and potato on each plate, starting with black pudding and finishing with a potato slice, seasoning with a little salt between the layers. Whisk together the oil and vinegar with a little seasoning and drizzle or dot this dressing over and around the stack. Serve at once.

Musselburgh Pie

In Musselburgh (the 'Honest Toun'), situated to the east of Edinburgh on the Firth of Forth, there have been oyster and mussel beds for many centuries. Clarissa Dickson Wright, in her charming book, *Hieland Foodie*, writes that these beds have been harvested since Roman times. Native British oysters, which were highly prized by the Romans, were transported in seaweed-lined barrels to the emperor's table in Rome.

In the days when they were literally two a penny, many of the oysters for Edinburgh's oyster bars came from the shoreline around Musselburgh. Now it is a polluted coastline, but this Musselburgh pie recipe, which combines oysters with rump steak, is a delightful remembrance of things past.

Serves 4

6 very thin slices of rump steak (called popeseye steak in Scotland), weighing about 750g/1lb 10oz in total

12 oysters

1 heaped tablespoon flour, seasoned with salt and pepper

50g/2oz butter

2 onions, peeled and chopped

250ml/9fl oz boiling beef stock

about 250g/9oz ready-rolled puff pastry

beaten egg, to glaze

Preheat the oven to 170°C/325°F/Gas 3. Cut the steak slices in half and lay them on a board. Open the oysters (see page 65), remove them from their shells and reserve the juices. Wrap each oyster in a piece of beef and dip them in the seasoned flour. Place in a 1.5 litre/2½ pint pie dish; they should fit snugly. Season well.

Heat the butter in a saucepan, add the onions and fry until tender, then tip them over the beef. Pour over the oyster juices and the boiling stock. Cover very tightly and cook in the oven for 1½ hours, then leave to cool completely.

Preheat the oven to 220°C/425°F/Gas 7. Cut a long strip off the rolled-out pastry. Wet your fingers lightly and dampen the edges of the pie dish. Place the pastry strip round the rim of the dish, then brush with some of the beaten egg. Place the remaining pastry over the top and press down to seal all the edges. Trim off any excess pastry and crimp the edges between your thumb and forefinger. Brush with egg, slit the top to allow steam to escape and bake for about 25 minutes, until golden brown.

Forfar Bridies

Bridies and pies are still very much a part of life in Dundee and Angus. And whereas the best pies have traditionally come from Dundee, the best bridies are from Forfar.

According to F. Marian McNeill, the first Forfar bridie baker was a Mr Jolly in the mid-nineteenth century. My recipe is based on Bill McLaren's, whose great-grandfather, James McLaren, learned the skills of bridie-making at Jolly's bakery. His family-run bakery, opened in 1893, has baked bridies to the same recipe ever since. When I visited him there, he taught me the essential 'dunting' and 'nicking' procedure to seal the horseshoe-shaped bridie.

There are also some recipes for venison bridies, which could be even more ancient than the now-traditional beef, since deer roamed the Highlands long before cattle.

Makes 4

450g/1lb shoulder or rump of beef
75g/3oz beef suet, grated
1 small onion, peeled and finely grated

For the pastry:

250g/9oz strong white flour
75g/3oz plain flour
a pinch of salt
75g/3oz unsalted butter, diced
75g/3oz white fat, diced

For the pastry, sift the flours and salt into a food processor. Add the fats and process until incorporated. Add just enough cold water (2½–3 tablespoons) to bind to a stiff dough. Gather it up in your hands, wrap in clingfilm and chill for at least 1 hour.

For the filling, roughly chop the beef – I use the pulse button on my food processor – or mince it very coarsely. Mix together the beef, suet, onion and plenty of salt and pepper. The mixture should be fairly stiff. Divide the pastry into 4 and roll each piece into an oval. Spoon the filling on to one half of each pastry oval, leaving a border all round it. Dampen the edges of the pastry and fold the uncovered half over the filling to enclose it. Trim the edges into a neat horseshoe shape (not a half-moon: that is the Cornish pasty). Now 'dunt' it by pressing down on the edges with the heel of your hand and 'nick' it by crimping with your forefinger and thumb to give a nice finish. Using a sharp knife, prick a small hole (for steam to escape) in the top of each bridie. Place on a lightly buttered baking tray and chill for an hour or so. Preheat the oven to 200°C/400°F/Gas 6.

Bake the bridies for 35–40 minutes or until golden brown. Serve warm.

Steak Pie

Steak pie used to be the main course on New Year's Day – and indeed, often on Christmas Day (which was, of course, just another working day) – for my parents' families. The pies were seldom home-made but were bought from the butcher's shop. The reason for this was not only that people were simply too busy but also a good butcher's steak pie was – still is – a thing of great beauty, and delicious, too. The enamel ashet (dish) was taken to the butcher's to be filled and baked, then all it required was reheating at home before being served with mashed potatoes and marrowfat peas or butterbeans.

When I make a steak pie myself, I start it the day before so that the stew has time to cool down and thicken up a little before I cover it with the pastry. I like to serve it with mashed potatoes, stir-fried cabbage and Brussels sprouts or peas.

Serves 6

50g/2oz dripping or butter

900g/2lb stewing beef, diced (my butcher recommends chuck (shoulder) steak)

40g/1½oz plain flour, well seasoned with salt and pepper

1 large onion, peeled and chopped

4 large carrots, peeled and thickly sliced

600ml/1 pint hot beef stock

1 heaped tablespoon tomato purée

1 tablespoon Worcestershire sauce

250g/9oz ready-rolled puff pastry

beaten egg, to glaze

Heat the dripping or butter in a heavy saucepan. Toss half the meat in the seasoned flour and brown it all over in the fat, then remove with a slotted spoon. Toss the remaining meat in the flour and brown all over. Remove with a slotted spoon, then add the onion and carrots to the pan (if necessary, add a little extra fat at this stage). Fry gently for about 5 minutes, until softened, then return the meat to the pan with the hot stock, tomato purée and Worcestershire sauce. Grind in plenty of black pepper and some salt, stir well and bring to the boil. Then cover and reduce to a simmer. Cook very gently for 2 hours, stirring once, then check the seasoning. Tip into a 1.8 litre/3 pint pie dish and leave to cool completely. Cover and refrigerate overnight.

The next day, preheat the oven to 220°C/425°F/Gas 7. Cut a long strip off the rolled-out pastry. Wet your fingers lightly and dampen the edges of the pie dish. Place the pastry strip round the rim of the pie dish, then brush with some of the beaten egg. Place the remaining pastry over the top and press down to seal all the edges. Trim off any excess pastry and crimp the edges between your thumb and forefinger. Brush with more beaten egg and use scissors to snip a hole in the middle. Bake for 30–35 minutes, until puffed up and golden brown. You might need to lay a piece of foil lightly over the surface for the last 10 minutes or so to prevent burning. Serve piping hot.

Scotch Pies

Made from beef or mutton, these are small raised pies with a pastry lid that sits down a little inside the top of the rim. They are never referred to as Scotch pies, except in books. In Dundee they are simply called pies (pronounced 'peh'). They are crucial to the average Dundonian, and even those ex-pats living elsewhere will stock up on pies from Dundee butchers and bakers and freeze them. There is some rivalry between the two professions, bakers insisting their pastry is best, butchers insisting their filling is best. David Craig of Robertson's butcher's in Broughty Ferry has come to the best compromise by buying shells from one of Dundee's top bakers and filling them with his own top-quality meat. Pies were traditional Saturday lunchtime fare, eaten hot with beans or peas, presumably as a quick meal that freed the men for the football in the afternoon.

David Craig has given me the recipe for his famous pies, which are so popular with locals. He recommends freezing them uncooked if you don't want to bake them all at once. If you do not want to make the pastry yourself, many good bakers and butchers in Scotland sell Scotch pie shells.

Makes 15–20

700g/1½lb lean minced beef
300g/10½oz white rusks
(baby rusks are fine), crushed
25g/1oz seasoning, made of 3 parts salt to
1 part white pepper)
beaten egg, to glaze

For the pastry:

225g/8oz lard or dripping
700g/1½lb self-raising flour
1 teaspoon salt

For the pastry, put the fat in a pan with 300ml/10fl oz water and bring to the boil until the fat has melted. Sift the flour and salt into a warmed bowl (to take off the chill) and stir in the liquid. Work with a wooden spoon until cool enough to handle, then knead until smooth. Cover and leave in a warm place until firmed up a little but still pliable. Roll out to fit 15–20 pie moulds (or large, deep bun or muffin tins). Roll out the remaining pastry and cut out lids to fit your tins. Leave the pastry shells and lids somewhere cool to harden overnight.

Preheat the oven to 190°C/375°F/Gas 5. For the filling, mix the mince and rusks with enough ice-cold water to bind to a stiff consistency, then add the seasoning.

Fill the pie shells about three-quarters full (no more), then press in the lids and glaze with egg. Slit a tiny hole in each lid. Bake for about 25 minutes or until the pastry is golden brown and cooked through. Serve piping hot.

Hotchpotch

It was difficult to know whether to put this into the soup or meat chapter, for it is really something in between. Chunky and hearty, it is a thick soup or sloppy stew that requires only some bread or baked potatoes as an accompaniment.

Originally from the French word, *hochepot*, meaning a mutton, beef or fowl ragout with turnips and chestnuts, hotchpotch now means a dish of mixed ingredients, such as a stew with vegetables. Interestingly, there is a very similar rustic Dutch dish called *hutspot*, with almost the same ingredients.

My recipe is a modernised version of the old recipes, using lamb instead of mutton and as many vegetables as can be crammed in. I have left out the chestnuts, although they were extremely popular in Scotland in the past. The secret of a good hotchpotch is slow cooking, in order to have tender pieces of meat and a richly flavoured broth. If you dislike a fatty taste to your broth, cook the first stage (i.e. for 2 hours), then cool and chill. Scrape off surface fat and reheat to boiling before adding the remaining vegetables.

Serves 6

900g/2lb neck and/or shoulder of lamb (traditionally the bone is left in), chopped into very large pieces

8 carrots, peeled but left whole

600g/1¼lb baby turnips, peeled but left whole

1 large onion, peeled and cut into sixths or eighths

3–4 sprigs of thyme

4 large (or 8 medium) spring onions, trimmed

1 small cauliflower, cut into florets

3 heaped tablespoons chopped parsley

Place the meat in a large, heavy casserole. Top with 2 whole carrots, the whole turnips, onion and thyme. Cover with 1.2 litres/2 pints of cold water, add some salt and pepper and bring slowly to the boil. Skim off any scum from the surface, then cover and cook over a very low heat for about 2 hours (skim again if necessary.) Remove the vegetables and discard. Then bring the mixture up to the boil, add the remaining carrots, the whole spring onions and the cauliflower florets. Cook, covered, over a medium heat for about 15 minutes, until the vegetables are just tender. Check the seasoning and stir in the parsley. Using a slotted spoon, divide between deep plates or bowls.

Roast Beef with Cucumber and Ginger Salad

Although this cucumber salad may not seem a typically Scottish accompaniment to roast beef, the inspiration came from B. Faujas de Saint-Fond's journal, *A Journey through England and Scotland to the Hebrides in 1784*. He describes a four-o'clock dinner that he took in Torloisk, Mull, consisting of soup, black pudding, mutton, woodcock, and hot roast beef with 'cucumbers and ginger pickled in vinegar'. This was followed by cream with Madeira wine and a pudding made of barley meal, cream and currants and cooked in dripping. The latter I could probably do without but the roast beef and ginger cucumbers comes highly recommended.

Serves 8

4-rib of beef, weighing about 4.25kg/9½lb

For the salad:

1 large cucumber, coarsely grated (unpeeled)

100ml/3½fl oz white wine vinegar

1 heaped tablespoon granulated sugar

½ teaspoon salt

4–5cm/1½–2in piece of fresh root ginger, peeled and coarsely grated

Preheat the oven to 230°C/450°F/Gas 8. Ensure the beef is at room temperature, not straight from the fridge. Season it all over, then place it in a roasting tin (without any extra fat) and roast for 15 minutes. Reduce the oven temperature to 170°C/325°F/Gas 3 and cook for a further 17 minutes per 450g/1lb. This will result in medium-rare meat.

For the salad, combine all the ingredients, then leave for an hour or so before serving.

Once the meat is cooked to your liking, remove from the oven and leave to rest for at least 15 minutes. Then carve and serve with the salad and some roast potatoes and green vegetables.

Steak with Claret and Anchovies

Inspired by a recipe in Mistress Margaret Dods' *Manual*, this quick dish is simplicity itself. In her 1829 book she recommended frying the steaks for 12–15 minutes but I think that is too long – even if you like them well-done rather than rare.

Claret was commonly drunk with food and sometimes used in the kitchen because of the Auld Alliance links between the Bordeaux region of France and the port of Leith. In Dorothy Wordsworth's *Recollections of a Tour Made of Scotland in 1803*, she describes a stay in a house in the Highlands. The lady of the house 'set before me red and white wine, with the remnant of a loaf of wheaten bread which she took out of a cupboard in the sitting-room, and some delicious butter'. I find this description both charming and enlightening, as it demonstrates that not only were the men claret consumers but the women were, too. And what better accompaniment to wine than a good loaf of bread?

Serves 4

4 sirloin or rib-eye steaks
25g/1oz butter
4 anchovy fillets, snipped
1 rounded teaspoon Dijon mustard
150ml/5fl oz red wine

Bring the steaks to room temperature, then season them while you heat a large frying pan (or use 2 smaller pans) until very hot. Add the butter, then once it has melted add the steaks. Fry for 2–3 minutes on each side, only turning after 2 minutes, to allow a good crust to form.

Transfer the steaks to a warm plate. Add the anchovies, mustard and wine to the pan and let them bubble away for about 3 minutes, until reduced. Season with pepper (no salt, since the anchovies are salty). Serve the steaks with the sauce – and perhaps some sautéed potatoes and spinach.

Gigot of Lamb

with Turnip and Caper Sauce

In traditional recipes for gigot (leg) of mutton, the meat is boiled with carrots and turnips and then served with caper sauce. Since few cooks use mutton in the kitchen now (delicious though it is), I have adapted the idea to give a recipe for roast leg of lamb with roasted turnip (swede), accompanied by a piquant caper sauce. Serve with roast potatoes and green vegetables such as spinach and broccoli.

Serves 6
1.8kg/4lb leg of lamb
25g/1oz butter, softened
1 turnip (called swede in England), about 600g/1¼lb peeled weight
2 tablespoons olive oil
1 tablespoon mushroom ketchup or soy sauce

For the caper sauce:
40g/1½oz butter
40g/1½oz plain flour
300ml/10fl oz lamb stock
300ml/10fl oz full-fat milk
3 heaped tablespoons drained capers

Preheat the oven to 190°C/375°F/Gas 5. Place the lamb in a roasting tin and smear the butter over it. Season well with salt and pepper. Peel the turnip and chop it into bite-sized chunks. Place these around the meat and drizzle them with the oil, then season well. Roast the lamb for 1 hour, then drizzle the mushroom ketchup or soy sauce over the turnip chunks. Return to the oven until done to your liking – about 20 minutes. Remove and allow to rest while you make the caper sauce.

Melt the butter in a saucepan, add the flour and stir well. Gradually add the stock, then the milk, whisking constantly until smooth. Cook for a couple of minutes, then stir in the capers. Season with salt and pepper to taste. Serve with the lamb and turnip.

Roast Bubbly-jock
stuffed with Oysters

Bubbly-jock – the Scots name for turkey – became a Christmas treat in Scotland only relatively recently. The New Year has always been the more important festival.

I love to stuff turkey with oysters, which was common in the big Scottish houses in those halcyon days when oysters were not regarded as a luxury. Old-fashioned stuffing recipes were based on a mixture of breadcrumbs, parsley, lemon, lemon thyme, suet and eggs. Mine omits the suet and is light, fresh and absolutely delicious.

Be sure to stuff the turkey just before cooking, because of the raw oysters. If you cannot find a small turkey, use an extra large chicken instead. The giblets can be boiled up with a carrot, onion, bay leaf and a few peppercorns to make a stock for the gravy.

Serves 6
2.2–2.5kg/5lb–5lb 9oz free-range turkey, giblets removed
2 tablespoons olive oil
plain flour
a little oyster sauce (optional)

For the stuffing:
8 oysters, shucked (see page 65) but still in their shells, so you don't lose any of the juices
grated zest of 2 lemons
150g/5oz fresh breadcrumbs
20g/¾oz parsley, chopped
2 large free-range eggs

Preheat the oven to 220°C/425°F/Gas 7. For the stuffing, slice each oyster into 2–3 pieces and put them in a bowl, adding any precious juice from the shells. Mix in all the remaining stuffing ingredients and season well with salt and pepper.

Place the turkey in a roasting tin. Put some of the stuffing in the neck end (don't fill it too tightly) and some into the body cavity. Rub the oil all over the bird and season with salt and pepper. Cover loosely with oiled foil and roast for 20 minutes. Reduce the oven temperature to 190°C/375°F/Gas 5 and continue to cook for 1 hour, then remove the foil and cook until done – another 40 minutes or so. Test by inserting a sharp knife or skewer into the thickest part of the flesh: the juices should run clear.

Transfer the turkey to a carving dish and leave to rest for 10–15 minutes. Meanwhile, make a gravy: put the roasting tin on the hob over a medium heat and stir a heaped tablespoon of flour into the pan juices (pour some away first if there is too much fat). Cook for a couple of minutes, then gradually stir in the giblet stock and bring to the boil, whisking constantly until smooth. Season to taste. I also like to add a splash of oyster sauce to enhance the oyster flavour.

Roast Hebridean Lamb
with Skirlie Stuffing

The idea for this delicious dish comes from Linda Wood, who runs Leachin House, a guesthouse in Tarbert, Harris. She always buys her lamb from Charles Macleod in Stornoway – 1 hour north in Lewis – and cooks it for guests, sometimes in the French style with garlic and rosemary but sometimes with skirlie. She marinates the meat first in a mixture of fresh thyme, soy sauce and olive oil. I prefer simply to rub it inside and out with good olive oil, then stuff it with the cooled, freshly cooked skirlie. Remember to ask the butcher for the bone once he has tunnel-boned the lamb, so you can make stock for the gravy. I just boil the bones up with 2 fresh bay leaves, half an onion and cold water to cover.

The lamb from the Stornoway butcher is from older animals than we might use on the mainland but the flavour is incomparable. The meat is from black-face and Cheviot lambs, from 6 to 15 months old. It goes without saying that Hebridean lambs are not intensively reared!

Serves 8
1 leg of lamb, weighing about 2.2kg/5lb, tunnel-boned (it should weigh about 1.8kg/4lb after boning)
olive oil
1 quantity of Skirlie (see page 113)
plain flour
lamb stock (see above)
a little red wine

Rub the meat inside and out with olive oil and leave somewhere cool for a few hours.

Preheat the oven to 220°C/425°F/Gas 7. Allow the skirlie to cool, then use it to stuff the lamb, taking care to pack it in neatly. Reshape the meat around it again and either tie it with string or simply tuck it into a tight-fitting roasting tin so it keeps its shape. Season all over with salt and pepper. Roast for 20 minutes, then reduce the oven temperature to 190°C/375°F/Gas 5 and roast for a further hour or so, until it is medium to well done, not rare.

Transfer the lamb to a serving platter and leave to rest for about 15 minutes before carving and serving with the skirlie. Meanwhile, make a simple gravy: put the roasting pan on top of the stove and stir about a heaped tablespoon of flour into the pan juices (pour some away first if there is too much fat). Gradually stir in the stock you have made from the bones and bring to the boil, whisking constantly. Add a splash of red wine and plenty of seasoning before serving.

Collops in the Pan

Undoubtedly another link with the Auld Alliance, the word collop, meaning a thin slice of meat (usually beef, venison or veal), is derived from the French *escalope*, which, according to *Larousse Gastronomique*, is 'slices of meat or fish of any kind, flattened slightly and fried in butter or some other fat'.

In old recipes, collops in the pan takes no more than 10 minutes to cook. I prefer to brown the onions well before adding the beef but it is still no longer than some 20 minutes from start to finish. Sometimes oyster pickle or walnut catsup was added to flavour it. I suggest using either mushroom ketchup (I think oriental oyster sauce would be inappropriate here) or Worcestershire sauce if you cannot find old-fashioned walnut catsup, or ketchup. Serve with mashed potatoes and a green vegetable.

Serves 4–6

50g/2oz butter

2 medium onions, peeled and sliced into rings

4 thin slices of rump steak, weighing about 1.1kg/2½lb in total

about 2 tablespoons mushroom ketchup, or Worcestershire sauce to taste

Heat the butter in a large frying pan (or 2 medium ones) and gently fry the onions for 10–15 minutes, until golden brown. Transfer to a plate with a slotted spoon. Increase the heat to high.

Cut the beef slices in half so you have 8 thin steaks. Season these and add to the pan. Cook for 4–5 minutes, turning once, until just done. Do not overcook.

Lower the heat, return the onions to the pan and add the mushroom ketchup or Worcestershire sauce. Stir and taste for seasoning, adding more ketchup or sauce if necessary. After a couple of minutes it should be ready to serve.

Haggis, Neeps and Tatties

Macsween of Edinburgh is famous worldwide for its haggis. From Hong Kong to Helsinki, its haggis (warm-reekin', rich, as Burns described it) has been consumed – no doubt with much whisky – anywhere and everywhere. Burns Night is, of course, the main time for haggis consumption but, according to marketing manager Jo Macsween, it is also popular throughout the year and is even served as a main course at weddings.

At Macsween's factory just outside Edinburgh, I watched the lamb lobes (lights) – which are the lungs – being cooked for some 3 hours, before being mixed with cooked beef fat, medium and pinhead oatmeal, onions and the special seasoning, which contains white pepper, mace, salt and coriander. After it has all been minced together, one of the Macsween family tastes it to check that the seasoning is correct. Then the mixture is used to fill the natural casings – ox bung or lamb's runner (intestine) that has been washed and salted. Then they are pricked and clipped at intervals, to allow for expansion, and cooked in the steam room for an hour or so before being left to cool overnight and vacuum packed. Because they are already cooked they only require reheating once you get them home. Typically they are served with neeps and tatties – and probably a wee dram. Or two.

The origins of the haggis are not set in stone. Although there are records of a similar 'sausage' in Greek writings, according to food historian Clarissa Dickson Wright the origins are more likely to be Scandinavian – a legacy of the Viking raids. The etymology supports this – the 'hag' part is linked to the Icelandic 'hoggva' and 'haggw', meaning 'to hew'.

However shrouded in mystery the history of the haggis may be, there is no disputing the fact that Robert Burns brought it into the limelight through his poetry in the eighteenth century. Before Burns it had been a homely, peasant dish. After his glorious poem, 'To a Haggis', it was – and is – 'Chieftan o' the Puddin'-race'.

Serves 4–6

1 haggis (the size depends on whether your guests are committed haggis eaters)
Bashed Neeps (see page 112) and Champit Tatties (see page 112), to serve

Preheat the oven to 180°C/350°F/Gas 4. Wrap the haggis in foil and heat it in the oven for about 45 minutes per 450g/1lb. Cut open the haggis and eat piping hot with neeps and tatties.

Stoved Howtowdie wi' Drappit Eggs

This delicious recipe is based on one in Meg Dods' 1829 *Manual* and is most definitely in the French style – the word stoved comes from the French *étuver*, which means to stew or heat in a stove. The chicken is browned all over, then stewed or cooked in the oven in stock until meltingly tender. Then some eggs are poached or dropped ('drappit') in the stock and these are served on spinach. A thin gravy is made with the stock once the eggs are done.

In my *Scots Thesaurus*, howtowdie is defined as 'a large young chicken for the pot, a young hen which has not begun to lay'. Some believe it comes from the Old French word *hutaudeau*, meaning a pullet. However, my former university lecturer, Dr Adamson, concluded that the derivation was in fact *hétoudeau* or *hétourdeau*, meaning capon, which seems more likely.

Be sure to use a free-range or organic chicken, whose flavour and texture will withstand long cooking better.

Serves 4

1 free-range chicken, weighing about 1.6–1.8kg/3½–4lb, giblets removed
1 white (mealie) pudding, skinned
75g/3oz butter
300g/10½oz shallots, peeled but left whole
700ml/1¼ pints hot light chicken stock
4 medium free-range eggs
300g/10½oz fresh spinach, washed and lightly cooked
1 heaped tablespoon cornflour

Preheat the oven to 180°C/350°F/Gas 4. Stuff the chicken with the white pudding. Heat the butter in a large flameproof casserole, then add the chicken and brown well all over. Tuck the shallots around it, pour over the hot stock and season well. Cover tightly with a lid (if it is not a good seal, use foil and a lid), transfer to the oven and cook for 1¼–1½ hours, until tender. Transfer the chicken and shallots to a large ashet (platter) and keep warm. Surround with the cooked spinach.

Place the casserole on the hob then, once the liquid is gently simmering, carefully drop in the eggs, one at a time, to poach (I like to draw the white gently around the yolk with a slotted spoon as they poach). After a couple of minutes, carefully remove the eggs with the slotted spoon and place on top of the spinach.

Mix the cornflour with 2 tablespoons of cold water and whisk this into the simmering stock. Cook for 5–10 minutes, whisking, until slightly thickened, then check the seasoning. Serve in a jug with the chicken.

6
game

At any time throughout the winter months, my butcher and game dealer has pheasant, roe deer, teal, widgeon, partridge, hare and rabbit, all of which are lean, flavoursome and healthy. They are also some of the most natural produce available, free from additives, hormones or chemical feed. And because they are wild, they have to work hard to obtain their food and so have very little fat on them. With our minds set firmly on reducing our fat intake these days, surely game constitutes an ideal modern food.

Although game was originally eaten by everyone (prehistoric man's diet was not all roots and berries), it gradually became exclusive to the privileged, and remained so until relatively recently. Images of massive haunches of venison served on large ashets with pomp and ceremony suggest baronial splendour – the landed gentry rather than Scotland's 'ordinary' folk. Grouse has definitely become a luxury item, mainly because of the ridiculous price on August 12th (when it should never be eaten, as it has not been hung). But although it is always fairly dear, later in the season prices come down and older, cheaper grouse can be used to make superb casseroles and terrines. Venison has also become less expensive, as it is now farmed. Provided you buy from a reputable supplier, farmed venison is excellent, and has the advantage of being available all year. If, however, you can buy some wild venison in season, such as fillet of roe deer, then do so, for a truly memorable treat.

This chapter contains some simple recipes using Scotland's game. Many are interchangeable, depending on availability. But with all the recipes, bear in mind that game is lean and so if you are roasting it, overcooking will ruin what should be a splendid feast. Casseroling and making pies or crumbles is a less unforgiving way of preparing it. Both ought to be tried, however, for game is one of the few culinary treats that have not been ruined by intensive production methods. It is a healthy food that deserves more acclaim.

Rabbit Pie

Rabbit used to be very popular cooked in stews and casseroles as a change from mince, or sometimes made into pies. This pie was inspired by a traditional 'Kingdom of Fife Pie' – rabbit joints and forcemeat balls tucked under a puff pastry crust and baked. I am not keen on meat still on the bone under pastry, so I cook the rabbit in advance and remove the meat from the bones. I also miss out the forcemeat, but keep in the characteristic sliced hard-boiled eggs. Eat this with mashed potatoes and a green vegetable or two.

Serves 4
1 plump rabbit, cleaned and jointed
1 heaped tablespoon flour, seasoned with salt and pepper
50g/2oz butter
110g/4oz smoked streaky bacon, chopped
1 onion, peeled and chopped
1 large leek, sliced
400ml/14fl oz hot chicken stock
3 thick sprigs of thyme
2 large free-range eggs, hard-boiled and sliced
250g/9oz ready-rolled puff pastry
beaten egg, to glaze

My butcher always advises rubbing wild rabbit with salt then rinsing well under a cold running tap, but if it is a farmed rabbit you probably will not need to do this.

Coat the rabbit joints in the flour, then fry in half the butter until browned all over. Transfer to a plate. Heat the remaining butter in the pan and gently fry the bacon, onion and leek for 10 minutes or so, until soft. Return the rabbit to the pan and stir in the hot stock. Add the thyme and some seasoning, bring to the boil, then cover and simmer over a low heat for 1 hour, until the rabbit is tender. Check the seasoning again while it is still hot, then leave to cool – I leave it overnight.

The next day, scrape off any surface fat and remove the rabbit joints. Take off all the meat and place in a 1.5 litre/2½ pint pie dish with the bacon and enough of the stock just to cover the meat. Top with the sliced hard-boiled eggs.

Preheat the oven to 220°C/425°F/Gas 7. Cut a long strip off the rolled-out pastry. Wet the edges of the pie dish and press the strip of pastry all around. Wet this and place the remaining pastry over the top. Press the edges to seal and then trim off any excess. Crimp the edges with your thumb and forefinger, then brush all over with beaten egg. Snip a couple of holes in the centre, then bake the pie for about 30 minutes, until puffed up and golden brown. Cover loosely with foil for the last 5–10 minutes if necessary, to prevent burning.

Serve at once.

Wild Duck with Juniper Sauce
and Glazed Shallots

This recipe is from Rosemary Shrager, chef at Amhuinnsuidhe Castle on the North Harris Estate in the Outer Hebrides. She uses duck from South Uist, south of Harris.

Serves 6

3 wild duck
extra virgin olive oil
a few sprigs of thyme
1 onion, peeled and chopped
20 shallots, peeled
but left whole
3 celery sticks, chopped
2 garlic cloves, peeled and
chopped
1 heaped tablespoon raisins
110g/4oz unsalted butter

For the sauce:
50g/2oz butter, plus a knob
2 bacon rashers, chopped
1 leek, chopped
600ml/1 pint red wine
600ml/1 pint chicken stock
1 tablespoon redcurrant or
bramble jelly
12 juniper berries, crushed

Remove the legs and breasts from the ducks and marinate these for 4 hours in a little olive oil with most of the thyme and some salt and pepper. Preheat the oven to 190°C/375°F/Gas 5.

Put the duck carcasses in a roasting tin (breaking them up if large), add the onion and roast for 20 minutes, until brown, then remove.

Place the shallots, celery and garlic in an ovenproof dish lined with a large piece of foil. Add the raisins and a little thyme and dot with the butter. Seal the foil and put into the oven for up to 1 hour, until tender.

Meanwhile, make the sauce: melt 50g/2oz of the butter in a medium saucepan and gently fry the bacon and leek in it for 5 minutes. Add the wine and boil until reduced by half. Add the chicken stock with the roasted duck bones and boil until the liquid is reduced to one third. Remove the bones, then add the jelly and juniper berries. Simmer until the sauce is reduced to about 225ml/8fl oz. Strain into a clean pan.

Heat a little olive oil in a large frying pan, add the duck pieces and seal quickly on both sides. Place in an ovenproof dish and roast (same oven temperature as the carcasses) for 8–10 minutes, depending on thickness – the legs will take a little longer than this. Remove and leave to rest for 5 minutes before serving.

To finish the sauce, reheat if necessary, whisk in the knob of butter, then check the seasoning. To serve, place a pile of the shallot and celery mixture in the middle of each serving plate. Slice the meat from the duck breasts and legs and place it on top, surrounding it with the sauce.

Pheasant and Lovage Crumble

Because of its dietary habits – it does not generally eat high moorland heather – pheasant has a much milder flavour than other game such as grouse. Indeed, some supermarket pheasant can taste rather like free-range chicken or turkey. Presuming your butcher hangs his pheasant well, however, the meat should be nicely – if not overtly – gamy. My game butcher, Alec Smith at George Bower, lets me know when it is time to sell 'old grouse' (casserole birds) cheaply, which means the pheasant season is nigh. The season lasts from 1 October to 1 February.

Lovage is an old-fashioned herb that was widely used in Scotland in the past and still grows in many people's gardens. If you cannot get hold of it, however, use parsley instead.

Serves 8
3 medium oven-ready pheasant
300ml/10fl oz chicken or pheasant stock
300ml/10fl oz dry cider
2 bay leaves
a handful of lovage stalks (use the leaves for the crumble topping)
50g/2oz butter
200g/7oz streaky bacon, chopped
1 large onion, peeled and chopped
4 celery sticks, chopped
200g/7oz button mushrooms
50g/2oz plain flour
150g/5oz whole cooked chestnuts (I use vacuum-packed)

For the crumble topping:
50g/2oz porridge oats
150g/5oz plain flour
1 heaped tablespoon chopped lovage leaves
50g/2oz hazelnuts, chopped
125g/4½oz butter, diced

Place the pheasant in a large pan with the stock, cider, bay leaves and lovage stalks. Bring slowly to the boil, then cover and simmer for 45–50 minutes, until the birds are just cooked. Remove from the heat and leave to cool, then strain, reserving the stock. Remove the meat from the pheasants and cut into large chunks. Heat the butter in a pan, add the bacon, onion, celery and the whole mushrooms and fry for about 10 minutes. Add the flour and cook, stirring constantly, for 1 minute. Then add the chestnuts and gradually pour in the reserved stock. Simmer over a medium heat for 3–4 minutes until thick, stirring constantly. Season to taste with salt and pepper and add the meat. Tip into a large gratin dish and leave to cool.

Preheat the oven to 180°C/350°F/Gas 4. For the crumble, place the oats, flour, lovage and nuts in a bowl and rub in the butter. Sprinkle this over the cooled pheasant mixture, pressing it down gently, and bake for about 1 hour or until golden brown and bubbling. Serve with crusty bread and salad.

Roast Grouse with Blaeberries

Rather than buying grouse at the beginning of the season, when they are expensive and haven't been hung properly, it's best to wait until early September, then enjoy young grouse for the entire month until the older birds come in for casseroling.

This simple roast dish calls for grouse to be stuffed with a mixture of butter and blaeberries, covered with bacon to prevent them drying out, then roasted in a very hot oven. Blaeberries are what we Scots call bilberries. If you cannot find them, use cultivated blueberries instead. Serve with Skirlie (see page 113), roast potatoes and a green vegetable.

Serves 2

2 young oven-ready grouse

125g/4½oz blaeberries

50g/2oz butter, softened

6 back bacon rashers

1 tablespoon blaeberry jelly

(or bramble/blackberry jelly)

2 tablespoons red wine

Preheat the oven to 230°C/450°F/Gas 8. Wash out the insides of the grouse and dry well. Mix the berries into the butter (gently, so they do not burst) and season with salt and pepper. Stuff this into each body cavity. Lay the bacon on top, trying to cover all the breast. Place the birds in a small buttered roasting tin and roast for 20 minutes, then remove from the oven. Tip out the contents of the birds' cavities into the tin. Place the grouse on a serving dish to rest in a low oven (if you have only one oven, leave them in it with the door open) for at least 10 minutes, loosely covered with foil. Place the roasting tin over a direct heat, add the jelly and wine and bubble away for 2–3 minutes, then season to taste. Pour the contents into a small sauceboat and serve with the grouse.

Game Loaf

This recipe was inspired by one in Elizabeth Craig's 1965 book, *What's Cooking in Scotland?*, which calls for young grouse breasts to be tucked inside a sandwich loaf with mushrooms and bacon, then covered in a rich game sauce and baked in the oven. I have developed her recipe – which is rather rich – to make a loaf that is lighter and more up-to-date. It is basically a variation on the famous shooter's sandwich, which is made with rump steak. This version is good to take on picnics or just for a simple winter lunch, perhaps after a warming bowl of soup.

I buy pheasant breasts from my butcher but if you can't, simply remove them from the bird (pheasant or grouse) by carefully running a sharp knife as close to the backbone as possible.

Serves 4-6

1 sandwich loaf,
weighing about 750g/1lb 10oz

4 tablespoons olive oil

6 pheasant breasts
or 6-8 grouse breasts

300g/10½oz large mushrooms,
thickly sliced

1 tablespoon thyme leaves

Cut one end off the loaf and set aside. Carefully remove much of the centre crumb, ensuring you leave a thickish crust – about 4cm/1½ inches all round. Heat half the oil in a large frying pan and add the game breasts. Season well and fry all over for 8–10 minutes, until just done. Tuck the breasts inside the loaf to form the first layer.

Add the remaining oil to the pan and fry the mushrooms for about 10 minutes, then add the thyme and plenty of salt and pepper. Tuck the mushrooms on top of the game and drizzle in all the pan juices. Replace the end of the bread, wrap the loaf in a double sheet of foil and leave in the fridge overnight, well weighted down (I use 2 orange juice cartons). The next day, remove the foil and cut the loaf into thick slices.

Roast Partridge

with Chanterelles

There are many elaborate recipes for partridge in old Scottish recipe books, from soups to soufflés. Because partridge is rather more of a treat nowadays – and expensive, too – I tend only to roast this fine bird, sometimes wrapped in bacon, sometimes stuffed with grapes. But I like to keep it simple.

If you can find fresh chanterelles, substitute about 150g/5oz for the dried ones, omitting the soaking.

Serves 2

20g/¾ oz dried chanterelles
100ml/3½fl oz dry white wine
2 tablespoons olive oil
2 oven-ready partridge
2 garlic cloves, peeled and chopped
½ small onion, peeled and finely chopped
1 heaped teaspoon plain flour
2 tablespoons double cream
a dash of truffle oil

Rinse the mushrooms and soak them in the wine for an hour or so.

Preheat the oven to 230°C/450°F/Gas 8. Heat half the oil in a small roasting tin on top of the hob, add the partridge and brown them all over. Season well, then transfer to the oven and roast for 5 minutes. Reduce the oven temperature to 200°C/400°F/Gas 6 and roast for a further 12–15 minutes, basting once. Test by inserting a skewer into the thickest part of the flesh; the juices should run clear or very slightly pink. Remove from the oven and leave to rest, loosely covered with foil, for at least 10 minutes.

Heat the remaining oil in a small saucepan and gently fry the garlic and onion in it for 5 minutes. Drain the mushrooms, reserving the liquid, and add them to the pan. Fry for 5–10 minutes, until tender, then increase the heat. Sprinkle in the flour and cook for 1 minute, stirring. Add the reserved wine and the cream. Simmer for 3–5 minutes, then season to taste with salt and pepper and a dash of truffle oil.

Serve the birds with the chanterelle sauce and either sautéed potatoes or tagliatelle and a green vegetable such as spinach or broccoli.

Roast Venison
with Blackcurrant Sauce

In the past, venison often appeared on the menus of the many inns for travellers throughout the Highlands, although it was perhaps not always treated with the greatest of respect. Writer Thomas Pennant, visiting Kinlochleven in the late 1700s, wrote, 'Breakfast on most excellent minced stag, the only form I thought that animal good in.'

This recipe makes rather more fitting use of venison, and is a splendid Sunday lunch alternative to beef or lamb. If you are using wild venison, it might be a good idea to marinate it first to ensure tenderness. In the Georgian period, venison was often marinated for many hours in a mixture of claret, vinegar and lemon juice, then the marinade was used to baste the haunch as it roasted. The original recipe for this was said to have been invented by the chefs of Mary of Guise.

If you cannot be bothered to make the sauce (though it's very easy), then serve the venison simply with a pot of blackcurrant or rowan jelly, a bowl of steamed new potatoes and some green vegetables.

Serves 6–8

50g/2oz butter

3 teaspoons blackcurrant jelly

1.3–1.8kg/3–4lb haunch (or saddle) of venison on the bone

3 tablespoons red wine

2 teaspoons blackcurrant (or raspberry) vinegar

300ml/10fl oz hot game or beef stock

3–4 sprigs of thyme

a handful of fresh blackcurrants

Preheat the oven to 230°C/425°F/Gas 8. Melt the butter and 2 teaspoons of the blackcurrant jelly in a large frying pan. Once sizzling, add the meat and brown it all over, then transfer it to a roasting tin, pouring all the butter over it. Season well with salt and pepper. Place in the oven and cook for 12–15 minutes per 450g/1lb – 12 minutes for rare, 15 for medium-rare; because it is such a lean meat, venison should not be cooked beyond medium. Then place the meat on a carving board, cover with a double sheet of foil (or place, uncovered, in a plate-warming oven) and leave to rest for about 20 minutes.

Meanwhile, make the sauce: pour off most of the fat from the roasting tin, leaving in only a teaspoon or so, then put the tin on the hob. Add the wine and vinegar and stir to scrape up all the bits from the base of the tin. Boil for a couple of minutes, then add the hot stock, the remaining teaspoon of jelly and the thyme and simmer for 4–5 minutes, stirring, until reduced to a sauce-like consistency. Season to taste, then sieve into a warmed serving dish or jug. Add the blackcurrants, stirring gently to heat them through.

Carve the venison into slices and serve with the blackcurrant sauce.

7

vegetables and grains

Whereas Scots have always been masters of the soup pot and mistresses of the rolling pin, vegetables have never quite been our thing. Apart from potatoes, turnips, kail, leeks, onions and carrots, they have never taken pride of place at the table. Unless, of course, they were in the soup pot. Depending on the season, some other vegetables, such as peas, cabbages and Brussels sprouts, were also eaten, but as a general rule everyday fare was root vegetables with an onion thrown in for flavour. Other vegetables were so simply cooked that they merit no recipe. I remember my sister and I picking from the long rows of peas in the garden. These would then be podded, boiled and served with nothing other than a good 'dod' of butter. I also remember my father thinning out his lettuces and pulling up some spring onions (often known in Scotland as 'sybies') for a fresh summer salad with cold meat, beetroot and tomato.

The few old-fashioned recipes for vegetables are much of a muchness. Colcannon and kailkenny are Highland and north-eastern variations of a potato and cabbage mash, with additions such as cream or turnip (swede). Clapshot and rumbledethumps are Orcadian and Borders versions of a mash of potatoes and turnip or cabbage, with the Borders dish being topped with grated cheese and baked in the oven. Stovies are sliced potatoes slowly cooked with onion in dripping and meat juices until soft and tender. Champit tatties are mashed potatoes, while bashed neeps are mashed turnips (swede).

There has, therefore, been little variety in traditional Scottish vegetables when served on their own. With our one-pot cooking ethos (the kail-pot over the peat fire) we tended to throw vegetables straight from the garden or kail-yard into a pot for stew or soup, thereby retaining all their goodness – there was method in our madness. And when we did come to cook vegetables separately, they were – and still are – of the finest quality, with a wonderful flavour. Simple, homely and delicious – Scotland's vegetables on a plate.

Stovies

This is a delicious dish of onions and potatoes fried in dripping (you can use the white fat on the surface of the meat jelly after pouring off the meat juices from your roasting tin and chilling), then cooked slowly in the meat jelly (or stock) until tender. Stovies are very similar to pan haggerty, a dish from the north-east of England consisting of sliced onions and potatoes cooked slowly in dripping in a deep covered frying pan. Just like stovies, this was traditionally served on Mondays after a Sunday roast.

Stovies are now classic pub fare throughout Scotland – understandably, since they are ideal for soaking up vast quantities of alcohol. They vary from region to region. In Arbroath and Aberdeen, corned beef or chopped roast meat is often added and they are served with oatcakes. In Orkney, pieces of brisket are stirred in.

Customers at my Edinburgh butcher's crumble Lorne sausage on top of the stovies as they cook, on the recommendation of the butcher's daughter, Audrey. However, they already have so much flavour from the dripping and meat jelly that I like them best served plain, with thick oatcakes and a glass of cold milk.

Serves 3–4
2 heaped tablespoons dripping
(use butter if you have no dripping)
2 onions, peeled and sliced
750g/1lb 10oz potatoes, peeled
and thinly sliced
2 tablespoons meat jelly (or beef stock)

Melt the dripping in a large heavy saucepan, add the onions and fry for 10–15 minutes, until golden. Add the potato slices and turn carefully in the fat: be careful the slices do not break up. Season well with salt and pepper, then add the meat jelly and heat until melted. Cover tightly and cook over a low heat for about 40 minutes or until the potatoes are tender and have absorbed all the liquid. Add a splash of hot water if they seem too dry. While they cook, shake the pan often to prevent sticking; do not stir or you will break up the delicate potato slices. Serve piping hot.

Clapshot

This dish from Orkney is similar to Northern Ireland's champ and also to colcannon, which is found in southern Ireland and the Highlands of Scotland. Clapshot differs by having turnips – called swede in England and, for short, neeps in Scotland – mixed with the potatoes instead of cabbage, spring onions or leeks. Because neeps and tatties are typical accompaniments to haggis, I suggest serving a dish of clapshot to ring the changes.

It also makes a very comforting vegetarian dish (if you use butter, not dripping), served in warm bowls with thick oatcakes and a glass of cold milk or buttermilk.

Serves 4–6
500g/1lb 2oz (peeled weight) potatoes, peeled and cut up
500g/1lb 2oz (peeled weight) turnip (swede), peeled and cut up
50g/2oz butter or dripping
1–2 tablespoons chopped chives

Put the vegetables in a pan of cold salted water, then cover and bring to the boil. Simmer for 15–20 minutes, depending on size, until tender, then drain. Return them to the pan, cover and shake the pan over a very low heat to dry them off completely. Remember, turnips are rather watery so unless you dry them off well the mixture will be sloppy.

Mash the vegetables with the butter or dripping, then add salt and pepper to taste and stir in the chives. Serve piping hot.

Grilled Dulse

Another idea from Margaret Horn of Auchmithie's But 'n' Ben. Dulse used to be a well-known snack in local pubs, roasted or grilled and served with a splash of vinegar. Given the innate saltiness of any seaweed, this was a fairly canny way of increasing thirst levels in the pub goer! The traditional way to grill dulse would have been to cook with a red-hot poker over the embers of a peat fire until it turned green.

Grilled dulse can be served with drinks instead of nuts or olives but it is also good as an unusual garnish on soups or pasta, or tossed over salads at the last minute. On the Isle of Barra, it was often eaten as a relish with potatoes.

When picking any wild seaweed, be sure it is from unpolluted water.

Serves 4
a large handful of freshly picked dulse, well washed
malt vinegar

Place the dulse under a hot grill for about 4–5 minutes, by which time it should be green and crisp (watch it like a hawk; it burns very quickly). Sprinkle with a little vinegar and eat hot or cold, but do not refrigerate.

Champit Tatties

Traditionally served with bashed neeps and haggis at a Burns Supper, this is Scotland's answer to the increasingly fashionable mash. You can flavour it with chopped spring onions, parsley or chives, adorn with crisp fried onion or bacon pieces, or sprinkle each mound with a fine mantle of Skirlie (see page 113) for a good contrasting crunch.

Serves 4–6
1kg/2¼lb floury potatoes
(e.g. King Edward, Fianna or Maris Piper),
peeled and chopped
100g/3½oz butter
100ml/3½fl oz hot full-fat milk

Cook the potatoes in boiling salted water until tender. Drain well and return to the pan over a low heat until thoroughly dry. Once dry, add the butter and mash with a potato masher, then add the hot milk and mash again, tasting and adding salt and pepper accordingly. Serve piping hot.

Bashed Neeps

Together with champit tatties, this is the traditional accompaniment to haggis. It is also good served with any roast meat or with grilled sausages. Although I suggest adding some nutmeg, Meg Dodds recommended a little powdered ginger in her mashed turnips, to help 'correct the flatulent properties of this esculent'!

What we in Scotland call neeps is actually short for turnip – which is in fact not what is called turnip down south but swede. I realise it is not everyone's favourite vegetable but I love it. A dish of piping hot, buttery bashed neeps is my idea of bliss.

Serves 4–6
750g/1lb 10oz turnip
(called swede in England),
peeled and cut into chunks
50g/2oz butter
freshly grated nutmeg

Cook the turnip in boiling salted water for about 20 minutes, until tender. Drain, then return to the saucepan and place over a low heat, shaking the pan often, to dry out completely.

Using a potato masher, mash the turnip with the butter, then add salt, pepper and grated nutmeg to taste. Serve piping hot.

Skirlie

Skirlie has the same ingredients as mealie puddings but is fried. The name derives from 'skirl in the pan' – the hissing noise it makes while frying, as in 'the skirl of the pipes'. In Aberdeenshire skirlie is traditionally served on a Saturday with champit (mashed) tatties. In other areas it is served as an accompaniment to mince but is also excellent as a stuffing for chicken, game or lamb. And I far prefer it with roast game birds to the more usual fried breadcrumbs. But perhaps that is purely national prejudice.

Most recipes recommend using medium oatmeal but sometimes coarse (half medium, half pinhead) is used, which gives a rougher, nuttier texture.

Serves 4–6
50g/2oz dripping or suet (or 25g/1oz butter and 2 tablespoons olive oil)
1 medium onion, peeled and finely chopped
100g/3½oz medium or coarse oatmeal

Melt the fat in a pan. Add the onion and cook slowly for at least 10 minutes, until softened and golden brown. Then add the oatmeal, stirring until the fat is absorbed. You might be able to add a little more oatmeal. Cook over a medium heat, stirring often, until it is toasted and crumbly – about 8–10 minutes.

Season to taste with salt and pepper. Serve piping hot, or leave to cool and use as a stuffing.

Big Peas and Lang Tatties

Big peas and lang tatties. Could there be a more evocative name for a dish? According to food writer Grace Mulligan, it was the name given to the portions of marrowfat peas and chips bought in the Overgate, in the centre of Dundee, for many years, certainly until the mid 1930s. My parents knew this as a 'Buster': chips and Buster (marrowfat) peas. For 1d (one old penny) you were given a deep, old-fashioned saucer full of chips and big peas, which were sprinkled with vinegar, the only flavouring apart from salt. Unlike mushy peas, which are often cooked up with onion or bacon, Buster peas are cooked dried peas, plain and simple.

The lang tatties, or chips, were, according to Grace Mulligan, cut from the giant potatoes that the potato merchants separated from their harvest. They often had splits inside them which you could not detect from the outside, and they would have been cheaper to buy and easier to peel. The chips were always fried in an unspecified fat, which presumably was beef dripping.

Grace can remember being taken by her grandfather to the market in Dundee, where they sat on wooden benches inside a tent-like structure in the middle of the old Dundee tenements. This is where they had the Buster stalls. The vats of hot fat and peas were cooked over open fires in big iron boxes, rather like old-fashioned ranges. This was quite dangerous, with small customers sitting directly underneath huge vats of boiling fat and hot peas!

These days I serve big peas at home when I am treating the children to fish and chips, which, in my humble opinion, beats Indian or Chinese takeaways any day.

Serves 4
For the big peas:
300g/10½oz dried marrowfat peas, soaked overnight and then drained
vinegar (malt is traditional; wine vinegar is also fine)

For the lang tatties:
4 large floury potatoes (e.g. Maris Piper, Record, Pentland Dell or Fianna)
fat or oil for deep-frying

Put the soaked peas in a saucepan and pour over enough boiling water to cover generously – about 1 litre/1¾ pints. Bring to the boil and cook, covered, for about 1¼–1½ hours, until tender. Drain off any excess liquid if necessary, then season with plenty of salt and sprinkle with vinegar.

For the lang tatties, peel the potatoes and cut them into thick chips (not dainty french fries). Place in a bowl of cold water to remove excess starch, then drain and dry thoroughly. Half-fill a deep-fat fryer or large deep saucepan with fat or oil and heat to 180°C/350°F. If you have no thermometer, drop in a chip; it should sizzle in a mass of tiny bubbles. Cook the chips for 5–6 minutes, then remove from the pan and drain. Increase the temperature to 190°C/375°F (or when a tester chip turns golden brown in about 1 minute) and cook the chips for about 3 minutes, until golden brown and crisp. Drain well, then sprinkle liberally with salt. Serve with the big peas.

Rumbledethumps

This is a Borders dish of potatoes and cabbage, topped with cheese and browned in the oven. My recipe also includes turnip, as this is how my mother prepares it. The name is meant to come from 'rumbled' (mashed or stirred together) and 'thumped' (pounded together). Chopped chives or spring onions can also be added.

Serves 4

600g/1¼lb (peeled weight) potatoes, peeled and chopped

400g/14oz (peeled weight) turnip (called swede in England), peeled and chopped

250g/9oz cabbage, preferably Savoy, finely sliced

75g/3oz butter

25g/1oz mature Cheddar cheese, grated

Preheat the oven to 180°C/350°F/Gas 4. Put the potatoes and turnip in cold salted water, cover and bring to the boil. Simmer until tender, then drain. Return the vegetables to the pan, cover and shake the pan over a very low heat to dry them off completely. Heat 50g/2oz of the butter in a pan, add the cabbage and cook until just tender but still bright green. Tip the cabbage and its butter into the pan of potatoes and turnips with the remaining butter and mash together well. Season with salt and pepper to taste and transfer to an ovenproof dish. Top with the cheese, then cover and bake for 25–30 minutes, until golden brown and piping hot.

White (or Mealie) Puddings

Mealie pudding is one of many traditional foods that bring back memories for me – this time of Dundee University in the mid 1970s. Late at night a group of us would traipse down to Greasy Pete's or Sweaty Betty's for a white pudding supper. This was a 'dressed' mealie pudding and chips. The pudding was denuded of its skin, then dipped in batter and deep-fried until crisp and golden on the outside, soft and squishy inside. There are few better tastes and textures if a bout of late-night hunger hits and it is stodge your body needs. The deep-fried Mars bar had not been invented at that time, otherwise it would definitely have been an option.

But mealie puddings are not unhealthy. Made from oatmeal, suet and onions, they were prepared – along with black puddings – whenever beef cattle were killed. The intestines were cleaned, then filled with the oatmeal mixture before being tied up and boiled. In rural Aberdeenshire the mealie mixture was sometimes packed into a scalded cloth and tied, leaving room for the oatmeal to swell, then boiled in the same way. Eaten traditionally as an accompaniment to mince and tatties or stew, they are also sliced on top of mince in Aberdeenshire and heated through in the oven, so that they absorb the fat from the mince. They also make the most sublime stuffing for chicken, too.

The following recipe comes from my Auntie Bette's mother-in-law, Granny Henderson. She was a stalwart of the Kirk and used to make dozens of mealies for church sales. Since she was boiling many at a time, she used her large washtub to boil up the puddings. I am sure it gave the socks an interesting flavour.

Makes 6–8
pudding skins
(natural casings are available
from good butcher's)
900g/2lb medium oatmeal
2 onions, peeled and finely chopped
450g/1lb beef suet, shredded
Jamaica pepper (ground allspice)

Prepare the skins by soaking them in salted water overnight and then rinsing well in clear cold water. Toast the oatmeal lightly in a moderate oven or under the grill. Mix it with the onions, suet and some salt and Jamaica pepper to taste. Stuff the mixture into the skins – not too full, since the oatmeal will swell. Tie the ends in a knot to secure and drop the puddings into a large pan of boiling water. Cook steadily for 1 hour, pricking the skins occasionally to prevent bursting. Once cooked, they will keep well for several weeks – preferably stored in a tub of oatmeal. When required, heat through either in simmering water or in a medium oven for about 20 minutes, until piping hot.

8

hot and cold puddings

Puddings are very dear to all Scots' hearts. It's that confounded sweet tooth of ours, which means that unless we finish a meal with a good slab of cake or have a scone with our cup of tea, we will be more than ready for pudding. If there is none, there will be a big sulk. Or a quick drive to the nearest petrol station or corner shop to indulge in some chocolate or sweeties. We didn't get our bad dental records for nothing.

Nowadays, people are more concerned about their sugar and fat intake and so are eating fewer puddings. But every now and then it is wonderful – and truly therapeutic – to make a lovely old-fashioned pudding that will be enjoyed by the whole family, safe in the knowledge that if it is home-made it will be a lot more wholesome than any commercial product.

Some of the recipes in this chapter are classics – Scots trifle, cranachan, Atholl brose. What would a Burns Supper be without one of these traditional dishes to round off the haggis and whisky-based meal? Others, such as cloutie dumpling or treacle duff, meant a lot to me during my childhood. I remember watching cloutie dumpling being mixed and lovingly wrapped in its floury 'clout', then boiled away for hours as I hung around, becoming more and more ravenous, waiting for the dumpling to emerge, plump and glorious, from its steamy bath. And treacle duff, a dark, sticky steamed pudding served in a puddle of custard, was another of my all-time favourites.

Finally there are some modernised versions of extremely old recipes – sticky toffee pudding, oatmeal praline ice-cream, apple frushie. All of them are easy to make and, as long as you use the best ingredients, all are absolutely delicious. Try them and see.

Treacle Duff

This is basically a steamed pudding flavoured with black treacle and is inspired by recipes in various old cookery books from the Kirk Women's Guild or WI, dating from the early 1900s. Treacle duff is among the usual roly-poly, seven-cup and canary puddings, beside lesser-known ones such as Brown George pudding (with mixed spice), Aeroplane pudding (with jam) and Auchingoul pudding (with lemon). My treacle duff recipe is similar to one called Marina pudding, a black-treacle-based mixture, but with the addition of a cup of raisins. Add these if you wish; with or without, this dark, treacly pud is truly memorable.

Serves 6

175g/6oz self-raising flour, sifted
1 teaspoon ground ginger
a pinch of salt
110g/4oz unsalted butter, softened
100g/3½oz dark muscovado sugar
2 large free-range eggs
2 level tablespoons black treacle

Place everything in a bowl and beat with an electric mixer for about 3 minutes, until smooth. Then tip into a lightly buttered 1 litre/1¾ pint pudding basin. To cover, fold a pleat in a double sheet of buttered foil (to allow room for expansion) and tie it securely over the basin with string. I make a string handle by threading the string twice from one side to the other so it is easy to lift. Scrunch up the edges of the foil so it does not sit in the water. Place the basin in a large saucepan over a low heat and pour boiling water carefully down the sides to come about half way up the basin. The water should be simmering gently, not boiling furiously. Cover the pan tightly and steam for 1¾–2 hours, topping up the water level if necessary. Leave for 5 minutes, then remove the foil, run a knife around the edge of the pudding and invert it on to a warm serving plate. Serve with custard.

Steamed Marmalade Pudding

The better the marmalade you use, the more divine this pudding will be. Serve with a large jug of custard.

Serves 6

2 heaped tablespoons Dundee
marmalade

110g/4oz butter, softened

110g/4oz golden caster sugar

2 large free-range eggs

175g/6oz self-raising flour, sifted

grated zest of 1 small orange

2 tablespoons milk

Butter a 1 litre/1¾ pint pudding basin and place the marmalade in the base. Cream together the butter and sugar until light and fluffy, then beat in the eggs one at a time, adding a little of the flour with each egg. Using a metal spoon, fold in the remaining flour, the orange zest and milk. Once well combined, spoon the mixture carefully on top of the marmalade and smooth the top.

To cover, fold a pleat in a double sheet of buttered foil (to allow room for expansion) and tie it securely over the basin with string. I make a string handle by threading the string twice from one side to the other so it is easy to lift. Scrunch up the edges of the foil so it does not sit in the water.

Place the basin in a large saucepan over a low heat. Pour boiling water carefully down the sides to come about half way up the basin. The water should be simmering gently, not boiling furiously. Cover the pan tightly and steam for 1¾–2 hours, topping up the water level if necessary.

Remove the pudding from the pan, wait 5–10 minutes, then remove the foil, run a knife around the edge and carefully invert the pudding on to a warm serving plate.

Cloutie Dumpling

My Auntie Muriel has been making cloutie dumpling for family birthdays for as long as I can remember. She will tie on her pinnie and stir together the ingredients, which she always says she couldn't possibly write down, for she tells me there's a 'ticky of this and a ticky of that'. No one ever used to write cloutie dumpling recipes, they just made them. But I have managed to pin her down and the following recipe is the one made for the family by her or often by her housekeeper, Mrs Patullo, who was Austrian and whose apple strudel was better than any shopbought one.

The word cloth is the origin of this dumpling recipe, as cloot or clout is Scots for cloth. It refers to the cloth in which the dumpling is boiled. Unlike other dumplings or steamed puddings, it forms a characteristic 'skin', made by sprinkling flour and sugar into the cloth before filling it with the mixture. Beware clouties without skin, as they are not authentic. The skin must be dried off before serving and nowadays this is done in the oven. But my mother tells me her task as youngest child was to dry the dumpling in front of the open fireplace. She would sit there on a stool for 15–20 minutes, turning the dumpling round and round until it was dried off and ready to eat. Since it was made only for special occasions such as birthdays (in which case there were silver threepennies hidden inside, similar to charms in a Christmas pudding), this was a chore worth doing well. It would then be eaten with custard, but is now also served with cream or ice-cream. Next day any leftovers would be fried in rendered suet and eaten with bacon for breakfast.

If you want to add coins, wrap 5p pieces or charms in waxed or greaseproof paper and add to the mixture.

Serves 8

225g/8oz plain flour, sifted
200g/7oz golden caster sugar
1 level teaspoon ground cinnamon
1 heaped teaspoon mixed spice
110g/4oz shredded suet
110g/4oz sultanas
110g/4oz currants
110g/4oz stoned dates, finely chopped
1 heaped teaspoon bicarbonate of soda
about 200ml/7fl oz milk, sour milk or cold tea
flour and caster sugar, for sprinkling

Mix the first 9 ingredients together in a bowl with enough of the liquid to give the dough a stiff dropping consistency.

Dip a large pudding cloth or tea towel into boiling water, then drain well and lay out flat on a table. Sprinkle with flour and then sugar (I use my flour and sugar shakers): you need an even, but not thick, layer. Place the mixture in the middle of the cloth, then bring the ends up and tie them together securely with string, allowing a little room for expansion. Place on a heatproof plate in a large saucepan. Top up with enough boiling water just to cover the pudding, then put a lid on the pan and simmer gently for 3¾–4 hours. Check the water level occasionally and top up if necessary. You should hear the reassuring, gentle shuddering sound of the plate on the bottom of the pan for the entire duration of cooking.

Preheat the oven to 180°C/350°F/Gas 4. Wearing oven gloves, remove the pudding from the pan and dip it briefly into a bowl of cold water – for no more than 10 seconds – so the skin does not stick to the cloth. Cut the string, untie the cloth and invert the dumpling on to an ovenproof plate. Place in the oven for 10–15 minutes, just until the skin feels less sticky. Sprinkle with caster sugar and serve hot, with custard.

Bramble and Butterscotch Crumble Tart

Blackberries are always called brambles in Scotland. Whether you pick them in the wild or buy cultivated ones, try this lovely tart, which can be served warm with thick cream, clotted cream or good vanilla ice-cream. If you cannot obtain dulce de leche, an Argentinian caramel spread, use a large can of condensed milk and boil it (unopened) in a large pan of water for 2–3 hours. Keep checking the water level and top up if necessary. Leave to cool before opening.

Serves 6
1 heaped tablespoon semolina
750g/1lb 10oz brambles (blackberries)
250g/9oz dulce de leche

For the pastry:
50g/2oz golden caster sugar
75g/3oz ground almonds
150g/5oz plain flour, sifted
110g/4oz butter, diced
1 large free-range egg

For the crumble:
75g/3oz plain flour, sifted
50g/2oz medium oatmeal
75g/3oz golden granulated sugar
75g/3oz butter, diced

Make the pastry in a food processor by processing the first 4 ingredients together, then adding the egg and processing briefly to combine (or make it by hand, rubbing the butter into the dry ingredients and mixing in the egg). Once amalgamated, bring it together with your hands, wrap in clingfilm and chill well. Then roll out to fit a deep 23cm/9in loose-bottomed buttered flan tin. Prick the base and chill again for at least 3 hours, preferably overnight.

Preheat the oven to 200°C/400°F/Gas 6. Sprinkle the semolina over the pastry, then scatter over the brambles. Gently warm the dulce de leche or condensed milk and spoon it over the berries.
To make the crumble topping, mix the flour, oatmeal and sugar together and rub in the butter. Sprinkle it over the berries and press down very lightly. Bake for 15 minutes, then reduce the oven temperature to 180°C/350°F/Gas 4 and bake for a further 25 minutes, until golden brown. Leave until barely warm before carefully decanting on to a plate.

Sticky Toffee Pudding

The Udny Arms in Newburgh, Aberdeenshire, claims to be the 'spiritual home of the famous sticky toffee pudding'. It was first served in the restaurant in the late 1960s, made by cook Pauline Wood, a local resident who had apparently modified a recipe from an extremely old cookbook she had found. Indeed, I have a recipe in my 1913 *Huntly Cookery Book* (Huntly is in Aberdeenshire) for a date pudding, by Mrs McGillivray, which is made with identical ingredients but is steamed instead of baked and has no toffee sauce. Instead there is a suggestion to serve it with a 'sweet sauce'.

But then there is Sharrow Bay, the famous Lake District hotel, renowned elsewhere in Britain (but not in Aberdeenshire) as the home of sticky toffee pud. Wherein lies the answer to the conundrum? According to food writer Simon Hopkinson, the Sharrow Bay pudding dates from around 1971 and originated from a traditional Lancastrian recipe. Whatever its mysterious origins, the most important fact is that it is a truly memorable pudding, rich, dark and sticky, ideal for wintry nights in the north – of England or Scotland.

Mackies, an ice-cream producer based on the family dairy farm near Rothienorman, Aberdeenshire, makes a sticky toffee pudding ice-cream by adding treacle toffee sauce, chopped dates, sultanas and syrup to softened ice-cream. The pudding is good on its own but, for the most hedonistic experience on the pudding trolley, serve sticky toffee ice-cream or plain vanilla as well as pouring cream on top of a bowlful of hot sticky toffee pudding. You might have problems moving afterwards, however.

Here is my version of the Udny Arms recipe.

128

Serves 8
100g/3½oz butter, softened
200g/7oz golden caster sugar
2 large free-range eggs
450g/1lb self-raising flour, sifted
250g packet of stoned dried dates, chopped
1 teaspoon bicarbonate of soda

For the sauce:
100g/3½oz butter
200g/7oz dark muscovado sugar
300ml/10fl oz double cream

Preheat the oven to 180°C/350°F/Gas 4. Cream the butter and sugar together until fluffy, then gradually beat in the eggs. Place the dates and bicarbonate of soda in a bowl and pour over 600ml/1 pint of boiling water. Stir around well to break the dates up. Fold the flour into the butter and sugar mixture, then add the date mixture. Once well combined, tip into a 2 litre/3½ pint round ovenproof dish and bake for 45–50 minutes, until a skewer inserted into the middle comes out clean (the timing will depend on the height of your dish). Remove from the oven.

To make the sauce, bring everything to the boil in a saucepan and boil for 3–4 minutes, then pour very slowly over the pudding. You may not be able to pour over all the sauce; offer any leftovers separately in a jug. Place under a preheated grill for about 2 minutes, or until bubbling and sticky (or return to the oven on a baking sheet – it might bubble over – for 3–4 minutes). Serve hot with pouring cream or ice-cream.

Scots Trifle

There are so many variations on trifle that an entire book could be written on the subject. But I must say we have some rather fine offerings in Scotland, with our wonderful raspberries, brambles and, of course, a good supply of whisky or Drambuie to drench the sponges. This version is pretty boozy, so reduce the Drambuie by half or substitute fruit juice if children are to be involved.

Serves 8
5–6 trifle sponges, halved
raspberry jam
150g/5oz packet of ratafias
(almond macaroons)
5–6 tablespoons Drambuie
250g/9oz fresh raspberries,
plus a few extra to decorate
300ml/10fl oz double cream,
lightly whipped

For the custard:
600ml/1 pint creamy milk (or half milk,
half double cream)
25g/1oz caster sugar
4 large free-range egg yolks

First make the custard: heat the milk (or milk and cream) in a heavy saucepan until just bubbling, then remove from the heat. Beat the sugar and egg yolks together, then slowly pour them into the milk, whisking all the time. Return to a gentle heat and cook slowly, stirring or whisking, for 5–8 minutes, until slightly thickened. Do not allow it to boil or it will curdle. Leave to cool, stirring occasionally to prevent a skin forming.

Spread the trifle sponges with jam and place over the base of a pretty glass dish. Scatter over most of the ratafias, keeping some behind for decoration. Slowly sprinkle over the Drambuie until all the sponges and ratafias are just soaked; do not drown them. Top with the raspberries, then pour over the cooled custard. Cover and chill. Shortly before serving, spread with the whipped cream and decorate with ratafias and raspberries.

Cranachan

There are many different versions of this delicious – and simple – pudding. Mine includes mascarpone cheese, to give a richer texture, and I use jumbo oats instead of pinhead or coarse oatmeal. According to Scottish food historian Catherine Brown, the traditional way of eating it is to sit down at a table spread with bowls of the various ingredients and each person would mix their own cranachan in their dish, according to taste. Less whisky and more honey for the children. The traditional ingredients are simply cream, crowdie (traditional hand-skimmed cottage cheese), toasted oatmeal, fresh soft fruit such as raspberries, blaeberries and brambles, heather honey and whisky.

If you are preparing this in advance, only mix it a short time before serving, otherwise the oats will lose their crunch.

Serves 6

125g/4½oz jumbo oats
(large rolled/porridge oats)
75g/3oz light muscovado sugar
250g/9oz mascarpone cheese
3–4 tablespoons malt whisky,
plus extra to serve
300ml/10fl oz double cream,
lightly whipped
250g/9oz raspberries
runny heather honey (optional)

Put the oats and sugar on a large sheet of foil and place under a hot grill for 3–4 minutes, stirring every 30 seconds or so. They burn quickly so watch carefully. Remove and leave to cool. Put the mascarpone in a bowl, add whisky to taste and beat until smooth. Fold this into the whipped cream with the cooled oat mixture. Once thoroughly combined, gently fold in the raspberries, taking care not to break them up. Tip into a glass bowl, cover and serve at once, or chill for no more than an hour. Offer an optional drizzle of whisky – and heather honey, if you like.

Drumlanrig Pudding

The Duchess of Buccleuch, whose Dumfriesshire home is Drumlanrig Castle, told me that until the First World War there was a huge walled garden there, with many different vegetables and fruits. Rhubarb would certainly have been a favourite and would have been cooked up regularly. Interestingly, after the great French chef, Florence (who worked for the Dukes of Buccleuch from around 1790 to 1840), almost all the cooks were women. I imagine it was one of these female chefs who transformed a regular summer pudding into a rhubarb pudding. After 24 hours in the fridge, the bread takes on a lovely pink hue from the glorious colour of the rhubarb.

Incidentally, the stunning walled garden at Drumlanrig was ploughed up and converted to the production of essential vegetables such as carrots during the Second World War, in order to feed the nation.

Serves 6

800g/1lb 12oz (trimmed weight) rhubarb, trimmed and chopped
100g/3½oz golden granulated sugar
about 200g/7oz sliced brown or wholemeal bread
(it should be fairly thickly sliced)
thick pouring cream or thick yoghurt, to serve

Put the rhubarb, sugar and 2 tablespoons of cold water in a pan, bring to the boil and simmer for 5–10 minutes, until the rhubarb is tender.

Use most of the bread to line the base and sides of a 1 litre/1¾ pint pudding basin or soufflé dish, cutting them to fit where necessary and making sure there are no gaps. Spoon in half the rhubarb, place a layer of bread on top, then top with the remaining rhubarb. Cover with a layer of bread, then put a plate or saucer on top that just fits inside the rim of the bowl. Place a weight on top of that and refrigerate for about 24 hours.

To serve, loosen the edges of the pudding with a knife and turn it out on to a plate. Serve with thick pouring cream or yoghurt sweetened with a little sugar.

Atholl Brose

Sometimes spelt Athole Brose, this is basically a drink, which I have converted into a pudding. And whereas I find the pudding delicious, served with crisp, buttery shortbread, I find it rather unpalatable as a drink – but then I am not a great whisky drinker. Shame on me, a Scot, I know!

Some versions of this ancient drink contain only honey, whisky and water. The classic recipe – credited to the fifteenth-century Duke of Atholl, who allegedly overpowered his enemies by making them drink from a well filled with this intoxicating drink – contains oatmeal, or simply the strained liquid after soaking oatmeal in water. But it was in Robert Louis Stevenson's *Kidnapped* that I found inspiration for my recipe, which has cream beaten in at the end. Stevenson writes: 'Duncan Dhu made haste to bring out the pair of pipes that was his principal possession and to set before his guests a mutton ham and a bottle of drink which they call Athole brose, and which is made of old whisky, strained honey and sweet cream, slowly beaten together in the right order and proportion.'

Serves 4
100g/3½oz medium oatmeal
2 tablespoons runny heather honey
200ml/7fl oz whisky
300ml/10fl oz double cream,
lightly whipped
shortbread, to serve

Mix the oatmeal with 200ml/7fl oz cold water and leave for 30 minutes–1 hour. Then press through a fine sieve to extract the liquid. Mix this with the honey and whisky and pour into a bottle. If using as a drink, shake well before serving.

For a pudding, gently fold 3 tablespoons of the brose into the whipped cream and transfer to a glass dish. Chill well to firm it up slightly, then serve with shortbread.

Apple Frushie

An apple frushie is an apple tart with short, crumbly pastry, the word frushie denoting the crumbly texture. I have moved this definition on a little to make a crumble instead of a tart, which is easier. This one is based on a delicious pudding I enjoyed while judging a competition in an Edinburgh girls' school. The contestant, Eve Smith, was only 11 years old yet produced one of the best crumbles – based on her grandmother's recipe – I have ever tasted.

Serves 6–8
1kg/2¼ lb cooking apples, peeled, cored
and thinly sliced
75g/3oz caster sugar

For the topping:
250g/9oz unsalted butter, diced
125g/4½oz plain flour, sifted
125g/4½oz medium oatmeal
a pinch of salt
150g/5oz light muscovado sugar

Preheat the oven to 180°C/350°F/Gas 4. Place the apples and sugar in a large ovenproof dish, stirring to coat the apples in the sugar.

To make the topping, rub the butter into the flour and oatmeal until crumbly, then stir in the salt and sugar. Tip this on to the apples and press down lightly. Bake for about 45 minutes, until the crumble is golden brown and the juices are bubbling through. Allow to cool for at least 10 minutes, then serve with vanilla ice-cream or thick cream.

Oatmeal Praline Ice-cream
with Berries

This ice-cream is divine served with berries (*au naturel*, or warmed slightly with a sprinkling of sugar until the juices run) in summer. In winter, melt some Dundee marmalade with a splash of whisky and serve this hot marmalade sauce over the ice-cream.

My recipe was inspired by F. Marian McNeill's 'Caledonian Ice', which is made by freezing sweetened whipped cream until almost hard, then stirring in some toasted coarse oatmeal. I like to make a custard-based ice-cream and fold in crunchy oatmeal praline just before churning. Although home-made is best, if you are feeling lazy you could simply mix the praline into a 1-litre tub of softened good-quality bought vanilla ice-cream.

Serves 6–8
500ml/18fl oz full-fat milk
300ml/10fl oz double cream
4 large free-range egg yolks
125g/4½oz caster sugar
seasonal berries, such as brambles, blaeberries and raspberries, to serve

For the praline:
150g/5oz pinhead oatmeal
140g tub of liquid glucose syrup
125g/4½oz caster sugar

Put the milk and cream in a heavy-based saucepan and bring slowly to the boil. Meanwhile, beat together the egg yolks and sugar until smooth. Just before they reach boiling point, pour the milk and cream over the egg and sugar mixture, stirring all the time. Then tip it back into the pan and return to a low heat. Stirring constantly, cook gently for about 10 minutes or until it has the consistency of double cream. It will thicken on cooling, so don't panic and think it is too thin. Leave to cool, stirring frequently to prevent a skin forming.

For the praline, toast the oatmeal either under the grill for a couple of minutes or in an oven preheated to 180°C/350°F/Gas 4 for 8–10 minutes, just until it smells nutty and toasty. If you use the grill, watch the oatmeal to make sure it does not burn. Tip it on to an oiled baking sheet. Place the glucose and sugar in a heavy-based saucepan and stir over a low heat until the sugar dissolves. Dip a pastry brush in cold water and brush quickly down the inside of the pan to loosen any sugar that is stuck to the sides. Then, without stirring at all, allow the mixture to bubble away for 8–10 minutes or until it is golden brown colour. During this time, swirl the pan around a couple of times. Then pour the mixture over the oatmeal, trying to cover it – but don't worry if the oatmeal is not all covered. Leave to cool, then break up and place in a food processor. Using the pulse button, process to coarse crumbs. Don't process too long or it will be powdery.

Once the custard is cold, stir in the praline, then pour into an ice-cream machine and churn. Or pour into a large, shallow freezer container, seal and place in the freezer. Remove after 2 hours, whisk madly (this helps prevent ice crystals forming) and return to the freezer. Repeat the whisking a couple of times, then freeze until firm.

To serve, transfer from freezer to fridge for about 20 minutes or until slightly softened. Serve with berries.

Whisky and Honey Ice-Cream

The character of this ice-cream alters completely depending on which whisky you use. I recommend either a Speyside or a Lowland one, not an Islay one: the peaty taste would dominate. The ice-cream packs a powerful punch. Serve it on its own, with poached apricots or fresh strawberries, or place a scoop on top of a hot pudding such as Sticky Toffee Pudding (see page 128) or Cloutie Dumpling (see page 124). Not traditional, I grant you, but exceedingly welcome nonetheless.

Serves 6
500ml/18fl oz full-fat milk
300ml/10fl oz double cream
2 tablespoons heather honey
4 large free-range egg yolks
100g/3½oz golden caster sugar
2 tablespoons malt whisky

Place the milk, cream and honey in a heavy-based saucepan and bring slowly to the boil. Beat the egg yolks and sugar together until smooth, then stir a little of the milk mixture into the yolks. Pour this into the pan and cook over a low heat, stirring constantly, for about 10 minutes, until slightly thickened. Don't let it boil or it will curdle. Pour the mixture into a jug and leave to cool completely, stirring occasionally to prevent a skin forming.

Once the custard is cold, stir in the whisky, then pour into an ice-cream machine and churn. Or pour into a large, shallow freezer container, cover and freeze – preferably on fast-freeze – for 6 hours, removing every 2 hours to whisk madly (this helps prevent ice crystals forming). Transfer the ice-cream to the fridge to soften up a little before serving.

Carragheen Pudding

Carragheen or Irish moss (*Chondrus crispus*) is found all round the British coastline and is used particularly in Scottish and Irish seaside towns and villages. Its gelatinous quality is useful for setting jellies and blancmange-style puddings, and it is often added to commercial ice-creams and jellies.

In the Hebrides many seaweeds are used as fertilisers, to enhance the flavour of new potatoes. A nourishing drink made by adding dried powdered carragheen to hot milk or water was popular in the Hebrides, especially as it had sedative qualities.

In the coastal Highlands, a restorative jelly made with carragheen used to be given to invalids. A milk pudding similar to the one below was also prescribed for those suffering from chest complaints, bronchitis or asthma because of its high mineral content, particularly iodine.

Flavourings such as rosewater, citrus zest or juice (Seville oranges being particularly good) and, of course, sugar can be added according to taste. I personally like it plain, perhaps served with some stewed rhubarb, which is the way Auchmithie cook Margaret Horn has eaten it all her life.

If using dried carragheen, you will need a minimum of 10g/½oz and it should be soaked in water for 15 minutes first.

Serves 6
50g/2oz freshly picked carragheen, well washed
1 litre/1¾ pints full-fat milk
sugar and other flavourings (optional)

Bring the carragheen and milk slowly to the boil, then simmer for 30–40 minutes or until the seaweed has become rather gelatinous. Add any flavourings now – sugar to taste, a dash of rosewater or some lemon or orange juice. Strain into a bowl and leave somewhere cold to set.

Eat on its own or with stewed rhubarb or apples.

9
baking

Another name for this chapter could be Teabreads, which, in many parts of Scotland, encompasses all manner of cakes, buns, biscuits, tarts, scones and fruit loaves. Teabreads are what you have with tea – after a simple hot dish such as eggs, smoked ('yellow') fish or oatmeal herring. In Aberdeenshire, a 'fly cup' (of tea) is invariably accompanied by a 'fine piece', which means something extremely tasty, usually sweet, often home-baked.

Home-baking is something we Scots have always excelled at, although, strangely, often without the use of an oven. F. Marian McNeill in her 1929 book, *The Scots Kitchen*, wrote, 'In Scotland, amongst the rural population generally, the girdle takes the place of the oven, the bannock of the loaf.'

But although the oven came into the Scots kitchen much later than the girdle, our skills at cakes, tarts and oven scones have come on apace with our innate girdle skills. Girdle is the Scots word for griddle. If you do not have a cast-iron girdle (griddle) you can use a heavy-based frying pan instead, although the heat distribution is not as even and it is not as practical to flip things over. I also find there is less chance of girdle scones or bannocks browning too much on a girdle, as it cooks them more quickly.

Sadly, nowadays, many people use neither girdle nor oven to bake. How deprived their tastebuds must be, for baking is one of life's greatest pleasures. It is also surely the most selfless of culinary arts, since it is all about sharing. Cakes, shortbread and scones are not only for the cook (although one of the great perks is scraping the bowl), they are made to be enjoyed by others.

Even if you have not done much baking before, I urge you to try some of the easy recipes in this chapter. The only proviso is that you must use good-quality ingredients: best butter for the shortbread, fine, plump raisins for the Border tart and rich, treacly dark muscovado sugar for the Ecclefechan tart. Then, once you have made some of the most intriguing-sounding recipes in the book – puggy buns, fatty cutties, broonie – all you have to do is sit back and wait for them to cool as the fabulously alluring smells of home-baking fill your house.

Scotch Pancakes

This is fast food as it was meant to be. From mixing the ingredients for these delicious little pancakes (called drop scones outside Scotland) to eating them warm takes as little as 10 minutes.

This is based on my mother's recipe, as it was part of her weekly repertoire, along with guggy cake (a boiled fruit cake), treacle scones and sultana cake. Sometimes the pancakes would be spread with raspberry jam, sometimes apple or blackcurrant jelly – all home-made. They are best eaten immediately but you could make a batch and freeze it for some later date. To reheat, thaw slightly, then wrap in foil and place in a moderate oven.

If you have never used a girdle before, it is easy: test whether it is hot enough by dropping a teaspoonful of the batter on to the surface. It should set almost at once and begin to bubble after 1 minute. It is the large bubbles that tell you the pancakes are ready to be flipped over. Those – and a growing impatience to devour the entire batch at once sitting – are the clue that it's time to put the kettle on, for tea is about to be served.

Makes 12–16

110g/4oz plain flour, sifted

½ teaspoon cream of tartar

¼ teaspoon bicarbonate of soda

a pinch of salt

1 teaspoon golden caster sugar

1 medium free-range egg, beaten

150ml/5fl oz milk

a little butter for the girdle

Sift the first 4 ingredients into a bowl. Stir in the sugar, then make a well in the middle. Add the egg and whisk together with a balloon whisk, then gradually add the milk, whisking all the time.

Continue whisking until you have a smooth batter. Heat the girdle (or a large heavy frying pan) over a medium heat. Using a wad of kitchen paper, smear a thin film of butter all over it. Once it is hot – mine takes about 3 minutes to heat up – drop spoonfuls of batter on to the girdle, 4 at a time. If you want dainty little ones, use a dessertspoon; for slightly larger ones, use a tablespoon. After about 1½–2 minutes you will notice large bubbles forming on top. Using a spatula, flip each one over and continue cooking for a further 1–1½ minutes until just done. They should take about 3 minutes altogether.

Remove and keep warm in a folded tea towel while you cook the rest. Serve with butter – and jam if you like.

Treacle Scones

I have always loved treacle puddings and bakes. Black treacle is popular in Scotland, whether in steamed puddings, gingerbread or scones.

As a child I had a different type of treacle scone at Hallowe'en. Then we would attempt to bite thick, floury, triangular scones that had been daubed in sticky black treacle. The snag was that they were hung by a string from the washing line in the kitchen (above a newspaper-lined floor, needless to say!) and our hands were tied behind our backs. Thankfully the next game was always dooking for apples, which involved immersion in tubs of freezing cold water to try and bite apples that always managed to bob away from you just as you were about to pounce. How come I recall these games as fun?

Makes 6–8

50g/2oz unsalted butter

1 heaped tablespoon black treacle

225g/8oz self-raising flour

a pinch of salt

½ teaspoon ground ginger

½ teaspoon mixed spice

about 50–70ml/2–2½fl oz milk

Preheat the oven to 220°C/425°F/Gas 7. Put the butter and treacle in a small pan over a low heat until just melted, then remove from the heat and leave to cool for about 5 minutes. Sift the flour, salt and spices into a mixing bowl. Make a well in the centre, then pour in the treacle and butter mixture with just enough milk to combine to a fairly soft dough. Add 3 tablespoons of milk at first, then add more if necessary.

With lightly floured hands, bring the dough together, using a very light touch with minimal handling, otherwise the scones will be tough. Pat out to a thickness of about 2cm/¾in (do not use a rolling pin). If there are any cracks, knead gently together until smooth. Using fluted or round scone cutters, cut out 6–8 scones. Place these on a buttered baking sheet and bake for about 10 minutes, until well risen. Transfer to a wire rack to cool a little, before eating warm with butter.

Aggie's Scones

My friend Aggie MacKenzie from Rothiemurchus has always raved about her granny's scone recipe, which she bakes frequently. Ina Campbell, Aggie's grandmother, handed on the recipe to Aggie's mum, who used to win prizes at all the local shows for her scones. The name Ina was short for Angusina and this adding on of Ina to any male's name in the family was traditional in the Sutherland area, where Ina Campbell came from. Aggie has an aunt called Hughina and a more distant relative called Hectorina Donaldina. Some traditions are better relegated to history . . . unlike the scone recipe, which is absolutely the best!

Makes 15–16

450g/1lb plain flour
1 heaped teaspoon bicarbonate of soda
1 rounded teaspoon cream of tartar
1 heaped teaspoon salt
40g/1½oz butter
1 tablespoon golden syrup
1 large free-range egg
300ml/10fl oz full-fat milk

Preheat the oven to its highest setting – 240°C/475°F/Gas 9. Sift the flour into a bowl with the soda, tartar and salt. Melt the butter and syrup together and cool slightly, then tip into the bowl. Beat the egg into the milk and add to the flour mixture. Stir together until combined to a soft dough, then, using well-floured hands, turn the dough on to a floured board and flattened gently to about 2.5cm/1in thick. The dough is very soft, so keep lightly flouring both hands and board. Cut out with a floured scone cutter and place on a very lightly greased hot baking sheet (I place it in the oven as it is heating up). Bake for 7–8 minutes, then transfer to a wire rack. Eat barely warm, with butter and jam.

Fatty Cutties

The fatty cuttie is a northern relative of those other famous girdle cakes, the Singin' Hinnie of Northumberland and the Welsh cake. My recipe was given to me by Mrs Scott, who used to live on the northerly Orkney island of Westray. It is similar to a recipe from Mrs Mathers of Stenness, in the west mainland of Orkney, but the mainland one uses double the amount of butter. Perhaps this is an indication of the relative affluence on the mainland.

According to Mrs Scott, the Orcadian fatty cuttie originated many years ago when people were very poor indeed. Daily bread took the form of a girdle bannock, usually made from beremeal. As people became slightly better off they began to use wheat flour instead of barley and also began to add fat (butter) to their girdle breads and cakes. Eventually the cakes came to be known as fatty cutties because they were enriched with fat and because they were cut into wedges before baking. A similar dish is the Shetland fatty brunnies, which are thick cakes of oatmeal and/or wheat flour baked on the girdle and enriched with a lump of lard to keep them soft.

Makes 8
175g/6oz plain flour
¼ teaspoon bicarbonate of soda
75g/3oz caster sugar
75g/3oz currants
75g/3oz butter, melted
about 1 tablespoon milk
a little butter for the girdle

Sift the flour and bicarbonate of soda into a mixing bowl. Stir in the sugar and currants, then pour in the melted butter and just enough milk to combine to a stiff dough. You may need to add another ½–1 tablespoon of milk. Knead very lightly and divide into 2 balls.

On a lightly floured surface, roll each ball into a circle, about 5mm/¼ in thick, then cut into 4 wedges. Heat your girdle to medium-hot, grease very lightly, using a wad of kitchen paper, then cook the fatty cutties for 3–4 minutes on each side, until golden brown. Serve warm without butter or cold with a thin smear of butter.

Shortbread

When I was *assistante* in a *lycée* in the Pyrenees, I often made shortbread for the pupils and staff. They absolutely loved it but always said how rich it was. This had never occurred to me, for it was such a part of my life that I just took it for what it was – simple and delicious, yet almost mundane. But considering it was originally a special-occasion biscuit (unlike the plainer bannocks and oatcakes), which has gradually become mainstream, it is not really surprising that first-timers consider it rich.

In her book on the Scots household in the eighteenth century, Marion Lochhead writes about tea parties of the day where the hostess 'must have a plate of bun and one of shortbread – either in a cake, broken into bits, or in little, round nickety Tantallon cakes, or in the favourite "petticoat tails". (I have no idea what nickety means either!) Many years on, shortbread still appears at all the best tea parties and also on special occasions such as Hogmanay (with black bun) but is also as regular a feature in Scottish kitchens as porridge or mince.

The following recipe is from my Granny Anderson's recipe book and my Auntie Muriel has dated it 14 January 1947. No one can recall this being a special occasion but the two brothers and two sisters were all back from their war duties and were living at home together once again. Feeding six adults every night must have been hard work but my grandmother was a strong character, having brought up four children pretty much on her own while her husband was away at sea. Shortbread would have been one of many items filling the biscuits tins, baked either by granny or her daughters, for visitors or family tea.

My granny's recipe is a rather frugal one – many recipes give a higher ratio of butter to flour. For a richer shortbread, see Petticoat Tails on page 148 or Moira MacAulay's Shortbread on page 149. All are exceptionally easy to make but only the best ingredients will give a good buttery, crumbly finish. Instead of semolina you could use rice flour (ground rice) for a similarly crunchy texture. Or use fine semolina (farola) or cornflour for a more melt-in-the-mouth feel. Simplest of all, of course, is to use only flour.

Remember that shortbread should never be kneaded for longer than it takes to bring the dough together quickly in your hands. Overworking it will toughen the shortbread. Indeed I never roll it with a rolling pin, I just press it out lightly to the required shape before baking. The lightest hand will give the lightest shortbread.

Makes about 16 pieces
110g/4oz slightly salted butter, softened
50g/2oz caster sugar
175g/6oz plain flour, sifted
50g/2oz semolina
caster sugar, for dredging

Preheat the oven to 170°C/325°F/Gas 3. Cream the butter and sugar together, then gradually add the flour and semolina. Bring together with your hands and knead briefly to combine to a ball. Using your fingers, lightly press it out to a rectangle, about 5mm/¼in thick, then cut it into fingers (it can also be pressed into two 20cm/8in sandwich tins or a shortbread mould). Place on a greased baking tray and prick lightly all over with a fork, then bake for about 20 minutes or until pale golden brown. Dredge with caster sugar and transfer to a wire rack to cool.

Variations

Highlanders: shape the dough into a long roll, roll this in milk then demerara sugar and cut into slices before baking.

Tantallon cakes: use rice flour instead of semolina, add the grated zest of 1 small lemon and cut into round biscuits.

Yetholm bannock: add 1 heaped tablespoon of chopped crystallised ginger and an egg yolk to the basic dough, which should be baked in an oblong.

Pitcaithly bannock: add 1 tablespoon each of chopped almonds and candied peel to the dough and bake in a large round.

Oaties

These deliciously crunchy oat biscuits are based on ones made by the Shortbread House of Edinburgh, which makes superb shortbread and other biscuits, all by hand. Obviously the staff were not keen to divulge its recipe but mine is cobbled together from their ingredients list – and lots of sneaky tastings! My biscuits are slightly less 'short' in texture. Both have their merits; both are good with tea or coffee.

Makes 18–20
110g/4oz butter
50g/2oz golden caster sugar
2 level tablespoons golden syrup
125g/4½oz rolled oats
75g/3oz plain flour, sifted
½ teaspoon bicarbonate of soda
100g/3½oz desiccated coconut

Preheat the oven to 180°C/350°F/Gas 4.
Melt the butter, sugar and syrup together in a large pan, then stir in the oats, flour, bicarbonate of soda and coconut. Drop spoonfuls of the mixture on to 2 greased baking sheets and bake for 12–15 minutes, until golden. Leave on the baking sheets for 2 minutes, then transfer to a wire rack to cool and firm up.

Petticoat Tails

This is just one of several recipes for petticoat tails. You could use all flour (no semolina) or substitute regular semolina for the farola if this is hard to find. Some old recipes suggest adding caraway seeds – a throwback to the days when caraway comfits (caraway seeds thickly coated in boiled sugar) were widely used as decoration.

Some believe that the name of these dainty shortbread biscuits is a corruption of the French *petites galettes*, meaning little cakes. Given the culinary interchange between France and Scotland, this is a possibility. But what is also possible is that the biscuits were named for their shape: they are identical to the individual gores of the full, bell-hooped petticoats worn by ladies at Court – probably in the sixteenth century at the time of Mary, Queen of Scots, who was said to be fond of them.

The classic shape of petticoat tails is a round with a small inner circle removed and wedges cut all the way around it. It is of, course, easier just to mark it into sixths or eighths, but if you wish to follow the traditional method, proceed according to the instructions in F. Marian McNeill's *The Scots Kitchen*:

'Cut out the cake by running a paste-cutter round a dinner plate or any large round dish inverted on the paste. Cut a cake from the centre of this one with a small saucer or large tumbler. Keep this inner circle whole and cut the outer one into eight petticoat-tails. Bake all these on paper laid on tins, serve the round cake in the middle of the plate, and the petticoat tails as radii round it.'

148

Makes 12–18
175g/6oz slightly salted butter
50g/2oz caster sugar
175g/6oz plain flour
50g/2oz farola (fine semolina)
caster sugar, for dredging

Preheat the oven to 150°C/300°F/Gas 2. Cream the butter and sugar together, then sift in the flour and farola. Mix together and knead very briefly until combined. Divide in 2 (or 3) and lightly press the pieces into two 20cm/8in (or three 15cm/6in) greased sandwich tins. Prick all over with a fork. Bake for 30–40 minutes or until pale golden brown. Remove from the oven and cut each round into 6 or 8 wedges. Dredge with caster sugar and leave to cool before decanting on to a wire rack.

Moira MacAulay's Shortbread

Moira MacAulay, mother of my university friend, comedian Fred MacAulay, bakes her shortbread regularly, to great acclaim. Fred's eldest son, Jack, declares Granny Moira's shortbread to be the best in Scotland – I am inclined to agree.

Moira insists there is no secret. In fact she developed her own recipe from one on the back of a cornflour packet many years ago. But she does insist that a really good, well-used baking tin is essential. Hers – an ancient one given to her by an aunt – is already the subject of fierce dispute between her daughters-in-law. Never mind the family jewels, who will inherit the shortbread tin?

Makes 20–24 pieces
225g/8oz butter
(I use slightly salted), softened
110g/4oz caster sugar
(I use golden caster)
225g/8oz plain flour, sifted
150g/5oz cornflour, sifted
caster sugar, for dredging

Preheat the oven to 150°C/300°F/Gas 2. Place the butter and sugar in a mixer or food processor and cream until pale. Add the flour and cornflour and blend briefly, just until thoroughly combined. Tip into a buttered 23 x 33cm/9 x 13in swiss roll tin and, using floured hands, press down so it is level. Prick it all over with a fork (do this carefully, so that you do not disturb the level surface), then bake for 50–60 minutes (Moira bakes hers for 1 hour; my oven requires only 50 minutes). It should be a uniform pale golden colour all over; do not allow it to become golden brown.

Remove from the oven and dredge all over with caster sugar, then cut into squares. Leave for 5 minutes or so, then carefully decant on to a wire rack to cool.

Parlies

Parlies are a type of gingerbread baked as biscuits. Although soft when you remove them from the oven, they firm up as they cool to become crisp but slightly chewy in the centre. It is important not to overwork the dough or they will be tough.

The name is short for parliament cakes, and it is said to derive from their popularity with members of the Scots parliament. In late-eighteenth-century Edinburgh, a lady called Mrs Flockhart ran a shop and tavern in Potterrow, at the back of what is now the Royal Scottish Museum in Chambers Street. Although the shop was a general one, the back room was the scene of her most profitable business. Her eminent customers – including Mr Scott (father of Sir Walter) and several Lords – would pass through the shop to the back room to partake of a dram or two and some gingerbread or biscuits. Her thin, crisp, square cakes were parliaments or parlies, the round ones snaps and the thick soft cakes were called white or brown quality cakes. I wonder if parlies are set to make a comeback now that Scotland has its own parliament again . . .

Fife's equivalent to parlies is paving stones (known as paving stanes). These are made from a gingerbread-type mixture that is shaped into old-fashioned oblong cobble shapes. After baking, a boiled sugar syrup is poured over them to form a crunchy coating.

Makes 4 extra-large or 16 small squares
110g/4oz unsalted butter
2 heaped tablespoons black treacle
225g/8oz plain flour
1 rounded teaspoon ground ginger
a pinch of salt
50g/2oz dark muscovado sugar

Preheat the oven to 170°C/325°F/Gas 3. Melt the butter and treacle together gently. Sift the flour, ginger and salt into a bowl and stir in the sugar. Pour in the melted mixture and stir briefly to combine.

Tip into a shallow 23cm/9in square buttered cake tin and, using floured hands, flatten down. Prick all over with a fork and bake for 20 minutes. Remove from the oven and cut into squares, then, while still warm, decant carefully on to a wire rack to cool. They will firm up as they cool.

Puggy Buns

Probably the oldest bakery in the UK, Adamson's of Pittenweem, was established in 1635 by a Dutchman called Hedderwick (this is doubtless an anglicised spelling). The East Neuk of Fife, which incorporates Pittenweem and other charming villages such as St Monans, Anstruther and Crail, used to trade regularly with Holland: the Dutch wanted Fife's potatoes, the Scots wanted Holland's wonderful tiles for their houses. The tiny bakery stands adjacent to the old Pittenweem castle (built some 10 years before the bakery), where Charles I dined on a visit to Scotland in 1635. Hedderwick was asked to bake something special to mark the occasion and the Hedderwick bun was born. When I asked the bakery owner, Kenny Adamson, for the recipe he looked at me as if I was mad. This was a secret that would possibly go with him to the grave. Then I asked if it was something like a Selkirk bannock, for it looks and tastes similar. His reply: 'You could say the Selkirk bannock is like the Hedderwick bun.'

But he did give me a recipe for another extremely old, traditional bun, the puggy bun. These look vaguely similar to Eccles cakes or Chorley cakes, although they don't contain dried fruit. They have been made in Adamson's bakery for many years – certainly since Kenny's grandmother, Agnes, bought the bakery in 1887. The old Scotch oven with the classic beehive roof is still in perfect working order, although it now runs on oil, not coal. The puggy buns, which are known locally as hypocrites – black inside, white outside – are filled with a gingerbread-type mixture called a gundy dough. Gundy is the old Scots word for a spiced confection or sweetmeat. The gundy dough can be made in advance and will keep for several weeks in an airtight container in the fridge. The outer dough used to be a barm dough, then later yeast dough, but now shortcrust pastry is used.

These Fife specialities can be enjoyed plain or spread with butter. Kenny likes to warm his under the grill before buttering.

Makes 6
275g/10oz plain flour, sifted
a pinch of salt
110g/4oz butter

For the gundy:
175g/6oz strong white flour
3 heaped tablespoons golden syrup, warmed
50g/2oz golden caster sugar
1 heaped teaspoon bicarbonate of soda
1 heaped teaspoon mixed spice
50ml/2fl oz milk

Make the gundy first: sift the flour into a bowl, add all the other ingredients and stir with a wooden spoon to combine. Wrap in clingfilm, then chill.

For the pastry, put all the ingredients in a food processor and process briefly until the mixture resembles breadcrumbs. Add enough cold water to make a firm dough – about 75ml/3fl oz. Wrap in clingfilm and chill for an hour or so. Preheat the oven to 190°C/375°F/Gas 5.

Roll out the pastry thinly and cut out six circles, about 15cm/6in in diameter. Divide the gundy into 6 and place a portion in the centre of each circle. Fold in the edges and pinch them together to seal, then turn over. Roll out each one with a rolling pin to form a rough circle about 10cm/4in in diameter. Place on a greased baking tray and slit the top of each bun 3 times. Bake for 20–25 minutes, until pale golden brown. Transfer to a wire rack to cool.

Orkney Broonie

Not to be confused with Shetland's fatty brunnies, which are thick girdle scones or bannocks made of wholemeal flour or oatmeal, the Orkney broonie is a light, moist gingerbread, not dissimilar to Yorkshire or Lancashire parkin. Both brunnie and broonie come from an old Norse word, *bruni*, which, according to F. Marian McNeill, means a thick bannock.

The broonie keeps well, wrapped in foil, and is good either plain or buttered, with a cup of tea. Or warm up thick slices and serve with butterscotch sauce and a great dollop of clotted cream for a truly memorable pudding.

Makes 1 Loaf

175g/6oz medium oatmeal
175g/6oz self-raising flour, sifted
a pinch of salt
85g/3¼ oz unsalted butter, diced
1 heaped teaspoon ground ginger
85g/3¼ oz light muscovado sugar
2 rounded tablespoons black treacle
1 medium free-range egg, beaten
150ml/5fl oz buttermilk (or fresh milk soured with ½ teaspoon lemon juice)

Preheat the oven to 170°C/325°F/Gas 3. Combine the oatmeal, flour and salt in a bowl. Rub in the butter, then stir in the ginger and sugar. Place the treacle in a small pan and heat very gently, then stir in the egg. Pour this mixture into the dry ingredients with the buttermilk or milk. Stir until thoroughly combined, then pour into a buttered, base-lined 900g/2lb loaf tin. Bake for 60–70 minutes, until a skewer inserted into the middle comes out clean. Set the tin on a wire rack and leave until cold before turning out.

Sultana Cake

It all came back to me as I licked the bowl. There I was, aged four, maybe five, kneeling on a kitchen stool and scraping my mother's mixing bowl just after she had put her sultana cake into the oven. Like tea loaf, scones and pancakes (the Scotch variety), sultana cake was available almost daily and so this was a frequent occurrence. And yet there was still something magical about climbing on to the stool and licking the bowl. Cynics among you might call it greed. I call it sharing baking duties – and, of course, quality time, had it existed in those days – with my mother. Afterwards we had to wait for the cake to be ready and, most agonising of all, wait for it to cool while the comforting smell of warm cake filled the house.

My mother cannot eat sultanas any more and she says this cake is one of the simple pleasures she misses. As I revisited my childhood, baking my mother's sultana cake after far too many years, I began to understand how she feels.

Makes a 18cm/7in cake
175g/6oz butter, softened
175g/6oz golden caster sugar
3 medium free-range eggs
225g/8oz plain flour, sifted
225g/8oz sultanas
1 level dessertspoon golden
granulated sugar

Preheat the oven to 170°C/325°F/Gas 3. Cream the butter and sugar together until pale. Beat in the eggs one at a time, with a third of the flour after each addition. Stir in the sultanas and combine well to make a fairly stiff dough. Turn into a buttered, base-lined, deep 18cm/7in cake tin and bake for about 1 hour or until a cocktail stick or skewer inserted in the centre comes out clean. Switch off the oven and sprinkle the top of the cake with the granulated sugar. Return to the oven for 3–4 minutes, then transfer to a wire rack to cool. Turn out of the tin when cold.

Dundee Cake

Dundee is famous for many things. Besides its marmalade and its pies, there is the cake. Dundee cake is known throughout the world but, strangely enough, it is seldom eaten in Dundee. It is one of those things – rather like haggis – which, although meant to represent the Scottish people's daily fare, is eaten only on high days and holidays. The rich ingredients would have made it an expensive cake for the average Dundee citizen.

Having said that, it is a cake to be proud of and its origins – according to David Goodfellow of Goodfellow & Steven (one of Scotland's best bakeries, established in Dundee in 1897) – are closely linked to the marmalade industry. The surplus of orange peel from Keiller's marmalade was used in Dundee cakes. A sign, therefore, of an authentic Dundee cake is the use of orange peel rather than mixed peel. Unless you are a purist, however, good-quality mixed peel will still make a very fine cake.

A well-made Dundee cake is a good alternative to a richer, darker Christmas cake and is also ideal for afternoon tea. It keeps well, tightly wrapped in a tin.

Makes a 18cm/7in cake
175g/6oz unsalted butter, softened
175g/6oz golden caster sugar
grated zest of 1 small orange
4 medium free-range eggs
175g/6oz plain flour
1 level teaspoon baking powder
½ teaspoon mixed spice (optional)
50g/2oz ground almonds
110g/4oz sultanas
110g/4oz raisins
110g/4oz currants
50g/2oz candied orange peel, chopped
about 1 tablespoon brandy or whisky
16–20 whole blanched almonds

Preheat the oven to 150°C/300°F/Gas 2. Cream together the butter and sugar until pale, add the orange zest, then beat in the eggs one at a time, adding a little flour if the mixture looks like curdling. Sift in the flour, baking powder and mixed spice, if using, then add the ground almonds. Fold in gently but thoroughly. Stir in the dried fruit and candied peel, with enough brandy or whisky to make a slightly soft consistency.

Spoon into a greased and lined deep 18cm/7in cake tin and smooth the top. Bake for 2½–3 hours, until a toothpick or skewer inserted in the centre comes out clean. Halfway through baking, remove from the oven, arrange the almonds on top and then return to the oven. Place a piece of foil loosely over the top if it becomes too brown during the last half hour or so. Cool completely in the tin before turning out.

Selkirk Bannock

Reputedly a favourite teatime treat of Queen Victoria, this rich, fruited sweet bread is a speciality of the Borders. It originated in the town of Selkirk as a means of using up spare bread dough. Good Selkirk bannocks are now made by bakers in other Border towns, such as Galashiels, Hawick and Kelso. Although some add the butter at the beginning when making up the dough, I prefer to follow the basic guidelines in F. Marian McNeill's *The Scots Kitchen*:

'Get 2 pounds of dough from the baker. Into this rub 4 ounces butter and 4 ounces of lard until melted but not oiled. Then work in ½ pound of sugar, ¾ pound sultanas and ¼ pound chopped orange peel. Put the dough into a buttered tin, let it stand for 30 minutes to rise then bake in a good steady oven.'

For those of us unable to buy 2 pounds of dough from the baker, here is my version for – I must say – a truly magnificent bannock that is easy to make and all too easy to consume. Since I am not keen on peel, I prefer to use sultanas alone. Besides, according to Theodora Fitzgibbon's *A Taste of Scotland*, it was originally made only with the finest Turkish sultanas. Orange or mixed peel seems to be a rather more recent addition – recent being a relative term, since *The Scots Kitchen* was published in 1929.

Makes 1 large bannock
900g/2lb strong white flour
a pinch of salt
2 x 7g sachets of easy-blend dried yeast
50g/2oz caster sugar
about 500ml/18fl oz warm semi-skimmed milk (or half milk, half water)
150g/5oz butter, softened
400g/14oz sultanas
1 medium free-range egg, beaten, to glaze

Sift the flour and salt into a bowl, then stir in the yeast and sugar. Add enough warm milk to combine to a soft but not sticky dough. Turn on to a floured board and knead well for 10 minutes or so, until smooth. Place in a bowl, cover and leave somewhere warm for 1–1½ hours, until well risen.

Cut the softened butter in 4. Flatten the dough, place a piece of butter in the centre and fold the dough over, then knead until thoroughly amalgamated. Repeat with the remaining butter. Work in the sultanas, a handful at a time. Shape into a bannock: a round, flattened dome about 28cm/11in diameter. Place on a buttered baking sheet, glaze with some of the beaten egg and leave, uncovered, for about an hour, until well risen. Preheat the oven to 220°C/425°F/Gas 7.

Glaze the bannock with the remaining egg and bake for 15 minutes. Then reduce the oven temperature to 190°C/375°F/Gas 5 and cook for a further 25–30 minutes, covering loosely with foil for the last 15–20 minutes to prevent the top burning. It is ready when it is golden brown all over and the base sounds hollow when tapped underneath. Leave to cool on a wire rack. Serve sliced and spread with butter.

Border Tart

This is based on one of my mother's teatime specials. These days, Border tart is a shortcrust pastry case filled with a rich, spiced raisin filling, to which I add grated lemon zest. Originally it was made with an enriched bread dough and filled with almonds, raisins, peel and marzipan, all bound together in an egg custard. The dough for the base would have been a portion taken from the weekly breadmaking.

Similar tarts can be found all over the Borders, most noticeably Eyemouth tart, which is also made with raisins and brown sugar but includes coconut, walnuts and glacé cherries, too. Ecclefechan Tart (see page 160) is another variation on the theme. Ecclefechan is just over the south-west border of the Borders, and so is a local variation gone somewhat astray.

Serves 8

100g/3½oz unsalted butter, softened
100g/3½oz dark muscovado sugar
2 large free-range eggs, beaten
400g/14oz raisins
grated zest of 1 large lemon
1 teaspoon mixed spice

For the pastry:

150g/5oz plain flour, sifted
50g/2oz ground almonds
125g/4½oz unsalted butter, diced
20g/¾oz caster sugar
a pinch of salt
1 large free-range egg, beaten

To make the pastry, place the flour, almonds, butter, sugar and salt in a food processor and process until the mixture resembles breadcrumbs. Add the egg and process briefly. Bring the mixture together with your hands, wrap in clingfilm and chill for 1 hour. Roll out the pastry and use to line a 23cm/9in tart tin. Prick the base all over with a fork and chill for at least 2 hours, preferably overnight.

Preheat the oven to 200°C/400°F/Gas 6. Line the pastry case with foil, fill with baking beans and bake for 10 minutes, then remove the foil and beans and bake for 5 minutes longer. Remove from the oven and reduce the temperature to 190°C/375°F/Gas 5.

For the filling, beat together the butter and sugar, then stir in the eggs, raisins, lemon zest and spice. Tip this into the part-baked pastry case, return to the oven and bake for 30 minutes, until set. You might need to cover the tart loosely with foil for the last 10 minutes or so to prevent the raisins burning. Leave the tart to cool, then serve in slices with tea or coffee.

Holyrood Tart

Since 1966, John Young has run the Breadalbane Bakery in Aberfeldy, where dozens of Holyrood tarts are baked and sold every week. He brought the recipe with him from Leven, in Fife, where he served his apprenticeship, but the Aberfeldy bakery is now the only one in Scotland baking these tarts. Similar to Border and Eyemouth tarts, they differ by having a lattice piped across the top to keep the fruit moist. Mr Young makes the lattice from a soft Viennese mixture but I have adapted his basic recipe to one with a stiffer lattice dough that can be cut instead of piped. I appreciate piping is not everyone's cup of tea.

Serves 6–8
75g/3oz sultanas
50g/2oz currants
25g/1oz glacé cherries, roughly chopped
50g/2oz walnuts, roughly chopped
1 heaped tablespoon pineapple jam
1 level tablespoon golden syrup
50ml/2fl oz water
2 tablespoons icing sugar, sifted

For the pastry:
225g/8oz plain flour, sifted
110g/4oz butter, diced
25g/1oz granulated sugar

For the lattice:
110g/4oz butter, softened
225g/8oz icing sugar, sifted
75g/3oz plain flour, sifted

First prepare the filling. Place the dried fruit, cherries, walnuts, jam, golden syrup and water in a saucepan and heat slowly until both jam and syrup have melted. Leave to cool (by which time the fruit will have swollen).

Make the pastry in a food processor by processing the flour, butter and sugar together, then adding about 50ml/2fl oz cold water to bind. (Alternatively make it by hand: rub the butter into the flour, stir in the sugar, then the water.) Wrap in clingfilm and chill for an hour or so, then roll it out and use to line a 23cm/9in tart tin, prick all over with a fork and chill again.

To make the lattice, cream the butter and icing sugar together, then gradually mix in the flour. Clingfilm and chill briefly.

Preheat the oven to 200°C/400°F/Gas 6. Spread the cooled filling over the pastry base. Roll out the lattice dough to form a large rectangle. Cut it into 6 long strips and use these to make a rough lattice. Don't worry if it is not beautiful – it spreads out a little as it bakes anyway. Bake for about 25 minutes, until golden. Meanwhile, make a simple glacé icing by mixing the icing sugar with 2 teaspoons of cold water. When the tart emerges from the oven, drizzle this all over the top. Eat at room temperature.

Ecclefechan Tart

Similar to Border Tart (see page 158), this rich, buttery, dried fruit tart is delightful served cold with a cup of tea, or warm with a dollop of thick cream for pudding.

This recipe is my adaptation of one from chefs Paul McCrindle and Angela MacKenzie at Peebles Hydro Hotel, where it is served for afternoon tea.

Serves 6–8

75g/3oz butter, melted

175g/6oz dark muscovado sugar

2 large free-range eggs, beaten

2 teaspoons white wine vinegar

225g/8oz mixed sultanas, currants and raisins

110g/4oz walnuts, roughly chopped

For the pastry:

225g/8oz plain flour, sifted

150g/5oz butter, diced

To make the pastry, place the flour and butter in a food processor and process briefly, then add about 1 tablespoon of cold water – enough to bind – and process again. Bring the mixture together with your hands and wrap in clingfilm, then chill well. Roll out and use to line a 23cm/9in tart tin. Prick the base and chill well again.

Preheat the oven to 190°C/375°F/Gas 5. Line the pastry case with foil, fill with baking beans and bake for 15 minutes. Remove the foil and beans and bake for another 5 minutes, then remove the pastry case from the oven. Reduce the temperature to 180°C/350°F/Gas 4.

Beat together the melted butter and sugar, then add the eggs and vinegar. Stir well, then mix in the fruit and nuts. Tip this mixture into the part-baked pastry case and bake for 30 minutes, until set. You might need to cover the tart loosely with foil during the last 10 minutes or so to prevent the dried fruit burning. Remove from the oven and leave to cool, then cut into wedges to serve.

Potato Scones

Known more commonly as tattie scones, these girdle scones are often served for breakfast or tea. Sometimes I add about 25g/1oz grated Cheddar to the mixture and serve them with a bowl of broth or lentil soup for lunch. They are best eaten as soon as they are made (leftovers can be toasted the next day) but they can also be made in advance, then loosely wrapped in foil and reheated in a low oven.

Makes 8
1 large floury potato
(e.g. Maris Piper, King Edward
or Pentland Dell),
weighing about 250g/9oz
25g/1oz unsalted butter
50g/2oz plain flour
½ teaspoon salt
¼ teaspoon baking powder
a little butter for the girdle

Peel the potato, cut it into chunks and cook in boiling water until tender, then drain well. Using a potato masher, mash the potato with the butter. Now weigh it: you need about 200g/7oz mash.

Sift the flour, salt and baking powder into a bowl. While the mash is still warm, stir it into the flour and combine well to make a dough. Using lightly floured hands, gently shape the dough into 2 balls, then turn them on to a lightly floured surface. Roll out gently with a rolling pin to form 2 circles about 5mm/¼in thick. Cut each circle into quarters and prick all over with a fork.

Heat the girdle (or a large heavy frying pan) to medium-hot, smear over a little butter with a wad of kitchen paper then, once hot, transfer 4 scones to it with a large spatula or fish slice. Cook for about 3–4 minutes on each side, until golden brown. Transfer to a wire rack to cool slightly before spreading with a little butter and eating warm.

Fochabers Gingerbread

This is a rich, fruited gingerbread made with beer. No one is quite clear why the name Fochabers is associated with it but presumably it was originally made by someone from Fochabers, a town near Elgin in Moray, in the north-east of Scotland. Just like Orkney Broonie (see page 152) this is a cake that keeps well, wrapped in foil in a cake tin. It is a good choice for fireside teas in the middle of winter or for hearty picnics in the hills, preceded by the obligatory Thermos of soup.

Makes 1 Loaf

175g/6oz butter, softened
175g/6oz light muscovado sugar
3 heaped tablespoons black treacle
1 large free-range egg, beaten
300g/10½ oz plain flour, sifted
50g/2oz ground almonds
50g/2oz raisins
50g/2oz currants
1 teaspoon ground ginger
1 teaspoon mixed spice
1 rounded teaspoon bicarbonate of soda
125ml/4fl oz beer

Preheat the oven to 150°C/300°F/Gas 2. Cream the butter and sugar together, either in a mixer or by hand. Heat the treacle very gently until melted, then tip it into the bowl, add the egg and mix together. Stir in the flour, ground almonds, dried fruit, spices and bicarbonate of soda. Once everything is well mixed, stir in the beer and combine thoroughly. Tip into a buttered, base-lined 1kg/2¼lb loaf tin and bake for about 1½ hours, covering loosely with foil for the last half hour or so to prevent burning. Begin to test for readiness after 1¼ hours, by inserting a cocktail stick or skewer into the centre: it should come out clean. Transfer to a wire rack and leave to cool, then turn out of the tin. Wrap in foil once completely cold.

Black Bun

In our house at Hogmanay there were some things that never changed. The home-made blackcurrant cordial might have been replaced by Advocaat and lemonade as we became older, but there was always the tall, dark man (my father) at the door at midnight with a piece of coal as the 'first-foot' of the year; and there was always black bun – rich, heavy and dense – served alongside the plate of shortbread with wedges of Cheddar cheese and sultana or cherry cake. Black bun was perfect for soaking up the copious amounts of whisky proffered at every household ('One more dram before you go'). And our house was not unique. Black bun and 'shortie' were *de rigueur* everywhere, as we did the rounds of neighbours' houses, first-footing until the wee small hours.

Black bun was supposedly the original Twelfth Night cake eaten in Scotland, before it became known as 'Scotch Christmas bun' during the first half of the nineteenth century: there is a recipe for one in Meg Dodds' book of 1829. It was traditionally a spiced fruit mixture encased in bread dough but the dough gradually gave way to a lighter shortcrust pastry case. According to Catherine Brown, it seems the term Scotch Christmas Bun had disappeared by around 1914 and the name black bun seems to have been used from the late 1920s.

Serves 12–16
450g/1lb raisins
600g/1¼lb currants
110g/4oz whole blanched almonds,
 roughly chopped
50g/2oz walnuts, roughly chopped
150g/5oz plain flour, sifted
75g/3oz caster sugar
1 teaspoon ground allspice
1 teaspoon ground ginger
1 teaspoon ground cinnamon
½ teaspoon cream of tartar
½ teaspoon baking powder
2 tablespoons whisky
about 4 tablespoons milk

For the pastry:
275g/10oz plain flour, sifted
½ teaspoon baking powder
juice and grated zest of 1 lemon
150g/5oz unsalted butter, diced
beaten egg, to glaze

For the pastry, sift the flour and baking powder into a bowl and stir in the lemon zest. Rub in the butter, then add the lemon juice and 3–4 tablespoons cold water – enough to bind to a stiff dough. Turn out on to a lightly floured board and roll out thinly. Use two-thirds to line a buttered, square 23cm/9in cake tin. Roll out the remaining pastry to fit as a lid, then cover and chill both the lid and the case for half an hour or so.

Preheat the oven to 140°C/275°F/Gas 1. For the filling, mix everything together except the whisky and milk (I do this with my hands, which is easier). Then add the whisky and enough milk to moisten the mixture. Turn into the pastry case and press down well.

Dampen the edges of the pastry and place the rolled-out pastry lid on top. Press together the edges to seal, then cut off any excess pastry. Prick all over with a fork. Using a very thin skewer, prick right through to the base of the tin: 6–8 pricks altogether. Brush the surface with beaten egg, reserving a little. Place in the oven and bake for 2–2¼ hours, until golden brown on top. Glaze with the remaining egg after 1 hour.

Cool in the tin for at least 2 hours, then carefully decant on to a wire rack and leave to cool completely. Wrap in foil and store in an airtight container for up to 4 months.

shivery bites and sweeties

10

A shivery bite is just that – a bite of something delicious while you are shivering. In my parents' day, going for a swim at Dundee Swimming Baths was the highlight of many youngsters' weeks. (Oh, that the young nowadays revelled in such simple pleasures.) After swimming in the exceedingly chilly waters and drying off in unheated changing rooms, there was no way you wouldn't have been shivering. And so the shivery bite would sustain you through chattering teeth as you left the baths to face the icy blast coming directly off the River Tay.

Also known as chattery or chattering piece or chitterin bite in other areas of Scotland, it was essential fodder to warm you up and comfort you as you gradually thawed out. The type of food brought by children as shivery bites varied enormously. Favourites in my parents' day were Abernethy biscuits (and the not dissimilar Heckle biscuits), jam sandwiches, treacle toffee and apples. But when it was really cold, a roll filled with a sausage – especially square Lorne sausage – was a great treat. In my childhood, it might have been digestive biscuits sandwiched together with butter, or a butterie with cheese. Of course, children were soon simply given money to buy crisps or chocolate from the machines at the Baths: not quite as interesting, but a shivery bite nonetheless.

There are also 'sweeties' in this chapter. And what delights we could buy at the many sweetie shops throughout Scotland, from gobstoppers and tablet to curlie-murlies, glessies and teuch Jeans. Sadly, many of these old-fashioned sweets are dying out, but one thing is for sure: Scotland's famous sweet tooth is not. You might not have thought of making sweets before, but why not try one of my childhood favourites: tablet, treacle toffee or puff candy. Just be sure to brush your teeth afterwards.

Treacle Toffee

My Granny Anderson's treacle toffee recipe from her 1947 handwritten recipe book said simply to boil everything together for 15 minutes until crisp. She used milk instead of water. And in the ingredients list after the sugar and treacle, she wrote, '¼lb margarine (if not 2oz)' – whatever that means!

So I have changed her recipe a little and given rather more explicit instructions so that, if you have never made toffee before, you will feel confident. It might not be good for the teeth but I happen to love it.

Makes about 30 pieces
450g/1lb golden granulated sugar
225g/8oz black treacle (the easiest way to measure it is to pour out half a 450g/1lb tin)
75g/3oz butter
1 teaspoon white vinegar
150ml/5fl oz water

Place everything in a heavy-based saucepan. Stirring often, heat gently until the sugar dissolves and the butter melts. Then increase the heat and bring to the boil. Boil, stirring occasionally, for about 10 minutes or until a little of the mixture, when dropped into a cup of cold water, forms hard threads that bend without breaking. If you have a sugar thermometer, it should register 138°C/280°F.

Pour into a well-buttered 20–23cm/8–9in square baking tin and leave to cool. Cut into pieces when half set, then remove from the tin as best you can once cold.

Tablet

The scene is a large garden somewhere in Scotland on a warm summer afternoon, circa 1965. The occasion is the church garden fête. I remember queuing up (probably in my best cotton frock) at the cake and candy stall with my 3d to buy a bar of tablet before the fête had even been opened. And I was not alone. Tablet, neatly wrapped in waxed paper, was first to sell out at any fête, and the people in the queue stretching past the bric-a-brac and tombola stalls invariably ignored the lady in the big hat who was officially opening the fête, as they politely attempted to edge up the queue a little more.

These days, when invited to help at my church fair or coffee morning, I am often asked to help on the cake and candy stall. It might be inside a hall instead of outside on rolling lawns, but the spirit is the same. The tablet is always first to go – and there is never enough.

Almost unknown south of the border, tablet is one of Scotland's oldest types of confectionery. It is rather like fudge with a bite to it. Marion Lochhead refers to it in her book, *The Scots Household in the Eighteenth Century*: 'Barley-sugar, tablet, crokain [from the French *croquant* = crunchy] are all old and honourable Scots confections. Tablet might be made simply by boiling a pound of sugar in two gills of water until it candied; with cinnamon or ginger added for flavouring.' By 1929, when F. Marian McNeill wrote her book, milk had been added, for her recipe requires granulated sugar, thin cream or milk and flavouring. For the latter, she suggests cinnamon, coconut, fig, ginger, lemon, orange, peppermint, walnut or vanilla.

Having been brought up on plain tablet, I like it with just the merest hint of vanilla, pure and simple. If ever there was a childhood memory to evoke happy thoughts of sunshine, laughter and lush green gardens, it is an indulgent bite of tablet. I leave the rather more rarefied confections such as madeleines to Proust.

Makes 16–20 bars

125g/4½oz unsalted butter
1kg/2¼lb golden granulated sugar
300ml/10fl oz full-fat milk
a pinch of salt
200g/7oz tin of condensed milk
1 teaspoon pure vanilla essence

Place the butter in a large heavy-based saucepan (only a reliable pan should be used, otherwise the tablet mixture will stick) and melt over a low heat. Add the sugar, milk and salt and heat gently until the sugar has dissolved, stirring occasionally. Bring to the boil and simmer over a fairly high heat for 8–10 minutes, stirring often (and making sure you get into all the corners with your wooden spoon).

Add the condensed milk, stir well, then simmer for 8–10 minutes, stirring constantly. The mixture should bubble, but not too fiercely. After 8 minutes, test if it is ready. It should have reached the 'soft ball' stage, which means that when you drop a little of the mixture into a cup of very cold water, it will form a soft ball that you can pick up between your fingers. On a sugar thermometer, it should read 115°C/240°F.

Remove from the heat at once and add the vanilla (or other flavourings). Using an electric hand-held beater, beat at medium speed for 4–5 minutes, just until you feel the mixture begin to stiffen a little and become ever so slightly grainy. You can, of course, do this by hand but it will take at least 10 minutes and it is hard work! Pour immediately into a buttered 23 x 33cm/9 x 13in swiss roll tin and leave to cool. Mark into squares or oblongs when it is almost cold. When completely cold, remove and store in an airtight tin or wrap the pieces individually in waxed paper.

Chocolate Shortbread Truffles

Be sure to use either home-made or good-quality bought all-butter shortbread for these delicious truffles, which are wonderful served with post-prandial coffee or liqueurs.

Makes 24
250g/9oz good-quality dark chocolate
(55–70 per cent cocoa solids)
100g/3½oz unsalted butter
100g/3½oz shortbread,
crushed to crumbs
1 tablespoon whisky or Drambuie
2 tablespoons cocoa powder, sifted

Melt the chocolate and butter together over a low heat, then stir in the shortbread and whisky or Drambuie and mix thoroughly. Transfer to a shallow bowl and leave to cool, then chill for a couple of hours to firm up.

Using a teaspoon, spoon out some of the mixture and form into balls with the palms of your hands. At first it will seem hard, but it will soon soften up with the heat of your hands. Place the cocoa powder in a small bowl and roll each ball in this, then place on a board while you make the rest. The truffles will keep for a few days in an airtight tin.

Raggy Biscuits

Raggy biscuits are just that: ragged around the edges. They date back to the days before biscuit cutters. Although they are a speciality of Fife, I also found them in the Breadalbane Bakery in Aberfeldy, where they are known as raggie (sic) teas, rather like Rich Tea biscuits, as they are often eaten with a cup of tea. Raggy biscuits are now also eaten with cheese, since they are not too sweet. They have a lovely crisp texture and keep well.

In bakeries a special stamp with 'prickles' or tiny spikes is used to produce the distinctive 'prickled' appearance of the biscuits, which prevents them blistering during baking. At home this can be done with the tines of a fork.

Makes 20–24

275g/10oz self-raising flour, sifted

50g/2oz plain flour, sifted

75g/3oz golden caster sugar

110g/4oz butter, softened

a pinch of salt

Preheat the oven to 180°C/350°F/Gas 4. Put the flours into a food processor or mixer (or into a mixing bowl), add the sugar, butter and salt and process briefly until the mixture resembles breadcrumbs. Add 125–150ml (4–5fl oz) cold water and mix to a dough. (Or do everything by hand: rub the fat into the flour, stir in the sugar, then add enough water to combine.)

Divide the dough into small balls. Flatten these slightly, then fold in the edges irregularly. Then turn them over and flatten again with a rolling pin. The edges should be nicely ragged – if not, tease some of the dough out to make them look less regular. They should be about 5mm/¼in thick. Any thicker and they will still taste good but will not be as crisp. Place on 2 greased baking trays, prick all over with a fork and bake for 18–20 minutes, until pale golden brown. Transfer to a wire rack. As they cool they will crisp up.

Abernethy Biscuits

My father remembers eating Abernethy biscuits as a shivery bite after emerging from the freezing cold waters of Dundee Swimming Baths. Opened in the early 1930s, the baths were filled with salt water, filtered from the River Tay.

The biscuits are easy to make – and even easier to consume. My father ate them plain, or sometimes with butter and cheese. Some recipes include a teaspoon of caraway seeds.

Makes 20–24
225g/8oz plain flour,
1 teaspoon baking powder
75g/3oz butter, diced
75g/3oz golden caster sugar
1 large free-range egg, beaten
about 50ml/2fl oz milk

Preheat the oven to 180°C/350°F/Gas 4. Sift the flour and baking powder into a bowl, then rub in the butter until the mixture resembles breadcrumbs. Stir in the sugar, then add the beaten egg and enough milk to form a stiff dough that you can bring together with your hands. Turn it on to a floured surface and roll out to about 5mm/¼in thick. Cut out into rounds with a 5–6cm/2–2½in cutter. Place on a buttered baking sheet, prick all over with a fork and bake for 12–15 minutes or until pale golden brown. Transfer to a wire rack to cool and firm up.

173

Millionaire's Shortbread

This is definitely a more modern shivery bite. But it was a great treat for me as a child, since I have always loved everything to do with toffee, caramel and fudge. I like to include chocolate chunks in the shortbread base to add even more texture and taste. If you can find Argentinian dulce de leche, then it means you don't have to boil up a can of condensed milk for a couple of hours, as we had to do in the good old days.

Makes 24 squares

400g/14oz tin of condensed milk (or 450g/1lb jar of Argentinian dulce de leche)

250g/9oz good-quality milk or plain chocolate

For the base:

300g/10½oz slightly salted butter, softened

175g/6oz golden caster sugar

150g/5oz good-quality milk or plain chocolate, chopped into small pieces

225g/8oz plain flour, sifted

110g/4oz semolina

If you are using condensed milk for the filling, start the day before: place the unopened tin in a deep pan with a lid and cover with water. Bring to the boil, cover and cook over a medium heat for 2 hours, then remove the tin from the water and leave overnight to cool down completely.

Preheat the oven to 150°C/300°F/Gas 2. For the base, cream the butter and sugar together until light and fluffy – I do this with an electric beater for 2–3 minutes. Stir in the chopped chocolate, then fold in the flour and semolina. Combine gently then tip into a greased 23 x 33cm/9 x 13in swiss roll tin. The mixture will look a complete mess so, using floured hands, press it into the tin to even the surface, then prick all over with a fork. Bake for 40 minutes, until firm around the edges and pale golden brown. Remove from the oven and leave to cool in the tin for about 30 minutes.

Open the tin of condensed milk (which will now be caramel) and pour it over the shortbread base (or use the dulce de leche, which you may want to warm up a little in the microwave first). Melt the chocolate and pour it over the caramel, spreading it all over. Once it has set a little, but before it is hard, cut into squares. Remove from the tin when completely cold.

Puff Candy

When I was little, my mother used to send me off to the local dairy for shopping. I used to love Moffats Dairy, as there were large trays of puff candy for sale beside the cheese, cream and butter. I was allowed to buy some of this golden confection and remember devouring it on the way home. Also called honeycomb, puff candy is just like a Crunchie bar without the chocolate coating. It is also what New Zealanders use in their wonderful hokey-pokey ice-cream. In fact you can make that with this recipe: just bash the puff candy up into small pieces and fold them into softened good-quality vanilla ice-cream: 1 litre/1¾ pints for this amount.

Makes a 18cm/7in tray
4 heaped tablespoons
granulated sugar
2 heaped tablespoons golden syrup
1 teaspoon bicarbonate of soda

Put the sugar and syrup in a heavy-based pan and allow to dissolve slowly over a low heat, stirring well. Increase the heat to medium and bring to the boil, stirring constantly. Once you see bubbles, reduce the heat slightly and simmer for about 3 minutes, still stirring constantly, until it is a rich golden brown. Do not allow it to become too dark or it will have a slightly bitter flavour. It should be the colour of a Crunchie bar.

Remove from the heat and stir in the bicarbonate of soda until the mixture froths up. Tip immediately into a well-buttered, base-lined 18cm/7in shallow baking tin. It is really important to butter the base and sides or the mixture will stick. Leave to cool completely. To remove, cut into large pieces or bash out the pieces with the end of a rolling pin. Eat plain, or melt some chocolate (I use half milk, half plain) and dip the puff candy pieces into it. Set on a board to cool.

Bibliography

Ena Baxter:
Scottish Cookbook
(Johnston & Bacon, 1974)

John Beatty: *Sula, the Seabird-hunters of Lewis*
(Michael Joseph, 1992)

Catherine Brown:
Scottish Cookery
(Richard Drew Publishing, 1989)

Catherine Brown:
A Year in the Scots Kitchen
(Neil Wilson Publishing, 1996)

Laura Mason & Catherine Brown:
Traditional Foods of Britain
(Prospect Books, 1999)

Hamish Whyte & Catherine Brown:
A Scottish Feast
(Argyll Publishing, 1996)

Lady Clark of Tillypronie:
The Cookery Book of Lady Clark of Tillypronie 1909
(Southover Press, 1994)

Elizabeth Craig:
What's Cooking in Scotland?
(Oliver and Boyd Ltd, 1965)

Clarissa Dickson Wright:
The Haggis, A Little History
(Appletree Press Ltd, 1996)

Clarissa Dickson Wright with Henry Crichton-Stuart:
Hieland Foodie
(NMS Publishing, 1999)

Mistress Margaret Dods: *Cook and Housewife's Manual 1829*
(Roster Ltd, 1988)

B. Faujas de Saint-Fond: *A Journey through England and Scotland to the Hebrides in 1784, Vols 1 & 2*

Theodora Fitzgibbon:
A Taste of Scotland
(Pan Books, 1971)

Willie Fulton: *The Hebridean Kitchen*
(Buidheann-foillseachaidh nan Eilian an Iar, 1978)

Denis Girard: *Cassell's New French-English English-French Dictionary*
(Cassell, 1962)

I. F. Grant: *Highland Folk Ways*
(Birlinn Ltd, 1997)

Peter Irvine: *Scotland the Best*
(Mainstream, 1996)

Samuel Johnson & James Boswell:
A Journey to the Western Islands of Scotland & The Journal of a Tour to the Hebrides (1773)
(Penguin Books, 1984)

Mark Kurlansky: *Cod*
(Vintage, 1999)

Robbie and Nora Kydd:
Growing Up in Scotland
(Polygon, 1998)

G. W. Lockhart:
The Scot and His Oats
(Luath Press, 1983)

Hollier-Larousse:
Larousse Gastronomique
(Paul Hamlyn Ltd, 1961)

Marion Lochhead:
The Scots Household in the Eighteenth Century
(The Moray Press, 1948)

Peter Martin:
A Life of James Boswell
(Weidenfeld & Nicolson, 1999)

W. M. Mathew:
Keiller's of Dundee
(Abertay Historical Society, 1998)

F. Marian McNeill:
The Scots Kitchen (1929)
(The Mercat Press, 1993)

F. Marian McNeill:
Recipes from Scotland (1946)
(Gordon Wright Publishing, 1994)

Gladys Menhinick:
Grampian Cookbook
(The Mercat Press, 1993)

Grace Mulligan:
Dundee Kitchen
(David Winter & Son Ltd, 1991)

Christina Noble:
The Story of Loch Fyne Oysters
(Oyster Ideas Ltd, 1993)

Judi Paterson:
The Scottish Cook
(Birlinn Ltd, 1995)

Judi Paterson:
Scottish Home Cooking
(Lindsay Publications, 1995)

Jenni Simmons:
A Shetland Cookbook
(The Shetland Times, 1978)

Tom Steel:
The Life and Death of St Kilda
(HarperCollins, 1994)

Janet Warren:
A Feast of Scotland
(Lomond Books, 1997)

Dorothy Wordsworth: *Recollections of a Tour Made in Scotland in 1803*
(The Mercat Press, 1981)

R. L. Stevenson:
Kidnapped (1886)
(Bloomsbury Books, 1994)

Eileen Wolf:
Recipes from the Orkney Islands
(Gordon Wright Publishing, 1978)

Useful Addresses and Mail Order

Aberdeen and Grampian Tourist Board
27 Albyn Place
Aberdeen AB10 1YL
Tel: 01224 288800

Angus and City of Dundee Tourist Board
21 Castle Street
Dundee DD1 3AA
Tel: 01382 527527

Argyll, The Isles, Loch Lomond, Stirling, Trossachs Tourist Board
Old Town Jail
St John Street
Stirling FK8 1EA
Tel: 01786 445222

Ayrshire and Arran Tourist Board
Burns House
Burns Statue Square
Ayr KA7 1UP
Tel: 01292 262555

Dumfries and Galloway Tourist Board
64 Whitesands
Dumfries DG1 2RS
Tel: 01387 245550

Edinburgh and Lothians Tourist Board
4 Rothesay Terrace
Edinburgh EH3 7RY
Tel: 0131 473 3600

Greater Glasgow and Clyde Valley Tourist Board
11 George Square
Glasgow G2 1DY
Tel: 0141 204 4480

The Highlands and Scotland Tourist Board
Peffery House
Strathpeffer
IV14 9HA
Tel: 01997 421160

Kingdom of Fife Tourist Board
Haig House
Balgonie Road
Markinch KY7 6AQ
Tel: 01592 750066

Orkney Tourist Board
6 Broad Street
Kirkwall
Orkney KW15 1NX
Tel: 01856 872856

Perthshire Tourist Board
West Mill Street
Perth PH1 5QP
Tel: 01738 627958

Scottish Borders Tourist Board
Shepherds Mills
Whinfield Road
Selkirk TD7 5DT
Tel: 01750 20555

Shetland Islands Tourism
Market Cross
Lerwick
Shetland ZE1 0LU
Tel: 01595 693434

Western Isles Tourist Board
4 South Beach
Stornoway
Isle of Lewis HS1 2XY
Tel: 01851 701818

Most of the following companies will supply mail order:

Arbroath smokies
R. R. Spink and Sons,
33 Seagate,
Arbroath DD11 1BJ.
Tel: 01241 872023.

Ayrshire bacon
Ramsay of Carluke,
22 Mount Stewart Street,
Carluke ML8 5ED.
Tel: 01555 772277.
www.ramsayofcarluke.co.uk

Beef
Donald Russell,
Harlaw Road,
Inverurie, Aberdeenshire,
AB51 4FR.
Tel: 01467 629666.
www.donaldrussell.co.uk

(Stornoway) black pudding and Hebridean lamb
Charles Macleod Butcher,
Ropewood Park,
Stornoway HS1 2LB.
Tel: 01851 702445.
www.charlesmacleod.co.uk

Black pudding (and baby pudding)
John Henderson Butcher,
67 High Street, Kircaldy.
Tel: 01592 260980.

Butteries
The Seafield Bakery,
11 Seafield Street,
Cullen AB56 4SG.
Tel: 01542 840512.

Aitkens Bakery,
Glenbervie Road, Aberdeen.
Tel: 01224 877768.

Dried carragheen, dulse and beremeal flour
Real Foods,
37 Broughton Street, Edinburgh.
Tel: 0131 557 1911.

Dundee cake
Goodfellow & Steven Bakers,
81 Gray Street,
Broughty Ferry DD5 2BQ.
Tel: 01382 730181.

Forfar bridies
McLaren Bakers,
Market Street, Forfar.
Tel: 01307 463315.

Fresh herbs
Scotherbs,
Kingswell,
Longforgan, near Dundee,
DD2 5HJ.
Tel: 01382 360642.
www.scotherbs.com

Game and beef
George Bower Butcher,
75 Raeburn Place, Edinburgh.
Tel: 0131 332 3469.

Game
Highland Game Ltd,
Baird Avenue,
Dundee DD2 3XA.
Tel: 01382 827088.

Haggis, black and white pudding
Macsween of Edinburgh,
Bilston Glen,
Loanhead EH20 9LZ.
Tel: 0131 440 2555.
www.macsween.co.uk

Holyrood tarts and Aberfeldy whisky cake
Breadalbane Bakery, Aberfeldy.
Tel: 01887 820481.

Lorne sausage, white puddings and Scotch pies
Robertson's the Butcher,
234 Brook Street, Broughty Ferry.
Tel: 01382 739277.

Oatmeal
Aberfeldy Water Mill,
Mill Street,
Aberfeldy, Perthshire PH15 2BG.
Tel: 01887 820803.

Oysters and kippers
Loch Fyne Smokehouse,
Ardkinglas, Argyll.
Tel: 01499 600217.
www.loch-fyne.com

Potted hough, haggis and meat roll
Forsyths Butchers,
21 Eastgate, Peebles EH45 8AD.
Tel: 01721 720833.

Puggy buns, raggy biscuits and Hedderwick buns
Adamson's Bakery,
Pittenweem.
Tel: 01333 311336.

Reestit (reested) mutton and sassermeat
James Smith Butchers,
177 Commercial Street,
Lerwick, Shetland.
Tel: 01595 692355.

Shortbread
Shortbread House of Edinburgh,
14 Broompark EH5 1RS.
Tel: 0131 552 0381.

Smoked salmon (hot and cold smoke), salt herring, smoked haddock and finnan haddock

George Armstrong,
80 Raeburn Place EH4.
Tel: 0131 315 2033.

Ken Watmough,
29 Thistle Street,
Aberdeen.
Tel 01224 640321.

(Farmed) Venison

Fletchers Fine Foods, Reediehill
Farm, Auchtermuchty, KY14 7HS.
Tel: 01337 828369.
www.fletcherscotland.co.uk

Index

Note: Page references in bold type indicate recipes; those in italics indicate illustrations.

Back from an attack on Berlin, the crewmen of a U.S. B-24 Liberator bomber head for a debriefing session at their base in England. The plane's prankish name, printed on its side, was "Arise My Love and Come with Me."

THE AIR WAR IN EUROPE

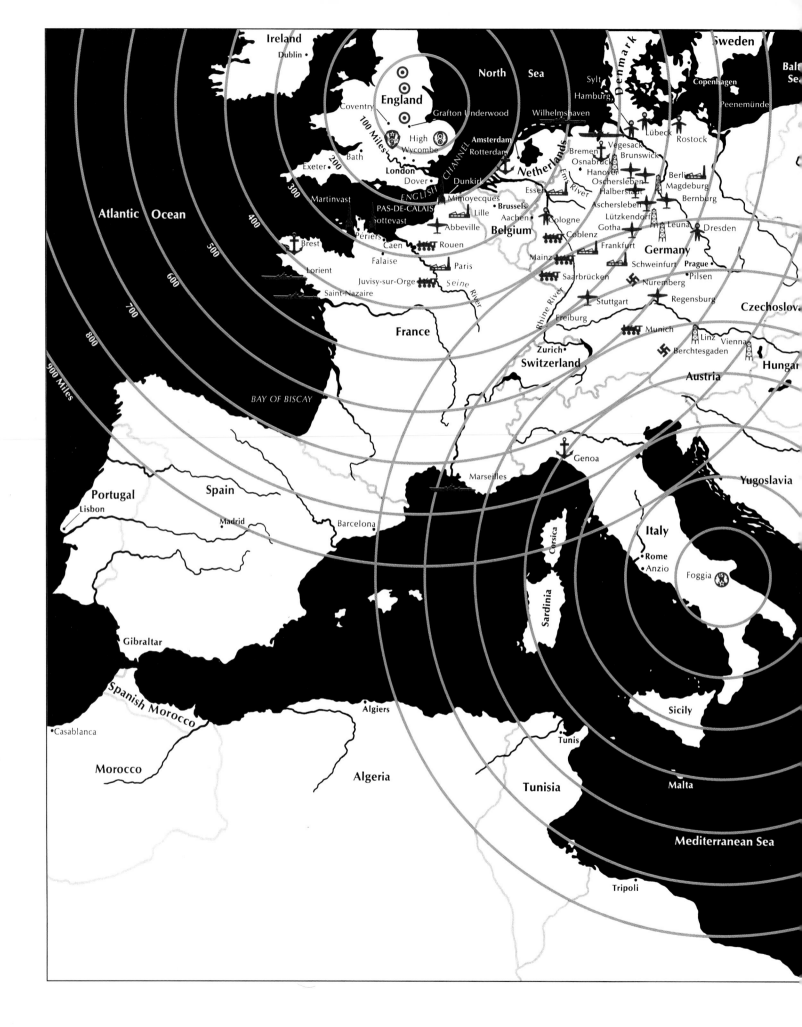

THE AIR WAR IN EUROPE: 1940–1945

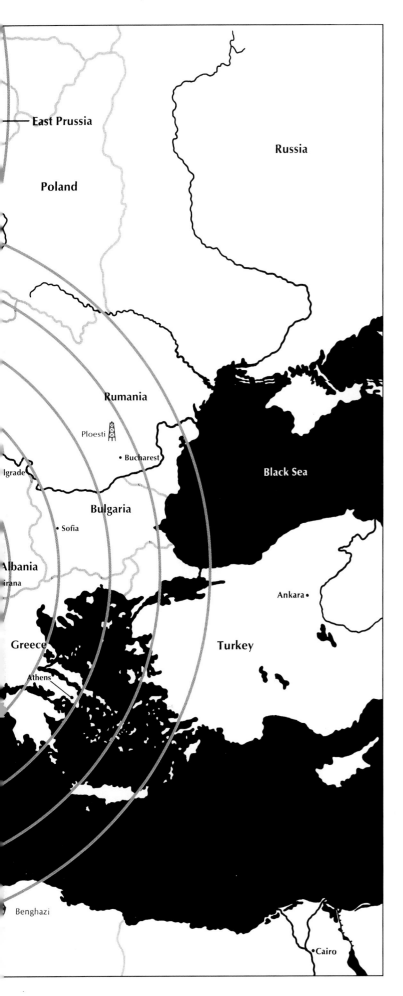

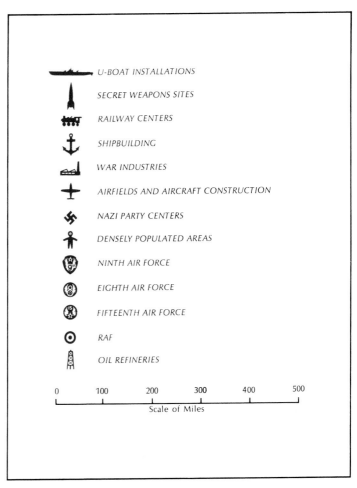

U-BOAT INSTALLATIONS	
SECRET WEAPONS SITES	
RAILWAY CENTERS	
SHIPBUILDING	
WAR INDUSTRIES	
AIRFIELDS AND AIRCRAFT CONSTRUCTION	
NAZI PARTY CENTERS	
DENSELY POPULATED AREAS	
NINTH AIR FORCE	
EIGHTH AIR FORCE	
FIFTEENTH AIR FORCE	
RAF	
OIL REFINERIES	

0   100   200   300   400   500
Scale of Miles

In the air war over Europe, RAF and U.S. Eighth Air Force bombers flew long distances (indicated by the concentric circles on the map) from their bases in England to attack not only industrial and military targets but also cities, in a concerted effort to undermine Germany's ability to carry on the war. Other bomber groups, flying from bases in North Africa, hit targets in southern Europe, and starting in 1943 the U.S. Fifteenth Air Force staged raids to the north and east from bases around Foggia.

TIME
LIFE
BOOKS

Other Publications:

HISTORY
Our American Century
What Life Was Like
The American Story
Voices of the Civil War
The American Indians
Lost Civilizations
Mysteries of the Unknown
Time Frame
The Civil War
Cultural Atlas

COOKING
Weight Watchers® Smart Choice Recipe Collection
Great Taste~Low Fat
Williams-Sonoma Kitchen Library

DO IT YOURSELF
Total Golf
How to Fix It
The Time-Life Complete Gardener
Home Repair and Improvement
The Art of Woodworking

TIME-LIFE KIDS
Student Library
Library of First Questions and Answers
A Child's First Library of Learning
I Love Math
Nature Company Discoveries
Understanding Science & Nature

SCIENCE/NATURE
Voyage Through the Universe

For information on and a full description of
any of the Time-Life Books series listed above,
please call 1-800-621-7026 or write:

Reader Information
Time-Life Customer Service
P.O. Box C-32068
Richmond, Virginia 23261-2068

This volume is one of a series that chronicles
in full the events of the Second World War.

WORLD WAR II · TIME-LIFE BOOKS · ALEXANDRIA, VIRGINIA

BY RONALD H. BAILEY
AND THE EDITORS OF TIME-LIFE BOOKS

THE AIR WAR IN EUROPE

Time-Life Books is a division of Time Life Inc.

TIME LIFE INC.
PRESIDENT and CEO: George Artandi

TIME-LIFE BOOKS
PRESIDENT: Stephen R. Frary
PUBLISHER/MANAGING EDITOR: Neil Kagan
VICE PRESIDENT, MARKETING: Joseph A. Kuna

WORLD WAR II

DIRECTOR, NEW PRODUCT DEVELOPMENT:
Elizabeth D. Ward
DIRECTOR OF MARKETING: Pamela R. Farrell

Dust Jacket Design: Barbara M. Sheppard

Editorial Staff for *The Air War in Europe*
Editor: Gerald Simmons
Picture Editor/Designer: Raymond Ripper
Text Editor: Henry Woodhead
Staff Writers: Dalton Delan, Brian McGinn, Tyler Mathisen,
Lydia Preston, Teresa M. C. R. Pruden
Chief Researcher: Oobie Gleysteen
Researchers: Kristin Baker, Loretta Y. Britten, Josephine Burke,
Mary G. Burns, Charles S. Clark, Jane Edwin, Nancy Friedman
Art Assistant: Mary Louise Mooney
Editorial Assistant: Constance Strawbridge

Special Contributor: Robin Richman (pictures)

Correspondents: Maria Vincenza Aloisi (Paris), Christine Hinze
(London), Christina Lieberman (New York).

Director of Finance: Christopher Hearing
Directors of Book Production: Marjann Caldwell,
Patricia Pascale
Director of Publishing Technology: Betsi McGrath
Director of Photography and Research: John Conrad Weiser
Director of Editorial Administration: Barbara Levitt
Production Manager: Marlene Zack
Quality Assurance Manager: James King
Chief Librarian: Louise D. Forstall

The Author: RONALD H. BAILEY is a freelance author
and journalist who was formerly a senior editor of *Life*.
He is the author of two volumes in the Time-Life Books
Human Behavior series, *Violence and Aggression* and
The Role of the Brain, and two volumes in the World
War II series, *The Home Front: U.S.A.* and *Partisans
and Guerrillas*. He has written a photography book,
The Photographic Illusion: Duane Michals, was a con-
tributor to *The Unknown Leonardo*, a book about the
inventive genius Leonardo da Vinci, and is now a con-
tributing editor for *American Photographer* magazine.
While at *Life* he edited a book of Larry Burrows' war
photographs, *Larry Burrows: Compassionate
Photographer*.

The Consultants: COL. JOHN R. ELTING, USA (Ret.),
is a military historian and author of *The Battle of
Bunker's Hill*, *The Battles of Saratoga* and *Military
History and Atlas of the Napoleonic Wars*. He edited
*Military Uniforms in America: The Era of the American
Revolution, 1755-1795* and *Military Uniforms in Amer-
ica: Years of Growth, 1796-1851*, and was an associate
editor of *The West Point Atlas of American Wars*.

ALFRED GOLDBERG received his Ph.D. from Johns
Hopkins University. A historian with the Eighth Air
Force and the U.S. Strategic Air Forces in Europe dur-
ing World War II, he later served as chief of the
Current History Branch, U.S. Air Force Historical
Division. He edited *A History of the U.S. Air Force,
1907-1957*, co-authored seven volumes of *The Army
Air Forces in World War II* and contributed to *D-Day
and the War Lords*. He taught at the University of
Maryland and the University of Southern California.

Library of Congress Cataloging-in-Publication Data
Bailey, Ronald H.
  The Air War in Europe

  (World War II)
  Bibliography: p. 204
  Includes index.
  1. World War, 1939-1945—Aerial operations. 2. World War
  1939-1945—Germany. 3. Germany—History—1933-1945.
  I. Time-Life Books. II. Title. III. Series.
D785.B26   940.54'21 78-2937
ISBN 0-7835-5704-3

© 1981, 1998 Time Life Inc. All rights reserved.
No part of this book may be reproduced in any form or by any
electronic or mechanical means, including information storage and
retrieval devices or systems, without prior written permission from
the publisher, except that brief passages may be quoted for reviews.
Printed in U.S.A.
School and library distribution by Time-Life Education,
P.O. Box 85026, Richmond, Virginia 23285-5026.

TIME-LIFE is a trademark of Time Warner Inc. U.S.A.

CONTENTS

FORGING A MIGHTY WEAPON

Practicing the art of formation flying, a group of British biplanes passes over London's Hendon Aerodrome in a rehearsal for an air show held there in 1935.

AIR POWER: THE PAINFUL BIRTH OF AN IDEA

At the weary close of World War I, air power was just a gleam in the eyes of a few farsighted men, notably British Chief of the Air Staff Hugh Trenchard and the assistant chief of the U.S. Army's Air Service, William "Billy" Mitchell. The wartime air forces had been novelties, and to most strategists of the day they seemed to have no military future. As French Marshal Ferdinand Foch put it, "Aviation is good sport, but for the Army it is useless."

Trenchard proclaimed otherwise to anyone who would listen, but he found his hands full merely defending the independent status of the Royal Air Force, then under attack by cost-cutting officials who saw no need for an air arm separate from the Army and Navy. In a strong, terse statement made public in December 1919, Trenchard argued for a small, well-trained RAF, adaptable to future needs and uninhibited by the tradition-bound military branches, which used planes "simply as a means of conveyance, captained by chauffeurs." Thanks largely to Trenchard's paper, the RAF remained unfettered. He said, "I have laid the foundations for a castle: if nobody builds anything bigger than a cottage on them, it will at least be a very good cottage."

In the United States, the visionaries of air power faced tougher going: the commanders of both the Army and the Navy, jealous of their prerogatives, successfully opposed the formation of a coequal air force. But Billy Mitchell's powerful opponents could not prevent him from demonstrating the terrible potential of what he termed "bombardment aviation." In a series of tests conducted in 1921 and 1923 off the Atlantic Coast, Mitchell's Martin MB-2 bombers sent to the bottom three warships confiscated from Germany and three more obsolete U.S. warships.

Neither Mitchell nor Trenchard worked miracles. In 1925 Britain still could not claim a single home-based squadron of bombers or fighters, and the U.S. had yet to produce a successor to its obsolescent Liberty engine, which dated to World War I. But as planes were improved by new technology, the idea of air power gained strength and followers.

Hugh Trenchard, British prophet of air power, stumps for the RAF at a 1934 ceremony opening the Hampstead headquarters of the 604th Bomber Squadron.

A 100-pound phosphorus bomb, dropped by a biplane in Billy Mitchell's September 1921 test, scores a direct hit on the crow's nest of a target warship.

Climbing to a record 33,113 feet with the aid of a newly developed supercharger, a La Pere biplane soars over McCook Field in Dayton, Ohio, in 1920. At that altitude the atmosphere was thin and the temperature –67° F., but the pilot wore an oxygen mask of his own design and also an electric, fur-lined flying suit.

TAKING THE GUESSWORK OUT OF FLYING

"A good pilot doesn't depend on his instruments," flight instructors warned their students in the 1920s. The admonition was a wise one, for navigational instruments available to pioneer aviators were dangerously inaccurate. The standard altimeter of the time was typical: it registered altitude 10 seconds late—obviously hazardous for planes flying in fog or low clouds.

Engines were not a lot better; they failed at a discouraging rate. Between 1918 and 1925, mechanical failures caused U.S. airmail planes to make some 1,600 emergen-cy landings. After one pilot had to put his plane down in a crowded cow pasture, his headquarters in Washington received this cheerless telegram: "Engine quit. Only place to land on cow. Killed cow. Wrecked plane. Scared me. Smith."

Year by year, trailblazing engineers extended the limits of aircraft performance. During the 1920s designers improved both the liquid-cooled and the air-cooled radial engine and introduced superchargers that pumped air into the engine, enabling it to function at high altitudes. And the barriers of clouds and darkness were penetrated by the appearance of many new navigational aids, including gyroscopic instruments and radio direction finders.

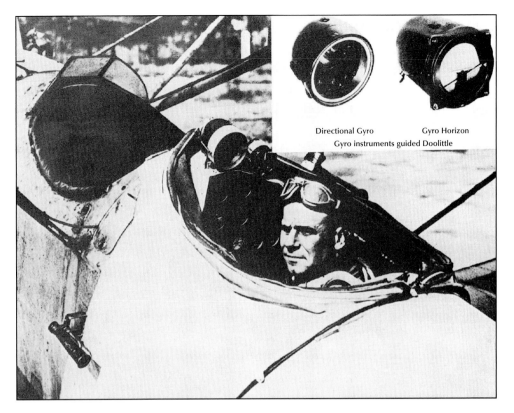

Directional Gyro   Gyro Horizon
Gyro instruments guided Doolittle

The Wright Whirlwind, the first dependable radial engine, was cooled by air flow rather than by the circulating liquid that was used for in-line engines. It powered Charles Lindberg's celebrated plane, the Spirit of St. Louis.

U.S. aviator Jimmy Doolittle, the first pilot to fly blind from takeoff to landing, looks out from the cockpit of his Consolidated biplane in 1929. Doolittle—flying under a canvas canopy, but with another pilot keeping watch— depended upon two gyroscopic devices (inset) invented by Elmer Sperry: a directional gyro (left), used to keep the plane on a straight course, and a so-called artificial horizon, which registered any deviation from level flight.

Before making a high-altitude research flight in 1934, U.S. aerial innovator Wiley Post takes a seat beside his Lockheed Vega "Winnie Mae" while assistants pump up his protective garb—a modified rubber diving suit. Post's plane was fitted with two superchargers: one for the engine, the other to pressurize his suit.

The barnstormers' indestructible Curtiss JN-4D—widely known as the Jenny—also saw duty as an Air Service trainer until the late 1920s. Light and maneuverable, the 90-hp Jenny needed only 1,000 feet to take off or land.

An early De Havilland Moth biplane, its wings conveniently folded, could easily be towed and stored in a garage. Forerunner of the Tiger Moth military trainer, the little craft could flutter to a landing at only 45 mph, and it consumed just a few gallons of gas per hour.

"BARNSTORMERS" AND "WHISTLING PIGS"

The men who first showed that airplanes could be reliable were not engineers but itinerant pilots who christened themselves "barnstormers" after the touring theatrical troupes. Flying cheap war-surplus Curtiss Jennys, they took countless thousands of thrill-seeking passengers on brief joy rides for a few dollars each.

Barnstormers' uncanny ability to keep their crates flying with scavenged parts did not persuade the military to invest heavily in airplanes. But convincing technological advances came thick and fast. Wood and cloth biplanes gave way to monoplanes made of light and durable aluminum alloy. Wooden propellers were replaced by metal blades—improved models of a crude prototype whose strange whirring sound earned it the nickname "whistling pig." Deicing equipment and wing flaps became standard. These and other developments produced, in 1933, a small but sure sign that air journeys were becoming as safe as surface travel: British Imperial Airways lowered its flight insurance premium from 12 shillings to one shilling per £1,000.

The first all-metal passenger plane, Germany's Junkers F-13 boasted a tough corrugated skin. Engineers soon discovered, however, that corrugation caused air friction, and later designs called for a smooth "stressed skin."

France's Latécoère-300, flown by the famous Jean Mermoz, provided regular air-mail service across the South Atlantic. Though flying boats were among the world's safest aircraft, Mermoz disappeared on his 24th ocean crossing, apparently a victim of engine failure.

At Calshot, England, a modified Supermarine S.6 seaplane is rolled out of the hangar for a speed trial. The plane was driven by a 2,300-hp Rolls-Royce engine—the forerunner of the Merlin engine of World War II fighters.

Daredevil Howard Hughes shows off his H-1 racer, with which he set a landplane speed record of 352 mph in 1935. Three years later, in a Lockheed Super Electra, he circled the globe in 91 hours, halving Wiley Post's record.

Jimmy Doolittle's speedy Gee Bee Super Sportster housed a huge 800-hp engine in a short, squat body.

IN HOT PURSUIT OF SPEED

"I have yet to hear of anyone engaged in this work dying of old age," wrote veteran flier Jimmy Doolittle after retiring from professional racing. Speed did kill: Doolittle had won the 1932 American Thompson Trophy race in a barrel-nosed Gee Bee; all of the seven Gee Bees built eventually crashed and killed six pilots. But speed like the Gee Bee's 250-plus miles per hour held a powerful fascination for everyone—especially the military.

The best aircraft designers were in the forefront of racing, and the innovations built into their streamlined planes were refined for aircraft of World War II. The British Supermarine S.6 racing plane gradually became the Spitfire fighter. And the German Messerschmitt-209, which set a speed record of almost 470 mph in 1939, influenced the development of some of the prominent German fighters of the War.

In addition to racing around measured courses, pilots set—and broke—innumerable speed records in flights from city to city and country to country. In 1933 Wiley Post caused an international sensation by circling the globe alone in less than eight days. Three years later Hollywood playboy Howard Hughes streaked east across the continent to Newark, New Jersey, in just over nine hours. All such flights included stops for refueling, however. The advocates of air power realized that speed alone was not enough, that military aircraft needed sufficient range to overfly enemy territory and return without landing.

The world's fastest prewar plane, the German Me-209, designed by Willy Messerschmitt, owed its speed to a compact 1,550-hp Daimler-Benz engine and a trim aerodynamic body.

The four-engined Curtiss NC-4 flying boat was the first plane to cross the Atlantic. The epic 1919 journey took the plane from Newfoundland to Lisbon via the

A World Cruiser, on a 1924 round-the-world flight for the U.S. Army's Service, passes a ship in Tokyo Bay.

The huge ANT-25, an experimental Russian

Striving for distance in a piggyback relay, the large Short-Mayo flying boat launches its light seaplane Mercury (top). The Mercury's airborne takeoff saved fuel and enabled it to set a distance record of 5,998 miles in 1938.

Azores and then on to England—all in 15 days.

bomber, comes to rest near San Jacinto, California, after a record 1937 flight over the Pole from Moscow.

REACHING FOR GREATER RANGE

Aircraft engineers' quest for range showed promise as early as 1919, when the U.S. Navy Curtiss NC-4 flying boat crossed the Atlantic Ocean by stages. Just eight years afterward, Charles Lindbergh stunned the world with his solo, nonstop transatlantic hop from New York to Paris. The U.S. Army Air Corps did not neglect the challenge of distance. The year 1935 saw the first flight of a plane that newspapers dubbed "the deadliest air weapon in the world." The aircraft was the prototype of a plane that could fly 3,300 miles unloaded, or nearly 2,300 miles packing 2,500 pounds of bombs; it went into production in 1936—as the B-17 Flying Fortress.

The need for a long-range transport was filled at about the same time. The Douglas Aircraft Company, creator of the renowned World Cruiser *(far left)*, produced the DC-3, with a maximum range of more than 2,100 miles. This work horse eventually transported 70 per cent of the total Allied air cargo.

Its design inspired by the RAF's call for a "bloody paralyzer" that could bomb Berlin, the tall Tarrant Tabor prepares for its first, and last, run in 1919. While taxiing, the behemoth nosed over, crushing its three officers.

The largest aircraft of its day, the Dornier Do X takes aboard passengers for its maiden flight. Powered by six pairs of back-to-back engines, it boasted three elaborate decks. The "X" in its name represented "unknown quantity."

ELEPHANTS OF THE AIRWAYS

"More likely to antagonize the air than pass through it," was how one observer described the U.S. Army's 21-ton Barling bomber, a huge, six-engined triplane that could lumber no more than 170 miles before it had to land for refueling. Although the only Barling made was scrapped in 1925, designers continued trying to construct immense, capacious planes whose great weight inevitably made them awkward, slow and short in range.

The largest aircraft of all were the flying boats, which carried dozens of passengers. Germany's enormous Dornier Do X made its formal debut in 1929 carrying 150 passengers, 10 crew members and nine stowaways. Though its ostensible purpose was commercial, the Do X was actually designed to study the feasibility of a warplane capable of both long-range reconnaissance and mine laying.

The mammoth planes posed all sorts of specialized problems for their builders and users. The British Tarrant Tabor triplane had to be assembled in a great balloon shed and then rolled out sideways on rails. And none of these early giants proved to be worth their weight in gasoline, which the Do X guzzled at the extravagant rate of 400 gallons per hour.

The RAF's huge Handley-Page Heyford biplane, built in the mid-1930s, proved to be the last big bomber with more than one wing. But by then the better qualities of these behemoths were being incorporated into smaller, more efficient bombers.

Flanked by two fighters, Russia's colossal 92,000-pound ANT-20 soars over a 1935 military parade in Moscow's Red Square. Named the Maxim Gorky by the Russians, but dubbed the "Maximum Gawky" by sensible fliers, the plane was kept aloft—briefly—by eight engines and a wingspread of 207 feet. One day an accompanying fighter smashed the Gorky's wing; the craft plummeted to destruction.

Britain's Handley-Page Heyford was able to carry one and a half tons of bombs—but only for some 900 miles at a rate of 140 mph.

Prototype of the Bristol Blenheim bomber, the 1935 "Britain First" could fly 285 mph with a full load. The plane also had an effective range of 1,000 miles.

Europe-bound travelers at Port Washington, New York, board one of the half dozen Boeing-314s that were used by Pan American Airways in its regular prewar transatlantic flights to Lisbon and Southampton.

PUTTING IT ALL TOGETHER

By the late 1930s, two decades of experiment and experience had begun to produce specialized but efficient and well-balanced airplanes. Instruments were now more than adequate: the first airborne radar system, which could spot a ship 10 miles away, was installed in a British Avro Anson in 1937. The Bristol-142, prototype of the Blenheim bomber, could fly nearly 50 mph faster than the fastest fighter the RAF then had. Pan American Airways' Boeing flying boats began commercial transatlantic service just in time to bring out hundreds of European refugees in 1939.

The two leading apostles of air power, Hugh Trenchard and Billy Mitchell, lived to see the U.S. adopt the B-17 bomber in January of 1936. Six and a half years later, the first wave of B-17s joined the British air assault on Germany and roared 200 miles from England to bomb enemy targets in occupied France. By then Mitchell's unlikely dream of "strategic aviation" was already an inescapable reality.

In an awesome display of accuracy in long-range navigation, a pair of war-ready

B-17 Flying Fortresses intercept and make a practice bombing run on the Italian oceanliner Rex as it steams along approximately 700 miles out into the Atlantic.

1

In the waning hours of September 3, 1939, the rumble of engines resounded at a Royal Air Force base at Linton-on-Ouse in northern England. That day Great Britain had declared war on Germany for invading Poland, and now 10 Whitley bombers began rolling down the flare-lit runway, primed to strike the RAF's first blow against the foe.

As the little force lumbered aloft and turned east in the darkness, it was singularly lacking in the discipline as well as the magnitude of the armadas that by 1944 would fill the air over Germany. The pilots made no pretense of flying in formation, but simply headed for their targets by whatever route each chose.

The Whitley was an ungainly plane with an angular fuselage and twin engines canted slightly upward so that it struggled along blunt nose down, like a comic-strip stork. Only five years off the drawing board, it was already considered obsolete. It had a cruising speed of less than 200 miles per hour and a ceiling limit of 17,000 feet. "The Whitley," remarked one pilot who flew it, "was not the sort of vehicle in which one should go to pursue the King's enemies."

The Whitleys' assault that night was aimed at the key German ports of Bremen and Hamburg and at half a dozen cities of the Ruhr Valley (map, page 61), Germany's industrial heartland. The Ruhr was so heavily defended by antiaircraft guns that RAF crews would in time flippantly dub it "Happy Valley." Just the previous month, Luftwaffe chief Hermann Göring, commander of Germany's air and ground defenses, had boasted: "We will not expose the Ruhr to a single bomb."

Before daybreak, the Whitleys had reached their targets, dropped their loads and turned for home. All got back safely except one bomber that was forced to land in friendly France because of heavy ice on its wings and propellers. But Göring's boast still stood: neither the Ruhr nor Bremen nor Hamburg had been exposed to British bombs. The entire 13-ton payload carried by the Whitleys, and stamped "Secret" to keep crewmen from prying, had consisted of nothing more lethal than 5.4 million pieces of paper—propaganda leaflets warning the Germans that no matter how long the War lasted, the Allies would eventually prevail.

To the men of RAF's Bomber Command, the leaflet raid came as a shattering anticlimax. For years they had been steeped in a radical concept of modern warfare, strategic

BRITAIN GOES IT ALONE

bombing, that now offered them their only way to hit the Germans at home. However, instead of bombs RAF planes were dropping clouds of paper politely urging the Germans to get rid of their Führer, Adolf Hitler. "The only thing achieved," said one crusty RAF officer of this and subsequent leaflet raids, "was largely to supply the continent's requirements of toilet paper for the five long years of war."

Certainly, the air marshals who ran the RAF would have preferred to pepper the Third Reich with bombs. But two important considerations held them back. The first was a concern for the opinion of other nations—particularly that of the United States, from which Britain was seeking aid in the struggle against Germany. The British were adhering to President Franklin D. Roosevelt's request—issued when Germany moved into Poland on September 1—that all combatants refrain from bombing civilian targets.

The RAF's second reason for holding back was even more compelling. Bomber Command simply was not ready. It could muster only 17 squadrons of bombers capable of making the round trip to and from the heart of Germany. Moreover, of the total of 209 aircraft on hand—Whitleys plus the newer twin-engined Wellingtons and Hampdens—many were not operational. And of those that were serviceable, only 80 per cent could be provided, on any given day, with crews. Additional planes were in production, but bigger, four-engined bombers were still in the planning stage. So were the expanded organization required to train new crews and the technology to help them find their targets.

Bomber Command's entry into the War as a paper tiger was more than a little ironic. Since the 1920s, the British had been the world's foremost proponents of strategic bombing. The military establishments of other countries were more familiar with tactical bombing, which was intended to support an army or navy in the immediate area of combat. The new strategic doctrine was far broader; it held that the way to defeat an enemy lay beyond the battlefield, in destroying the ultimate sources of his power—his arms factories, his economic strength, his very will to fight.

One of the reasons for Britain's early embrace of the doctrine stemmed from recent experience. During World War I the Germans had sent their twin-engined Gothas and their huge lighter-than-air Zeppelins to drop nearly 400 tons of bombs in a series of air attacks on London and other English cities. The raids killed about 1,400 people. But the attacks were intended more to inspire terror than to destroy strategic targets, and the Germans themselves failed to recognize the potential for future conflicts. When their defeated and dismantled air force was reborn in the early 1930s as the Luftwaffe, its primary function was foreseen as tactical bombing, specifically in support of ground forces.

But a few farseeing individuals in Britain and elsewhere drew on the lesson of the German air raids of World War I to help shape the new theory of strategic bombing. One of the concept's major prophets was an Italian military thinker, General Giulio Douhet, who published his views in 1921 in a book entitled *Command of the Air.* Douhet argued that aerial attackers should give priority to industrial rather than military objectives, and that they should inflict a "merciless pounding" upon the enemy's cities as well. "The time would soon come," he wrote, "when, to put an end to horror and suffering, the people themselves, driven by the instinct of self-preservation, would rise up and demand an end to the war—this before their army and navy had time to mobilize at all!" Douhet's notions were anathema to most of the world's generals and admirals for a special reason of their own: he insisted that strategic bombing required an air force that was independent of an army and navy and that would, in fact, make them obsolete.

This heresy was shared by many airmen—and most particularly by a pugnacious American who was assistant chief of the U.S. Army's fledgling Air Service: Brigadier General William "Billy" Mitchell. Not only did Mitchell irk the Army by demanding that the Air Service be removed from Army control and made a separate entity, he also enraged the Navy by asserting that the bomber spelled doom for sea power. In bombing tests off the Atlantic Coast in the early 1920s, Mitchell's planes sank three obsolete American battleships and three German prizes of World War I, including the supposedly "unsinkable" battleship *Ostfriesland.*

Despite Navy protests that results would have been otherwise had the ships not been anchored, unarmed and unmanned, Mitchell's demonstration provided a dramatic glimpse of air power's potential. But his habitual bluntness proved his undoing. A statement in which he accused the War and Navy Departments of "criminal negligence" and

experience was typical. In the course of a single mission it was hit first by an electrical storm, then by a blizzard.

But after mid-May of 1940 the bomber crews no longer needed to endure such trials in the service of mere pieces of paper. On May 10 the phony war ended; Germany launched its blitzkrieg against Belgium, Holland and France. On the same day Britain's air-power advocates rejoiced as their staunch friend Winston Churchill succeeded Neville Chamberlain as Britain's Prime Minister.

Churchill had been fascinated by flying even before the First World War. He had taken lessons, giving them up only after the crash of his trainer, from which he was lucky enough to walk away. As Secretary of State for War and Air after World War I, he had helped beat back attempts to deprive the RAF of its separate identity, and in subsequent Cabinet posts he had consistently pushed its interests.

Among the dilemmas that Churchill immediately faced as Prime Minister was the need to speed the production of RAF fighter planes. With the Germans imminently in control just across the Straits of Dover, and an assault on England clearly in the cards, a stepped-up output of fighters to cope with the Luftwaffe's inevitable attacks was crucial. But even as Churchill put Britain's aircraft builders on a seven-day, round-the-clock work week, he kept his characteristically long view. As he was to put it: "The fighters are our salvation, but the bombers alone provide the means of victory."

Churchill lost no time warning the Germans that any air raids on civilian areas would bring an "appropriate" response. Coincidentally, on the very day he took office bombs fell on the city of Freiburg in southwestern Germany, killing 57 people and provoking an outraged charge by Hitler that the British were guilty of "inhuman cruelty." But it turned out that the offending bombers were German—Heinkel-111s that had lost their way in heavy clouds en route to an attack on a French air base.

Five days later, however, RAF Bomber Command went into action. On May 14 the Germans bombed Rotterdam, killing more than 800 civilians. The following night, 99 RAF bombers dispatched at Churchill's order roared over the Ruhr Valley's oil refineries and railways. This time the planes carried not leaflets but bombs, and Göring's boast about the Ruhr's impregnability was belied.

The strategic air offensive against Germany had begun at last. It would go on for almost precisely five years and constitute, in the words of Bomber Command's official history, "probably the most continuous and grueling operation of war ever carried out." At the moment, with the Germans rapidly pushing the British expeditionary force back to the beaches of Dunkirk and out of France, it was Britain's only means of hitting at the enemy.

With the memory of the disastrous daylight raids still fresh, RAF Bomber Command now decided that the air strikes at Germany would, with only occasional exceptions, take

place at night. To many of the men aboard the planes, the very act of dropping bombs was a new and strange experience, but doing so at night magnified the strangeness. A daytime mission, if low enough, might afford glimpses of people on the ground—friendly, if furtive, waves in occupied Holland, clenched fists of anger in Germany. At night, however, the life below was unseen, eerily suggested only by the faintest glimmers of light.

A perceptive young Whitley pilot named Leonard Cheshire often thought about the night bomber's remoteness from earthbound reality. Flying home at dawn from a mission in June of 1940, he wondered about the British troops still fighting somewhere below him in France. "I was going back to a warm bed and breakfast, but what had they to look forward to? Felt a curious sense of detachment: almost unreal, like being at a cinema."

Cheshire, who was to become one of the RAF's most decorated heroes, was flying missions four nights out of five that summer. He later recalled marking the tiresome six-hour round-trip passages by a succession of coastlines: "English coasts and Dutch coasts and German coasts coming and going, not once but often: sometimes in the brilliant light of the moon, sometimes lurking in the virginity of darkness. And in coasts such a wealth of meaning. If hostile, the expectancy of wondering whether it is the right landfall, the thrill of knowing at last the fight is on. And then, if friendly, the thought: 'God, *how* friendly?' Never shall I forget the warmth of those dawn receptions. One day, just out to sea, a bird escorted us home to the coast. I do not know what sort of a bird it was: I never shall know. I only know it was soft and fluffy and that it flew along just beside the port wing-tip."

Like many other bomber pilots, Cheshire went into the air war with an overblown image of himself as "a fully-groomed operational pilot wanting but a short experience of gunfire to be complete." Soon, however, he was caught up in the practical problems of preparing himself for his new combat role. Between missions he would sit in the grounded plane wearing a blindfold and grope about the cockpit "until I could lay my hands on everything without the use of eyesight." He also learned every task of his three-man crew, from loading the guns to setting the bombsight. Cheshire came to realize that "bombing is technical, a matter of knowledge and experience, not of setting your jaw and rushing in."

As one observer noted, the men of Bomber Command and Fighter Command were "two very different breeds, different both by temperament and by virtue of their jobs." About all they had in common was their slang: a crash was a "prang"; something that failed to work was "U.S.," for unserviceable; a dead pilot had "got the chop"; a coward had "LMF," or lack of moral fiber.

A natural rivalry sprang up between the "Bomber Barons" and the "Fighter Glamour Boys," and it was exacerbated late in the summer of 1940 by the fact that the Barons had to take second place in public esteem to the Fighter Boys, who were daily engaged in defending England against Luftwaffe attacks. Moreover, the two knew little about each other's job. The bomber pilots, catching up on their sleep during the day, seldom saw the fighters in action. And because the short range of the fighter planes precluded their escorting the bombers to Germany and back, the Fighter Boys never saw the Whitleys, Wellingtons and Hampdens in action.

The rivalry became acute only when both groups invaded the same pub on the same night. One squabble that began over tankards of ale led to a bizarre, if bloodless, private war. Three Hampden pilots touched it off by zooming low over a fighter base and dropping a cascade of toilet tissue and old propaganda leaflets. The Fighter Boys responded by landing at the bomber base, kidnapping the wing commander, flying him back to their own base and forcing him to pick up all the litter. Only the intervention of higher authorities—and the reminder that there was a real war going on—kept the feud from escalating to even more imaginative levels.

The top-priority targets of the strategic air offensive during that first summer were Germany's aircraft factories, synthetic oil plants and railway marshaling yards. But in August, when Luftwaffe raids on England began to mount, the British public's desire for revenge claimed precedence. It was intensified by London's baptism of fire on the night of August 24. The bombing was, in fact, unintended, and was contrary to Hitler's current standing order to the Luftwaffe to avoid London; two German pilots, on their way to another destination, had strayed off their assigned course and

Encircled by their planes, British airmen of the 216th Bomber Transport Squadron turn out for a parade in 1937 on the runway at Heliopolis, an RAF base in Egypt. In prewar years, about two dozen squadrons manned British air bases from Suez to Hong Kong. They were occasionally called into action to suppress intertribal fighting or to quell local uprisings. But the fliers logged much more air time delivering smallpox vaccine to remote areas and searching for parties lost in deserts or jungles.

had decided to unload their bombs before heading home.

Churchill knew opportunity when it knocked. Swift retaliation would help satisfy the growing British thirst for vengeance. It would undoubtedly spur reprisal raids on London. But these, in turn, were bound to fire up the American sympathy and support that Churchill urgently needed.

And so, on the night following the London episode, 81 British bombers made their first appearance over Berlin. Though ostensibly the targets were industrial, the intent was simply to hit back at the Germans. As Churchill later phrased it to prolonged cheers in the House of Commons: "On every side is the cry, 'We can take it,' but with it there is also the cry 'Give it them back.' "

The raid on Berlin caused little damage; the cloud cover over the city was unusually thick that night. But the audacity of the British in striking at the German capital stunned Berliners. "They did not think it could ever happen," the American correspondent William L. Shirer recorded in his diary the next day. Shirer had been arguing that very point with a censor in the German Propaganda Ministry minutes before the air-raid sirens sounded; the censor had flatly declared it impossible that any enemy bombers could get at the proudest city of the Third Reich.

The RAF bombing of Berlin—repeated three more times in 10 nights—cheered the British as much as it shocked the Germans. Indeed, the boosting of morale on the home front was a cardinal function of the strategic air offensive. However, government propaganda and press accounts exaggerated the importance of every raid, and false optimism took hold. Even within Bomber Command itself, officers who

Aboard a Whitley bomber over enemy territory in 1940, an RAF crewman waits for the signal to drop propaganda leaflets through a specially adapted photoreconnaissance flare chute. The paper bombardment, prepared within the Political Intelligence Department of Britain's Foreign Office, attempted to drive a wedge between the German people and their Nazi leaders. Said the leaflet at right: "The Gestapo ravage entire lands and call it peace. Is that the Lebensraum that you are fighting for?"

should have known better tended to accept uncritically any encouraging news that leaked out of Germany via secret agents and neutral businessmen. According to one intelligence report, industrial output in the Ruhr plummeted by more than 30 per cent during the summer of 1940. This estimate was based on reasoning that was equally erroneous: the RAF's night raids, the report asserted, had kept the Ruhr's workers from getting any sleep, and thus had lowered their productivity.

The truth was that the bombing had little more than nuisance value. Britain did not yet have enough bombers to do a bigger job, and many in the existing force had to be diverted to attack the barges massing across the English Channel for Operation *Sea Lion*, Hitler's projected invasion of England.

Bomber Command rarely could dispatch more than 100 planes to Germany in any one night. Moreover, the fuel required to get there and back meant that each plane could carry no more than a ton of bombs, and the biggest bomb in Britain's arsenal in mid-1940 was a 500-pounder. And the bombs were seldom concentrated on a single target but were distributed among half a dozen or so. A typical raid in August of 1940 had to spread its impact over two synthetic oil plants, a power station, a naval armaments factory, two aircraft plants, a storage facility for aircraft parts, two railway yards and a metal castings factory.

The individualistic approach that had characterized the early leaflet raids still pervaded the air offensive. Bombers still flew to their objectives separately rather than in formation. Over the target, each plane's captain selected the time and the altitude for dropping its bombs. Even the takeoff time was left to his discretion. One pilot, Guy Gibson, recalled delaying takeoff for a mission against oil tanks in Hamburg simply because he and a crew member wanted to attend a movie that night.

Fortunately for the British, Germany's defenses were also in their infancy. They relied almost entirely on 450 heavy antiaircraft batteries that were clustered around such key industrial areas as the Ruhr. The guns fired 22-pound shells that exploded into 1,500 fragments of shrapnel. But in the 25 seconds a shell was on its way, a bomber could take evasive action.

Defenders and attackers acquired a special language. The Germans called their antiaircraft guns *Fliegerabwehrkanonen,* then mercifully shortened this to *Flak* to signify the fire that the guns spewed up at the rate of 15 to 20 rounds per minute. The British called it "ack-ack," derived both from antiaircraft and from the sound itself. They also invoked a venerable English word, "jinking," a kind of artful dodging, to describe the rapid turning-and-weaving that was used to confuse the enemy's aim.

As an American military observer later noted, a heavy bomber in the process of jinking "suggested an elephant trying to waltz on roller skates." Moreover, bombs released during evasive action were likely to miss their target. The Germans, in fact, regarded this as a secondary purpose for their flak: if the antiaircraft failed to hit the attacker, it could at least reduce his accuracy. To some RAF pilots, however, the very act of trying to dodge the enemy shells became an exciting, if deadly, interlude in an otherwise long, dull flight. Cheshire called it "the gripping, priceless attraction of night-bombing."

At first, the Luftwaffe's vaunted fighter planes were even less of a peril than the exploding shells. Though the speedy Me-109 was a terrible threat to the occasional British plane attempting to bomb in daylight, it proved unsuitable as a night interceptor. It lacked the endurance necessary to track a target at night, and because of its short radio range, it could not travel far afield without risking the loss of vital information supplied by ground control. The pilot, the Me-109's sole occupant, had his hands full just flying the plane in darkness—let alone hunting down an unseen bomber.

During the summer of 1940, the Me-109 was being replaced as a night interceptor by the Me-110. Dubbed "The Destroyer," the twin-engined Me-110 had failed to live up to the name in the role for which it was originally designed, as a bomber escort. In the Luftwaffe's raids on England, it proved far too slow to cope with Britain's Spitfire interceptors. But its speed—approximately 300 miles per hour—was adequate to overtake the lumbering British bombers, and it possessed special advantages for night fighting. The Me-110 could remain in the air for as long as three and a half hours without refueling; moreover, it carried two men. The crewman could operate the radio and handle navigation while providing the pilot with a second set of eyes for the difficult task of spotting enemy bombers in the dark.

The Me-110 crews disliked being relegated to defense of the home front. It seemed too humdrum an assignment compared with fighting the air war over England. They also grumbled that it was impossible to see in the dark, and they gobbled quantities of vitamin pills and yellow turnips in a vain attempt to improve their night vision. In their first few weeks on the job, they managed to bring down just one plane—one of their own. The Me-110's twin-finned tail closely resembled that of the Whitley bomber.

On the night of July 20, 1940, one of the loudest complainers, a 29-year-old former banking apprentice named Werner Streib, was at the controls of his Me-110 over the Ruhr. He and his squadron mates had been alerted by a radar station on the German coast. The Germans' radar—

named Freya for the mythological Teutonic goddess who looked after the souls of dead warriors—had a range of 75 miles. Though it could determine the direction in which an intruder was flying, it could not fix the altitude. But the night of July 20 was clear and moonlit, and as Streib and his crewman looked around, they suddenly glimpsed the shadowy outline of another plane. To make sure it was a Whitley and not another Me-110, Streib crept in until he was flying practically wing tip to wing tip with the enemy bomber. Then he turned and came in from behind. At 250 yards the Whitley's tail gunner opened fire.

Streib countered with two short bursts from the machine guns and cannon mounted in the Me-110's nose. He then pulled away to await the foe's next move. "His starboard engine was burning mildly," Streib later reported. "Two

In a crowded shop, English metalworkers knock brass and iron fittings off aluminum kettles, pots and pans—a fraction of the thousands of tons of cookware contributed by citizens after an appeal by the government. Once the fittings had been removed, the pots were melted down and the aluminum sent in ingots to aircraft manufacturers, who needed more than 15,000 pounds of aluminum for a typical heavy bomber.

dots detached themselves and two parachutes opened out and disappeared into the night. The bomber turned on a reciprocal course and tried to get away, but the plume of smoke from its engine was still clearly visible even by night. I attacked again, aiming at the port engine wing, without this time meeting counterfire. Two more bursts and engine and wing immediately blazed up."

German night fighters had made their first score. Two nights later, Streib bagged another bomber. By the middle of October, he had accounted for eight more, including three Wellingtons that he managed to shoot down in the space of just 40 minutes.

Streib's successes and those of his comrades heralded a stiffening of the Reich's defenses. But the small British losses were considered tolerable by Bomber Command's leaders. What bothered them more than flak or night fighters was the basic problem of how to find and hit the target. The darkness that enabled the bombers to fly over Germany with relative impunity also hid the targets from them. The problem was succinctly summed up by one RAF group commander as "a never ending struggle to circumvent the law that we cannot see in the dark."

In time, improved airborne radar would help to solve the difficulty, but in the autumn of 1940 airborne sets were in limited use even by the fighters that were defending England itself; they relied instead on ground-based radar, which directed them to Luftwaffe attackers with great precision. In this respect, Britain's night interceptors enjoyed an advantage over Germany's night interceptors. Conversely, however, the German bombers had the advantage over the British bombers in night raiding; the German bombers were guided to their targets in England by a system of intersecting radio beams known as *Knickebein* (crooked leg), while the British bombers had to try to make their way to their targets in Germany by the hit-or-miss method that the mariners of old had employed when they could not go by the stars—dead reckoning.

Navigation by dead reckoning was so undependable that Bomber Command later labeled it getting there "by guess and by God." Using elementary tools—map and compass—the navigator would plot a course based on the speed of the aircraft and the predicted wind velocity en route. Theoreti-

cally, this course would take the plane to the target in a given number of hours.

But things almost never worked out that way. Any disturbance could throw the plane off course—flak or a shift in the winds over the Continent, which were notoriously unpredictable. On the 600-mile trip to Berlin, for example, an unexpected side wind of 20 miles per hour could blow a Wellington off course by as much as 66 miles.

Navigators constantly tried to correct the course en route to the target. There were several ways of doing this, none of them easy. Bearings broadcast by radio from ground stations in England could provide a fix on the plane's precise position, but only for the first 200 miles from home base. Farther along, if the moonlight was bright enough—the so-called bomber's moon—the navigator could try to get a visual fix on some identifiable feature, such as a river or forest, that appeared on his map. But dipping low enough to see the ground brought the plane perilously close to the Germans' antiaircraft guns.

If the sky was clear, the navigator could shoot the stars with a sextant. But this required the aircraft to be flown level for several minutes—an extremely difficult feat. And once he had gathered all the necessary information about wind speed and direction, the location of the stars, and the speed and direction of his plane, the navigator had to do a series of complex mathematical calculations to determine where he was—or where he had been when he began. As one navigator described this nerve-racking exercise: "It was rather like sitting in a freezing cold stair cupboard with the door shut, the Hoover running, and trying to do calculus."

Reaching the general area of the target—coming within 20 miles was regarded as first-rate navigation—was only half of the problem. The navigator now had to try to spot either the target itself or a recognizable landmark that was nearby. He would attempt to do so by the unreliable light of the moon or the stars, or perhaps by the light of a dropped flare—although this would reveal the bomber's presence. It was not uncommon for a bomber to spend a precious half hour or more cruising around trying to locate its assigned target.

The German ground defenses, like those in England, did their best to complicate the task of an enemy navigator by means of decoy targets. A decoy could be as simple as a brushwood fire, deliberately ignited to persuade the navigator that preceding bombers on the mission had already set the target ablaze. Other elaborate decoys, placed in the countryside, were constructed to suggest entire towns. They had *papier-mâché* buildings, fake lighting systems and even sparking devices to simulate the flashes of moving trolley cars. RAF pilot Guy Gibson remembered one decoy so improbably sophisticated in its design that it became a familiar landmark for the British, serving to point them to their actual objective nearby.

After the navigator had spotted the target, or something plausibly approximating it, his work was not done. He had to double in brass as the bombardier—in RAF parlance, the "bomb aimer." Having spent three or four hours poring over his lighted charts, he now had to recover his night vision, issue careful instructions to the pilot throughout the final bomb run, and then release his load at precisely the right moment.

Not surprisingly, a navigator would sometimes get so hopelessly confused that his plane would drop its bombs on a dummy city, the wrong city or even, occasionally, on an RAF base back in England. In one notorious instance, a Whitley plowed through an overcast sky, unloaded its bombs on an airfield below, then ran out of gas and crash-landed in a cabbage patch. All four men aboard scrambled out safely and set fire to the plane to keep it from falling into enemy hands. Then, hoping to make a getaway by daylight, they hid in a nearby barn. They were confronted

During a 1938 gathering of the enthusiastic aeronauts in the Oxford University Air Squadron, young Leonard Cheshire, who became the most decorated British bomber pilot of the War, signs his flight plan before taking off in a Hart Trainer airplane. Cheshire and many other RAF airmen piloted their first planes as members of one of the dozens of flying clubs that promoted aviation in England between the Wars. Although Cheshire later flew more than 100 combat missions over Europe, he confessed: "I've always been terrified of heights, even in a plane."

there a few minutes later by an apoplectic RAF group captain who had watched the whole affair through binoculars from his own control tower.

For all the mishaps that marred the strategic air offensive in the fall of 1940, its leaders continued, even in private, to express confidence that Bomber Command was finding and hitting its targets. With virtually no evidence except the rosy reports brought back from the raids on Germany, they went on assuming a theoretical average bombing error of only 300 yards—a figure that was derived from prewar experiments conducted in broad daylight and unhampered by enemy flak or fighters.

In December of 1940 the climate of optimism began to change. Prime Minister Churchill himself contributed to the new mood. Though he had not questioned the RAF estimate of the accuracy of the night bombing, the tonnage figures of the bombs dropped on Germany worried him: the figure for December—992 tons in all—was less than the Luftwaffe had dropped in just five nights over England.

An urgent message bearing a bright red sticker marked "Action this day" was sent off to Chief of the Air Staff Sir Charles Portal. The gist of the message was blunt and Churchillian: "I am deeply concerned at the stagnant condition of our bomber force."

Doubts about the bombers' performance were beginning to penetrate even Bomber Command. Among the growing skeptics was Air Vice-Marshal Robert Saundby, the senior staff officer. One day at Bomber Command headquarters he stood studying an impressive wall map checkered with red and black squares. As the officer in charge of the map explained it, the red squares represented Germany's synthetic oil plants, the black squares those plants that had been flattened by British bombs. The officer was certain that the plants marked in black had been destroyed. It had been shown statistically, he said, that 100 tons of bombs would destroy half of an oil plant; hence, 200 tons would do the whole job. By such reasoning, in fact, one civilian expert had concluded that Germany's synthetic oil production had been reduced by fully 15 per cent.

Saundby patiently heard out his subordinate, then politely set him straight. "You have not dropped 200 tons of bombs on these oil plants," he said. "You have *exported* 200 tons of bombs, and you must hope that some of them went near the target."

As it happened, Bomber Command was just starting, at the end of 1940, to employ a new device that could demonstrate conclusively how many—or how few—bombs fell near or on a target. The device was the aerial reconnaissance camera, and it had entered the RAF's arsenal by a somewhat circuitous route.

Back in 1939, with war clearly threatening the British Empire, an Australian civilian named Sidney Cotton had undertaken to find out everything he could about what was going on in Germany. He was aware of the hazards of spying, but he was an adventurous man, and RAF intelligence gave him its blessing. As a cover, Cotton set up a business he called Aeronautical Research and Sales Ltd., whose ostensible activities included the marketing of color film in Germany. Cotton made frequent trips there at the controls of an American-built plane, a Lockheed-12A, which had three cameras concealed in the cabin floor.

For months before the outbreak of war, Cotton roamed the skies over Germany, making aerial photographs of arms factories and military installations. On one occasion, scarcely five weeks before hostilities began, he brashly dropped in on a Nazi air rally in Frankfurt. Curious Luftwaffe colonels and generals clustered around his unusual aircraft, which was painted a duck-egg green to make it harder to detect at higher altitudes. Cotton genially took the Luftwaffe officers for a ride. Even as they enjoyed the view, he casually flicked an inconspicuous switch, activating the cameras to click away at future targets of the RAF.

In November of 1940, Bomber Command formed its own Photographic Reconnaissance Unit. One of the unit's first assignments was to photograph the effects of a major raid on the city of Mannheim in southwestern Germany. The raid took place on the night of December 16, under unusually favorable conditions. The moonlight was perfect and the bomber force one of the biggest of the period—134 planes. To make the task of hitting the target even easier, the crews were not assigned to pinpoint specific industrial plants, but were instead instructed simply to aim at the center of town.

Five days later, a Spitfire succeeded in photographing Mannheim by daylight. The photographs revealed that although there was considerable damage, many bombs landed wide of the main target.

These and later photographs that showed less damage to other targets did not in themselves prove that the bombers were failing badly. Conceivably, the Germans were repairing or camouflaging the damage with lightning speed. To check out this possibility, special photographic systems were installed in the bombers themselves. The system consisted of a camera and a flash—itself a small bomb—synchronized so that the ground would be illuminated at the instant the bombs hit. The resulting photographs, when matched against preraid pictures of the target, would show precisely where the bombs fell.

The bomber crews disliked the new gadgetry. It was like having a snooper along on their missions. Moreover, the cameras were conveying messages that clearly spelled out the failure of some of the missions. Many crewmen refused to believe the photographs, and so did some higher-ups. But there were other officers in Bomber Command who were sufficiently disturbed over the photographic evidence to show it to an aide of Lord Cherwell, Churchill's scientific adviser, in the hope that Cherwell would mention it to the Prime Minister.

The ploy worked; Churchill ordered a full-scale investigation. Cherwell's aide, David Bensusan-Butt, was set to analyzing some 650 photographs taken in June and July of 1941 in the course of 100 missions over France and Germany, involving a total of 4,065 sorties. He compared the bombing photographs not only with prior photographs of the target areas but also with the claims of the crews.

The Butt report, presented on August 18, shocked even those who were already inclined to take Bomber Command's claims with a grain of salt. Of all the planes in the bombing photographs, only one in five came within five miles of the target. In the case of the Ruhr Valley, where smoke and the glare of searchlights compounded the attackers' difficulties, the news was still worse. Only one in 10 of the crews that claimed to have hit the target there actually dropped their bombs within five miles of it.

After reading these dismal conclusions, Churchill could not resist taking a sarcastic poke at Bomber Command. "It is an awful thought that perhaps three quarters of our bombs go astray," he wrote in a note to Chief of the Air Staff Portal.

"If we could make it half and half, we should virtually have doubled our bombing power."

Churchill's enthusiasm for the strategic air offensive was beginning to fade. Fully a year had passed since he had predicted that Britain's bombers alone would provide "the means of victory." And since that rousing declaration, made on the first anniversary of Britain's entry into the War, he had gone out on another large limb. With the German invasion of Russia on June 22, 1941, he had promised his new ally, Soviet dictator Josef Stalin, that British aid would include an intensified punishment of the Reich from the air—"a heavier discharge of bombs, making the German people taste and gulp each month a sharper dose of the miseries they have showered upon mankind."

At the end of September of 1941, Churchill gave notice that his ardor for strategic air warfare had cooled to the chilling point. Before him was a new RAF plan to destroy "beyond all hope of recovery" 43 German cities with a total population of 15 million. The proposal envisioned the need for a minimum of 4,000 British bombers—approximately 10 times the number that was currently available for operations over Germany.

"It is very disputable whether bombing by itself will be a decisive factor in the present war," Churchill wrote in response. "On the contrary, all that we have learnt since the war began shows that its effects, both physical and moral, are greatly exaggerated. The most we can say is that it will be a heavy and I trust a seriously increasing annoyance."

Churchill had further cause for his change of attitude. Not only was the RAF having a hard time finding its targets, the bombers were not always getting through to Germany. The Luftwaffe, though it had been fought to a standoff over England, was demonstrating a new ferocity over the western approaches to Germany.

German air defenses were now in large part deployed in occupied France, Belgium and Holland. To reach the Reich, British bombers had to run a gauntlet of searchlights and night fighters stretching from Denmark in the north to the French-Swiss frontier in the south (map, preceding the title page). Many bombers were being knocked down en route.

The gauntlet was known as the Kammhuber Line, after its designer, Major General Josef Kammhuber. Formerly com-

THE LUFTWAFFE'S SPANISH PROVING GROUND

In July of 1936, Hitler seized an opportunity to test his fledging Luftwaffe in combat. At the request of Spanish insurgent leader Francisco Franco, he supplied planes to transport Franco's Nationalist forces from Morocco to Spain to battle the Republicans in the Civil War. Soon afterward, he made a more direct contribution, sending Franco some 6,000 Lutwaffe airmen who fought under an impressive name invented for the occasion: the Condor Legion.

For nearly three years, the men of the Condor Legion honed their skills in strikes against military and industrial targets, cities and towns. German engineers drew on the lessons of combat to improve planes that would long be Luftwaffe mainstays—the Messerschmitt-109, Heinkel-111, Dornier-17 and Stuka Ju-87 dive bomber.

The Condor Legion won its practice war handily, downing 277 Republican aircraft against just 96 losses. More significant, the airmen gained the experience and confidence that would pay big dividends in Hitler's blitzkrieg and the air war.

Triumphant Condor Legion men parade on motorcycles at the airport in Madrid in 1939.

A Heinkel-111 showers bombs on Valencia Harbor.

A German pilot marks time as ground crewmen prepare his Me-109 for its next sortie.

mander of a bomber wing, Kammhuber had taken charge of his country's night air defenses in July of 1940 at the order of Göring himself. Göring was no longer in a mood to boast about Germany's defenses; he now frankly described them as his country's "Achilles' heel." Kammhuber was an excellent choice for his new job. Though he had a taste for good living—he installed himself in a handsome 17th Century castle near the Dutch city of Utrecht—he had a great gift as an organizer. Methodically, he began building a massive barrier against the British bombers.

First, he had the powerful German searchlights moved west, away from the gun-encircled German cities, and positioned them in a belt up to 20 miles wide. Here, his Me-110 night fighters would have no fear of being shot down by German flak when they engaged enemy bombers that were caught in the searchlights' glare. And the glare was unending; one searchlight would pick up a bomber in its beam, then follow the plane until another searchlight took over. One British tail gunner reported that it was like being "in the center of an enormous lighted but empty circus, waiting for the unknown." Then the Me-110 interceptor would appear, "a faint ghostly shape entering the circle of light."

Kammhuber's searchlight barrier became even more effective in 1941 with the introduction of a radar-controlled master light. This would lock onto a bomber automatically and hold it in a pale blue beam until the manually operated searchlights picked it up.

The searchlights were only part of Kammhuber's arsenal; if the British got past them, they were greeted by radar-directed gun batteries. Kammhuber also had at his disposal some 30 light bombers—Junkers-88s and Dornier-17s that had been converted for use as night fighters. Their function was to head for England and shoot up the RAF bombers just as they were taking off for a raid and before they had attained sufficient air speed to evade the intruders. The German planes launched their mission upon an alert by specially trained radio operators in Holland who tuned in on RAF frequencies. When the eavesdroppers heard a whistling and chirping, they knew that the radio operators in the bombers at the RAF bases had switched on their sets to check them out before takeoff.

Kammhuber's intruders would also hit the air bases in England just as the bombers were returning from a raid, sometimes boldly queuing up with the Whitleys and Well-

An array of seven towers forms one of 20-odd radar installations that guarded England's east coast in 1939. Aerials on the three 350-foot towers at left transmitted microwave signals, which bounced off aircraft up to 110 miles away and returned to antennae on the shorter towers at right. The course of the approaching planes was plotted by a radar technician, and the RAF dispatched fighters to intercept the intruders.

ingtons as they waited to come in for a landing. "If I want to smoke out a wasps' nest," Kammhuber explained, "I don't go for the individual insects buzzing about, but the entrance hole when they are all inside."

His Junkers and Dorniers were so successful against the British that by October of 1941 they claimed more than 100 kills. But on the 13th of that month Hitler ordered Kammhuber's intruder force transferred to the Mediterranean to take on the increasingly troublesome British stronghold on the island of Malta. In any event, Hitler declared, shooting down bombers in faraway England did nothing to improve the morale of the German people: they wanted to see the enemy bombers brought down closer to home. Kammhuber protested in vain.

Yet he still had aces in the hole—night-fighter aces. One was 25-year-old Prince Heinrich of Sayn-Wittgenstein, a Danish-born aristocrat. Unlike most of his comrades, who disdained home-front defense duty, the Prince relished the hide-and-seek life of the night fighter. In order to savor it he had, in fact, given up flying bombers after 150 missions. Intense and high-strung, he was, in the words of one admirer, "as out of place in a bomber squadron as Hitler at a Churchill dinner party." But in a fighter plane the Prince came into his own. "He had an astonishing sixth sense—an intuition that permitted him to see and even to feel where other aircraft were," one of his commanders recalled. "It was like a personal radar system." Whatever his gifts, Prince Heinrich was destined to be credited with a remarkable total of kills of enemy bombers—seven in one night, six in another night and five in another—before his own death in the air in January of 1944.

By late 1941, the RAF's bombers were finding it more and more difficult to get across the Kammhuber Line. The defending Me-110s and Junkers-88s no longer had to rely solely on the searchlights to help them spot the enemy aircraft. They could home in on the incoming foe with the guidance of a powerful ground-based German radar system, the Würzburg. Unlike the earlier Freya system, which could track only the direction of an enemy plane, the Würzburg could also determine its altitude.

With the Würzburg's introduction, Kammhuber set up a new chain of defenses in front of the searchlight barrier. It consisted of overlapping rectangular zones about 20 miles in length and width—roughly the effective range of the Würzburg. The Germans called these zones "boxes."

Each box had its own fighter-interceptor, a Freya radar, two Würzburg radars and a ground-control station. The Freya radar served to give early warning of the approaching enemy aircraft. One Würzburg then plotted the course of the British bomber as it crossed the box. The other set plotted the course of the German interceptor. At ground control, the two courses were displayed on a frosted glass screen. A spot of green light indicated the position of the bomber; a red light showed the position of the interceptor. It was the job of the ground controller, talking by radio to the two-man interceptor crew, to give directions that would bring the two dots so close that the fighter pilot could actually see the bomber.

These new tactics created a hell for the RAF bombers. Until late 1941, British losses had been running at a rate of just 2.3 per cent—mostly attributable to flak, mechanical failure and other noninterceptor causes. But on the night of November 7, 1941, when some 400 RAF bombers set out across the newly reinforced Kammhuber Line en route to targets in Cologne, Berlin and other German cities, they were caught between the enemy fighters and flak, and 37 British planes failed to return. This was nearly double the 5 per cent loss rate deemed acceptable by Bomber Command. And among the bombers that headed for the Ruhr, risking the most formidable sector of the Kammhuber Line, the loss rate was a frightening 21 per cent.

Churchill knew that such losses could not be sustained. This realization, and the photographic evidence that Bomber Command had scattered 40,000 tons of bombs on the German countryside with negligible impact, forced him to a painful decision. On November 11, four days after the costly raid, Churchill imposed a drastic cutback on Bomber Command's activities; it amounted to a virtual ban on the bombing of Germany for the coming winter. Only small bomber forces were to be sent, and then only to the nearest targets and only in the most favorable weather.

In his melancholy order to the air chiefs, Churchill wrote: "It is now the duty of . . . Bomber Command to re-gather their strength for the spring." The man who had unleashed the bombers against Germany 18 months earlier had now reined them in.

HARD TIMES FOR THE RAF

Wellington bombers take off at dusk for a raid on Germany. Fondly nicknamed "Wimpys," Wellingtons carried the main load of the RAF's offensive through 1942.

MEN, PLANES AND AN INVINCIBLE SPIRIT

Prepared for a raid over enemy territory, RAF air gunners head toward their bombers laden with ammunition belts, logbooks and parachutes.

Britain in the summer of 1940 stood stripped of allies by the German blitzkrieg and facing an enemy that vowed to "eliminate the English motherland." The burden of defense—and later of a token offense—was dropped squarely on the shoulders of an outnumbered and underequipped RAF. Against a potential attack force of some 2,000 German aircraft, the British mustered barely 600 fighter planes. Many RAF men were boys of only 19 or 20, fresh from flight school. But they fought with an insouciant verve that made them a match for their battle-hardened adversaries.

Fighter pilots characterized their deadly encounters with the Luftwaffe as "a rather noisy game of hide and seek." Bomber crews spoke of their nighttime raids over Berlin, Hamburg and Cologne as "visits." One crewman said of the missions that it was "a wonderful thing to have an evening's entertainment provided for you."

RAF Wing Commander Guy Gibson had no illusions concerning his chances for survival: once he skipped a dental appointment because he "didn't see any point in having my teeth fixed when I was likely to die within the next few days." But Gibson was well aware of the dangers of fatalism, and he took his crews on boisterous rounds of the pubs to keep them together and, he said, to "lead them into thinking they were the best: that they cannot die."

The spirit that drove these young fliers captured the imagination of Frank Wootton, an artist who had volunteered for the RAF at the approach of the War. To his dismay, he was put to work making drawings of bombsights and other equipment for use as training aids. But he also found time to paint the fliers' aircraft: to him, the dashing Spitfire fighters, the great grim Lancaster bombers, were as full of heroic personality as the men who flew them.

Wootton eventually was appointed the official RAF artist and given free rein to paint pictures of the planes and their battles. His vivid images, some of which are reproduced on these pages, revealed the beauty of the planes, and paid eloquent tribute to the indomitable RAF fliers who saved Britain in the desperate early years of the War.

An RAF student pilot maneuvers his Tiger Moth biplane into a loop high above the training field. The trainee's flight instructor is seated in the rear cockpit.

Flying high above a plowman on England's coast, a squadron of Defiant fighters heads for the Channel en route to Dunkirk, there to cover the evacuation of

BEHIND THE PILOTS, A "MIGHTY PANORAMA" OF SUPPORTING PLAYERS

A Short Sunderland, one of the Coastal Command's flying boats, flies over the Southampton docks on a patrol.

the defeated British and French forces.

Destined for bomber duty, a student gunner trains his machine gun on a model Messerschmitt fighter.

Behind the celebrated RAF pilots stood a large contingent of lesser known but no less important personnel. Every pilot was backed by mechanics, ground crews, and Coastal Command reconnaissance and rescue teams. And on bombers each pilot relied on the further support of his crew.

Bomber pilot Leonard Cheshire recalled sensing a still wider indebtedness during a raid over the Ruhr in 1940. He saw the mission as "a mighty panorama" with himself in the spotlight and the whole island of Britain standing in the wings as supporting players. "A vast organization has been created to provide a pilot capable of executing these orders, and equally a whole system of supply and maintenance of aircraft and bombs and guns and petrol and countless other tools . . . has been created to allow one pilot to drop one bomb."

Moments from a kill over France, Spitfire pilot Robert Stanford Tuck goes into a dive to fire on an Me-109. The Luftwaffe formation attacking the bombers at

Three weary RAF fighter pilots give an intelligence officer an account of their just-completed mission.

"Pretty and precious looking as a cavalier's jeweled rapier" was an admirer's phrase for the slim Spitfires flown by many of the pilots of RAF Fighter Command. The description was felicitous in more ways than one. Some RAF fighter pilots adhered to the code of the gentlemen swordsmen of an earlier age; rules of honor, fair play and courtesy provided a framework for their duels to the death.

Luftwaffe fighter pilots had a kindred code, as British ace Robert Stanford Tuck discovered when he was shot down and taken prisoner in 1942. His Luftwaffe captors treated him chivalrously, and before he was sent off to prison camp, Tuck was entertained at dinner by a group of pilots commanded by ace Adolf Galland. Over cigarettes and Scotch, the two men chatted amiably in English about the earlier encounter depicted at left, in which both Galland and Tuck had scored victories. So, said Galland, he and Tuck could part company "even Stevens."

lower left was led by ace Adolf Galland.

On patrol high over southern England, Spitfire fighters search the autumn skies for enemy aircraft in 1940.

Ground crewmen feed bombs into the bays of a pair of Hampdens at an RAF airfield at Waddington.

A base commander awaits bombers returning from a raid.

Hidden from searchlights by heavy clouds,

Life in RAF Bomber Command offered little of the continuous headlong excitement of fighter combat. An anonymous tail gunner with a six-man Wellington crew said of his night missions over Germany: "We get shot up, iced and fed up, but for the most part our outings lack the Hollywood element. The highlights of combat come only now and then. At the end of seven and a half hours in the tail turret, one rather sighs for them."

The RAF bomber crewmen concentrated on further developing their skills and on perfecting the disciplined teamwork that was, in itself, a kind of reward for those who served in Bomber Command. "Crew life becomes unendingly intimate," continued the Wellington tail gunner. "Without being sentimental, there is a sense of comradeship about the venture. None of you would probably have chosen each other if crews were made on the picking up principle, but after a bit you would not dream of changing."

Blenheim bombers fly over a German target in 1940. Lightly armed and highly vulnerable to German fighters, Blenheims were gradually phased out of service.

LONG WAITS FOR THE "HIGHLIGHTS OF COMBAT"

Roaring over the Alps, a formation of Lancasters heads for the Italian port of Genoa, whose lightly defended docks and shipping yards were popular targets for

RAF bomber crews. Six such raids on the port city in the autumn of 1942 helped prevent Italian naval forces from opposing the Allied invasion of North Africa.

2

Soon after he took over RAF Bomber Command in February of 1942, Air Chief Marshal Arthur Harris was hurrying to his headquarters at High Wycombe west of London when he was stopped for speeding. On the front fender of his Bentley convertible was an official sticker exempting him from the speed limit. Seeing the sticker, the policeman gave Harris a bit of polite advice instead of a ticket.

"I hope you will be careful, sir," he cautioned. "You might kill somebody."

"My dear man," Harris replied, "I'm paid to kill people."

The bluntness of this remark said a good deal about Harris. A martinet with strongly held opinions and a tart tongue, he had risen from World War I pilot to group commander to deputy chief of the Air Staff by sheer tenacity of purpose. Now, at 49, he was at the top of Bomber Command and in a position to further his most cherished aim—the relentless bombing of Germany. So single-minded was his dedication to the eventual aerial destruction of the Reich that the press called him "Bomber" Harris. His air crews were later to hit on a different name for him. Partly in admiration of his hard-driving methods and partly in resentment over the high human cost of some of his missions, they came to call him "Butch"—for "The Butcher."

Harris took charge of Bomber Command at a time when it desperately needed his forceful leadership. Its morale was ebbing, its detractors multiplying. Its much-touted ability to find and hit targets in Germany by night had proved more mythical than real, resulting in Churchill's cutback of the air offensive in November of 1941. In the three months since, the bombers' chief assignments—a lot closer to home than Germany, and undertaken by day as well as by night—had ended in another dispiriting failure.

The assignment, carried out under the direction of Harris' predecessor, Air Marshal Sir Richard Peirse, called for the destruction of three German warships sitting just across the English Channel in the harbor of Brest, on France's northwestern coast. Since defeating the French, the Germans had made Brest a major way station for their ships en route to and from the intensifying Battle of the Atlantic. The trio targeted by RAF Bomber Command—the 26,000-ton battle cruisers *Scharnhorst* and *Gneisenau*, and the 10,000-ton cruiser *Prinz Eugen*—had already scored heavily against the British. The *Prinz Eugen* had helped dispatch the mighty

"BOMBER" HARRIS TAKES OVER

battle cruiser *Hood*; the *Scharnhorst* and the *Gneisenau* had sunk the carrier *Glorious* and sent 115,000 tons of merchant shipping to the bottom.

The three warships were in Brest for repairs and refitting, and blasting them as they lay in dry dock proved impossible. After 1,875 sorties by Bomber Command, in which 1,962 tons of bombs were dropped, the targets were still intact. Moreover, the antiaircraft guns that were massed around Brest's dock area and vigorous defensive action by Luftwaffe fighters cost the British 43 bombers. The jubilant Germans saw added cause for satisfaction. Their warships, by serving as what one Luftwaffe commander described as "a sort of flytrap," had diverted the enemy aircraft from what might have been productive missions elsewhere.

The crowning humiliation for Bomber Command came on February 12, 1942. Late the previous evening, the *Scharnhorst*, the *Gneisenau* and the *Prinz Eugen* left Brest to make a dash through the Channel toward Germany. Hitler, in a sudden onset of prudence, wanted the ships near home in order to avoid further risk. Escorted by seven destroyers, some 50 smaller vessels and a fighter cover of 250 planes working in relays, the three ships steamed through the Straits of Dover virtually under the noses of the British— although heavily cloaked in mist and rain.

Bomber Command, belatedly alerted on the afternoon of February 12, sent 242 planes in pursuit. The weather was so bad that only 39 of them found the ships. Then the ceiling was so low that the bombs had to be dropped from as little as 200 feet, and they literally bounced off the armor-plated decks of the ships. The quarry escaped with only minor damage—and that was caused by mines that had been previously sown in the sea.

To the British public, the fact that bombing conditions were almost hopeless that day was no excuse for what was clearly a fiasco. As one blunt critique put it: "The plain truth seemed to be that Bomber Command . . . couldn't even hit a target 250 yards long in broad daylight on its own doorstep." The popular reaction was so furious that Churchill himself, attempting to gauge it, came to the conclusion that it was even worse than the response to a second, more spectacular calamity the same week: the surrender of Britain's Far Eastern bastion, Singapore, to the Japanese. "It was certainly not strange," the Prime Minister wrote, "that pub-lic confidence in the Administration and its conduct of the war should have quavered."

The Prime Minister's personal response to the Channel episode was to come out fighting. Two days later he lifted his ban on missions deep into Germany and ordered a full-scale resumption of the bombing offensive. Ten days later Bomber Command had a change of chiefs. Air Marshal Peirse was sent to India to head the RAF force based there, and Bomber Harris took over in his place.

Harris was on the spot, and he knew it. He recalled: "I had to prove, and prove quickly, to the satisfaction of those who mattered, that the bomber force could do its work if it was large enough and if its efforts were not frittered away on objectives other than German industry as a whole."

Beefing up the bomber force was the paramount priority. Harris, who had spent more than half of 1941 in Washington on an RAF supply mission, was dismayed on settling in at Bomber Command to find that its frontline strength was scarcely greater than at the start of the War two and a half years earlier. He had available a daily average of little more than 300 long-range bombers—and only 69 of these were heavy bombers. Though 18 new squadrons had been organized during 1941, some had been sent to support the ground forces fighting the Germans in the North African desert, and the rest had been turned over to RAF Coastal Command to support naval operations against the U-boats in the Atlantic.

More vexing to Harris, the War Office wanted additional bombers for an expected new offensive by the redoubtable chief of Germany's Afrika Korps, Lieut. General Erwin Rommel. The Navy wanted at least eight and a half more squadrons, including two to try to cope with the Japanese now rampaging through British possessions in the Far Fast.

Still, Harris saw a number of reasons for optimism. Britain's aircraft factories were producing at a faster rate than ever. New types of four-engined heavy bombers—Stirlings, Halifaxes and Lancasters—were coming into service. Bomber Command's sorry record in finding and hitting targets in Germany had spurred the development of new means and methods of aerial attack.

Above all, Harris was heartened by a basic shift in government policy concerning the air war on Germany. So-called precision bombing, the pinpointing of specific targets, was to be replaced by generalized "area bombing." Precision bombing had been hampered to begin with by the government's inability to decide which German factories or railheads or shipyards should be attacked; at one point the leadership's vacillation had led one exasperated member of Parliament to offer the Air Ministry a memorandum on priorities prepared by his greengrocer. But even when a firm choice of a target had been made, the RAF's bombers had trouble hitting it; the results were nowhere near as crippling as the economic experts in London had predicted, and Germany's industrial machine kept chugging along.

Britain's own experience at the hands of the Luftwaffe helped clinch the argument for area bombing. The German raid on Coventry in November of 1940, while primarily directed at industrial targets, had devastated some 100 acres of the city; the havoc to workers' housing and to such public services as transportation, water and electricity had apparently delayed the return to war production more than the bombing of the factories themselves.

The possibility that damage to morale might outweigh damage to key factories in the prosecution of the War seemed worth investigating, and subsequent German raids on Birmingham, Hull and other cities prompted a survey of the effects on the inhabitants. The results were then analyzed by none other than Lord Cherwell himself, the man whose scientific judgment Churchill most trusted. Cherwell, a physics professor on leave from Oxford, drew two conclu-

sions: that the worst damage to morale came from the loss of one's house—"people seem to mind it more than having their friends or even relatives killed"—and that this finding should be utilized in carrying the war to Germany.

Cherwell bolstered his case with statistics. He figured that for every ton of bombs the Germans had dropped on the cities in the survey, between 100 and 200 people had been made homeless. By this measure, a British bomber, assuming it lasted long enough to make 14 sorties, could "de-house" 4,000 to 8,000 Germans. Cherwell noted that much of the German population—22 million people—was concentrated in 58 cities. He estimated that if these cities were subjected to area bombing over a period of 18 months, the RAF could "de-house" at least a third of the entire German population and thus "break the spirit of the people."

Cherwell's statistics were hotly disputed by others in the scientific establishment—one dissenter pronounced them "at least 600 per cent too high"—and in time both German and British civilians would disprove Cherwell's assumption that the stress of losing one's house was bound to shatter morale. Churchill, however, was smitten by the clarity and certitude of his mentor's analysis. Even before he received Cherwell's finished report in March of 1942, he moved to make area bombing official government policy. In late February, when Air Chief Marshal Harris took over at Bomber Command headquarters at High Wycombe, he found formal notification of the policy shift awaiting him.

Harris, who had long opposed precision bombing because it dealt with what he dismissed as mere "panacea" targets, was delighted. The new orders from the Air Ministry authorized him to attack Germany "without restriction," and added: "The primary object of your operations should now be focused on the morale of the enemy civil population and in particular, of the industrial workers." Translated into practical terms, this meant that in attacking Germany's cities, British bombers would henceforth drop their lethal loads on heavily built-up and densely populated districts without attempting to pinpoint one or another site within the designated area.

Bomber Command scored its first major success under Harris less than two weeks after he was chosen to lead it. Ironically, the raid involved precision bombing, and the

Four-engined Stirlings—Britain's first heavy bombers—receive servicing at an RAF bomber station. The big bombers, which made their combat debut in February 1941, had several shortcomings. They could not carry a maximum bombload above 16,500 feet, their bomb bays were unable to hold anything larger than 2,000-pound bombs, and their landing gear had a tendency to collapse. As improved bombers replaced them, Stirlings were increasingly used to tow gliders and transport troops.

target was not even in Germany. On the night of March 3, he dispatched 235 bombers to attack the huge Renault works at Billancourt, near Paris. Instead of automobiles, Renault was now busy turning out tanks and other armor for the Germans, performing a vital service for Hitler's war machine. All but 12 of the raiders hit the target. By one estimate, the Germans lost the output of enough armor and transport to have supplied five motorized divisions, and almost four months were to elapse before Renault could get back to full production.

Though the target was nowhere near Germany, Harris' preferred arena of operations, at this early stage of his stewardship he needed a quick triumph to restore the confidence of his crews, and of the British public, in the mettle of Bomber Command. Renault was easy to reach and far less heavily defended than the Reich's own industrial concentrations. It also made a good choice psychologically—as an object lesson to industrialists in occupied countries.

What gratified Harris most about the Renault attack was the high level of effectiveness his bombers achieved, thanks in large part to two innovations that he had decided to test. One was a way of marking a target so that it would be readily spotted by the incoming bombers and easier for their bombs to hit. The mission was divided into three waves of planes, all carrying as many flares as their bombloads would permit. The first wave, using the most highly trained crews, dropped some of their flares, then their bombs; they then dropped the rest of the flares to windward to serve as beacons for the next wave. The second wave repeated the process for the third wave. The target was thus continuously illuminated for the raid's duration.

The other innovation was also tactical. Instead of sending in his bombers at random during the night, Harris scheduled them to arrive within a one-hour period. The concentration of the attack not only saturated the light antiaircraft defenses around the Renault plant but also overwhelmed the fire-fighting crews attempting to contain the damage.

Five nights after the Renault raid, Harris launched his first attack on Germany itself—and his first attempt at area bombing. He sent 211 planes to attack Essen, the chief city of the Ruhr (map, page 61). By the criteria of the new British policy, Essen was a prime objective. It was so heavily industrialized and built up that—according to the experts in

Britain's Ministry of Economic Warfare—a bomb could be dropped on the city at random and still stand "an even chance of hitting some work of man."

Though the attackers were instructed to aim their bombs at the large square in the center of Essen's old town, with no precise targets specified, it was fully expected that extensive damage would befall the gigantic Krupp steelmaking and armaments enterprise, which made its home in Essen. This outcome seemed to be inevitable; Krupp factories sprawled everywhere in the city. But Krupp emerged virtually untouched by the raid of March 8—and by a follow-up raid the next night. The brunt of the attack was borne not by the center of Essen but by its outskirts and neighboring towns.

The trouble lay with one of the two innovations Harris had employed with such success at the Renault works. Sending in the bombers on a tight time schedule proved its worth in breaching the formidable Kammhuber Line that guarded the approaches to the Ruhr; the German interceptors along the line, accustomed to dealing with the enemy bombers on a one-to-one basis, could not cope with their concentrated numbers. But over Essen itself, the Harris plan to have the advance force light the way for the main force went awry. The flares that were dropped to start with burned out before they could serve as guidelines for the incendiary bombs that were dropped next; as a result, many of the incendiaries went astray, and the fires they set were scattered enough to mislead the incoming main force in aiming its own bombs.

A third innovation also proved to be something of a disappointment. This was a radio signaling system known as Gee, and it was primarily intended to guide a bomber to an objective without the need for making visual fixes en route. Synchronized signals from three ground transmitters in England appeared as pulses on a special receiver aboard the aircraft. The navigator measured the time intervals between pulses and related the figures to coordinates that had been previously prepared and printed on a chart of Europe overlaid by the lines of a grid ("Gee" simply stood for "grid"). These calculations determined the location of the plane at a given moment.

Gee got high marks as a navigational guide to Essen but flunked an important secondary task that the British had hoped it would fulfill—as an aid to so-called blind bombing. They had assumed that Gee would eliminate the need for visual fixes not only en route to the objective but also over it, and could thus serve to direct the dropping of bombs without any help from the human eye. It had failed in that mission, dismally.

Harris was bent on offsetting the fiasco at Essen by a clear-cut success elsewhere, soon. The objective he chose was Lübeck, a historic north German port on the Baltic. The city was a tempting target. It served as a supply funnel for German operations in Norway and Russia. Its antiaircraft defenses were not especially strong. And it was bound to burn fast. Lübeck was, in fact, a veritable tinderbox. It dated back to medieval times and was largely built of wood. Harris planned accordingly: about half the 300 tons of bombs his planes were to carry were incendiaries.

On the night of the 28th of March, 234 RAF bombers left for Lübeck. Those in the vanguard had Gee receivers— "goon boxes," the crews now called them. Though the city lay beyond Gee's maximum range, 400 miles, the goon boxes got the lead planes nearly four fifths of the way. Then an easily identifiable landmark, the mouth of the Trave River, provided an excellent visual fix of position.

That night Lübeck won the distinction of becoming the first German city to go up in flames. The raiders were able to swoop as low as 2,000 feet to disgorge their fire bombs. Some 200 acres, about half the city, were totally laid waste.

Lübeck's 12th Century cathedral was destroyed, along with the central power station, factories and warehouses. By the Germans' own count, 15,707 people were—in Cherwell's word—"de-housed."

In Germany the high-level reaction to Lübeck was delayed; the dimensions of the disaster took a while to sink in. That weekend Propaganda Minister Joseph Goebbels noted in his diary that the raid had "thoroughly spoiled" his Sunday at home. An entry a week later was less casual. "I have been shown a newsreel of the destruction," Goebbels wrote. "It is horrible." He speculated about the possible demoralizing effects on the people of Lübeck, then drew some comfort from the traditionally tough fiber of the region's inhabitants. "Thank God it is a North German population," he noted.

In England the men of RAF Bomber Command added a new term to their vocabulary: "to do a Lübeck," which meant "to flatten."

On the day after the success at Lübeck, Harris issued an order that typified his autocratic style of leadership. He forbade wives of the bomber crews to live within 40 miles of the bases at which their husbands were stationed; he wanted no distractions from the job at hand. He was well on his way to giving his men a new sense of purpose, while inspiring a healthy terror of their new chief.

Moreover, Harris was managing to make his presence felt

by remote control. He seldom visited his air bases. The majority of his crews never even saw him. To keep informed about what the men were thinking and saying, he relied on his deputy commander, Air Vice-Marshal Saundby. They were friends of long standing. Two decades earlier in Iraq, Harris, as commander of a bomber squadron, and Saundby, as his senior flight officer, had helped police rebellious tribesmen; together they had worked out an ingenious tactic for aiming a bomb from a prone position rather than over the side from the cockpit. They simply sawed a hole in the wooden floor of an old Vickers Vernon.

When Harris became head of Bomber Command, he invited Saundby to share his Victorian home near headquarters so that they could stay in constant touch. Saundby was so devoted to Harris, and to bombing Germany, that he later refused a promotion to an RAF command of his own.

The two men complemented each other. Harris was hard-bitten and aloof, Saundby gentle and sociable. Saundby often had an afterhours drink with subordinates, talking of matters far removed from the War, including his favorite hobbies—catching fish and catching butterflies. Unworried about appearances, he was sometimes seen in his air vice-marshal's uniform chasing butterflies with a net.

Saundby's twin passions figured in his choice of code names for the bombing targets in Germany. He was torn between fish and butterflies but, as Harris later reported, "there were not enough short names of butterflies and moths to go round and it would obviously be inconvenient to use words like 'Broad-bordered bee hawk.'" Fish won the day; Berlin became Whitebait, and Cologne was code-named Trout.

Harris spent much of his time casting his net of persuasion over "the people who mattered"—newspapermen, politicians and government officials all the way up to Churchill, with whom he met almost weekly. On such occasions, Harris could abandon his usual gruffness and summon up the artistry of a born public-relations man. What he aimed to sell was the concept of strategic air power. In the spring of 1942, he recalled, "I had to regard the operations of the next few months not only as training or trial runs from which, and only from which, we could learn many essential lessons, but also as commercial travelers' samples which I could show to the War Cabinet."

Harris meant "commercial travelers' samples" quite literally. Among them was his Blue Book, an album of aerial photographs showing the destruction wrought by the raids on Lübeck arid other German cities. Copies of the Blue Book, regularly updated, were sent to the Prime Minister and to Buckingham Palace—and to Stalin, Britain's new ally in Moscow—as evidence of Bomber Command's rebirth.

Harris continued his proselytizing afterhours. By the end of the War, he and his attractive young wife, Jill, had entertained an estimated 5,000 visitors at their home. After dinner, the host—wearing a plum-colored velvet smoking

At RAF Bomber Command headquarters 30 miles from London, Air Chief Marshal Arthur Harris pores over his Blue Book—a group of photographs surveying damage caused by RAF bombers—with his second-in-command, Air Vice-Marshal Robert Saundby (on his right), and two aides. The main building of the headquarters complex was a closely guarded underground shelter (right), hidden beneath a grassy hill and heavy layers of concrete.

drove home humming an old war tune and enjoying a new sense of buoyancy.

Soon afterward, Harris scheduled Operation *Millennium* for May 27 with either Hamburg or Cologne as the target, depending on the weather. But on May 26 unexpected trouble loomed. Harris was suddenly confronted by a steep drop in the number of planes he had counted on: the subtraction of 250 bombers that Coastal Command had agreed to lend him. Though organizationally a part of the RAF, Coastal Command came under the Navy's operational control, and the Admiralty had decided that the Navy had nothing to gain from helping Harris. If the Thousand Plan failed, as the admirals thought likely, the Navy stood to lose many of the bombers it now had. If the plan succeeded, Harris would have a strong argument for denying the Navy the added bombers it sought for the Battle of the Atlantic.

With just over 24 hours to go, Air Vice-Marshal Saundby set out to plug the gap left by the withdrawal of one fourth of the Thousand Plan force. He dug deeper into Bomber Command's plane reserves; he put together more crews made up of students still in training units, along with their instructors. He was also able to juggle some personnel as a result of a recent change in the composition of the heavy-bomber crews. These bombers no longer carried a second pilot; he had been replaced by a flight engineer. By the morning of May 27, Saundby had scraped up enough planes and men to make a grand total of 940 aircraft and crews.

At that point the weather intervened to delay Operation *Millennium*. For three days in a row, thundery conditions and thick clouds persisted over most of Germany, and three times Harris reluctantly had to order a postponement. Clear skies were even more essential than usual for this colossal mission, to reduce the risk of aerial collisions and to enable the half-trained student crews to find the target.

In fact, the weather delay proved to be a boon for the British. While it lasted, ground crews working for 18 hours at a stretch managed to put into shape nearly 100 bombers that had been regarded as unserviceable. At 9 a.m. on Saturday, May 30, when Harris strode through a grove of beech trees at High Wycombe and down into his underground headquarters for his daily planning conference, his available force of planes exceeded 1,000.

The conference followed the customary ritual. Harris sat at his desk while Saundby and a group of top aides stood clustered around him. From an office across the hall, a stern-faced little Scotsman emerged—chief meteorologist Magnus T. Spence, bearing his weather charts. As he spread them over Harris' desk and began spelling out his predictions, Harris and the others listened in respectful silence.

Spence's report that morning was almost as discouraging as on the three previous days. Thunder clouds still covered much of Germany; Hamburg was blanketed. However, the weather to the south was improving. "There's a fifty-fifty chance," Spence said, "that the cloud in the Cologne area will clear by midnight."

Harris sat staring at the weather charts through his glasses while he considered the forecast's implications. The Thousand Plan had engaged him in the biggest gamble a commander could take. Not only was he committing all his reserves, but by using student crews and the instructors who trained them, he was risking the very future of Bomber Command. The weather was chancy, yet time was running out on the full moon. Another postponement would mean putting off the raid for nearly a month. By then, Bomber Command might be "frittered away," as Harris later put it, to other fronts.

The drama of the decisive moment was described by one of the aides, Group Captain Dudley Saward:

"The C.-in-C. moved at last. Slowly he pulled an American cigarette carton from his pocket, and, flicking the bottom with his thumb, selected the protruding Lucky Strike. He lit the cigarette and then drew from his right breast pocket a short, stocky cigarette holder. Very deliberately he pressed the cigarette into the end of the holder and grasped it firmly between his teeth. He continued to stare at the charts and then slowly his forefinger moved across the continent of Europe and came to rest on a town in Germany. The pressure on his finger bent back the end joint and drove the blood from the top of his finger nail, leaving a half circle of white." Harris turned to Saundby.

"The Thousand Plan tonight."

"His finger," wrote Saward, "was pressing on Cologne."

That afternoon, 53 air stations across England resonated with what one chronicler later called "the dreadful note of preparation." At little-known places such as Binbrook,

The Ruhr region of west-central Germany—a cluster of key industrial cities near the confluence of the Ruhr and Rhine Rivers—was one of the prime targets of the Allied strategic bombing offensive. The British estimated in 1943 that the Ruhr processed more than 60 per cent of Germany's steel and two thirds of the country's high-grade alloyed metals for weapons and aircraft engines. During the next two years, this production was repeatedly reduced by Allied bombing—and restored by the Germans.

Feltwell, Alconbury and Marston Moor, ground crews readied the aircraft and loaded them with bombs ranging from high-explosive 4,000-pounders to four-pound incendiaries. The air crews, in the meantime, tried to snatch a little sleep. There were 1,046 crews in all, an unprecedented air army of some 6,000 men—Englishmen, Scots, Canadians, Australians, New Zealanders, Rhodesians, South Africans, Poles and five Americans. The Americans included a boy from Brooklyn, Charles Honeychurch, and a pair of Texans, Bud Cardinal of Fort Worth and Howard L. Tate Jr. of Dallas, who proclaimed themselves members of the "RTAF"—Royal Texan Air Force.

The crews had known for several days that they were in for a "really big show," but they did not learn until 6 p.m. just how big and where. In the briefing rooms at the 53 stations, the windows were closed, blinds drawn, doors locked. Then, with suitable ceremony, the sheet of paper covering the target map was ripped away to reveal the night's destination. The sight of the name brought an audible surge of relief. Many of the men had been to Cologne before and knew that the city was heavily defended; it was ringed by some 500 antiaircraft batteries and 150 searchlights. But there could have been a much worse mission in store; one rumor was that Harris planned to send the crews on a suicidal low-level daylight mission to Hamburg.

Relief gave way to astonishment when the crews were told that 1,000 aircraft would take part in the raid. At one station the men leaped to their feet cheering, and began to dance about and pound one another on the back.

The main concern expressed at the briefings was one that had bothered Harris from the first. With more than 1,000 planes concentrated over the target in a 90-minute period, the specter of collisions loomed frighteningly large. But Harris' technical experts—whom the crews called "boffins"—had assured him that this danger would be minimal if three different aiming points were designated and if the attack force was divided into three parallel bomber streams over the target.

The briefing officer at one station reported: "The boffins are confident that the risk is negligible. They have assessed the chances at one in a thousand." There was a murmur of skepticism as the audience pondered the likelihood that the congestion caused by all those planes twisting, turning, diving and climbing over the target could result in only one collision. After a time someone piped up: "Have the boffins worked out which two aircraft it will be?"

A gale of laughter broke the tension. The briefing officer then read a special message sent from Harris himself, urging the crews "to strike a blow at the enemy which will resound, not only throughout Germany, but through-

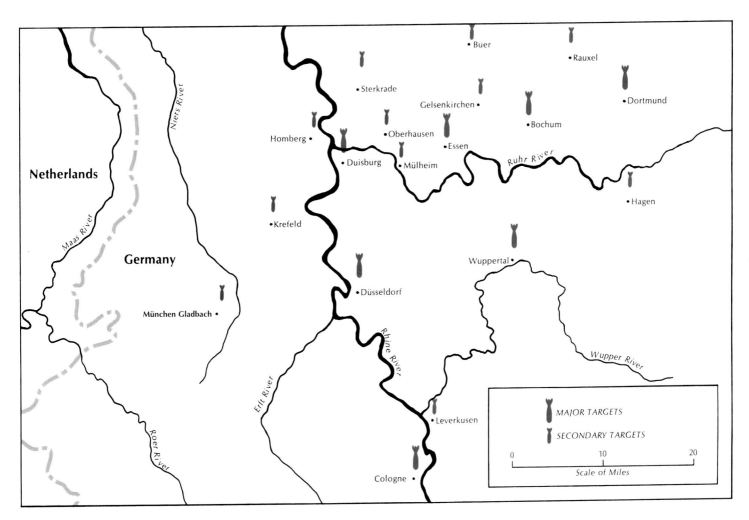

out the world. . . . Let him have it—right on the chin."

When the first bombers rumbled down the flare-lit runways at about 10 p.m., however, Harris was not there to see them off. He was just sitting down to dinner at Chequers with the Prime Minister and selling the merits of his night offensive to Churchill's other guests, a delegation of American brass that included the commanding general of the United States Army Air Forces, Henry H. "Hap" Arnold.

By midnight the planes had taken off. The bomber stream stretched across the North Sea into Holland. It was an awesome procession, some 70 miles long, with the planes flying at various altitudes over a span of about 4,000 feet.

The planes were a mixture of the old and the new. About 70 per cent of the force was made up of the old more-or-less reliables—the twin-engined bombers that had been waging war against Germany for almost three years now and were soon to be replaced. Among them were the ungainly Whitley and the odd-shaped Hampden, whose crews called it the "frying pan." By far the best as well as the most numerous of the old bombers was the fabric-covered Wellington, better known as the "Wimpy," named for the hamburger-loving character in the Popeye cartoons, J. Wellington Wimpy. The Wellington's rugged "basket-weave" construction enabled it to absorb considerable battle damage and keep flying. Some 600 Wellingtons were taking part in the raid.

The remainder of the force consisted of 338 of the newer heavy bombers—the twin-engined Manchester and the four-engined Stirling, Halifax and Lancaster. Of these, the Stirling and the Manchester had already proved so disappointing that they were gradually being phased out of long-range bombing. The Stirling was limited by a ceiling of about 16,000 feet as a result of design specifications drawn up to fit conditions in the late 1930s: its short 99-foot wingspan had been dictated by the 100-foot width of RAF hangar doors in those days.

The twin-engined Manchester was woefully underpowered. That weakness, however, had led to the birth of a powerful bigger brother. The basic Manchester had been redesigned and equipped with four Rolls-Royce Merlin engines, the same power plant used on the agile Spitfire fighter. The new plane had been rechristened the Lancaster; Harris was later to claim that it was "the greatest single

factor in winning the war." With a seven-ton load of bombs, the Lancaster could cruise at 210 miles per hour over a range of 1,660 miles. It could climb on two engines and come home on one.

Bringing up the rear of the bomber stream were approximately 75 Lancasters and 130 Halifaxes, the heavy bombers that ranked next to the Lancasters in performance. The job of this last bomber wave was to spend the final 15 minutes of the raid over Cologne delivering the knockout blow with high-explosive 1,000- and 4,000-pounders.

The bomber stream lacked fighter escorts, but an intruder force of 50 planes had been sent ahead to keep the German night fighters busy. The intruders—light bombers from Bomber Command and fighter-bombers from RAF Fighter Command—attacked enemy night-fighter bases in the areas of Holland, Belgium, northern France and western Germany straddling the bomber-stream route to Cologne.

Before too long, however, the bomber stream started to shrink. A few of the planes were pounced on by German fighters, Messerschmitt-110s and Junkers-88s, as they crossed the Kammhuber Line. Many more, especially the patched-up older aircraft, developed mechanical problems or ran into severe icing conditions over the North Sea and were forced to turn back. These so-called boomerangs totaled more than 100.

As the Gee-equipped lead planes approached the German border, less than an hour from Cologne, the predicted break in the weather was nowhere to be seen. Then, suddenly, as they moved toward the target, the clouds broke; the full moon flooded the night with light. The crews of the lead Stirlings and Wellingtons could see the Rhine glistening some 15,000 feet below them. Like a great crooked arrow, the river pointed toward the heart of Cologne.

Among the first planes over the target were a pair of Stirlings piloted by Wing Commander J. C. Macdonald and Squadron Leader R. S. Gilmour. Their aiming point was an area known as the Neumarkt, which was located in the center of Cologne's old city on the left bank of the Rhine. The aiming points of other planes lay a mile to the north and a mile to the south.

Macdonald and Gilmour could see Cologne's celebrated 13th Century cathedral northeast of the Neumarkt. The

During a raid staged on March 8, 1942, British bombs score direct hits on the Matford works, a German-run truck factory in Poissy, France. This attack was followed up by two more in April, reducing the factory's production level from close to 1,000 vehicles per month to a mere trickle.

cathedral was not a target, though some of the student crews from the training units had been ordered to aim at its twin towers. That, so the reasoning went, was bound to ensure the cathedral against damage—and, in fact, the damage proved to be relatively minor.

At 12:47 a.m.—eight minutes ahead of schedule—the two Stirlings released their incendiary bombs to start fires as beacons for the bombers to follow. Below them, the residents of Germany's third-largest city were hurrying to underground shelters, roused from their predawn Sunday sleep by the routine wail of air-raid sirens half an hour earlier. In all, since the War's start, the 800,000 residents of Cologne had endured 106 bombing attacks. But the British took pains to inform them that this one would be worse than the rest. Along with the falling incendiaries, the vanguard planes dropped leaflets warning: "The offensive of the RAF in its new form has begun."

For the first 15 or so minutes of the raid, the new form of offensive was chaotic. The 100 planes of the first wave, carrying incendiaries to mark the way for the next wave, ran into heavy flak and began weaving to avoid being hit. Some pilots—either confused or unable to break their old freelance habit of approaching a target in whatever way they found convenient—ignored briefing orders to follow predetermined paths and made direct bombing runs on their own. Others dropped their bombs, then lingered, circling the city to watch while Cologne began to burn. "There were aircraft everywhere," a crew member recalled. "The sky over Cologne was as busy as Piccadilly Circus."

With the planes converging willy-nilly from every direction, the risk of collision multiplied. A Wellington rose slightly; the Stirling above it dipped. The propellers of the Wellington sheared off the tail of the Stirling. The Wellington blew up; the Stirling plummeted into the flaming city. It was the first of two collisions—only twice the number predicted by Harris' "boffins."

Shortly after 1 a.m., just as the second wave of bombers—the main force—reached Cologne, the German gun batteries suddenly went silent. Searchlights continued to probe the crowded skies, apparently setting the stage for the German night fighters to enter the arena. But because of an administrative mix-up at the local air-defense command, the interceptors remained on the ground. When the German batteries finally started firing again, they were overwhelmed by the RAF bombers. Bomber crews later reported that the defenses—plus the few interceptors that did get off the ground—seemed "weak and confused."

Most of the bombers in the main attack force thus encountered little difficulty over Cologne. The exceptions tended to be the underpowered twin-engined Manchesters. The 20-year-old pilot of one Manchester, Flying Officer Leslie Manser, found that he had to fly at about 7,000 feet—less than half the altitude of many of the other bombers—because his engines overheated if he tried to climb. At that height his Manchester found itself alone, a stray that was now a sitting duck for the frustrated German searchlight and gun crews. Caught in a cone of searchlights, Manser held the plane straight and level over the aiming point. Then his navigator, Richard Barnes, who was known as "Bang On" Barnes for his accuracy in getting to a target, reported: "Bombs gone." Almost immediately, the Manchester was rocked by a direct flak hit in the bomb bay.

Manser had to fight to control the plane. To elude the searchlights, he resorted to the classic tactic, "Fly straight down the beam," and went into a steep dive. At 800 feet, he wrestled the control stick back and began climbing into the darkness. But his port engine overheated under the strain and burst into flame.

The five men of Manser's crew, watching the fire spread along the wing toward the fuel tank, were ready to bail out. Manser told them to hold on; he hoped they could somehow make it back home or at least to the English Channel. The fire on the port wing stopped short of the tank, but the starboard engine began to fail. Some time later, when the plane was over Belgium and rapidly losing altitude, Manser ordered the bailout. A crewman named Leslie Baveystock tried to fasten Manser's parachute on him but was thrust away. There was scarcely time left for Baveystock to escape—and none for Manser. Less than 200 feet from the ground, Baveystock jumped. Though his parachute did not open completely, the water in a drainage ditch broke his fall. Some 100 yards beyond the ditch, the Manchester crashed and burned, with Manser still at the controls.

Bang On Barnes was captured by the Germans. Baveystock and the other three members of the crew, with the help of the Belgian underground, eventually made it back to England. Their story of Manser's heroism resulted in his receiving the posthumous award of the Victoria Cross, Britain's highest military honor.

Cologne had been under attack for 75 minutes when the heavy Lancasters and Halifaxes of the third and final wave began their approach. The city was burning with such fury that the crews first saw the crimson glow while flying over the Dutch islands nearly 150 miles away. Leonard Cheshire, piloting a Halifax, thought that it was "the most monstrous sight in all the history of bombing" and later recalled feeling "a slight chill in my heart." Then his thoughts turned to his brother Christopher, a bomber pilot who had been shot down and was now in a German prisoner-of-war camp, and the chill faded.

When the third wave reached Cologne, the aiming points were dense with flames: an area three miles long and two miles wide was solidly ablaze. Many of the newly arrived bombers sought out peripheral targets. At 2:25 a.m., precisely on schedule, the last bombs were dropped and the planes turned for home.

All, that is, but one lone straggler. A Lancaster piloted by Flight Lieutenant George Gilpin had taken off so late that, as it flew high over the North Sea, it met bombers returning from the raid. But Gilpin had been so determined to go on the raid that he had put together a scratch crew, including a navigator to serve as one of his gunners.

Now, though he was aware that his plane would never make it home under the cover of darkness—the 2:25 a.m. deadline for the final bombing had been set for just that reason—Gilpin flew on. Alone over Cologne at 3:10 a.m., his Lancaster released its bombs into a pillar of smoke that rose 15,000 feet above the city. The bombs brought the total dropped by the British to 1,455 tons. When Gilpin's Lancaster finally limped home on three engines, daylight had long since descended on his base at Syerston. His was the 898th plane to bomb the target that night and return home safely.

In Cologne the glare of the burning city outshone even the sun. Some 600 acres lay in flaming ruins. More than 250 factories—including metal and rubber and chemical works, and plants that manufactured machine tools and submarine engines—were either destroyed or badly damaged. The dead numbered 474. More than 45,000 people were homeless, and the roads leading out of Cologne were clogged with refugees. So many people were fleeing the stricken city that local officials fretted about the demoralizing effect on the rest of Germany and made a futile attempt to hush up eyewitness accounts of the horror.

Air Chief Marshal Harris, with one massive stroke, had restored British confidence in strategic bombing and given new hope to the Allies, at a time when they were still in retreat on other fronts. The cost of the Cologne mission was less than either Harris or Churchill had anticipated—40 of 1,046 bombers, or 3.8 per cent. Soon after the raid Harris was knighted. On June 17, 1942, "Sir Bomber" Harris—as the irreverent now called him—wrote Churchill a memo on how to win the War. It began: "Victory, speedy and complete, awaits the side which first employs air power as it should be employed."

But in the weeks following Cologne, Harris could not repeat his success. On June 1, two nights after Operation *Millennium,* he launched another huge strike against Essen. Though he sent forth 956 bombers, a combination of cloudy weather, heavy flak and the lack of easily identifiable landmarks prevented them from attaining good concentration over the Ruhr city. Three weeks later, on the night of June 25, Harris sent 904 bombers against the North Sea port of Bremen, a submarine-building center, with only limited success and the loss of 49 planes.

Meanwhile, less than a month after its ordeal by fire, Cologne was returning to normal, a sign of the remarkable resiliency of Germany's city dwellers. As Harris later conceded: "Not one or two such strokes, but the cumulative effect of hundreds of them, would be needed before the enemy felt the pinch."

Such an offensive could not be sustained by Bomber Command until it grew bigger. By mid-August of 1942, Harris was averaging fewer than 300 planes on major attacks, and he could no longer rely on Gee, which the enemy was beginning to jam.

Harris needed some help in his night offensive, and he thought that he could get it from the Americans, who were now building up a bomber force in England. But the Americans, even though they were extremely impressed by the master stroke against Cologne, had their own ideas about how to bomb Germany out of the War.

ALL-SEEING EYES IN THE SKY

AIR RECONNAISSANCE COMES OF AGE

Early in the War, the RAF dispatched a series of Blenheim bombers to photograph German naval operations in the North Sea; the lumbering Blenheims were all shot down or driven off before they could complete the job. The failure nettled Sidney Cotton, an intrepid Australian flier who, in the guise of a salesman of aeronautical products, had delighted British officials with his prewar airborne espionage across Germany. Cotton, now a civilian photographic consultant to the RAF, took off in his swift, camera-equipped spy plane *(left)* and returned in hours with the photos.

This flight proved Cotton's then-radical concept of wartime aerial photography: the plane had to be fast enough to evade Luftwaffe fighters, and it should be stripped of guns and radio to make room for extra fuel. The RAF put Cotton in charge of revamping its reconnaissance service and began switching its cameras from Blenheims and Ansons to 392-mile-per-hour Spitfires.

Cotton also led in developing the techniques and personnel needed to exploit high-altitude photography. Announcing that photo interpretation required "the patience of Job and the skill of a good darner of socks," he organized a corps of specialists, including many members of the Women's Auxiliary Air Force. By 1942, photos taken by RAF pilots and analyzed by experts were supplying priceless information on the disposition of enemy defenses, the effectiveness of bombing and the location of camouflaged war plants.

Despite the British successes, the new intelligence tools were adopted slowly by the Americans. Early reconnaissance models of the twin-engined Lightning were no match for Luftwaffe fighters. One U.S. recon unit lost more than a quarter of its pilots in its first three months of active duty.

But by 1943 the Americans were catching up. Pilots who had scorned recon flights as unmanly work were now volunteering for the risky missions. One veteran, Lieut. Colonel Karl Polifka, was judged too old, at 33, to fly low-level missions, so he signed up as a Lieutenant Jones. His daredevil dives to photograph German positions at point-blank range made him the best-known recon pilot of the War.

Pioneering aerial espionage, Sidney Cotton boards the Lockheed-12A from which he covertly photographed German war preparations in 1939.

An RAF photographer, seated at the open observation port of a Blenheim bomber in 1940, focuses his cumbersome F.24 camera upon a ground target.

Two U.S. fliers (left) are briefed for a night mission while a sergeant carries a flash bomb for taking photos in the dark.

Two ground crewmen adjust the

Huge telephoto lenses, to be used on high-altitude flights, are checked by a technician for their power to capture details

...aerial cameras in a Lightning's nose. Most Lightnings took three wide-angle cameras for general coverage and two long-lens cameras to zero in on target areas.

NEW EQUIPMENT FOR HIGH-ALTITUDE PHOTOS

As reconnaissance pilots flew higher in order to escape German flak, they discovered that the altitude was as formidable an opponent as the gunners below. In the sub-zero temperatures encountered above 30,000 feet, film cracked inside the cameras and lenses frosted over with condensation. Fortunately for the Allies, Sidney Cotton found an answer: he improvised

ducts that sent warm air from the Spitfire's engine blowing across the cameras.

Cotton's crude heating system eventually was replaced by electrically heated camera covers. Later models of reconnaissance planes were able to photograph at even greater altitudes, using 40-, 50- and 60-inch lenses *(left)* that took clear pictures from as high as eight miles up.

The man who was primarily responsible for the high-powered lenses was George W. Goddard, the U.S. chief of photo research. Goddard also extended photore-

connaissance into the hours of darkness by inventing the "flashlight bomb" *(top left)*, a 50-pound cylinder of magnesium whose explosion illuminated a ground area and, at the same time, tripped a photoelectric camera shutter. For fast, lower-level reconnaissance, Goddard helped to develop an ingenious shutterless camera that recorded enemy positions on a continuous strip of film. And to speed film processing, Goddard designed portable field laboratories and a printing machine that churned out 1,000 photos per hour.

On a low-level reconnaissance of the Saar River, U.S. Captain Robert Holbury photographed an uncompleted bridge and German fortifications. His Lightnin

LOW-LEVEL FLIGHTS INTO ENEMY GUNFIRE

Photographs of strategic targets, such as the German war plant at top right, were usually taken at flak-free high altitudes. But when ground commanders required

detailed tactical reconnaissance of enemy positions, pilots flew risky low-level sorties, which the British called "dicing runs" because they were gambles with death.

On a dicing run shortly before D-Day, U.S. Captain Charles Batson sped at treetop level along the invasion coast of Normandy. He returned with his engines full

of twigs and leaves and with 130 bullet holes in his plane. But photos by Batson and others pinpointed nearly every German gun and landing obstacle in the area, doubtless saving the lives of thousands of troops on D-Day. Dozens of recon pilots, however, made one flight too many and failed to return; Batson was among them

was so badly shot up that it had to be junked.

Photos taken before and after an RAF raid reveal that bombs nearly destroyed a Cologne tire factory

SEEING THROUGH THE CAMOUFLAGE

Without waiting for prints, a pilot and an interpreter make a preliminary study of negatives.

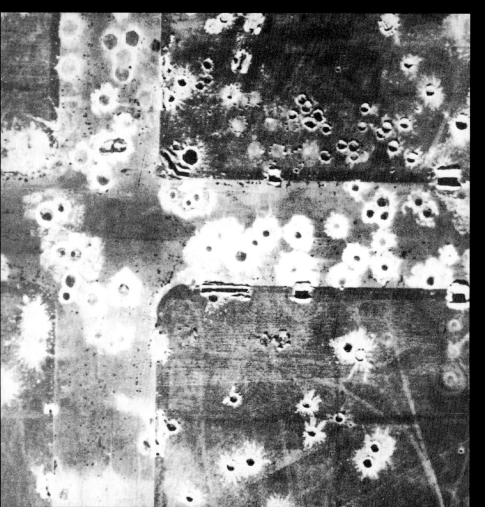

As Allied air forces began their heavy day and night bombing of Germany in 1943, the Germans tried with increasing desperation to hide their vital installations from the prying eyes of reconnaissance planes and the bombers that soon followed them. Enormous camouflage nets were draped over navigational landmarks—such as Berlin's broad boulevard Unter den Linden —to confuse Allied bombardiers. German specialists in camouflage applied paint in ingenious ways to disguise factories and military depots. And in Rumania, carpenters constructed an enormous wood and canvas replica of a refinery, complete with fire-making devices that sent up plumes of oily smoke.

But Allied photo interpreters rose to the challenge. They detected camouflaged installations by studying pictures taken at various times of the day; painted shadows did not move with the sun. A German airfield, camouflaged with painted extensions of the irrigation ditches from a nearby farm, was finally discovered when water in the real ditches froze and produced a telltale reflection in aerial photos.

The very thoroughness of German camouflage artists was sometimes their undoing. At U-boat shipyards in Kiel, camouflage nets were neatly extended as each section of the hull was completed; simply by measuring a lengthening net, Allied experts could predict exactly when the submarine would be launched.

Laborers drafted by the Germans built a wood and canvas replica of
Czechoslovakia's Škoda arms works (above and below left) to draw Allied
bombers away from the real factory in Pilsen (below right), three miles
away. The decoy was close enough to fool Allied airmen on one mission.

THE PUZZLING VIEW FROM MILES UP

Before their unit moved ahead to Europe, inexperienced American photograph analysts made an embarrassing mistake in the North African campaign. In studying a set of photos, they interpreted a suspicious line as a column of German tanks. British mobile forces raced some 60 miles to intercept the tank column, only to find out that it was actually a camel caraven.

The reason for the novices' mistake is unmistakably clear in the 11 aerial views of occupied Europe shown on these pages. Like most recon photos, they were taken at very high altitudes, and ground objects show up as baffling shapes and patterns. Well-seasoned analysts were expected to solve hundreds of such visual riddles every day—and they usually did.

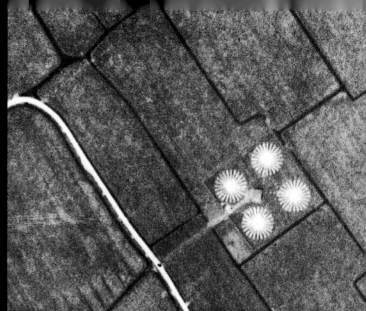

GERMAN DIRECTION-FINDING RADIO MASTS

HERRINGBONE PATTERNS OF DRAINAGE DITCHES

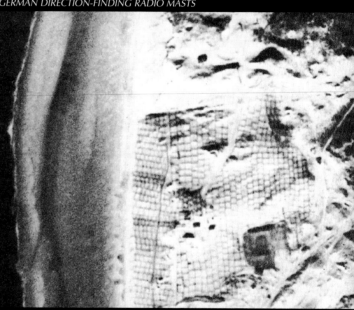

PATCHES OF GRASS ON SAND DUNES

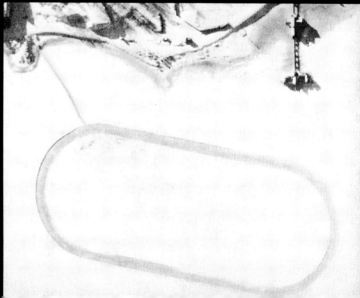

ROWS OF CIRCULAR TENTS IN A GERMAN CAMP

A SUBDIVISION OF THREE-WING HOUSE

HUTS AND PENS OF A FOX FARM

UNDERWATER SHELLFISH-CULTURE BEDS

Peering through a stereoscope, a photo interpreter moves two prints until the separate images seem to merge into a single three-dimensional view.

TRANSLATING PICTURES INTO THREE DIMENSIONS

The intelligence gleaned from aerial photos was usually disseminated in the form of written target reports soon after the recon pilot returned. For particularly important operations, expert craftsmen translated the evidence of the photographs into three-dimensional models of the target area.

After studying pairs of photos under a stereoscope *(above)*, interpreters provided the modelmakers with the precise dimensions of objects in the target area. The craftsmen then constructed a scale model that included each natural and man-made feature more than three feet high. Artists painted this miniature landscape, taking care to reproduce the foliage colors of the season.

Bomber crews found the models invaluable for target recognition and analysis of enemy defenses. By walking around the models, they could see, in depth, exactly what their objective would look like on approach from any direction or altitude—information that not even the sharpest aerial photograph could provide.

man synthetic-oil refinery in painstaking detail. It includes every bomb crater from previous raids and even shows the different crops in the surrounding fields.

3

The American fliers who began swarming into England in the summer of 1942 brought to the air war a flamboyant style and a controversial bombing strategy. Equally free with their money, their emotions and their opinions, they were the first Americans to inspire the celebrated British lament that "the trouble with the Yanks is they're overpaid, oversexed and over here."

A graphic example of the American style was the way the air crews personalized their big bombers. In contrast to the RAF crews, who gave their planes such staid names as "E for Edward," the Americans came up with suggestive puns like "Ima Vailable" and "Dinah Might"—and with illustrations to match. One visiting U.S. congressman, after inspecting several of these raffish displays on the sides of American planes, advised adding some clothes to the female figures to avoid offending any chance viewers. The proposal was impassively received and promptly forgotten.

The projected strategy of the Americans unsettled the British even more than their style. The newcomers intended to attempt something the RAF believed was just about hopeless—to bomb Germany successfully by day. The RAF had tried daylight bombing periodically since the start of the War and had suffered severe losses; its night attacks had proved more effective and less costly. Air Chief Marshal Harris and his staff at RAF Bomber Command were convinced that if the U.S. joined the RAF's night missions, the War could be shortened by many months. But in their efforts to push this idea, they found themselves up against a stone wall. "War without allies," Air Vice-Marshal John Slessor observed, "is bad enough—with allies it is hell."

The Americans preferred the daylight-bombing strategy for a variety of reasons. They felt that their four-engined bombers—the B-17 Flying Fortress and the B-24 Liberator—were well equipped to stave off attacks by the Luftwaffe's day fighters; they were better armed than the British bombers, normally carrying up to ten .50-caliber machine guns. And installed on board each B-17 and B-24 was the new Norden bombsight, which was said to be so accurate that the bombardier could "drop a bomb in a pickle barrel" from 20,000 feet. The Americans expected that with the help of this remarkable device they could make short work of German airplane factories, synthetic oil plants and other so-called pinpoint targets. In their view, precision bombing

BOMBING ROUND THE CLOCK

had a pronounced advantage over area bombing, the British practice. They believed that precision bombing could cripple Germany faster and more efficiently while causing fewer civilian casualties. Besides, the very notion of precision bombing appealed to the American psyche: it summoned up the old frontier pride in marksmanship.

British planners were cool toward the projected American strategy, and none more so than Harris. The leader of Bomber Command had already heard the case for precision bombing from a number of his own countrymen; once, in a moment of fury, he had suggested that such "panacea mongers" were the tools of a German plot. Though he sometimes employed precision bombing when it suited a particular mission, he regarded it as essentially a futile exercise. The Germans, he argued, could easily repair or otherwise compensate for the damage to a pinpoint target.

Harris also opposed the American plan on a technical basis. He did not share the Yanks' high regard for their Flying Fortresses. Early in 1941, a score of Forts—as they were called—had been sent across the Atlantic for the British to use on daylight missions and, in Harris' words, "got the hell shot out of them." From their performance in action, he had concluded that they were too slow and clumsy. Worse still, they accommodated only about half of the bombload carried by his beloved Lancaster. Harris clearly felt that the Americans could better apply their rising industrial might to turning out Lancasters.

As for the Norden bombsight, Harris pointed out that its only tests thus far had taken place under ideal circumstances: during practice missions in the sunny, cloudless—and flak-less—skies of the U.S. Southwest. The skies over Germany were seldom as benign; thick cloud cover, or the haze and smoke of German industry, could turn the bombsight into a useless toy. Allan Michie, an American war correspondent who interviewed Harris, reported his summing up of the problem in one pithy sentence: "In order to hit a barrel from 20,000 feet, *you must first see the barrel.*"

Behind these specific criticisms lay a basic worry that Harris left unspoken. The British now saw themselves cast in the irksome position of a seasoned veteran confronted by a younger brother who has suddenly acquired new muscle and a know-it-all air to boot. Though they genuinely admired the Americans' talent for organizing and zest for experimenting, they felt that they had a lot to teach the novices from the States.

The Americans, for their part, genuinely admired the RAF's battle record, particularly the 1,000-plane raid on Cologne, but they did not feel that experience guaranteed freedom from error. They believed, for example, that the British had botched the handling of the Flying Fortresses sent over for their use in 1941. While conceding that these planes—an early model known as the B-17C—needed improving, the Americans were annoyed by the British failure to exploit the Fortresses' strong point. Forts were intended to fly in massed formation, a dozen or more together, so that their firepower could be brought to bear collectively against an attacker. RAF Bomber Command had chosen to avoid large formations and had dispatched the Forts instead in twos and threes—with costly results.

The Americans' irritation at this outcome reached all the way to the top. General Arnold, chief of the Army Air Forces—whose nickname "Hap" was short for Happy, his normal disposition—later recalled the Fort episode in blistering terms. The first B-17s, he wrote, "were so badly mishandled by R.A.F. Bomber Command's people that it was obvious it was their place to learn; and they didn't."

Clearly, the Americans did not intend to be treated as younger brothers, or even as junior partners.

Unlike the British, the Americans who believed in air power had been compelled to campaign long and hard before their cause was won. One of their first problems had been to persuade doubters of the basic worth of the airplane. In 1921—three years after the Royal Air Force had been officially accorded equal status with Britain's Army and Navy—the people of San Francisco engaged in a spirited debate as to which traveled faster: a plane or a pigeon. A local newspaper had raised the issue, and the man who finally laid it to rest was Hap Arnold, then a major in the Army's Air Service. Arnold got a coop of carrier pigeons from the Signal Corps, released them at Portland, Oregon, and raced them to San Francisco. The birds made it in 48 hours, Arnold's plane in seven and a half—and his lighthearted stunt earned a handsome publicity dividend for the cause.

Arnold and his friends in the Air Service openly rallied around Billy Mitchell when America's most vocal advocate of air power was court-martialed in 1925. Their show of support did not sit well with General Mitchell's foes among the Army's top brass. Arnold, for one, was exiled from Washington, where he held a post as an information officer, to Fort Riley, Kansas, where he was put in charge of a squadron of rickety observation planes.

Clearly, the argument that the plane had enormous military potential needed more evidence of a solid sort. Such evidence could be amassed only by the development of new aerial devices and techniques and by patient probes of the airplane's capabilities. Much had been achieved along those lines in the early 1920s. The effort was now intensified in an all-out drive "to expand the limits of aeronautical knowledge," as one account described it.

Among the successes of import for the future were several record-breaking feats of long-range and endurance flying. In January of 1929, a trimotor Fokker monoplane named "Question Mark" took to the skies over Southern California and—thanks in part to the recently developed technique of refueling in mid-air—remained aloft for an unprecedented stretch of more than 150 hours. The plane also made history of another kind. The project's leader was

Major Carl "Tooey" Spaatz, the chief pilot Captain Ira C. Eaker. Spaatz, 13 years later, was to be chosen to direct all American air operations over Europe as commander of the U.S. Eighth Air Force; Eaker was to direct the Eighth's bombers in their strikes at German targets from bases in England.

Throughout the 1930s, the champions of air power kept pleading their cause with a largely uncaring government in Washington. They sought greater autonomy within the Army; though the Air Service had been renamed the Air Corps, it was answerable to the Army General Staff and had little authority of its own. More important, the Corps wanted money to train many more pilots and to finance the building of many more planes—especially heavy bombers.

The opposition was multiple: from Army chiefs unwilling to yield any meaningful control to the Corps, from others in the military with a total faith in ground and sea power, from congressmen dead-set against large-scale spending. The economic depression of the 1930s was itself an obstacle. With the drop in federal revenues, every request for appropriations was closely scrutinized; even when it was approved, the funds did not always follow.

The Air Corps also ran into trouble by harping on the need for heavy bombers. Most military thinkers strongly disagreed. They believed that the function of the Corps in a war would be to help the Navy defend America's coasts and to provide support for the Army's ground forces—and that neither task would require heavy bombers. Aircraft of such power suggested independent offensive missions, and these were flatly ruled out by a special fact-finding board set up by the War Department in 1934. Independent air missions, the board concluded, "have little effect upon the issue of battle and none upon the outcome of war." After two years, the Air Corps managed to win approval to order the first of its heavy bombers—the Flying Fortress —but by 1939 it had only 13 on hand and 40 on order.

More than a decade before becoming air war commanders, Captain Ira C. Eaker and Major Carl Spaatz (second and fourth from left) stand with associates alongside their Fokker monoplane "Question Mark," after setting an endurance record of more than six days in the air. The marathon flight, in January 1929, was made possible by a series of 43 mid-air linkups with a Douglas C-1 transport (upper plane, above), which poured fuel into the Fokker through a borrowed fire hose.

The outbreak of war in Europe that September, and the sudden boom in the U.S. aircraft industry as a result of a rush of British and French orders, muted much of the antagonism to air power. But the last vestiges of opposition faded only after the fall of France in June of 1940 attested to the Luftwaffe's might. Later that month Hap Arnold, now chief of the Air Corps, went to Capitol Hill to talk about appropriations. He was assured that any amount he named would be granted. Senator Henry Cabot Lodge Jr. told him: "All you have to do is ask for it."

The Air Corps took full advantage of its blank check. From the 26,000 men and 800 first-line combat planes it had numbered in September of 1939, it expanded to 354,000 men and 2,846 planes just before Pearl Harbor in December of 1941; by then the Corps had been reconstituted as the Army Air Forces. By the spring of 1945, the AAF would reach a peak strength of 2.4 million men and nearly 80,000 planes.

Less than three months after Japan's attack on Pearl Harbor plunged the U.S. into the War, Ira Eaker, now a brigadier general, arrived in England to set up headquarters for the newly formed Eighth Air Force's Bomber Command and to arrange the reception of its first combat units. Luck attended Eaker's own trip to England. Since military aircraft for such uses were still scarce, he and his advance staff of six took a commercial airliner, by way of neutral Portugal, and narrowly escaped an apparent attempt by a German interceptor to shoot down the plane over the Bay of Biscay.

By coincidence, Eaker reached England shortly before Air Chief Marshal Harris took over RAF Bomber Command. That Sunday the two men walked to church together, talking all the while about the hellfire they intended to visit upon Germany, and formed an immediate liking for each other. Like Harris, Eaker had been an early and fervent convert to strategic air power and had never swerved in his belief; he had even put his military career on the line by serving on the defense staff at Billy Mitchell's court-martial. The affinity that Eaker and Harris felt for each other was not only personal but also professional—what a sentimentalist once described as "the bond that makes all airmen one."

Harris invited Eaker to stay at his home until Eaker could get settled. On April 13, Harris' 50th birthday and Eaker's 46th, they held a joint celebration. They also shared a few laughs about the headquarters Eaker had chosen near Harris' command post at High Wycombe—an imposing country house that had served as an exclusive school for the daughters of what Harris called "the port-drinking classes." On the night the Americans moved in, the duty officer was startled to hear a sudden cacophony of bells. It turned out that each of the bedrooms contained a relic of its recent past as a girls' dormitory—a placard proclaiming, "Ring twice for mistress"—and the new tenants were complying.

Once settled in, Eaker had to deal with a logistical problem of staggering dimensions. Sites for his bomber bases had to be selected and built up to house personnel and planes. Much of the Americans' equipment, including the bombers, had to be ferried by air nearly 3,500 miles across the North Atlantic in the face of fierce weather. The logistical problem was further complicated by the Americans' penchant for clinging to little bits of home. The amused aeronautical correspondent for the London *Times* reported: "They have actually brought with them their own dustbins—garbage cans, they call them."

Eaker had the wholehearted cooperation of Harris in his gigantic task. Harris smoothed the way for the establishment of the first of some 60 bases that the Eighth Air Force eventually occupied and helped to ease the training headaches of Eaker's embryonic bomber force. Many of Eaker's gunners had never practiced firing from a moving aircraft; some of his new radio operators were still unfamiliar with Morse code. Harris provided facilities where the rookie American crewmen could brush up on their skills.

Harris' growing regard for Eaker was soon echoed in other British quarters. At one point Eaker was introduced at a community gathering in the town of High Wycombe. The audience, including many British soldiers and sailors, no doubt expected the cocksure American of legend, or at least a facsimile of Harris at his most theatrical. Eaker turned out to be a model of soft-spoken tact. "We won't do much talking until we've done more fighting," he told the crowd. "We hope that when we leave, you'll be glad we came."

Though such modesty would later prove appropriate, the results of the early U.S. bomber raids exceeded expectations. The first raid oganized by Americans took place on the 17th of August, 1942. A dozen Flying Fortresses left their base at Grafton Underwood in eastern England. Protected by four squadrons of RAF Spitfire fighters, they flew 200 miles to the French city of Rouen, northwest of Paris, and dropped 18.5 tons of bombs on railway marshaling yards and repair shops. All the Forts returned safely, though two sustained slight damage from German flak.

By the standards of the RAF, which had been bombing Germany for 27 months with payloads up to 80 times the tonnage dropped on Rouen, the raid was scarcely what the British called a "really big show." But it was a promising beginning. Only after experimental pinpricks against lightly defended nearby targets in France, Holland and Belgium would the American airmen be ready for what they called "the big league"—Germany.

Eaker himself went along on the mission to Rouen because he wanted a close-up look at combat conditions and because, as he later put it, "I don't want any American mothers to think I'd send their boys someplace where I'd be afraid to go myself." His plane was aptly named "Yankee Doodle," and the following day he received a congratulatory telegram from his British counterpart. "Yankee Doodle certainly went to town," Harris had written, "and can stick yet another well-deserved feather in his cap."

Two days after their mission to Rouen, the Americans returned to France to bomb a German fighter base at Abbeville near the Channel coast. The reconnaissance photographs from this raid, and from the one at Rouen, showed such bombing accuracy that even the reticent Eaker could not contain his jubilation. Extrapolating from the results of both raids, he submitted an excessively optimistic report to Eighth Air Force. Eaker predicted that 10 per cent of the bombs dropped would be dead on the aiming point and that fully 90 per cent would be within a one-mile radius of

it. By comparison, the British night offensive was getting only 5 per cent of the bombs within a mile of the aiming point. "It is safe and conservative to say, therefore," Eaker concluded, "that high-level day bombing will be at least ten times as effective for the destruction of definite point targets as night area bombing."

By early October of 1942, "Eaker's amateurs"—as some RAF officers liked to call them—had flown 13 missions against German targets in France, Belgium and Holland. Despite dire British predictions, they had lost only two bombers to German interceptors and flak. Skeptics began to take notice of qualities they had overlooked. An article in London's *Evening Standard,* remarking at the stamina that enabled American crews to operate from such high altitudes as 26,000 feet without passing out, speculated that they were superior physical specimens—the result no doubt of playing baseball. The superspecimen legend grew when a British doctor went up with one American crew to study the effects of high-altitude flying and quickly fainted. Apparently he had improperly fitted the oxygen mask that was required gear under such conditions.

Some of the steam began to go out of the RAF campaign to convert the Americans to the night-bombing strategy. In a private memorandum to Chief of the Air Staff Portal, Air Vice-Marshal Slessor wrote of the Americans: "They are, I think, a bit unwarrantably cock-a-hoop as a result of their limited experience to date. But they are setting about it in a realistic and business-like way. . . . I have a feeling they will do it. . . . They have hung their hats on the day bomber policy and are convinced they can do it."

On October 9 the Americans mounted their most ambitious raid to date, a mission against the steelworks at Lille in

A Yank in the RAF, Eugene "Red" Tobin prepares his Hurricane fighter for takeoff from a British air base in 1941. Tobin was a member of one of three RAF Eagle Squadrons composed entirely of Americans who volunteered to fight before the United States entered the War. The squadrons were responsible for destroying more than 70 German aircraft from February 1941 until they were incorporated into the U.S. Army Air Forces in September of 1942.

northern France. The force of 108 bombers included, for the first time, B-24 Liberators. A friendly rivalry had already developed between the crews of the Liberators and the Flying Fortresses. Liberator crewmen boasted about their plane's 225-mile-per-hour speed—14 miles an hour faster than the Fort's—and its greater bombload capacity. Fort crews touted the B-17's ability to fly at higher altitudes and to withstand greater damage, and scoffed at the Liberator's graceless, boxlike fuselage. The Liberator, they joked, was actually the crate that the Fort was shipped in.

That day over Lille, the crews of neither Liberators nor Forts had much to brag about. Due to mechanical failures and human error, only 69 planes managed to reach the primary target; only nine bombs fell within 500 yards of the aiming point. Moreover, the crews had their first taste of heavy opposition from the Luftwaffe. "Lille was our first real brawl," one navigator later recalled.

Still, the Americans returned to base feeling that they had scored a triumph. Against the loss of three Forts and a Liberator, they claimed no fewer than 56 German fighters shot down. The claims proved to be preposterous. Double-checking by Allied intelligence cut the estimate by almost half, while the Germans' own records put their fighter loss at exactly two. In the confusion of battle, some American gunners had laid claim to the same plane. The German fighter pilots had compounded the chance for error by playing possum—deliberately deceiving the enemy by flipping over their planes and plunging them earthward with smoke pouring from the exhausts (smoke pots were sometimes installed to enhance the illusion).

The inflated claims of the Americans reflected their euphoria at this stage in the air war. Eaker's airmen had been flying under excellent conditions: fighter escort to and from the French coast by British Spitfires and U.S. Lightnings and—before Lille—relatively little show of interest by the Luftwaffe. Now, however, the problems began piling up.

The weather itself became a prime obstacle. Eaker was receiving extremely accurate forecasts of conditions over Europe through Ultra, the remarkable British system for cracking German coded messages, and the reports were mostly bad. The weather over England was no better. For the American airmen, it was a new experience, as an officer said, "to start down the runway in sunshine and before clearing the ground to be in the midst of a downpour."

In the 12 days after the raid on Lille, the weather forced cancellation of 11 U.S. missions, and only 12 were flown all through November and December. Many of the cancellations came after the bombers were airborne—a special blow to morale since abortive missions did not count toward the 25 that were required to complete a tour of duty in England. One American gunner later estimated that he had gone through briefings for 65 missions but had completed only 15; all the rest had been scrubbed.

Another major problem was thrust upon Eaker by the Allied invasion of North Africa in November of 1942. This massive operation not only cost the Eighth Air Force its top-priority claim on new planes and crews but also compelled the transfer of two of its bomber groups from England to support the invaders. Eaker lost nearly 100 of his planes, about a third of his strength. And to prevent U-boat attacks on American and British convoys bound for North Africa, the rest of Eaker's bombers were sent to blast the German submarine bases on France's Atlantic seaboard. The missions proved largely ineffective. The German submarine pens were so massive—the concrete roofs were as much as 12 feet thick—that many of the one-ton U.S. bombs bounced off as harmlessly as marbles on a city pavement.

Moreover, the Luftwaffe's fighters were becoming increasingly aggressive. On November 23, a squadron led by Lieut. Colonel Egon Mayer confronted a number of Flying Fortresses over the submarine base at Saint-Nazaire and dealt them a nasty surprise. Instead of attacking the Forts from the rear—the standard tactic—Mayer and his comrades came at them head on. To make such a frontal assault required nerves of steel; the combined speeds of the bomber and fighter added up to a closing rate of nearly 600 miles per hour, posing the risk of collision. But the Forts were vulnerable up front: the nose lacked a power-operated turret and the hand-maneuvered machine guns mounted there had a limited field of fire. That day, Mayer's head-on tactic cost the Americans four of their 56 Forts. The Germans lost seven of their fighters.

By the end of 1942, the daylight offensive that had begun so hopefully in August was bogging down. Only 27 U.S. missions had been flown in all. The loss rate was only 2 per

this day afforded them at least one luxury: real eggs instead of the customary powdered substitute. Inside the drafty metal Nissen briefing huts on the airfield proper, they struggled, groaning, into their fleece-lined flight suits and gathered together their bulky gear—parachute harness, oxygen mask, escape kit complete with foreign currency in case they were shot down.

So far it had been a normal mission day. In the briefing room, however, they learned that this was to be no ordinary mission. On the big map, the path from home base to target was marked, as usual, by a strand of yarn. But this time the strand did not stop short in France, Belgium or Holland. "Gentlemen," the briefing officer began. Then, with a subtle change in tone that stilled the sleepy murmuring and the idle foot shuffling, he went on: "Gentlemen, the target for today is Germany."

Out of the silent audience came one airman's emphatic response: "Goddam."

The target was Wilhelmshaven, the submarine-building center on the North Sea. It was not, in fact, very far into Germany—only 40 miles from the Dutch border. But none of the previous American raids over occupied territory had involved so long a stretch of time and distance. Getting to Wilhelmshaven and back required a 600-mile flight, most of it without benefit of escort.

The sheer duration of the flight magnified the discomforts, giving the bomber crews a grim preview of what even-longer missions into the Reich would entail. Flying at more than 20,000 feet over France had introduced them to the rigors of cold at high altitudes, but now the cold was protracted; it knifed through layers of clothing to infuse the flesh with a seemingly ineradicable chill. Oxygen masks chafed the cheeks and nose and chin, but they could not be held away from the face for more than 15 or 20 seconds; any longer risked mortal peril.

The need to urinate was another agony, one of the great unmentioned hazards of the air war. Though the planes were supplied with so-called relief tubes, they very rarely worked. The men were compelled to wait many painful hours to use the latrines back at base.

Underlying all the physical torment was a natural human emotion that each man tried to conceal from the others: the fear of dying. As one B-24 copilot later put it: "You don't know what it is to be really scared until you're up in the sky, your fighter cover gone, and you suddenly see an Me-109 coming at you from out of nowhere, with guns blazing. All you can do is listen to your gunners firing back—and pray."

Over Wilhelmshaven that day there was much to be scared about. Of the 91 Fortresses and Liberators that had set out on the mission, only 53 reached the city. More than 100 Luftwaffe fighters swarmed up to meet them. In the savage combat that followed, the Americans claimed seven fighters downed but lost three of their own bombers—a loss rate of more than 5 per cent. Moreover, the cloud cover made accurate bombing difficult; the results of the mission, as one U.S. report described them, were "only fair."

Still, back at base that night the men were in high spirits, jovially arguing at mess about which of their planes had been the first over German soil. But the issue was less than momentous. What mattered was that the Americans had hit Germany at last.

Eaker's amateurs were now in "the big league," and the Germans were impressed. Luftwaffe Lance Corporal Erich Handke, who was aboard one of the twin-engined Me-110s that had taken on the American bombers over Wilhelmshaven, recalled: "The sight put me into a bit of a flap, and

In the company of an armed guard, two student bombardiers (left) head for their plane toting a canvas-covered section of a top-secret Norden bombsight. This section (at top, above) comprised a telescopic sight and a mechanical calculator that computed bomb trajectories, allowing for the plane's speed, altitude and drift. The sight was linked to the plane's automatic pilot; as the bombardier operated the sight, the sight flew the plane.

the others felt the same. We seemed so puny against these four-engined giants."

But the Germans, faced now with defending the homeland against the Americans as well as the British, soon overcame their surprise. When the Eighth Air Force returned to Wilhelmshaven a month later, on February 26, Luftwaffe fighters shot down seven U.S. bombers.

Six American correspondents went along on the mission, the first time that newsmen had been permitted to accompany a U.S. raid over Europe. It was a rugged introduction to what the crewmen had to endure as matter of course—not only the German flak and interceptors but also the intense cold of high-altitude bombing. Frigid air blasted in through the large openings on either side of the fuselage where the waist gunners were stationed. The United Press correspondent, Walter Cronkite, reported that above 20,000 feet he and his colleagues could no longer make notes; the cold actually froze the lead of the pencils. Cronkite summed up the mission as "an assignment to hell—a hell 26,000 feet above the earth."

As aids to survival in this environment, the Eighth Air Force kept devising new equipment and tactics. The crewmen were given new "vests" to protect them from flak. Made of overlapping two-inch-square steel plates on top of heavy canvas, the flak vest proved to be so effective that one bombardier survived unhurt when a 20mm cannon shell exploded only two feet away from his chest. Another innovation that was gradually replacing the crews' leather and fleece-lined clothing was the electric flying suit; it could be plugged in at receptacles inside the bomber.

The new tactics that were worked out had two principal aims: to increase bombing precision and to make the massed bomber formations more invulnerable to Luftwaffe attack. Some of the methods were devised by an irascible, cigar-chomping 36-year-old Ohioan, Colonel Curtis E. LeMay, who commanded the 305th Bombardment Group. LeMay was such a slave driver that his men called him "Iron Ass." In their dispatches home, American correspondents softened the term to "Iron Pants," only to earn LeMay's scornful charge that they feared "offending some delicate old-maid type readers."

LeMay was never to curb his notorious penchant for plain speaking, but in the winter of 1943 he was better known for two tactical innovations. The first was the flying formation known as the "combat box." In contrast to the loose bomber stream used in the British night missions, the Americans' choice of a daylight strategy had required their planes to be tightly bunched for effective defense against attack. Le-May's combat box further strengthened the defense. It consisted of as many as 21 planes staggered vertically and horizontally in such a way that the bombers' guns provided maximum firepower all around, and especially against head-on attacks. On large raids, three of these boxes were formed into a combat wing, with one box in the lead and the others stacked 1,000 feet above and below it.

LeMay's second innovation, designed to increase bombing accuracy, was to place his most proficient crews in the lead planes of the combat boxes. All the planes in the box dropped their bombs simultaneously—but only at the signal of the lead crew. The result, at least in theory, was a closely packed pattern of hits on the target.

These tactics, combined with new flight-control gadgetry,

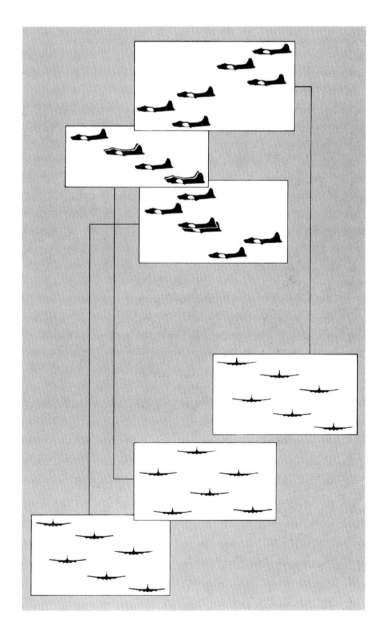

Three squadrons made up of six or seven planes each—here isolated in individual compartments and shown from both the side and front—formed one "combat box," a compact defensive formation devised by Colonel (later General) Curtis E. LeMay to protect unescorted U.S. bomber groups from head-on attacks by Luftwaffe fighters. From the side, the combat box resembled a slanted flying wedge, with the lead squadron in the middle; as seen in the front view, other squadrons were stacked 250 feet to the lead squadron's right and left. This arrangement opened up a clear field of fire for the bombers' forward-firing gunners and enabled them to catch the attacking fighters in coordinated cross fire.

helped the Eighth Air Force achieve its most successful raid to date. The mission, against the submarine-building yards at Vegesack in northwestern Germany, involved an unusually large force of 97 bombers and was carried out on March 18, 1943. The Forts were equipped with the new AFCE—automatic flight control equipment—which provided a link between the bombardier and the aircraft's automatic pilot. This gave the bombardier control of the plane during the crucial bombing run: he flew the plane simply by lining up the cross hairs on his Norden bombsight, which was connected to the automatic pilot. Largely thanks to AFCE, the attackers put 76 per cent of their bombs within 1,000 feet of the aiming point at Vegesack.

Individual acts of heroism also contributed to the mission's success. A Texan, First Lieutenant Jack Mathis, was the bombardier in the 359th Squadron's lead plane. Less than a minute before Mathis was due to release his bombs, flak exploded just outside the nose compartment. The shrapnel nearly severed his right arm and hurled him back nine feet. In great pain, Mathis crawled forward to his bombsight, released the bombs and started to call out over the intercom, "Bombs away." He never finished the familiar phrase; in a few moments he slumped over dead. But he had released his bombs on time and on target, enabling the planes in his box to lay down an effective pattern. Posthumously, Mathis became the first member of the Eighth Air Force to be awarded the Congressional Medal of Honor.

The results at Vegesack—seven U-boats damaged and two thirds of the shipyards destroyed—led Eaker to call a press conference at which he indulged in a rare bit of puffery. Vegesack, he told the assembled reporters, marked "a successful conclusion to long months of experimentation in daytime, high-level precision bombing. After Vegesack comes a new chapter."

Eaker's elation masked some nagging worries. His average daily operational strength in March of 1943 barely exceeded 100 bombers. To replace combat losses, he desperately needed more planes and crews, and he was receiving very few of either. The extent of the manpower shortage was signaled in early April, when Eaker raised from 25 to 30 the number of missions that crews were required to fly to complete a tour of duty. His men now joked that if they didn't survive 25 missions, it wouldn't be so bad—at least they wouldn't have to fly the extra five.

Another of Eaker's problems stemmed from the growing realization that despite the vaunted ability of his bombers to go it alone in the face of enemy attacks, they would fare better with fighter-escort protection. But there were no planes with sufficient range to accompany Eaker's bombers all the way to Germany. The available fighters—the British Spitfire and the American Thunderbolt—had a radius of action of no more than 175 miles, enough to escort the bombers only partway to the target and partway home. The gravity of the problem was underscored in mid-April, when 16 of a mission of 115 Forts were lost in a raid on an aircraft factory in Bremen.

Eaker had to wait for the arrival of new and improved fighters, but meanwhile he could and did demand more bombers. While his crews continued to hit points in Germany, he launched a paper blitz against Washington. He wrote letters, sent cables and asked his RAF allies to bombard Washington with pleas for more bombers. At dinner with Eaker one night, Prime Minister Churchill jocularly proposed they send a joint cable to General Arnold that would say: "We are dining together, smoking your cigars, and waiting for more of your heavy bombers."

Arnold was waging his own battle over airplane priorities on the home front; the Navy was badgering him to divert more bombers to the war in the Pacific as well as to anti-submarine duty in the Atlantic. But Arnold was a skilled political infighter, and 35 years in the Army had taught him that something in writing could be a useful weapon.

Arnold had Eaker and his staff draw up an elaborate proposal, documented with statistics and projections of sweeping results, that would rescue the Eighth Air Force from its current plight. The proposal evolved into the Combined Bomber Offensive Plan. Similar to the preceding Casablanca Directive, it outlined the respective day and night bombing roles of the Americans and the British and listed top-priority targets.

But it also contained some new elements. The Allied bombing was envisioned as specific preparation for the invasion of Western Europe, now scheduled for 1944, and—in recognition of the growing effectiveness of the Luftwaffe—aircraft factories rather than U-boat shipyards topped the

Spraying a fountain of light as it detonates at a preset altitude, a target-marking bomb illuminates a French aircraft-engine plant for an RAF night raid. British marker bombs flamed in yellow, red or green, thwarting German efforts to confuse the raiders with hastily lighted decoy fires.

priority list. Most important, the plan pledged the U.S. to enlarge the Eighth Air Force to numerical parity with RAF Bomber Command; Eaker was to receive an additional 944 heavy bombers by July 1, 1943, and nearly double that number by the year's end. The plan was approved by the U.S. Joint Chiefs of Staff on May 4 and formally issued as a joint Anglo-American commitment on June 10 under the portentous title of Pointblank Directive.

By then, the paper war waged by Eaker had already helped ease the strain on the Eighth Air Force. On a single day in mid-May, for example, the number of available combat crews jumped from 100 to 215. New U.S. bases began to dot the English landscape, giving the island the appearance of an enormous aircraft carrier. One Englishman recalled: "The sky was never still."

Eaker was able to step up the size of his attacks on Germany while continuing his missions against targets in the occupied countries. The new momentum of the U.S. offensive gave him a sense of personal triumph, but before long it also brought him a somber reminder of the face of war as seen by the men that were under his command.

In late June the Eighth Air Force launched its Mission No. 69, a raid in two parts. The main force of 191 bombers was dispatched to the U-boat pens at Saint-Nazaire. A diversionary force of 50 bombers was sent to hit a German airfield on the outskirts of Brussels. As was customary when there was a risk of killing friendly civilians, the crews of the diversionary force had been especially cautioned at the premission briefing about hitting anything but the designated target.

The approach to the German airfield took the 50 planes directly over Brussels. It was the safest route, since the Germans seldom wasted flak protecting occupied cities. As the U.S. force passed over the Belgian capital, the bombardiers prepared for their attack by opening bomb-bay doors and checking bombsights. The lead bombardier in one of the three combat groups happened to notice a large rectangular park in the middle of a residential area. He selected it as a simulated aiming point to rehearse the bombing run he would make over the targeted airfield. Suddenly, to his horror, he felt the jolt of bombs being released. Behind him, the other bombardiers in his combat group took the cue and also dropped their loads. The explosions ripped a path

of destruction through the park and the houses alongside.

American bombs had gone astray before, killing civilians sympathetic to the Allied cause, but never had an entire group of bombers dropped its payload in one huge collective error. Two days later the pilots, bombardiers and navigators of the lead crews were summoned to the headquarters of Brigadier General Robert Williams, commander of the 1st Bombardment Wing. The meeting opened with the customary postmission critique of the main raid on Saint-Nazaire. And then came the moment that the men had been awaiting in dread.

The bombardier who had caused the accident over Brussels rose and stepped forward. Colonel Budd Peaslee, who had led the diversionary raid, later remembered him as "a slight blond young man wearing the silver bars of a first lieutenant, hardly out of his teens but with the face and expression of a man twice his age." The room was dead silent as he attempted an explanation. "I don't know how it happened," he concluded. "Whatever the cause, I alone am to blame—the bombs of the entire formation are on my head. . . . I can only say I have regretted the day I was born."

Then General Williams spoke again, his one eye sternly fixed on his audience—he had lost the other eye in a German bombing raid while on a stint as an observer during the Battle of Britain. After noting how often the men had been warned about the possibility of bombing errors, Williams revealed that an investigation of the Brussels incident had been made "through agents in Belgium and other intelligence sources."

He paused, and the men braced for the verdict. "We find these results are not so bad as had at first been feared," Williams said. "As a matter of fact we are informed that the German occupation command considered the park area and the better-class adjoining residences an excellent locale for the billeting of troops. The entire circumference of the park was used for this purpose. We are informed there were 1,200 casualties among these forces and only a few Belgians were injured or killed. Across the Channel this accident is

being called a remarkable exhibition of American precision bombing. Such are the fortunes of war, gentlemen. This meeting and the incident are now closed."

The fortunes of war were also looking up for RAF Bomber Command. Like the Eighth Air Force, it had spent most of the past winter in frustrating attacks on the virtually bomb-proof U-boat bases along France's coast. But by March 1943, Air Chief Marshal Harris, taking advantage of a build-up of planes and new technological devices, turned his attention back to what Bomber Command considered its main job: "to render the German industrial population homeless, spiritless and as far as possible, dead."

On the night of March 5, a force of 367 RAF planes roared in over Bomber Command's toughest and most resistant target, Essen. The Ruhr city, ringed by guns and shielded by perpetual haze, had thus far defied Harris' best efforts to make a dent in it; in 1942 alone he had lost a total of 201 bombers there. Now, however, the British possessed new ways and means of getting at Essen.

The attack was led by the Pathfinder Force, an elite group of Bomber Command's most proficient crews. In the van guard were eight Mosquitoes. The Mosquito was to prove to be the most versatile plane built during the War, serving variously as a bomber, fighter and photoreconnaissance plane. It could exceed 400 miles per hour in level flight—faster than most fighters—climb above 30,000 feet and carry a two-ton bomb. And it required only a two-man crew.

But the most remarkable fact about the Mosquito was that it was largely made of wood. This not only allowed the British to build parts of it in woodworking shops—easing the burden on the country's metal supplies—but it also enabled the Mosquito to elude detection by enemy radar.

In the raid on Essen, the Mosquitoes carried their own variety of radar, a target-finding device known as Oboe because it transmitted a continuous note that sounded a lot like the wood-wind instrument. Oboe depended upon pulse signals transmitted from two ground stations in Eng-

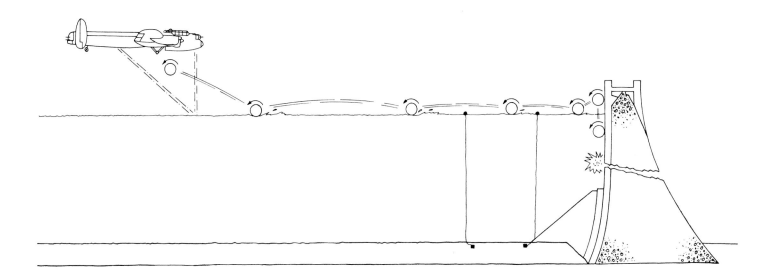

land. Signals from one station, code-named Mouse, kept the bomber on course. Signals from the Cat station told the bombardier precisely when his plane had reached the predetermined point for releasing the bombs.

On cue from Oboe, the Mosquitoes dropped special target-marking flares over the center of Essen. These target markers exploded at 3,000 feet, sending out a spray of brilliantly colored lights—yellow followed by red—that ignited like Roman candles and showered to earth in great pools of fire. In the wake of the Mosquitoes came 22 heavy bombers, also part of the Pathfinder Force, which supplemented the red indicators with a barrage of green markers. When the main bomber force arrived moments later, a giant Christmas-like display of red and green festooned the target, lighting the way for the RAF's deadly gifts.

More than 600 acres of Essen were either destroyed or badly damaged that night, and four more RAF raids were to come. The Krupp steelmaking complex was left in such ruins that after the head of the family, Gustav Krupp von Bohlen und Halbach, viewed the wreckage, he suffered a stroke from which he never recovered.

Essen was only the start of a sustained RAF campaign against the Ruhr. The operation was to exact a high price from the attackers: 872 bombers carrying more than 5,000 crewmen failed to return. During the next four months, more than two thirds of Bomber Command's missions concentrated on the area, and the centers of several cities were burned out. To a British pilot, looking down upon the flaming Ruhr one spring night, "the clouds were like cottonwool soaked in blood."

Cities were not the sole targets during the Battle of the Ruhr. The most memorable mission of the RAF offensive was one that Harris himself strongly opposed; it was executed only after he had been overruled by his superiors on the Air Staff. More than ever intent on area bombing, he resented going back to pinpointing specific objectives.

But the Air Ministry's planners sharply disagreed with Harris in the case of the projected mission—a raid on three of the big Ruhr dams that supplied the valley's water and hydroelectric power. By knocking them out, the argument went, the RAF's bombers could not only flood the valley but also paralyze Germany's entire armaments industry. This assessment was later to be confirmed by the Reich's own production czar, Albert Speer. Had the mission entirely succeeded, Speer said, it would have had the same effect as removing the ignition from a motor—rendering it useless.

The dams—the Möhne, the Eder and the Sorpe—were enormous piles of concrete, masonry and earth, some 150 feet high and nearly as thick at the base, and they were virtually impervious to conventional bombs. But early in the War a British aeronautical engineer named Barnes Wallis had come forward with an ingenious design for a dam-busting bomb. It was a barrel-shaped cylinder, five feet long and four feet in diameter. Weighing nearly five tons, it was designed to be slung crosswise in a special cradle beneath a Lancaster bomber. A belt-drive motor attached to the cradle would impart a rapid backspin to the bomb just before it was released at a low altitude. The backspin would make the bomb skip across the surface of the water. When it hit the dam, the backspin would force it down to a depth of 30 feet, where its pressure-sensitive fuse would go off. The explosion, magnified by water pressure, would function like a small man-made earthquake and breach the dam.

In mid-March, shortly after the first successful strike at Essen, a squadron of 147 men, hand-picked for the dam mission, began training for low-level flight without knowing their ultimate target. The new squadron's chief, Wing Commander Guy Gibson, was at 24 already a legend in the RAF. Once rejected by the peacetime RAF because his "legs were too short," Gibson had since flown 173 missions in both bombers and fighters.

The requirements for the projected mission far exceeded any in Gibson's experience. To elude radar detection, the squadron would have to fly all the way to the targets at altitudes under 1,500 feet. Then, over each dam, they would have to swoop down in their big Lancasters to a precisely fixed bomb-release point—exactly 60 feet above the water and 425 yards from the dam-while flying at a speed of 220 miles per hour. A crude bombsight, fashioned from a peephole, a piece of plywood and two nails, was devised to aid the task of the bomb aimer; he would line up the two nails with a pair of towers at either end of each dam. A more difficult problem involved finding a device that would tell the crews when they had come down to 60 feet. This was finally solved with the help of simple trigonometry. Spot-

The RAF's ingenious "bouncing bombs," which breached two of the hydroelectric dams near Germany's Ruhr industrial region, were released by Lancaster bombers with a rapid backspin to send them skipping over antitorpedo nets (vertical lines in diagram) and caroming downward after hitting the top of the dam wall. As the bomb reached a depth of 30 feet, a hydrostatic fuse triggered the five-ton explosive charge, whose force was concentrated upon the dams by the pressure of the surrounding water.

ANATOMY OF A MISSION

Speeding toward a target in occupied France, U.S. Eighth Air Force bombers and their faraway fighter escorts lace the sky with snow-white vapor trails.

A LONG ORDEAL FOR A BRIEF BOMB RUN

At the end of an arduous mission over Germany, an exhausted, unshaven bomber pilot completes his official flight report back at home base.

By the winter of 1943-1944, the strategic bombing missions of the U.S. Eighth Air Force were nearing their ultimate form. Tactics, teamwork and equipment had been greatly improved, and the percentage of plane losses was being cut by the potent long-range P-51 Mustang and other fighters equipped with drop tanks that permitted them to escort bombers deep into Germany. Yet for all these hard-won gains, the essential character of a mission had changed very little since the first American aircrews set out to prove that daylight bombing was just as safe as the RAF's night raids, and even more effective.

A mission was still a protracted ordeal. Many airmen spent five to 10 miserable hours jammed into a cramped duty station and weighted down with about 60 pounds of gear. Besides a parachute, they wore steel-reinforced vests to protect them from flak splinters, a bulky flight suit to keep them warm in the frigid upper altitudes, and oxygen masks that felt, said a B-24 copilot, "like a clammy hand clutching the lower part of your face." In this regalia even the simplest tasks required concentrated effort.

Discomfort was accompanied by grinding tedium. Every few minutes the navigator calculated and logged the plane's position. Hour after hour, the radio operator listened to static in his earphones, and the pilot and copilot struggled to hold the plane close—but not too close—to the bombers around it. Interminably, the gunners scanned the skies for Luftwaffe fighters, trying to stay awake and alert.

More than anything else, a mission was hard, complicated work—and not just for the aircrews. For a routine raid, many tens of thousands of men—headquarters planners, operations officers, mechanics and specialized personnel—toiled for hundreds of thousands of man-hours to put several hundred B-17s and B-24s over a German target for about five minutes each. But a successful bomb run made all the travail worthwhile, and an airman could say with satisfaction, as one did after a raid on the port of Emden: "When those Germans start putting those fires out they won't have enough water left to make a good pot of tea."

Getting ready for takeoff, the crewmen of a B-24 Liberator bundle up in their flight suits—vital protection against temperatures of 40° below zero at 25,000 feet.

Contending with Britain's wintertime mud, maintenance men wrestle a replacement tire for a bomber along a narrow boardwalk leading from a storage building.

The order for a mission usually reached the headquarters of the various bomber groups late in the day preceding the raid, and it always set off intense activity along the hardstands—the paved areas in which the planes were parked. A corps of specialists assigned to each squadron hurried to complete any servicing or repairs of the bombers' sheet metal, oxygen equipment, instruments, guns and propellers. But most of the work on each bomber was the responsibility of two or three permanently assigned mechanics. The plane was their pride and joy; they boasted of the number of missions it had flown and suffered—and sometimes wept—when it failed to return.

Toiling all night if need be, the mechanics swarmed over their plane, testing the controls, inspecting the brakes and landing gear, checking tires for burns and rubber-lined fuel tanks for leaks. Most important, they tuned and retuned the plane's four engines, listening intently for any sound of trouble. Replacements of flak-damaged or overtaxed, worn-out engines were common. In one year, the mechanics in the 398th Bomb Group changed 140-odd engines on the squadron's bombers.

Mechanics replace a B-17's four engines. They often salvaged sound parts from discarded engines and used them to rebuild others.

LOADING THE PLANES: A DELICATE BALANCE OF FUEL AND BOMBS

A fueling team fills up a gas-guzzling B-17. Fully loaded, a Fortress burned 400 gallons an hour climbing to cruising altitude, 200 an hour en route to the target.

Cradled in a hoist, a 500-pound bomb swings toward the bomb bay above. Bombs sometimes broke loose and crushed a crewman's feet.

Early on the morning of a mission, fueling teams and ordnance men rolled out to the paved hardstands in their trucks to top off the gas tanks and load the planes with bombs and ammunition. The exact weight of fuel and bombs had been specified by mission planners, whose calculations took into account many factors—the distance to target, the expected wind speed and the planned cruising altitude. Typically, fuel made up more than half the total load. Both the B-17s and the B-24s consumed gas ravenously and required nearly 2,800 gallons, or about nine tons, for a mission deep into Germany.

No matter how carefully the load was apportioned, unforeseeable circumstances might cause emergencies. The allocation of gasoline assumed a return flight without bombs, with the lightened planes getting appreciably better mileage. However, unexpected bad weather sometimes forced the bomber formation to turn back short of the target. In such cases, the mission commander faced a Hobson's choice: to head for his preselected alternate target, choose a target of opportunity or simply order his pilots to jettison their bombs. A few German towns devoid of military targets were hit by bombers forced to drop their payloads out of self-preservation.

At the "time-tick" in the briefing room, airmen synchronize their watches to the official time announced by an operations officer.

In an orderly procession, B-24 Liberators taxi down the runway—"just like a gaggle of geese going to a pond," remarked one navigator.

P-47s on escort duty pass over a base whose bombers have left one B-17 behind. The speedy fighters gave the bombers a head start.

OUT OF THE BRIEFING ROOM AND INTO THE SKY

Early on mission day, usually before daybreak, runners roused the aircrews. The airmen dressed quickly, downed as much breakfast as their jittery stomachs could take and headed for the briefing room. When all the airmen were present or accounted for, the operations officers locked the doors and drew open the curtains that concealed the mission map and the length of yarn that stretched across its surface from England to the target in Germany.

In careful detail, the officers described the weather outlook, the target, the proper approach to it, the kind of flak and fighter opposition to expect. Reports of stiff German defenses were often greeted by whistles, groans, nervous laughter and wisecracks. The ritual of synchronizing watches brought the session to a close. Navigators usually had a special briefing afterward.

Then the men climbed into their planes with all their gear. Pilots and copilots ran through the long preflight check list. The bombers got into line on the taxiways and then, 30 seconds apart, thundered down the runways and struggled into the air. When every plane was in position, and squadrons, groups and wings had joined forces, the formation headed for its rendezvous with the fighter escorts.

Waiting for the bombers' return, ground crewmen and a fire fighter wearing an asbestos suit stand beside a fire truck, prepared to spring into action in case of a crash landing.

A tight formation of bombers usually loosened up as returning pilots sighted the English Channel. Everyone was edgy, weary, eager to land. The Channel was, declared one airman, "the shortest stretch of water in the world when you're going out —the longest when you're coming back!"

As the planes approached their bases, crews aboard bombers carrying wounded men shot off red flares, signaling that they must land first, and ambulances—"meat wagons"—rushed out to greet them. After medics removed the wounded, the rest of the crew members piled out. Invariably, some men celebrated their safe return: a few would run their fingers through the grass or kiss the ground, and those who had just finished their last mission before being rotated cheered and jumped for joy. Then, as the airmen tramped off to their debriefing session, the sheet-metal workers started to measure the damaged aircraft for patches, and an engineering officer made a count of the bombers that were still combatworthy.

Signaling from a jeep and the checkered trailer of their mobile control station, air-traffic controllers direct bombers to a safe landing.

Wounded in the leg by flak, a pilot is helped from his bomber by medics at base. His crew gave him first aid en route from Germany.

A pilot demonstrates an attacking fighter's maneuvers for two interrogation officers (right). His crew, waiting at the rear for their turn to report, were free to add details to his account.

Gathering in the debriefing rooms for interrogation after a mission, crews milled about, smoked and consumed hot chocolate, gray coffee and Spam sandwiches. They were also offered a shot of whiskey to help them unwind. If the mission had been an easy one, the airmen's talk was loud and animated. After a "rugged deal," they barely talked at all; everyone glanced about furtively to see who had made it back and listened for the sound of crippled bombers limping home.

Intelligence officers interrogated every aircrew as a group. Each man in turn reported the mission as he had seen it from his post. The interrogators reconciled discrepancies and ran through a check list of questions, probing for information about the enemy's response. Did the Luftwaffe employ any new tactic or send up fighters with an unfamiliar unit insignia? Was the flak heavier or lighter than expected?

After interrogation, the intelligence officers rushed their Flash Report—the raw facts of the raid in tabulated form—to the headquarters staff for analysis. Later, when aerial photos of the strike had been developed, they were taken by small plane to be air-dropped at headquarters. The headquarters staff began at once to study the results, looking for clues uncovered in this mission to help in planning the next one.

Safely back at the base, a pilot and copilot stand on a wing of their Flying Fortress and survey the heavy

damage it suffered during a costly raid on an aircraft assembly plant near Brunswick, Germany, in January of 1944. Sixty bombers did not return from the run.

INNUMERABLE WAYS TO DIE IN A PLANE

Every combat airman flew in the face of constant danger, knowing all too well that he might not come back from his next mission. The most obvious perils—food for troubled thought in the agonizing waits between sorties—were enemy fighter planes and antiaircraft fire. But fliers were killed in innumerable other ways. They died in crashes caused by fog and unexpected storms, by errors in judgment or just plain carelessness, and by "gremlins"—inexplicable mechanical bugs, such as clogged fuel lines and malfunctioning controls, which kept cropping up in spite of meticulous maintenance. On one occasion, the wind played a part in an American disaster. During a B-17 raid on Merseburg in November 1944, steady head winds slowed the bombers and helped German gunners shoot down or cripple 56 Flying Fortresses.

Another hazard was purely psychological. As Allied airmen watched their friends perish, they grew ever more anxious about their own chances of surviving the 25 or more missions needed to become eligible for relief from combat duty. In the second half of 1943 almost a third of U.S. bomber crew members failed to complete their quota of missions. The mounting strain on the survivors' nerves impaired their efficiency, contributing to still more casualties.

The life expectancy of German fliers was even shakier. Because the Luftwaffe never adopted a rotation policy, veteran pilots and crewmen had to serve until they were killed or incapacitated by wounds or combat fatigue. Superstitious Germans and Allies alike felt that their luck would run out at some preordained moment, no matter what they did—a notion that undoubtedly led some fliers to get themselves killed in reckless stunts or pointless heroics.

There was a ready antidote to the fliers' foreboding: the knowledge that many airmen survived mishaps that should have proved fatal. American gunner James Raley plummeted 19,000 feet in the severed tail section of his B-17 and landed safely in a tree. Perhaps most encouraging was the charmed life of Luftwaffe ace Georg Peter Eder. He was shot down 17 times but kept flying until the end of the War.

Allied airmen, all of them survivors of crash landings in France, wait at an emergency airstrip for a plane ride back to their bases in England.

Spraying thousands of gallons of flame-smothering foam, fire fighters try to save a B-24 that caught fire as it crash-landed at a U.S. Eighth Air Force bomber base.

Trailing a thick plume of smoke, an attacking British Spitfire roars past a German Heinkel-111 bomber. The fighter was hit by the guns of a third plane from which the picture was taken.

The nose-gunner on a Luftwaffe bomber brings his weapon to bear on a Spitfire. Strength and quickness were key attributes for a gunner.

DEADLY DUELS ALOFT

"One of the most unnerving things I have ever witnessed was a group of B-24s being annihilated by German fighters," wrote American copilot Jim Fletcher. "They were way out ahead of us and we could see bombers being picked off. Every so often one would get hit and explode. Seeing it like that had far more impact; you had time to think what might soon be happening to you."

Dizzyingly swift and agile, the enemy fighter planes made many bomber crewmen feel as helpless as swimmers pursued by sharks. British navigator William Anderson, whose bomber was the target of a Luftwaffe fighter over the Ruhr Valley in 1942, later acknowledged, "Then I knew fear. Somewhere outside there was someone crouching behind guns circling round to come in again and kill me. . . . In that brief moment when I watched a pattern of holes appearing in the fuselage beside me I discovered that I was a coward, hopelessly and horribly afraid of fighters."

Furthermore, said Anderson, fighter pilots used "a lot of nasty tricks. A very old one was to turn on their lights. Then, while the bomber crew was watching, another fighter would sneak quietly in from the other side." Anderson also reported that the fighters "liked to sneak up from below and rake the bombers' belly with cannon shells." As the shells pierced a bomber's skin they could gouge out holes big enough for a man to fall through.

U.S. pilot Charles W. Paine cited other deadly fighter tactics. "When they peeled off to attack, they came in so close together that by the time one ship had shot us up and banked away, the next in line had his sights on us." A second maneuver, said Paine, "was to pretend to come in on one of the other ships, and then do a twenty-degree turn and shoot hell out of us." Paine, too, came under cannon fire from Luftwaffe fighters, and he was hard put to describe the harrowing experience. "It was," he later said, "like sitting in the boiler of a hot-water heater that was being rolled down a steep hill."

A German pilot tumbles from the cockpit of his Focke-Wulf 190 and begins his parachute descent to earth as the plane catches fire.

A B-24 Liberator bomber flies through flak over Vienna. The plane, on a mission in October 1944, managed to get back to its base in Italy.

THE GAUNTLET OF ENEMY FLAK

Some of the airmen were fascinated by the flak that set their hearts pounding. Radioman Edward Gibson remembered: "It was scary, but you sat too with a certain awe at the sheer beauty of it. You'd sit there and watch it come up, and it seemed to drift rather like a waterfall upside down. But if they hit you, there was a rending of metal and then the thunking crash of broken glass." Larger shells of heavy flak, which detonated at predetermined altitudes rather than on contact, enthralled U.S. pilot Al Gilles, who called them "lazy black fingers making puffs." But he added, "I wasn't kidding myself. More than once I'd seen a single burst of flak turn a powerful throbbing four-engine plane into an enormous ball of orange flame."

In fact, flak was deadlier than most airmen knew. In 1944, German flak destroyed 3,501 American planes—nearly 600 more than Luftwaffe fighters.

A B-26 Marauder, set afire by flak over France, loses an engine from a flaming wing. Minutes later, it crashed.

Scattered scraps of metal on an English airfield are all that remain of a P-38 Lightning, destroyed by a foolish, forbidden stunt. The pilot buzzed the base at 100

CASUALTIES CLAIMED BY CARELESSNESS

Of the problems of formation flying, U.S. General Curtis E. LeMay wrote: "Once in a while some muttonhead wouldn't be on the ball, and we would have mid-air collisions." Unfortunately, mid-air collisions were only one variety of aerial disaster caused by negligence or by simple mistakes that should have been avoided. All too frequently, fighter pilots and gunners on bombers shot down planes in their own formation. Pilots who neglected to check their instruments or to follow instructions from ground control splattered themselves and their planes all across the landscape. And airmen on both sides of the conflict miscalculated their positions or mistook landmarks with calamitous consequences: they strayed or bombed their own airfield.

...few complete a loop and was killed in the crash.

To prevent such blunders, airmen had to concentrate at all times on even the most routine aspects of flying their planes. Flight instructors repeatedly cautioned their students to keep thinking, to anticipate trouble, to follow normal procedures unless otherwise ordered. The fate of those who failed to do so was set forth in doggerel by an RAF training manual. Parodying "Ten Little Indians," the verses recounted the tragic adventures of "ten little bomber boys" who broke all the rules: taxied too fast, did damage to their engines by overrevving them, forgot their emergency boat drill, cut through balloon barrages and so on—with each error and oversight proving fatal. By the end of the poem, all the little bomber boys were dead:

*One expensive aircraft
Will never fly again,
With their ten expensive aircrews...*

Powered by German machine guns, a B-24 collides in mid-air during flight, merely able to pose a ripple as planes bank to base several hundred miles away

TAKING OFF OVERLOADED, COMING IN ON A PRAYER

The first two or three minutes of a bomber's mission were often truly the most harrowing of all. B-24s roared down the runway, laden with so low, the bombs they often weighed thousands of pounds more than the plane was designed to fly, and frequently would labor to attain enough power to get a fully burdened plane aloft.

3

4

7

10

11

4

Hitler's reaction to the catastrophe at Hamburg disturbed even his most devoted lieutenants. Though they were aware of his aversion to viewing the results of Allied air raids—he always ordered the shades drawn when his train passed through bombed-out areas—they felt that the special ferocity of the attack on Hamburg had earned its people the right to a personal visit by the Führer. But repeated pleas from the city's gauleiter for such a visit went unheeded. So did his request that Hitler at least receive and commend some of the harried rescue crews.

Minister of Armaments Albert Speer fared no better when he decided to warn Hitler of the ominous implications of the Hamburg attack. The scale of the devastation, Speer later admitted, "put the fear of God in me." On August 1, 1943, while Hamburg was still under siege, he managed a meeting with the Führer and bluntly predicted that a series of such attacks on six more major cities would bring Germany's war production to a total halt. Hitler waved the warning aside. "You'll straighten all that out again," he said.

Luftwaffe chief Göring did not share Hitler's detached attitude toward the catastrophe, though his initial response was typically insensitive: instead of visiting Hamburg himself, he sent the gauleiter a telegram expressing routine condolences to the people of the city. Prudently, the gauleiter decided not to publish the text of the message, and even a high-ranking Luftwaffe officer later admitted that it "would have created a riot."

Göring's second reaction to the catastrophe was more constructive. As the man ultimately responsible for Germany's air-defense system, he could scarcely deceive himself about its failure at Hamburg. The city's ordeal was still going on when he called an urgent conference of the Luftwaffe's high command to consider ways of ensuring that no such humiliation would ever recur.

The meeting took place at the so-called Wolf's Lair at Rastenburg in East Prussia—the fortress-like headquarters, deep in a pine forest, from which Hitler was supervising Germany's latest military moves. Göring's decision to convene his staff at Rastenburg struck them as a hopeful sign in itself. For months, the Reich Marshal had been sitting out the war at his palatial retreat near Berlin, growing ever fatter and indulging once again in his old addiction to morphine and its derivatives. He had passed much of his time admir-

THE LUFTWAFFE FIGHTS BACK

ing the Rembrandts and Goyas he had plundered from occupied Europe or playing with his jewel collection—"like a little boy with his marbles," one visitor reported.

But the Hamburg debacle roused Göring from his torpor, and at Rastenburg he displayed flashes of the same vigor and spirit that had marked his build-up of the Luftwaffe in the 1930s. No longer inclined to denounce reports of its failings as craven lies, he was now ready to accept a realistic appraisal by the men who knew the Luftwaffe best: what had once been the world's most powerful and up-to-date air force was lagging behind its Allied counterparts in new technology. Moreover, it was being stretched dangerously thin—not only by Hitler's strategy of involvement on many fronts but also by the necessity of defending Germany itself against round-the-clock bombing attacks.

To remedy the situation, strong measures would have to be taken. Fighter production would have to be boosted to more than 1,000 a month—twice the previous year's rate. The defense of the homeland would have to be given top priority. This, in turn, would require diverting planes and seasoned pilots from the support of ground units fighting on the Russian and Mediterranean fronts. Göring's deputy, Field Marshal Erhard Milch, put it baldly: "The soldier on the battlefield will just have to dig a hole, crawl into it and wait until the attack is over. What the home front is suffering now cannot be suffered very much longer."

Lieut. General Adolf Galland, who as chief of the fighter arm of the Luftwaffe had been pressing for such action for months, was cheered by the atmosphere of unity at the conference. He was one of the few men present with a firsthand knowledge of modern aerial combat; a fighter pilot during the Battle of Britain in 1940 and 1941, he had scored 94 kills and won acclaim as one of Germany's boldest aces. In his more recent role as an administrator, he had come to detest the maneuvering that usually went on at high-level meetings, and he was relieved by its absence at Rastenburg. "It was as though under the impact of the Hamburg catastrophe everyone had put aside either personal or departmental ambitions," Galland recalled later.

When the sessions ended, Göring declared that all that remained for him to do was to go to the Führer's bunker and get approval of the measures the Luftwaffe proposed. He returned looking shattered; without a word, he walked past his waiting staff into his office. After a while Galland and another officer were told to go in. They found Göring with his head buried in his arms, mumbling incoherently.

"We stood there for some time in embarrassment." Galland remembered. "At last Göring pulled himself together and said we were witnessing his deepest moments of despair. The Führer had lost faith in him. All the suggestions from which he had expected a radical change in the situation of the war in the air had been rejected. The Führer had announced that the Luftwaffe had disappointed him too often. A changeover from offensive to defensive in the air against the west was out of the question. He would give the Luftwaffe a last chance to rehabilitate itself. This could be done by a resumption of air attacks against England, but this time on a bigger scale. Now as before, the motto was still: Attack. Terror could only be smashed by counterterror."

Up against what Galland called "an invincible barrier—the Führer's orders," the Luftwaffe set about complying with Hitler's demand for a renewed assault on England. But the task of assembling the bomber force of new Junkers-188s and Heinkel-177s would take months, and meanwhile the immediate threat of more Allied raids had to be faced. Barred from making the changes they had urged at Rastenburg, the Luftwaffe's leaders had to rely on their existing air-defense setup. But they were under no restraints against improving and refining the fighters' tactics and trying some new combat tricks, and on this they rested their hopes.

By mid-August, within three weeks of Hitler's rebuff of Göring, three massive U.S. raids on targets crucial to the German war machine gave the Luftwaffe's leaders reason to believe that they might stem the Allied air tide. The first raid took place on August 1, the day Speer warned Hitler that continuing Allied attacks could halt the Reich's war production. The Americans' choice of a target was the oil fields of Ploesti, in Germany's satellite, Rumania. Ploesti was, in Churchill's phrase, "the taproot of German might." From its refineries flowed a third of the Reich's petroleum needs.

Ploesti, located in the southeastern corner of Rumania, was too far to reach from England. Instead, the mission was launched from bases across the Mediterranean in Libya. Two groups of Liberators from the U.S. Ninth Air Force, which had received its baptism of fire while helping the RAF beat back Rommel's Afrika Korps in 1942, joined with three groups on loan from the Eighth Air Force to deal what was expected to be a decisive blow at Hitler's oil supply.

The plan called for the bombers to fly in radio silence and—in order to elude the enemy's radar—at minimum altitude. Since the German ground defenses were concentrated south of the oil fields, the planes were to cross Rumania to a point northwest of Ploesti, veer back to the target, drop their bombs and then return to North Africa. But just about everything went wrong for the raiders. The Luftwaffe's early-warning network destroyed the essential element of surprise by intercepting the routine American radio transmissions at the time of the planes' takeoff. Over Rumania, the command bomber of the first group turned too soon, misleading another group, and both groups approached Ploesti from the heavily defended south.

Thanks to their early-warning network, the defenders were ready and waiting. Flying in at virtually treetop level, the Americans ran into a solid wall of flak. The antiaircraft crews were able to zero in on them simply by visual sighting. German gunners fired from hidden positions in haystacks, church steeples and even a gun-mounted train that pursued the bombers by rail. German interceptors pounced from above, braving their own flak. Then, as the attackers turned for home, the interceptors overtook them, hanging on "like snails on a log," according to one account.

Of the 177 Liberators on the mission, 53 were shot down; 55 returned to Libya so badly damaged that many were fit only for salvage. Nor did the raid seriously impair Ploesti's oil production. Though an estimated 40 per cent of its capacity was knocked out, Ploesti had sufficient reserve facilities to keep pouring out its monthly quotas for the Luftwaffe and other sectors of the German military.

On August 17, the Americans turned their attention back to Germany itself, and to two targets whose destruction would have crippled the enemy's war effort almost as effectively as a shortage of oil. The first objective was Regensburg, where a Messerschmitt plant was turning out nearly 30 per cent of the Luftwaffe's single-engined fighters. The second objective was Schweinfurt, site of factories that accounted for half of Germany's production of ball bearings; the tiny steel balls, essential to keeping precision machinery free of fric-

tion, were required by the Luftwaffe alone in quantities of several thousand per plane.

Regensburg and Schweinfurt represented the Americans' biggest challenge thus far. Both cities lay deep in southeastern Germany, farther from the U.S. bases in England than any Eighth Air Force planes had yet penetrated. The range of their fighter protection—British Spitfires and American Thunderbolts—extended only as far as Aachen, just inside Germany's border with Belgium and Holland. The attacking bombers would have to go it alone the rest of the way, across vast stretches of hostile and unfamiliar air space.

For the Luftwaffe, the Americans' double strike provided a major test of its new resolve. Alerted by long-range Freya radar, its first interceptors were aloft a few minutes after 146 Flying Fortresses, bound for Regensburg, began to cross the English coast at 9:35 a.m. The German fighters—the vanguard of 300 that were to defend the homeland that day—bided their time while the armada crossed Holland and headed for the German border. As the last of the enemy escorts peeled off and turned back, the Germans moved in. Long before Regensburg, a furious battle was on.

Never before had the U.S. bombers faced such an array of aerial firepower—cannon and machine-gun shells, mortar rockets, even bombs. Single-engined Focke-Wulf 190s and Messerschmitt-109s blazed away with 30mm heavy cannon that fired at the rate of 10 rounds per second. Me-110s—the slower, twin-engined aircraft normally used only at night—cruised just beyond the range of the Fortress gunners and lobbed time-fused rockets. These missiles, adapted from the Germans' infantry mortar, were fired from as many as four tubes slung under the wings of the fighters. They were four feet long, weighed 248 pounds and exploded with the power of a small artillery shell. Meanwhile, other German fighters flew above the Forts to give them a dose of their own medicine: 500-pound bombs, carried under the fuselage, fused to explode in the middle of a bomber formation.

The Germans' game was to break up the bomber formations, each consisting of three tiers of tightly stacked combat boxes of as many as 21 bombers per box. Along with the unprecedented firepower, the Me-109s and FW-190s unveiled new tactical twists and refinements the Americans had never encountered in previous raids on Germany. Some innovations had been tested in mock battles with Forts that had crash-landed in occupied Europe; the Germans had patched up the bombers to make them airworthy again and then turned them over to a special training unit called the Traveling Circus. The Circus toured the Luftwaffe's interceptor bases, allowing fighter pilots to practice maneuvers against the Forts and even to fly them. More than once the Germans had infiltrated a few of the patched-up planes into U.S. bomber formations to determine their speed and course and even to open fire on the unsuspecting crewmen.

The Americans bound for Regensburg found that the adversary had honed his skills well. Many of the fighter attacks came en masse, with six or so interceptors boring in wing to wing on a combat box. Other fighters sped along parallel with the bombers, then raced ahead and turned to meet them—queuing up "like a bread line," one U.S. navigator said. Still other fighters concentrated on the so-called coffin corner of each bomber formation—the corner occupied by the combat box that was stacked below and slightly behind the other two boxes in the three-tier formation. The Germans quickly broke up the coffin corner occupied by the U.S. 100th Bomb Group, then set upon the stragglers, as one account put it, "like wolves on wounded deer."

It took the U.S. bombers 90 minutes to cover the 300 miles from the German border to Regensburg, and they were hounded all the way. From interceptor bases that lined the attack corridor on either side, the Luftwaffe's fighters rose in relays. When one unit exhausted its fuel and ammunition, it landed and a fresh unit from the next base took off.

The carnage suffered by the raiders would have been even worse but for a move the Germans had not anticipated. After the badly mauled formations dropped their bombs on the Messerschmitt factory, they turned south across the Alps on a preplanned route to U.S. bases in Algeria. This enabled the Americans to elude the refueled and rearmed Luftwaffe fighters awaiting the bombers' return along the expected route to England.

The second phase of the U.S. mission that day, the attack on Schweinfurt, was to have started only 10 minutes after the first wave of bombers left for Regensburg—a plan designed to overtax and confuse the Luftwaffe. But a sudden heavy fog that descended on England delayed the takeoff for Schweinfurt by more than three hours.

When the 230 Fortresses of the second armada reached the German border, the full fury of some 300 Luftwaffe fighters was again unleashed. This time the Germans were able to hammer at the Americans not only all the way to the target but back to the border, pulling off only after the Thunderbolt escorts came to the aid of the Forts.

During the battle, an Me-109 ace named Hans Langer slipped up from below and joined a box of Fortresses, flying along between two bombers so closely that he could see the startled faces of the American waist gunners on either side of him. Neither gunner fired, for fear of hitting the other Fort. Langer, who just weeks before had been decorated by Hitler himself for shooting down 45 Allied planes, opened fire on the Fort directly ahead of him. The wing exploded and the crippled bomber flipped over and collided with another Fort. The impact flung Langer's own plane out of the formation, but he managed to land safely.

Despite the punishment they took, both the Regensburg and Schweinfurt raiders managed to inflict substantial damage on their targets. At Regensburg, every important building of the Messerschmitt complex was hit by incendiary or high-explosive bombs. At Schweinfurt, the production of

Luftwaffe chief Hermann Göring (center) adds to the smiles in an informal portrait of the Luftwaffe staff at an unidentified country retreat. But beneath the apparent camaraderie lay constant dissension and intrigue that led General Staff chief Hans Jeschonnek (fourth from right) to commit suicide in August 1943.

ball bearings plummeted by 38 per cent. But the price exacted by the Luftwaffe made many of the Americans wonder whether the bombing results were worth it. Against German losses of 25 fighters, 60 of the U.S. bombers were shot down and 47 others were so badly damaged that they had to be scrapped. For the total of 376 Fortresses sent into action that day, the loss rate was more than 15 per cent. One alarmed American noted that a week of such operations would wipe out the Eighth Air Force.

For the RAF's night missions, the Luftwaffe had other innovations in store. One stemmed from the Hamburg experience. The Germans now knew that they could no longer trust radar to help them find incoming enemy bombers in the dark; the RAF's dropping of Window—the strips of metal foil that appeared on radar screens as blips—had thoroughly confused the ground controllers and sent the Luftwaffe's fighters off on fruitless sweeps through their stations along the Kammhuber Line on Germany's western approaches. To eliminate this waste of time and effort, the Germans decided on a new defensive plan that posed a high risk, but seemed worth the gamble. The plan called for circumventing Window by waiting until an attack on a city was already under way—at which point an alert by area ground control would send the pilots speeding directly there. In the glare of searchlights—and burning buildings—they would have no trouble spotting and engaging the enemy. Moreover, the illumination would allow the Luftwaffe to use day fighters as well as night interceptors.

The new plan required a special sort of airman—one who would rely on his own judgment, ingenuity and daring rather than on conventional ideas of combat. To find such men the Luftwaffe's high command turned to 30-year-old Major Hans-Joachim "Hajo" Herrmann, a veteran of 300 bombing missions against England and Malta. Herrmann was famous in the Luftwaffe as a tireless promoter of inventive ideas; one of his more imaginative proposals had envisioned an aerial attack on the United States by huge flying boats that would take on fuel and bombs from U-boats stationed off America's East Coast. Herrmann's latest concept called for putting together a special group of Luftwaffe fighter pilots who would, in effect, act as freelancers in battling the British. Herrmann code-named his group *Wilde*

Sau—Wild Boars. One Luftwaffe general characterized the men as "a motley collection, loosely organized and rather like guerrilla bands in their attitude to authority."

About a dozen Wild Boars, flying FW-190s and Me-109s, had been sent into action as an experiment during an RAF raid on Cologne in late July, with some success. The experiment was expanded on the night of August 17. Hours after the last American planes had landed in England from the afternoon's raid on Schweinfurt, the British were poised for an attack of their own. The RAF's target that night was Peenemünde, site of a top-secret German research station on a small island in the Baltic Sea. The veil over activities there had been pierced by British intelligence agents. At Peenemünde, Hitler's scientists were perfecting and test-firing two pilotless projectiles—"vengeance weapons" that the Führer planned to unleash against England in the wake of the renewed bomber assault: the V-1, a jet-powered flying bomb, and the V-2, a liquid-fueled rocket.

Thanks to an intercepted RAF radio message, the German night-fighter chief, General Kammhuber, knew that the British were coming that night, though not where. From his headquarters in Holland, he put on alert the largest force of night fighters yet assembled—more than 200 pilots, including many who had flown against the Americans earlier that day and who were exhausted but exhilarated. Among them were 55 Wild Boars, primed to put their own tactics to use.

The British, too, had a trick up their sleeve. To divert the Germans from the real target, eight Mosquito bombers flew to Berlin and dropped flares that ordinarily would have signaled a major attack. In the meantime, at night-fighter headquarters in Holland, communications cables connecting General Kammhuber with the rest of his ground-control network inexplicably went out of commission—possibly the work of two British undercover agents.

Kammhuber was cut off from the battle, and his ground controllers, fooled by the decoy raid on Berlin, dispatched the German fighters to the capital. When they roared in, the ground units manning the antiaircraft batteries assumed that the main force of RAF bombers had arrived. They opened up, firing some 11,000 rounds at their own planes.

As the outraged German pilots dodged the flak, some of them spotted the yellow glow of target-marking bombs over Peenemünde, 100 miles to the north. They radioed the

A low-flying B-24 Liberator skims a cluster of towering smokestacks during an attack in August of 1943 on Astra Romana, the largest of 11 refineries operated by the Germans in Rumania's Ploesti oil fields. Even though Astra Romana's main facilities were heavily damaged and two nearby refineries were knocked out, the results were disappointing. Astra Romana possessed an enormous reserve capacity, and the refinery soon outstripped its preraid production by approximately 33 per cent.

Berlin ground controller, asking permission to go on to Peenemünde; unaware of the target's top-secret importance, he ordered them to remain over the capital. As the planes continued to circle, they began to run out of fuel—the single-engined planes of the Boars had virtually none left—and landing became imperative. At one field, about 100 fighters came down almost simultaneously; in the resulting jam, 30 crashed, so littering the runways that take-offs were impossible.

But some of the more experienced pilots who had refueled at other fields ignored the ground controller's orders and sped north. Not all of them were Herrmann's Wild Boars, but all were now following the basic Wild Boar dictum that authority was to be flouted when circumstances warranted. In all, 30 fighters got to Peenemünde in time to intercept the final wave of the 597 RAF planes on the mission. They bagged 29 of the 40 bombers lost by the British—a hint of what they might have achieved with an earlier start. But the British dropped a total of 2,000 tons of bombs, killing several of Germany's leading scientists and setting back the V-1 and V-2 programs by four to six weeks.

The Wild Boars got another chance at the foe less than a week later, on the night of the 23rd of August. This time Berlin was the RAF's true target, and the Luftwaffe's ground controllers were not fooled. Nearly an hour before the 727 British bombers reached the capital, German fighters were

heading for the city from bases throughout Western Europe.

The Berlin sky was lighted up like a stage. Along with the usual searchlights, Herrmann had arranged for extra lighting effects—incandescent rockets sent up by the gun batteries. Combined with the glare of the British target-marking flares, the illumination supplied by the Germans turned night into day. Berliners scurrying for shelter found the spectacle bizarre. They had gone through three years of strict blackouts during which it had been a punishable offense even to light a cigarette in the open. Now it was possible to read in the street. From their vantage points high in the sky, the Luftwaffe fighter pilots could look down and see the silhouettes of the RAF bombers moving across the illuminated clouds "like flies on a tablecloth," as Field Marshal Milch jubilantly described it. Between them, the fighters and the ground batteries downed 56 of the raiders. An additional 67 RAF planes fell to the newly confident night defenses when Bomber Command returned to Berlin in force twice more within a fortnight.

Göring was so pleased that he promoted Hajo Herrmann to lieutenant colonel and ordered him to triple the strength of the Wild Boar units. Herrmann had no trouble recruiting. His units quickly attracted scores of free-spirited airmen, among them a number of fliers with black marks on their records who hoped to redeem themselves.

The Luftwaffe's new successes, trumpeted by the German press and radio, served as a national tonic. Popular morale had remained remarkably steady in spite of the earlier Allied onslaughts; now it stiffened even more. The embattled Berliners gave full play to the sarcastic humor for which they had long been noted. One wag tacked a sign on a gutted warehouse announcing that it was now "open day and night." Watching the piles of bomb rubble grow more and more mountainous, people told one another: "A Third World War and Berlin's in the Alps!" Instead of saying the usual goodbyes, friends parted with the wry admonition to make sure "you're left over"—from the next Allied raid.

Any feelings of despondency beneath the humor were kept private. "The Nazi regime was not prepared to tolerate any depression," wrote Hans Rumpf, who, as the wartime inspector general of fire prevention, was in a special position to assess civilian reactions to the Allied bombings. Fear of being punished for defeatist talk was, in fact, one of several reasons for the Germans' impressive display of backbone. Rumpf cited additional reasons. Some people, he noted, simply became too numbed emotionally to feel any fright at the bombings. In others, a deep-seated urge to "live dangerously" came to the fore. Still others took refuge in religion, accepting their sufferings as "acts of God."

By and large, however, people just adapted to the ordeal—as they would have done to recurrent earthquakes or floods—and went on as best they could. Many Germans, indeed, resisted efforts to evacuate them from their devastated cities, or found ways to return. Less than a year after the catastrophe at Hamburg, when four fifths of the city still lay in ruins, 900,000 citizens—almost two thirds of the normal population—were back there again.

Germany's war production proved to be as resilient as the people. The bombs that destroyed the structure of a factory did not necessarily wreck all of its machines and machine tools, and assembly lines could operate without benefit of a roof overhead. Moreover, Germany had an asset of incalculable value in a conscript force of some six million laborers who could be moved at will—sometimes by the hundreds of thousands—to speed the repair of damaged installations. This immense reservoir of manpower, composed largely of prisoners of war and workers forcibly recruited in occupied lands, made it possible for German industrialists to rack up a startling record for 1943. Throughout the year, despite the enemy's intensified air offensive, German factories—unlike their Allied counterparts—remained on a single daily shift and had no need to hire women.

In a curious way, the Allied bombings gave the Reich's industrialists a new sense of freedom, a release from hectoring by the Nazis' economic bureaucrats and from the reams of paper work they ordinarily demanded. Preoccupied by having to wage war at home as well as abroad, the regime loosened some of its hold on the industrial sector, leaving the practical-minded men who ran it more and more to their own devices—and to their skills at improvising. In this they had the full blessing of one of the few men around Hitler who took a long and objective view of Germany's situation: Minister of Armaments Speer.

With Speer's approval, priorities for critical raw materials and essential machine parts were quickly reassigned, when necessary, from one plant to another. Factories were dispersed; some were relocated in Germany's satellite countries to the southeast; new factories were built underground to produce airplane engines. Despite Hitler's disenchantment with the Luftwaffe's fighter arm, the monthly output of fighter planes rose from less than 700 in December of 1943 to a new high of more than 2,000 by April of 1944.

Aside from their own stepped-up efforts, the Germans profited from a mistake in Allied strategy, as later attested by Speer. His country's war machine would have come apart much earlier, he reported, had the Allies been more persistent in their attacks on key targets. He cited Schweinfurt as a case in point. By failing to follow up immediately on the raid of August 17, 1943, the Americans provided the Germans with a vital breather. While the factories at Schweinfurt were being repaired, the gap in the production of ball bearings was filled by other factories in Germany as well as in Switzerland and Sweden, and the simpler slide bearings were also used as a substitute.

The Americans did not return to Schweinfurt for almost two months. In the interim, the Eighth Air Force had largely confined its missions to targets in France, the Low Countries and Germany's western fringes. These targets were near enough so that the bombers could receive fighter protection all the way there and back to England. But Schweinfurt was still uppermost in the minds of the U.S. strategists, and on the morning of October 14 they sent the bombers back there for a second showdown.

There were 291 Flying Fortresses in the armada—61 more than on the first raid. But the Germans, too, were better prepared. Some 300 newly installed antiaircraft batteries of 88mm guns stood ready around Schweinfurt. Along the air corridor from Aachen east to the target, more than 300 interceptors waited. Each pilot was under Göring's orders to fly at least three separate sorties against the Americans, landing and refueling between one and the next.

Added to the Me-109s, Me-110s, FW-190s and Ju-88s that the Luftwaffe had used in the earlier raid, there were speedy new twin-engined Me-210s, Stuka dive bombers, and even four-engined bombers—H-177s and FW-200s—which flew just out of the firing range of the Americans to report on the progress of the battle. It seemed, said one Fortress crew-

man, that "the whole goddamned Luftwaffe is out today."

Once again, the U.S. bombers had to fly through a seemingly unceasing hail of machine-gun fire, cannon shells and rockets. The intensity of the onslaught was later measured in the reports of American crewmen who survived: in a single minute, they counted at least 40 attacks by the German fighters on just three of the bomber groups.

Colonel Budd Peaslee, one of the American commanders on the mission, later described the feeling of utter helplessness that overcame the bomber crews as their cumbersome craft seemed to crawl across the skies toward Schweinfurt: "I think of the Middle Ages. I see myself strolling across an open plain with a group of friends. Suddenly we are beset by many scoundrels on horseback. They come from every direction, shooting their arrows. We defend ourselves as best we can with slings and swords, and crouch behind our leather shields. We cannot run, we cannot dodge, we cannot hide—the plain has no growth, no rocks, no holes. And it seems endless. There is no way out—then, or now."

The battle went on for more than three hours and was to be one of the most savage aerial encounters of the entire War. The results reflected the carnage: the Luftwaffe lost 38 fighters, the Americans 60 bombers. But despite the decimation of the U.S. planes, General Eaker initially described the raid as a great success for the Eighth Air Force. His report to Washington rated the Luftwaffe's virtuoso performance "as the last final struggle of a monster in his death throes," adding: "There is not the slightest question but that we now have our teeth in the Hun Air Force's neck."

Eaker's misplaced optimism was based in part on the claims by his crews that 186 German fighters had been shot down and in part on photographs showing heavy damage at Schweinfurt. The fact is that though the damage disrupted production for six weeks, no German plane or tank failed to be built for the lack of ball bearings.

Eaker soon had sober second thoughts about the outcome at Schweinfurt; he called a halt to big raids deep into Germany. The bombers would not return there until they could be escorted all the way to their target and back by fighters—American rather than German.

With the Americans temporarily sidelined, the Luftwaffe could focus on the British and the night war. More than ever, during the closing months of 1943, night fighting became a battle of wits and electronic wizardry. Göring was openly envious of Britain's advanced technology. "They have the geniuses and we have the nincompoops," he said. "After this war's over I'm going to buy myself a British radio set." The RAF's continuing use of Window to confound German radar was a particular source of frustration for the Reich Marshal. In search of a technical solution to the problem, he funded a nationwide competition with prizes of up to 162,500 reichsmarks—the equivalent of $65,000— but none of the submitted schemes proved feasible.

Further improvements in tactics appeared to offer a better bet than technology, and so the Luftwaffe's planners embraced an idea that had come from their own midst—put forward by Colonel Viktor von Lossberg, an ex-bomber pilot serving on the general staff of the night-fighter force. The Lossberg plan called for a more effective use of the conventional twin-engined interceptors that guarded Germany's western approaches. These planes were to operate under the code name of *Zahme Sau*—Tame Boars—to set them apart from the Wild Boars; but they, too, were to employ more freedom of action. Instead of being confined to patrolling fixed zones along the Kammhuber Line, they were now to rove far afield in seeking out the foe.

Like the Wild Boars, the Tame Boars took off at an alert from ground control. But rather than speeding to a city already under RAF attack, they aimed to get into the British bomber stream en route to the target. To do so, they moved from one radio beacon to another—there were 21 in all dotted through the western approaches—to get ground control's running commentary on the probable location of the enemy bombers. Ironically, the controllers were able to use the Window device to advantage in determining the likely area—by watching for the biggest concentration of blips on their radar screens. They would direct the Tame Boars to the area indicated, and the interceptors would begin their own visual search for the enemy, then close in.

There were five ground control centers in all, one for each Luftwaffe air division assigned to the defense of the homeland. The centers were underground, in bunkers so elaborately outfitted that one German described them as "battle opera houses." An enormous wall map of frosted glass showed Europe. Opposite the map, in amphitheater-like rows, sat dozens of young women Luftwaffe auxiliaries, wearing headsets and listening for word on the whereabouts of the enemy bombers. The reports came from a vast network of monitoring posts: ground observers, radar stations and new electronic devices that could track the radar impulses emitted by the British navigational aid, H2S. With each report on a bomber's location, the auxiliary would train the beam of a small spotlight at the appropriate point on the frosted-glass map. This function gave the women their special name, *Leuchtspucker*—light spitters.

The ground controller, from his seat up in the balcony, watched the points of light scuttling about the map and then dispatched the Tame Boars accordingly. Sometimes he found himself directing as many as 200 fighters. He was only as good as the information that he received, but the best controllers also employed intuition and educated guesswork to predict the target accurately and to get the Tame Boars to the right radio beacons. The controllers were aware of how much rode on their decisions. A correct assessment could bring the entire night-fighter force to bear on the RAF bomber stream. A wrong one could send the Tame Boars roaming through the skies without firing a shot.

The British did their utmost to fox the ground controllers. They installed powerful radio transmitters in England and aboard Lancaster bombers over Germany and jammed the ground controllers' running commentaries to the Tame Boars with electronic noises. Then they began broadcasting their own bogus running commentaries, using fake ground controllers who could speak German. Further to confuse the Tame Boars, the British broadcast phony weather reports; once they even got the German fighters to land prematurely by predicting the onset of a heavy fog.

Since the British were employing men as their fake controllers, the Germans countered by using a woman controller. But shortly after she began her commentary, the British went on the air with a woman who spoke flawless German. And when Luftwaffe ground control resorted to a musical code to identify the evening bombers' probable target—a waltz meant Munich, jazz signified Berlin—the British retaliated with a barrage of ringing bells, band music and phonograph records blaring Hitler's strident speeches.

On the night of November 18, 1943, the British launched the campaign they called the Battle of Berlin. It lasted for four and a half months, through the end of March of 1944, and included 35 major raids that used an average of more than 500 bombers a night. Nineteen of the raids were directed against various cities scattered around the Reich in an attempt to keep the German air defenses from ganging up. But 16 missions concentrated on Berlin itself—the greatest assault yet mounted against a single target.

Air Chief Marshal Harris was bent upon repeating the kind of devastation that had been heaped upon Hamburg the previous summer. Berlin, as the seat of Nazi power, attracted him much as Schweinfurt's ball-bearing factories had drawn the Americans. On November 3, the leader of Bomber Command wrote Prime Minister Churchill: "We can wreck Berlin from end to end if the U.S. Army Air Forces will come in on it. It will cost between us 400 and 500 aircraft. It will cost Germany the war."

The Americans, still recovering from their heavy losses at Schweinfurt, could not go along with the Harris plan. Nor would they have chosen to in any case. By now, they were under orders to concentrate their efforts on knocking out the Luftwaffe in preparation for the invasion of Europe. This was the officially affirmed aim of the British as well, but Harris clung to the belief that he could somehow bomb Germany out of the War without an invasion. With Prime Minister Churchill's enthusiastic approval, Harris plunged ahead with the Battle of Berlin.

Though Harris vowed to keep hammering away at Berlin "until the heart of Nazi Germany ceases to beat," the capital proved to be an extraordinarily difficult target. Because much of it was built of brick and stone, and because its broad streets served as natural firebreaks, it was harder to burn than the older city of Hamburg. It was too far from England for the RAF bombers to make use of the Oboe target-finding device, and too sprawling to provide clear-cut images on their H2S viewing screens. The Luftwaffe had made the target-finding task even tougher by constructing decoy targets out in the countryside, including a full-sized, plywood-and-cardboard replica of Berlin measuring nine miles in diameter.

Moreover, the new night-defense system proved increasingly efficient, racking up some of the Luftwaffe's best scores of the War: 55 attacking bombers were downed over Magdeburg on January 21, 1944, another 43 over Berlin on January 28, and 78 over Leipzig on February 19. On such nights, it was not unusual for several German pilots to shoot down four or five bombers apiece in a couple of hours. The Luftwaffe's recordkeepers had a relatively liberal system of awarding "kills," and some of the night aces, like the German day aces, were piling up kill totals that would ultimately far surpass those of the top American and British fighter pilots. At least in part, the high scores of the Germans were attributable to the Luftwaffe's practice of not rotating its pilots. The men were kept flying until they were killed or seriously injured.

The Luftwaffe's night fighters accounted for about two thirds of the bombers shot down during the Battle of Berlin, and antiaircraft batteries accounted for the rest. Up to now, some of the Luftwaffe's top brass had questioned the worth of these ground units. By one estimate, shooting down a single enemy bomber required an average of 3,343 88mm shells at a cost of 267,440 reichsmarks—about $107,000. It was also argued that the system tied down guns that could have been put to profitable use on the Russian front, since they had proved to be deadly against tanks. Ironically, the

The deadly flak met by Allied bombers came in many forms and sizes, from 22-pound explosive shells that could be hurled six miles high or more by 88mm batteries (far left) to the 37mm and 20mm tracer shells seen greeting RAF night bombers over an unidentified German city at near left. The smaller guns, which had effective ranges of about one mile, were aimed visually with the help of the tracer trails. In most cases, 88mm guns were brought to bear on their distant targets by radar.

personnel of the antiaircraft units in the Battle of Berlin included Russian prisoners of war, as well as German women, old men and teen-age boys. This fact led one jocular battery commander to address his unit as "Ladies and gentlemen, fellow workers, schoolboys and comrades."

Despite the debate over the worth of the ground batteries, the Luftwaffe had managed over the past year to increase the number of guns by more than a third, including many 128mm's with a much higher reach and greater radius of burst. This weaponry was concentrated in *Grossbatterien,* huge groupings of up to 40 guns each that hurled rectangular patterns of shellbursts known as box barrages. Ordinarily, the British bomber stream was carefully routed around the heaviest concentrations of flak. But on the night of March 24, when the RAF planes visited Berlin for the 16th time in little over four months, unusually fierce winds drove them into the thick of the shellfire. The result was the best score of the War for the antiaircraft guns. They accounted for at least 50 of the 72 bombers shot down that night.

For the British, this ill-fated mission marked the final attempt on Berlin during the long winter campaign. Harris had failed to fulfill his vow to wreck the city. But the last big battle of the campaign was still to be fought. On the night of March 30, Harris dispatched 795 bombers to Nuremberg in southeast Germany.

Nuremberg was relatively unimportant from a strategic standpoint. It was not a major industrial center. It was, however, a celebrated symbol of Nazi power—long associated with the grandiose party rallies held there. But after choosing it as a target, Harris let down his guard on the night of the raid. Instead of routing his bombers on a zigzag course to confuse the German ground controllers, he sent them virtually straight in. And though he anticipated some cloud cover to shroud the bomber stream, the skies proved so clear that the ground controllers could scarcely believe their good fortune.

By 11 p.m. the Germans' early-warning network had detected two separate streams of bombers approaching the coast of Europe. One was a force of 50 old Halifaxes, intended by the British as a decoy. These planes were cruising over the North Sea and dropping the metal-foil strips of Window to jam the German radar. The Nuremberg-bound force, 795 planes, was crossing the English Channel toward Belgium.

By tracking emissions from the H2S radar aboard the bombers, the German ground controllers correctly guessed which bomber stream was bigger, and immediately ordered the Tame Boars to assemble over a radio beacon code-named Ida, about 50 miles east of Aachen.

It turned out to be a fortuitous move for the Luftwaffe. The bomber stream was entering Germany through an area that was known to the British as the Cologne Gap—a 20-mile-wide corridor that would make it possible for the raiders to pass between the big flak concentrations at the southern edge of the Ruhr Valley and a smaller one farther south. Ida was 15 miles to the north of the Cologne Gap.

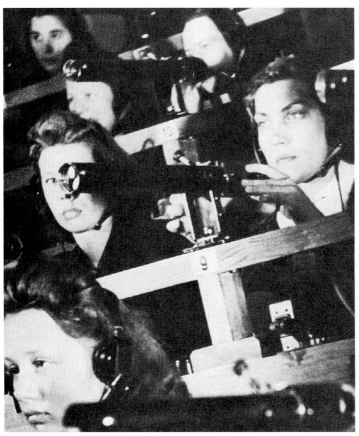

The lead elements of the bomber stream entered Germany at midnight and threaded their way safely through the Cologne Gap. But the planes in the middle of the bomber stream ran into winds of up to 90 miles per hour and drifted north into the orbiting assemblage of Tame Boars.

Many of the German planes were newly equipped with two devices that the Luftwaffe had managed to keep secret from the British. One was a new variety of airborne radar, Lichtenstein SN-2, which operated on a wave length that made it impervious to jamming by the deceptive strips of metal foil; it could detect a bomber at a range of up to four miles. The Germans had been so anxious to prevent SN-2 from falling into the hands of the British that when an Me-110 equipped with the device landed in Switzerland by mistake, they persuaded the Swiss to blow it up. The Swiss price was a squadron of brand-new single-engined fighters.

The Luftwaffe's other new device consisted of a pair of 20mm cannon mounted on top of the Me-110 in such a way that they could fire upward from beneath a British bomber. Because the cannon slanted slightly forward, this innovation was known as *schräge Musik*—literally, "slanting music," but idiomatically translated as "jazz music."

Jazz Music had evolved from a series of accidents in which night fighters, while flying in their traditional *von unten hinten* position of attack—from under and behind the bomber—had shot down their own comrades. Ordered to fly directly underneath their quarry to obtain positive identification before firing, the night fighters had discovered that the British bomber crews could not see them. On the few previous occasions when Jazz Music had been tried, the RAF crews did not, in fact, know what had hit them. Nearby crews, seeing a bomber suddenly explode, had refused to believe the evidence of their eyes and had assumed that the Germans were trying to scare them with a bizarre flak shell that simulated the flash of a bomber exploding.

As the Tame Boars employed their new devices against the Nuremberg-bound bombers, they also received some assistance from nature. The moon, although it was not full, was unusually bright that night, and the temperature was so cold that the steam pouring out of the bombers' exhausts condensed, leaving brilliant phosphorescent trails to follow. One British airman had the impression of "being on a well-lit main road and being shot at from unlit side streets."

The odds against the bombers were stacked so high that many of the raiders suspected a betrayal; they were convinced that the details of the raid had somehow been revealed to the Luftwaffe in advance. In the first hour after midnight, bombers went down at the rate of one per minute, marking part of the 300-mile route from the German border to Nuremberg with their blazing wrecks.

And when the British finally reached the target after flying so vulnerably through clear, moonlit skies, they found clouds nearly two miles thick obscuring Nuremberg. Many of their bombs fell in open country. Some fell as distant as 55 miles from Nuremberg—on Schweinfurt, the Americans' ball-bearing target that Harris had insisted was too small for his planes to find at night.

By the time the bombers turned for home, a number of Luftwaffe aces had boosted their personal kill scores. First Lieutenant Helmut Schulte destroyed four Lancasters with just 56 shells from his upward-firing Jazz Music. Near Nuremberg, he framed a fifth Lancaster in his sights only to find the Jazz Music jammed. Schulte switched to his conventional forward-firing cannon, but the Lancaster, piloted by Warrant Officer Howard Hemming, went into a weaving corkscrew maneuver and the shells passed harmlessly over the bomber's wings.

Schulte pursued the Lancaster for about five minutes, jockeying for the *von unten hinten* position. Every time he fired, however, Hemming expertly corkscrewed his bomber and eluded the shells. Sometime past 1:30 a.m., after Schulte had been aloft more than two hours, the German decided to let the Englishman off the hook. "He had been through as much as I had," Schulte recalled years later. "We had both been to Nuremberg that night—so I decided that was enough." Hemming thus made it safely back to England, but 95 of the 795 British bombers did not. The Germans lost no more than 10 fighters. It was Bomber Command's worst night of the War—and the Luftwaffe's best.

In all, the Battle of Berlin cost the British 1,047 bombers, more than their total frontline strength on any given night. Like the American strategists after Schweinfurt, Harris at last knew that the bomber alone was not enough. He, too, needed fighter escorts to fend off the resurgent Luftwaffe. Only eight months after its humiliation at Hamburg, it now ruled the night skies over the Reich.

In an underground Luftwaffe fighter control center, women aides (far left) receive telephoned reports of approaching Allied bomber forces and project the planes' positions onto the rear of a translucent map with beams of light. Other aides, silhouetted behind the screen (left), plot the bombers' course, and liaison officers in front of the map radio the formations' latest positions to Luftwaffe fighters. Photographs were made of the map every five minutes for later study of fighter tactics.

THE LUFTWAFFE'S ELITE

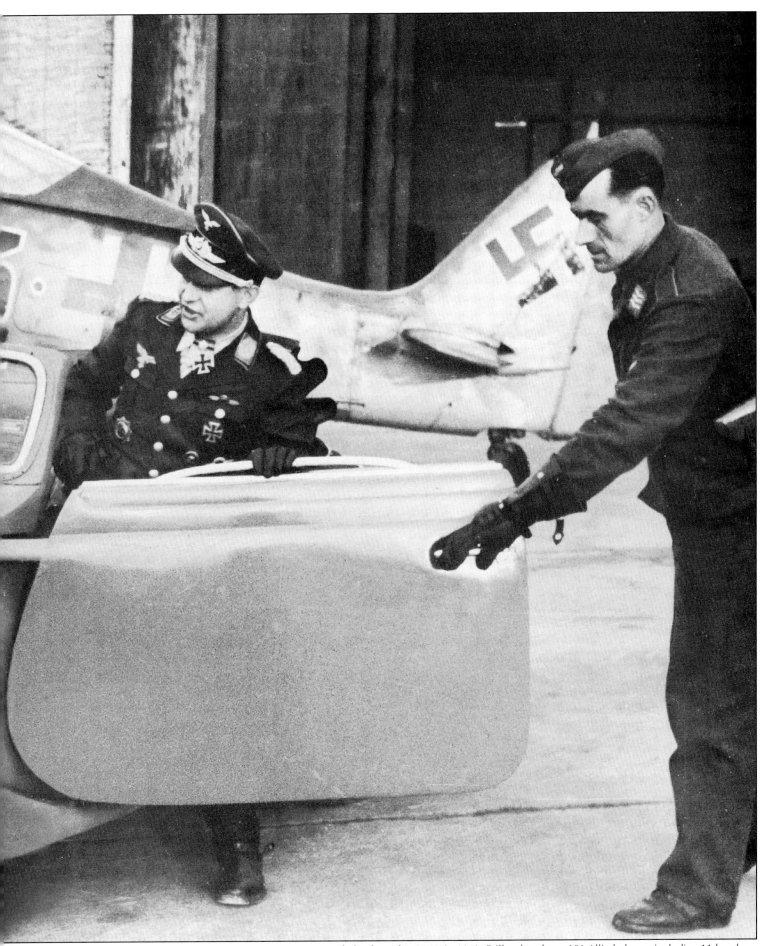

Major Josef Priller, the head of a Luftwaffe fighter wing in France, is helped into his BMW in 1943. Priller shot down 101 Allied planes, including 11 bombers.

GERMANY'S FAVORITES BECOME SCAPEGOATS

As the spearhead for Hitler's blitzkrieg in 1939 and 1940, the Luftwaffe fighter command was an elite force that could do no wrong. The pilots fought with gallantry and devastating skill, racking up hundreds of kills. They were idolized and rewarded with French wines, Russian furs, Balkan tobacco, beautiful women and, of course, Iron Crosses. Luftwaffe commander Hermann Göring set aside scarce transport planes to take the fliers home on leaves, and he spent more than one million reichmarks (about $250,000) to set up a mountain resort solely for the distinguished Richthofen squadrons. Hitler's headquarters staff boasted, "The Luftwaffe can do anything."

But the Luftwaffe's days of glory abruptly gave way to years of crisis. The first crucial reverse came as early as 1940, when the Luftwaffe failed to knock out the RAF in the Battle of Britain. At that point, wrote ace Adolf Galland, the myth of Luftwaffe invincibility "had been exploded." Galland and other Luftwaffe realists foresaw an inexorable war of attrition: the Allies, endowed with more manpower and production facilities, would send hordes of bombers to wear down the Luftwaffe fighters. Field Marshal Erhard Milch later warned that "the enemy knows that he must wipe out our fighters. Once he has done that, he will be able to play football with the German people."

Month after critical month, Hitler took no emergency measures to beef up the fighter command. He believed the steady stream of reports he received from self-serving production personnel, who misled him with scrambled and hopelessly overoptimistic figures on aircraft output, which did increase sporadically, but not nearly enough. According to Milch, Hitler was convinced that "he had done too much for the fighters." The Führer seemed determined to punish the hard-pressed pilots for their failure to put an end to the Allied bombing raids.

True to Galland's forebodings, the odds against the fighter pilots mounted steadily. They battled on courageously, but by 1944 they were in the same desperate plight that their RAF counterparts had been in just four years before.

Fighter commander Adolf Galland signs his autograph on an admirer's back. In 1942, at the age of 30, he became Germany's youngest general.

German fighter pilots take a well-earned break between sorties. When the air war turned against Germany, Hitler accused the fighter command of laziness.

REDOUBLED EFFORTS TO STEM THE ALLIED TIDE

"That was a lot of fun," said a diehard Luftwaffe fighter pilot after returning from a mission late in the War. "Why don't we refuel and go again?" The fact is that by then back-to-back missions had become a sheer necessity. Göring ordered that every pilot refuel at least three times before being allowed to quit a battle. Some men flew more than five sorties in a single day. Many pilots chalked up 500 missions and more than 1,000 combat hours—far more than their adversaries.

Fighter commander Galland, who continued to fly combat missions in addition to his administrative duties, gave his comrades due credit for an "aggressive spirit, joy of action, and the passion of the hunter." But the price of gallantry kept rising until it was higher than the Luftwaffe could afford. Galland said, "Each incursion of the enemy is costing us about fifty aircrew." With few exceptions, he said, "our aces fought until they were killed."

Hard-working ground crewmen of a Richthofen fighter squadron rearm and service a Focke-Wulf 190.

Admiring airmen greet ace Günther Rall, landing after a sortie. Rall was grounded by a back injury in a 1941 crash, but returned to combat nine months later.

An exultant pilot indicates his victory as he springs from his cockpit.

A fighter pilot relives a maneuver he used to down an enemy plane.

Putting the finishing touches on his latest victory, a Luftwaffe pilot painstakingly paints the tail of his Messerschmitt fighter with a stripe denoting a kill.

Modified to attack tanks, a Junkers-87 dive bomber carries a pair of 37mm cannon under its wings.

A belly gas tank added to an Me-109 extended

Me-109s raid England on a two-hour fuel supply. On one sortie, 12 109s ran out of gas and had to ditch.

GETTING MORE OUT OF LESS

"Fighters, fighters, fighters, that's what we need!" railed Ernst Udet, Luftwaffe production chief, in 1941. But his output remained pitifully small—fewer than 1,400 single-engined fighters in six months—and he soon committed suicide in despair.

Though Udet's successor, Erhard Milch,

its range by about 170 miles and also increased its fighting time. Fighters equipped with these tanks frequently lurked aloft to get the jump on bombers.

upped production to more than 9,600 in 1943, the combat odds failed to improve. By 1944, the Luftwaffe was shooting down a bomber for every fighter it lost—a remarkable record, except for the fact that the Allies were outproducing the Reich in airplanes by more than 2 to 1. The problem was compounded by the woeful inadequacy of repair facilities: fully one third of the Luftwaffe's single-engined fighters were out of action in September of 1943.

Hitler had contributed to the shortage of planes by placing the Luftwaffe in fifth place on his priority list for urgently needed metals. Incredibly, the fighter force was allowed to suffer for the lack of aluminum, which was being used to build termite-proof barracks for the postwar occupation of Germany's tropical colonies.

To make do with what they had, the Luftwaffe commanders jury-rigged fighters with extra armament, bombs, spare gaso-line tanks and whatever else could extend their utility. But pilots complained that the added load detracted from the planes' speed and maneuverability, and increased the casualty rate. The truth was inescapable—there were simply not enough fighters to go around. When Milch later was asked what the Luftwaffe's biggest mistake had been, he delivered the answer with bitter vehemence: "One hundred and forty thousand unbuilt fighter aircraft!"

Luftwaffe recruits watch attack techniques demonstrated with models. The wires attached to the enemy B-24 showed fields of fire that pilots had to avoid.

Fledgling pilots prepare to test-fire an Me-109's guns at a combat base. They completed their studies there because of the shortage of training facilities.

BELATED REACTIONS TO THE MANPOWER PINCH

"The only raw material that cannot be restored in the foreseeable future is human blood," cautioned Field Marshal Milch in 1943. By then, the cumulative effect of fighter-pilot losses was overtaking a training system with far too little depth. Germany had entered the War with only one school for fighter pilots, and the Luftwaffe at first replaced the casualties by faster, sketchier training. General Galland noted that the student pilots suffered "immense casualties during training, which were only justifiable because of the extraordinary state of emergency."

In a belated effort to make amends, the Luftwaffe opened 10 new schools in 1944. But the youths who graduated were so poorly prepared for combat that the main contribution they made was to the list of casualties. Said Galland, "Between January and April 1944, our day fighter arm lost more than 1,000 pilots."

Freeing men for combat, women staff a Luftwaffe fighter control station in occupied France in 1944.

A day fighter gets ready for a night mission. Skimpy training for blind flying at night and in bad weather contributed to the Luftwaffe's alarming loss rate.

Once the terror of the skies, an FW-190 lies hidden in a forest in France.

THE FIGHTER COMMAND IN BATTERED DISARRAY

In 1944, all of the Luftwaffe's losses and shortages came home to roost. The fighter pilots were opposed by vastly superior numbers—8 to 1 in some aerial battles that spring and summer—and they also faced a worsening fuel shortage. The Allies had turned their attention to Germany's crucial gasoline refineries, and production of aviation fuel plunged from nearly 200,000 tons in May to a mere trickle of 7,000 tons by October. The fighter pilots "retired to the forests," Galland said, camouflaging their planes to escape Allied attacks.

Incredibly, the German fighters would be able to mount a major counteroffensive. But in general, bitter recriminations were now the only things still flying. Hitler bellowed at Göring, "Your Luftwaffe isn't worth a damn!" Predicted production chief Milch, "We shall be forced to our knees before the coming year is out."

Luftwaffe crewmen cautiously push a lone Focke-Wulf fighter onto an airfield

in France in 1944. At the time of the Allied invasion, Galland later wrote, "the danger of being detected and destroyed by the enemy was ever present."

5

At the age of 31, Adolf Galland was one of the youngest of the Luftwaffe's generals, and one of the shrewdest. Despite his fighter pilots' successes on the home front in the second half of 1943 and early 1944, he harbored no illusions that their winning streak would continue. And he knew when the turning point would come: when Allied bombers began to appear deep inside Germany with a protective shield of fighter escorts.

Galland kept worrying about this eventuality and watching for signs that it impended. One day in late September of 1943 his forebodings were confirmed by an incident at Aachen. This ancient city, just inside Germany's western border, marked the point beyond which Allied fighters did not ordinarily venture. Once they had accompanied their bombers to the German border, they would turn back, unable to go farther into Germany because of the limited amount of fuel they could carry without impairing their speed and maneuverability. On that September day, several of the escorts—American P-47 Thunderbolts—were shot down and proved to be equipped with auxiliary fuel tanks that would have taken them beyond their usual range.

As it happened, Galland soon had the chance to convey these tidings directly to Hitler. Summoned to discuss what could be done to prevent the Americans' daylight raids, he reiterated his standard plea for more fighters, but he raised his estimate of the number that would be needed. Thwarting the enemy attacks, Galland estimated, would require a Luftwaffe fighter force three or four times the size of the U.S. bomber force. Even this numerical superiority would be insufficient, Galland added pointedly, if the Americans increased their fighter escorts and sent them ever deeper inside Germany.

Hitler, who had listened without demur to Galland's proposal for an expanded fighter force, bristled at the suggestion that the U.S. escorts could extend their penetration of the Reich. Saying he had Göring's own assurance that such a possibility was completely out of the question, he curtly dismissed Galland.

Later that day, Galland paid what he thought would be no more than a routine call on his Luftwaffe boss; Göring was about to leave on his special train for a hunting trip at a forest preserve in East Prussia, and Galland went to bid him goodbye. What ensued instead was a scene so tense that

SUPREMACY IN THE SKY

Minister of Armaments Speer, who happened to be present, never forgot it.

Göring, he recalled, was clearly out of sorts. Galland, self-assured as usual, stood at ease, his general's cap slightly askew, and the ever-present long black cigar clamped between his teeth; in his days as a fighter ace, he had even installed a special holder in the cockpit of his Me-109 so he could park an unlighted cigar while flying on oxygen.

Göring got right to the point. "What's the idea of telling the Führer that American fighters have penetrated into the territory of the Reich?" he snapped.

"Herr Reichsmarschall," Galland coolly answered, "they will soon be flying even deeper."

"That's nonsense, Galland. What gives you such fantasies? That's pure bluff!"

"Those are the facts," replied the young general. "You might go and check it yourself, sir; the downed planes are there at Aachen."

Göring then lamely suggested that the planes had actually been shot down west of the German border and "could have glided quite a distance farther" before they crashed. Galland insisted that the planes were over Aachen at the time they were shot down.

Finally, Göring erupted: "I herewith give you an official order that they weren't there! Do you understand? The American fighters were not there!"

As the Reich Marshal stalked off, Galland smiled cynically and called after him: "Orders are orders, sir!"

By early 1944 Galland no longer needed to argue his case. More and more, the American bombers that appeared in the daylight skies over Germany flew in the company of "Little Friends"—their radio terminology for Allied escort fighters. To the Luftwaffe pilots, the newcomers were soon known as *Indianer,* in reference to the savage warriors of the American Wild West.

The feisty Little Friends, all single-seaters, came in a variety of shapes and sizes. The biggest, the P-38 Lightning, had two engines mounted on twin fuselages. The single-engined P-47 Thunderbolt had a blunt nose and a stubby body. The single-engined P-51 Mustang was the smallest and trimmest of the three; one early model weighed only 8,800 pounds, less than half the weight of the Lightning.

The Mustang was to prove to be the bombers' most reliable friend and the best all-around fighter plane of the War. Its development was due not to the Americans but to the British. Built to their order by a U.S. plane manufacturer in 1941, the Mustang was at first largely ignored by American air strategists. The early models lacked power at high altitudes, and the British had to relegate the plane to a tactical role in low-level support of infantry.

But in 1942 they fitted the Mustang with a bigger engine, the Rolls-Royce Merlin, which also powered their Spitfires. Flight tests demonstrated that the new model Mustang, the P-51B, could achieve what had been regarded as a technical impossibility: the performance of a fighter coupled with the long range of a bomber. It had a big fuel capacity plus an economical engine that burned only about half the gasoline of other U.S. fighters' engines. It could reach a top speed of 440 miles per hour at 30,000 feet. In all, the tests suggested that the Mustang could outspeed, outclimb and outdive any fighter the Luftwaffe had in service.

Despite the Mustang's exciting potential, the Americans were still reluctant to mass-produce the plane for their own use; they believed that its liquid-cooled engine was far more susceptible to damage by enemy gunfire than the radial air-cooled engine of the Thunderbolt. In any case, some U.S. strategists were not yet convinced of the need for long-range fighters; they continued to cling to the belief that their big bomber formations could defend themselves over Germany.

This faith was shaken by the disastrous losses incurred in the U.S. raids on Regensburg and Schweinfurt in August of 1943. Production of the Mustang was stepped up, and by late November the first few dozen were at Eighth Air Force bases in England, ready for action along with the Thunderbolts and Lightnings that had previously seen escort duty as far as the German border.

Like the Mustang, these older planes were now outfitted with auxiliary fuel tanks. The tanks were at first slung under the fuselage; later they were placed under the wings. Once the fuel in them was exhausted, the pilot could jettison them; relieved of the added weight, he could achieve greater speed and maneuverability in combat. But while in use, the drop tanks gave the Little Friends "extra legs," as Army Air Forces Chief Arnold put it. The Mustang had the longest legs of all: with a 108-gallon tank under each wing, the P-51B and later models would eventually be able to fly all the way to Poland and back to England, a 1,700-mile round trip.

While the fighter force was being expanded and improved, increasing numbers of Flying Fortresses and Liberators were also arriving from the States, along with the crews to man them. By the end of December 1943, the Eighth Air Force was prepared to mount missions of as many as 720 bombers—almost twice the capability it had at the time of the second raid on Schweinfurt only 10 weeks earlier. In addition, it was to have help in the renewed bombing offensive from the U.S. Fifteenth Air Force, now established in the Foggia area in southeast Italy, in the wake of Allied ground advances up the Italian peninsula.

The Fifteenth was a much smaller force than the Eighth, and in need of training and seasoning. But its role in the bomber offensive was critical. From its bases in Italy, the Fifteenth could strike at enemy targets far beyond the reach of the Eighth, hitting at Germany itself through the Reich's southern approaches and at German-held bastions in the Balkans and Greece. Moreover, the flying weather around the Mediterranean was generally better than in northern Europe—though many a Fifteenth pilot, watching his plane ice over as he crossed the Alps into Germany or Austria, would soon argue otherwise.

Before long, the Fifteenth was to shake off its initial assessment as a "pretty disorganized mob." The critique was General Eaker's, who—to his own surprise—was now running the Allied air war in the Mediterranean. Eaker, who had headed the Eighth through its blooding in 1943, had been reassigned so that the original commander of the Eighth, General Spaatz, could return to England from North Africa to oversee all U.S. air operations in Europe. Spaatz was the choice of the newly designated Supreme Commander of the Allied Expeditionary Force, General Dwight D. Eisenhower. The air general had served under Eisenhower in the invasion of North Africa; as Ike moved to England in January of 1944 to prepare for the invasion of the European continent, he wanted Spaatz with him again. Spaatz brought with him a new commander for the Eighth, Lieut. General James H. Doolittle. As a lieutenant colonel, Jimmy Doolittle had lifted the spirits of the American public by a daring carrier-based bombing raid on Tokyo in April of 1942; more recently, he had commanded the U.S. Twelfth Air Force in the Mediterranean.

Eaker was bitterly disappointed at his transfer. He wanted to finish the job he had begun over Germany, and in an emotional appeal to his boss in Washington, General Arnold, declared that it was "heartbreaking to leave just before the climax."

Eaker was somewhat mollified after a stopover in Casablanca en route to his new headquarters in Italy. He had received a message asking that he pay a call on a mysterious "Colonel Holt"—who turned out to be Winston Churchill. Traveling incognito, Churchill was in Casablanca recovering from pneumonia. He received Eaker at the same villa where,

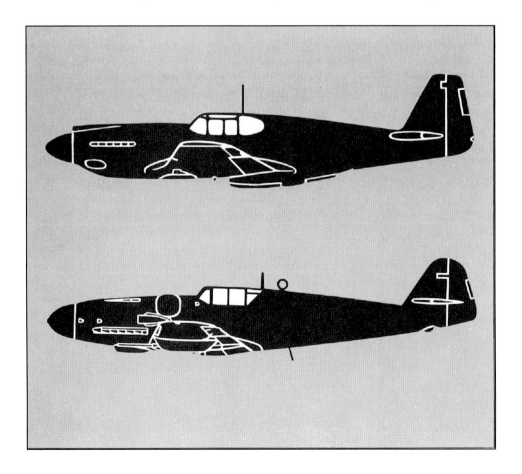

Profile silhouettes of the Messerschmitt-109 (bottom) and the P-51 Mustang (top) reveal the planes' confusing degree of similarity in size and contour. On a number of occasions—many of which understandably were never reported—the resemblance prompted bomber gunners or fighter pilots to shoot down friendly planes that suddenly flashed into view.

just one year earlier, the American general had sold the Prime Minister on round-the-clock bombing. "Your representations to me at that time have been more than verified," Churchill said. "Around-the-clock bombing is now achieving the results you predicted."

The goal of the American air build-up was summed up by General Arnold in a New Year's message for 1944 to his new commanders in Europe. "This is a MUST," he wrote. "Destroy the Enemy Air Force wherever you find them, in the air, on the ground and in the factories."

The goal was essentially the same as the one set forth in the Pointblank Directive in June of 1943. But its realization was now more crucial than ever. As long as Messerschmitts and Focke-Wulfs swarmed the skies over Europe, the projected Allied invasion of France was likely to entail a prohibitive cost in human lives. The date tentatively set for the landings was May 1, 1944, and the time available for removing the threat posed by the Luftwaffe was, in fact, even less. January and February could not be counted on for flying; in midwinter, Europe's weather made most missions chancy. A day without heavy cloud cover was exceptional, a rare opportunity to be watched for and seized.

On January 11, 1944, the Eighth Air Force had a report of clear skies over north-central Germany and quickly went ahead with a mission of special import: this was to be the first large-scale American raid with fighter protection deep into the Reich. The targets, in three cities clustered about 90 miles west of Berlin, figured as high priorities in the Luftwaffe's operations. Most of its FW-190s were produced at a factory in Oschersleben. A plant at Halberstadt was believed to be building wings for Ju-88s. Me-110 parts were made and the planes assembled at three plants in and around Brunswick.

The U.S. strike force consisted of 663 Fortresses and Liberators, divided into three formations. Their fighter escort was made up of 11 groups of Thunderbolts, two groups of Lightnings and a single group of Mustangs—the only one available, numbering 49 planes. Bombers and escorts were to rendezvous over the Dutch coast. The Lightnings and Thunderbolts were to accompany the bombers to within 70 miles of the target and meet them about 100 miles from it on the way back to the coast. Only the Mustangs, with their more extended radius of action, were to stay with the bombers all the way to the target, provide support there and escort them back.

The weather was so bad over England that the mission had trouble taking off and assembling. Conditions en route proved to be even worse, and rapidly deteriorating. The overcast became so thick that a decision was made to recall all planes that had not yet penetrated far into Germany; about two thirds of the bombers turned back, and so did many of the Lightnings and Thunderbolts.

For the planes that flew on, the Luftwaffe provided a reception as tumultuous as the one that had greeted the American raiders at Schweinfurt. The German interceptors were not only out in force but also newly equipped with drop tanks. The extra fuel allowed them to bide their time aloft until the shorter-range enemy escorts had peeled off, then swoop in on unprotected Fortresses and Liberators. A total of 60 U.S. bombers went down—a loss equal to that suffered over Schweinfurt in October.

The raiders managed to inflict heavy damage on the Focke-Wulf factory at Oschersleben, where half of their bombs fell within 1,000 feet of the aiming point, and on one of the three targets near Brunswick, where three quarters of the bombs found their mark. But the brightest spot in the day's picture was the Mustangs' performance. Split into two sections to cover the operations at Oschersleben and Halberstadt, the 49 Mustangs proved more than a match for the Luftwaffe's interceptors. The Mustangs suffered no losses and destroyed an estimated 15 enemy planes.

At one point, some of the Mustang pilots looked down and saw Me-110s and Me-109s below the bombers, "climbing," one pilot recalled, "like a swarm of bees." A voice came over the radio: "Go down and get the bastards!" The fighter pilots swooped to the attack; in the ensuing combat, the eager Mustang rookies shot down nine German interceptors without a loss. But in their headlong dive they had left their bombers unprotected.

As this thought occurred to Major James Howard, the Mustangs' leader, he pulled his plane up short and climbed back. Unlike most of his men, Howard was a veteran of air war—a former Navy pilot who had fought in China with the Flying Tigers against the Japanese before going to Europe.

When Howard reached the bombers, they were under

assault by some 30 German fighters. Ordinarily, an escort pilot was supposed to engage in combat only if his wingman was protecting his rear. Howard took on the entire enemy force alone.

His first victim was a relatively easy target, a slower-moving twin-engined Me-110. "I went down after him," Howard recalled, "gave him several squirts and watched him crash. He stood out very clearly, silhouetted against the snow that covered the ground." Next was a much-faster single-engined FW-190, "cruising along beneath me. He pulled up into the sun when he saw me. I gave him a squirt and I almost ran into his canopy when he threw it off to get out. He bailed out." In short order, Howard attacked four other fighters. During one of these encounters, three of his four .50-caliber machine guns jammed, but he kept hammering away with the fourth.

The entire episode was over so quickly that Howard was not sure how many German fighters he had gunned down. When he returned to England, dangerously low on fuel, he claimed two planes destroyed and brushed aside his performance with a flippant "I seen my duty and I done it."

But the bomber crews who had witnessed Howard's feat —"the greatest exhibition I have ever seen," declared the bomber-formation leader, Major Allison Brooks—claimed four to six kills for him; in the end, he was credited with four. For his solo battle with the Luftwaffe, Howard was awarded the Congressional Medal of Honor, one of the few fighter pilots to win it for aerial combat over Europe.

The Mustang still had a few bugs. As Howard had found, its guns tended to jam during high-speed maneuvers when the force of gravity caused the ammunition belts to clog. This problem was solved on later models by the addition of small auxiliary motors that kept the belts moving.

A second problem was posed by the fact that in silhouette the Mustang closely resembled the Luftwaffe's Me-109. Recognition posters were distributed at the bases in England, and as an added precaution the Mustangs were painted with a yellow band around the chord of the wing. But these measures did not always work. On a number of occasions during the winter of 1944, Mustangs were mistaken for Me-109s and jumped by other American fighters. Another case of mistaken identity might have proved fatal to Mustang pilot Jack T. Bradley. Flying escort over Germany, he lost sight of his squadron mates and radioed a request for their location. Following instructions, he caught up with a formation and settled into his normal slot. After cruising along for several minutes, he glanced casually out the side window and discovered that he was flying in a formation of Messerschmitt-109s. Almost simultaneously, the Me-109s recognized Bradley's plane and started to go after him. Bradley dropped his auxiliary fuel tanks in order to gain speed, then dived out of the formation, leaving his unwanted companions behind.

In spite of the minor problems, American pilots yearned to fly Mustangs and complained that there were not enough of them available. But by the middle of February of 1944, more Mustangs had arrived from the States. In addition, the performance of the Thunderbolt was upgraded. Its range was lengthened by rigging two drop tanks under the wings instead of one under the fuselage. And its climbing speed was increased by a new water-injection system that boosted the engine's horsepower.

Buoyed by their growing fighter and bomber strength, the

General Dwight D. Eisenhower pins the Distinguished Service Cross on American ace Captain Don Gentile at a ceremony in Debden, England, in 1944. At right is Gentile's commanding officer, Colonel Don Blakeslee of the high-scoring 4th Fighter Group.

Americans began preparing for their biggest blow thus far at Germany's aircraft factories, specifically those turning out fighter planes or fighter components. The operation, code-named *Argument,* called for a series of coordinated attacks by the Eighth Air Force from England and the Fifteenth Air Force from Italy, though with the Eighth carrying the main load. But a succession of clear days was required, and the usual forbidding winter weather of the Continent compelled repeated postponements. Finally, on February 19, the meteorologists forecast a break in the skies over Europe. Early on the morning of February 20, when England itself was blanketed by clouds and snow, General Spaatz sent word from his intertheater headquarters at Teddington outside London: "Let 'em go."

That morning the Eighth hurled virtually its entire operational strength against a dozen targets in central Germany and western Poland. For the first time, more than 1,000 U.S. bombers took part. Nearly as many fighters—Mustangs, Thunderbolts, Lightnings and British Spitfires—accompanied them at various stages of their journey. The fighters, clustered in flights of four about 200 yards apart, were positioned like four outstretched fingers of a hand—an arrangement originally devised by the Luftwaffe to guard against enemy attack from all directions.

In a typical deployment of a fighter group, two flights flew "top cover," about 3,000 feet above each bomber formation, while others flew on either side of it. Others flew in front, some up to 10 miles ahead of the formation so as to intercept the Luftwaffe fighters before they could get close to the bombers. To maintain station as they patrolled, the escorts had to keep weaving; otherwise, they would have far outstripped the slower bombers.

The U.S. commanders were braced for the loss of as many as 200 of their bombers on the first day of Operation *Argument.* But the protection afforded by the escort planes, combined with an unexpected show of timidity by the Luftwaffe, paid off. Although 21 bombers went down, the loss rate was only about 2 per cent.

Five more days of massive U.S. raids followed. During "Big Week," as the Americans came to call it, some 3,800 sorties were flown over the targets, 3,300 by the Eighth Air Force and 500 by the Fifteenth, and about 10,000 tons of bombs were dropped—a tonnage roughly equal to that dropped by the Eighth throughout its entire first year of operation. In all, 226 U.S. bombers and 28 fighters were lost.

Big Week destroyed or damaged more than half of the plant facilities of the German aircraft industry. At Leipzig, center of a third of all Me-109 production, 350 combat-ready fighters were demolished, along with hundreds of others that were only half finished on the assembly lines. Heavy damage was done at Gotha, where most of the twin-engined Me-110s were built, and to the Ju-88 factories located at Aschersleben and Bernburg.

The planners of Big Week concluded that the German aircraft industry had been dealt a crippling blow; they were wrong. The shock of the saturation bombing galvanized the Germans into an urgent program of plant dispersal and reconstruction. Fighter aircraft production, up to now the jealously guarded preserve of Reich Marshal Göring, was placed under a special agency in the efficient hands of Minister of Armaments Speer. At his direction, huge quantities of vital machine tools were salvaged from the wrecked plants; roughhewn shelters, hidden in wooded areas, were speedily built to house airframe and final-assembly operations; the legions of conscript labor were set to work anew. By May, fighter output was to total more than 2,200—a new monthly high.

As it turned out, more damage was done to the Luftwaffe in the sky than on the ground. Aerial combat with the U.S. escort fighters and bombers during Big Week cost the Germans 225 of their airmen dead or missing and 141 wounded. Though the Americans, too, suffered grievous losses—some 2,600 killed, missing or seriously wounded—the German losses were proportionately far higher. They represented fully a tenth of the personnel that was available to man the Luftwaffe's interceptors.

In the wake of Big Week the Luftwaffe's commanders became increasingly cautious. Though their resources were still formidable, they began conscious efforts to conserve, backing away from full-scale confrontations with the U.S. bombers and choosing where and when they would send up interceptors in strength.

The Americans took the opposite tack, seeking out rather than avoiding concentrations of enemy interceptors. The Little Friends were encouraged to break away from their escort stations and force the Luftwaffe to do battle. As a German fighter pilot later put it: "No longer was it a case of their bombers having to run the gauntlet of our fighters, but of our having to run the gauntlet of both their bombers and their fighters."

The hope of luring the reluctant Luftwaffe into combat helped dictate the Americans' choice of their next big target—Berlin. Though by now the British were beginning to incur almost unbearably heavy losses in their own four-month-long assault on Berlin by night, the Americans felt confident that they could do much better. They were certain that the German day fighters would rise up in swarms to defend their capital and that the Mustangs and Thunderbolts—now equipped with larger wing tanks enabling them to make the 1,200-mile round trip—could best the Luftwaffe over the heart of Hitler's domain.

The first American attempt on Berlin, made on March 4, had more psychological than practical value. Overcast skies forced the recall of all the 502 bombers that set out, except for 30 bombers that failed to get the radioed message. Escorted by about 20 Mustangs, they scattered their payloads on a suburb of Berlin and turned for home without encountering as much opposition as they had expected. Göring himself saw the Mustangs flying over the capital and could no longer refuse to believe that American fighters were penetrating deep into the Third Reich. "I knew the jig was up," he later admitted.

The Mustangs' leader on this mission was Colonel Don Blakeslee, commander of the 4th Fighter Group. Blakeslee was 27, a square-jawed six-footer from Ohio who—said one of his staff officers—"appeared to be made of cast iron laced together with steel cables." Like some of his pilots, Blakeslee had served earlier with the RAF, flying Spitfires in one of the Eagle Squadrons, which were made up of American volunteers. He was nearing the end of a three-year tour of duty, during which he piled up more than 1,000 hours in combat and flew more missions than any U.S. fighter pilot in Europe. To avoid being rotated home after 200 to 300 combat hours, as most fighter pilots were, he had practiced the simple stratagem of doctoring his logbooks.

Above all, Blakeslee was a superb combat leader. "He was everywhere in the battle," wrote his unit's historian,

"twisting and climbing, bellowing and blaspheming, warning and exhorting. His ability to keep things taped in a fight with 40 or 50 planes skidding and turning at 400 miles an hour was a source of wonder."

That first day over Berlin, Blakeslee jumped an Me-109 only to find that his guns had jammed. Swearing loudly, he overtook the German plane, flew alongside and waved in mock courtesy. The German waggled his wings in bewildered acknowledgment, then slipped away.

Two days later Blakeslee again led the Mustangs to Berlin. On this mission there were so many Little Friends—more than 800—that they outnumbered the bombers. They flew in relays across Western Europe. Groups of Thunderbolts and Lightnings flew cover as far as they could, and the Mustangs took the bombers all the way into the target.

Still, there were gaps in the fighter protection, and these were exploited by the largest force of German interceptors the Americans had tangled with since Big Week. One group of interceptors went directly for the bombers while another group engaged their Thunderbolt protectors. The resulting battle raged for 45 minutes along the route to Berlin. Fortunately for the escorts, many of the German fighters were of the slow twin-engined variety more often used for night fighting. These cumbersome planes were so easily outperformed by the Little Friends that the American pilots considered them "meat on the table." The Luftwaffe soon stopped sending them up during daylight hours.

Statistically, the day's combat was a standoff: 80 American aircraft—69 bombers and 11 fighters—went down, many of them to flak. The U.S. pilots claimed 82 German kills. But the Americans now had a seemingly limitless reserve of bombers and fighters to draw on. The Luftwaffe's losses, by contrast, totaled a fifth of the force it sent up that day. When the Americans returned to Berlin on March 8, there were fewer enemy planes to greet them.

This third strike proved to be a particularly memorable one for two of Blakeslee's best pilots: Captain Don Gentile, another Ohioan, and his wingman, Lieutenant John Godfrey, a Rhode Islander. By nature Gentile was low key, Godfrey devil-may-care; but in action their teamwork was faultless. As Gentile and Godfrey rendezvoused with the Fortresses over Berlin, they ran into a swarm of perhaps 20 Me-109s that were attacking one of the bomber formations.

AIR ACES OF THE WESTERN FRONT

Germany

Heinz-Wolfgang Schnaufer—121 kills

Helmut Lent—110 kills

Adolf Galland—104 kills

Great Britain

James Edgar Johnson—38 kills

Adolf Gysbert "Sailor" Malan—35 kills

Pierre H. Clostermann—33 kills

United States

Francis S. Gabreski—28 kills

Robert S. Johnson—27 kills

George E. Preddy—26.83 kills

To a large extent, the victory totals racked up by the top aces in Western Europe depended on length of service. Of the nine aces shown here—three from each major power—the Germans led their rivals by a wide margin primarily because they alone fought for the duration of the War. In turn, the British aces led the U.S. fliers because of longer tours of combat. Contributing to the Americans' totals were partial scores awarded for sharing in a victory; thus one ace amassed the odd total of 26.83 kills.

"Johnny, cover me," Gentile called over the radio. "I'm diving on the Jerry at three o'clock."

"Right behind you, Don," said Godfrey. He followed Gentile down, watched as he closed in on the Me-109, then looked up, down and around and reported: "Go to it, Don, your tail is cleared."

With Godfrey keeping watch, Gentile pulled the trigger on his control stick and blew his quarry apart. Then, taking turns at providing cover for each other, the pair went after more Germans. Climbing, banking, diving, pushing their Mustangs to the limit, each man shot down two Me-109s and shared one more kill.

The day's work was not yet done. On the way home, Gentile and Godfrey spotted an American straggler, a Fortress flying alone with one of its engines out. Godfrey, who by now was completely out of ammunition, called to Gentile: "There's a Big Friend that needs company, Don. How's your ammunition?"

Gentile was running low, but they decided to fly the weaving escort pattern over the Fort to bluff away any German interceptors that might show up. They moved in close, approaching carefully; as Godfrey later explained, Fortresses "had a bad habit of shooting at anything that came in their range." But the bomber crew was so elated to have friendly company that as Godfrey came near he could see, in the open waist gunner's positions, "first one man and then another throwing kisses at me."

He and Gentile kept the stricken Big Friend company until the lonely three-plane formation reached safety over the English Channel. Then the two Mustangs raced for home. Godfrey paused only to buzz a hospital where his girl friend worked as a nurse. Later, back at base, he bought drinks for the house—with money borrowed from Gentile.

The U.S. raids on Berlin proved conclusively that the Americans had gained the upper hand in the skies over Germany. When 669 bombers returned to Berlin on March 22, German fighters downed only one or two of the dozen attackers that were lost: flak and accident accounted for the others. U.S. bombers, with the help of their Little Friends, could now attack targets anywhere in Germany with decreasing peril.

As the Luftwaffe threat lessened, the Americans' lust for action and glory increased. To many fighter pilots aerial combat became, in Don Blakeslee's words, "a grand sport." The prospect of outdueling an enemy interceptor, and of running up one's personal total of victories, compensated for such unappealing aspects of the job as sitting strapped in a tiny cockpit for as long as seven hours.

A fighter pilot's score was a subject of intense interest and sometimes bitter contention. Obtaining confirmation of a kill was a relatively straightforward matter: a kill had to be witnessed by another pilot or by bomber crewmen, or it had to be documented by the movie cameras in the wings of the fighters that were activated every time the guns were fired. But some pilots resorted to trickery to fatten their scores. A pilot seeing a squadron mate about to shoot down an enemy plane might yell "break!"—the radio warning to pull away from an onrushing enemy attack from the rear— so that he could move in and grab the kill for himself. Another source of dissension was the current policy of recognizing victories for enemy planes destroyed on the ground as well as in the air.

Rivalry for kills was keenest at the group level—most notably between the Mustangs of Don Blakeslee's 4th Fighter Group and the Thunderbolts of the 56th Group, commanded by Colonel Hubert Zemke of Missoula, Montana. Like Blakeslee, Zemke was a gifted aerial tactician and an inspiring leader who instilled in his men what he called "an inner urge to do combat." Zemke's aggressive tactics in combat won his group the nickname of "Wolfpack." On days off, the Wolfpack's Thunderbolts and the 4th's Mustangs could often be seen in mock dogfights over England. Over Germany the rival groups engaged in what the 4th Group's chronicler described as "a sort of Hun-killing tournament that sparked and stimulated the aggressiveness of all the other outfits."

During March of 1944, Zemke's Wolfpack led the tournament by almost 3 to 2 in total planes destroyed. The group included a pilot who was soon to become a leading American ace in Europe, Major Robert S. Johnson. An Oklahoman who had unaccountably failed gunnery school during flight training, Johnson shot down four German planes on March 15 alone, raising his total kill score to 22.

In April, Blakeslee's Mustangs surged ahead of the Wolfpack, scoring 31 kills in just one day. Early in May, Johnson scored his 26th and 27th kills, surpassing ace Eddie Rickenbacker's World War I record of 26—the highest previous score for an American in Europe. In the end, victory in the tournament was to go to Blakeslee's Mustangs, though by a narrow margin. Their total of 1,016 German aircraft destroyed was 10 more than the Wolfpack's score.

Bent on adding to the destruction, the Eighth Air Force decided on a calculated campaign to go after the Luftwaffe fighters on the ground. If they did not come up, the reasoning went, the Americans would go down and get them. Beginning early in April, armadas of 600 or more U.S. fighters flew strafing missions against airfields in France and Germany. These forays proved extremely successful. On some days U.S. claims of enemy planes destroyed on the ground climbed over the 100 mark.

But skimming over an airfield at more than 400 miles per hour posed its own great dangers. During April three times as many American fighters were lost to flak and accident on strafing missions as in aerial combat. A number of American aces who had survived dozens of battles in the air went down while attacking parked Messerschmitts and Focke-Wulfs. One of the aces was Lieut. Colonel Francis S. Gabreski of the 56th Group, who finally topped all U.S. pilots in Europe with 28 aerial victories. In July Gabreski flew so low on a strafing run in Germany that the propeller of his Thunderbolt hit the ground. He pulled up the plane, but the engine began to fail. Gabreski belly-landed in a nearby wheat field and got out, unhurt, as the plane burst into flames. He was captured and taken to a prison camp. There he was soon reunited with the Wolfpack's commander, Colonel Zemke, who was forced to bail out over Germany during an air battle, and with one of their old dueling rivals from the 4th Group, Lieutenant Godfrey, who also fell victim to the dangers of low-level strafing.

At the end of April 1944, General Galland sent his superiors in the Luftwaffe's high command a despairing memoran-

Enjoying a smoke after seven hours of escort duty, a P-51 pilot displays the briefing-session instructions he wrote on the back of his hand for ready reference aloft. The notations gave the times for starting engines, taking off, setting course and rendezvousing with the bombers, as well as the compass heading to follow as the planes left the target and turned for home.

dum. "The time has come," the fighter chief wrote, "when our force is within sight of collapse."

What had led Galland to this grim conclusion was not a dwindling supply of planes but a shortage of pilots. The Germans, in fact, were now producing more planes than ever before; as a result of the emergency program instituted after Big Week in February, relocating or rebuilding plants and imposing a 72-hour week on laborers, they were, said one Luftwaffe officer, "virtually drowning in aircraft." But planes were useless without pilots.

Galland's memorandum noted that the Luftwaffe's losses during the past four months had not only included more than 1,000 aircraft—day fighters—but also some of "our best officers." One of them—shot down by a Thunderbolt on March 2—was Colonel Mayer, the 26-year-old commander of the elite Richthofen fighter unit. Mayer had been flying combat since December of 1939 and had pioneered the use of the deadly head-on attacks against U.S. bombers in 1943. In more than four years of action, he had been credited with 102 aerial victories, including 25 bombers.

Such men, Galland knew, were irreplaceable; in fact, there were not enough trained pilots of any kind. The Luftwaffe's flight schools were beset by difficulties. They lacked good teachers; the best pilots stayed in the front line until they were killed or disabled. The schools also lacked enough fuel to give trainees adequate air time. Rookies were being sent to operational units with only 112 hours of flight time, well under half that of American trainees.

The implications of Galland's memorandum were clear: when the Allied forces launched their invasion, the Luftwaffe would need a near miracle to do its job against the invaders. It would have to exploit its newly expanded air fleet with a diminishing number of seasoned pilots.

In England, meanwhile, the planners of Operation _Overlord_—the invasion—were debating how best to use Allied air power in the weeks remaining before D-Day. A ticklish matter of national pride had to be resolved first. Eisenhower insisted that overall control of the bombers—British as well as American—should reside with him as Supreme Commander. The RAF, reluctant to yield up the independence of its Bomber Command even temporarily, opposed the idea and was firmly backed by Churchill. But according to Eisen-

hower's aide, Captain Harry C. Butcher, Ike threatened to "go home," and the Prime Minister quickly caved in. Eisenhower took over direction of both the U.S. and British bombers, though in using the aircraft he actually relied heavily on his British deputy supreme commander, Air Chief Marshal Sir Arthur Tedder.

The issue of how to employ the bombers most effectively stirred far more contention, and this time the split was not along national lines. The chiefs of the U.S. and British bomber forces, General Spaatz and Air Chief Marshal Harris, were in thorough agreement: they felt they could best contribute to _Overlord_ by continuing their air offensives against the German homeland—the British by night against the cities, the Americans by day against key industries. In particular, Spaatz wanted to deploy the bulk of the American bombers against Germany's oil-producing facilities. This offensive, he believed, would deny vital fuel to the German ground forces fighting the Allied invaders. Moreover, Spaatz was certain that oil installations would be heavily defended by the Luftwaffe, giving his escort fighters the opportunity to shoot down many enemy interceptors and to extend Allied superiority in the air.

Spaatz and Harris were opposed in the debate by advocates of what was called the Transportation Plan. The plan envisioned using the U.S. and British bombers to cripple the main German lines of communication in northwest Europe. Rather than just temporarily interdicting roads, bridges and rail lines, the bombers would carry out a systematic attack aimed at totally disrupting German traffic. The principal targets were to be some 80 railway marshaling yards and repair centers in Belgium and northern France. Their destruction, proponents argued, would create "a railway desert" around the intended Allied beachheads in Normandy, sealing off the Germans from supplies and reinforcements.

The man who originated the Transportation Plan was an imaginative 39-year-old British scientist named Solly Zuckerman, then a civilian adviser to _Overlord_'s air planners. He had solid credentials as an air strategist. When it was deemed vital to seize the heavily fortified Mediterranean island of Pantelleria before the invasion of Sicily in 1943, Zuckerman's calculations about such seemingly arcane matters as the density of bomb strikes needed to silence gun batteries had helped make it possible to win the island's surrender simply by bombing. But Zuckerman had his detractors. Air Chief Marshal Harris could not resist harping on Zuckerman's academic background: he had been a zoologist specializing in monkeys. The chief, one of Harris' aides said, "felt that Zuckerman did not necessarily qualify as a competent authority on air strategy by virtue of his exceptional knowledge of the sexual behavior of anthropoid apes." (Later, after Zuckerman had been elevated to the peerage as Lord Zuckerman, he acknowledged the incongruity by titling his memoirs *From Apes to Warlords*.)

To the consternation of Harris and Spaatz, the Transportation Plan gained backing at the highest levels. Deputy Supreme Commander Tedder, formerly the Allied air commander in the Mediterranean, had seen Zuckerman's ideas bear fruit. Tedder, once described by a superior as "a practical thinker" with "a great gift for getting his priorities right," was able to look beyond the prevailing dogmas of strategic

bombing. He wanted the most direct help he could get from the bombers in making Normandy safe for invasion. So did his boss; Eisenhower approved the Transportation Plan.

Even then, the plan faced opposition from a formidable adversary. Prime Minister Churchill came down on the side of Harris and Spaatz, attacking the alternative proposal ostensibly for humanitarian reasons. The raids on the rail yards, Churchill argued, would result in the "cold-blooded butchering" of civilians who were living nearby.

Churchill probably had less lofty reasons for the stance he took. Worn and edgy after more than four years as Britain's war leader, he was increasingly concerned with the political future, and killing Frenchmen in bombing raids was not likely to improve Anglo-French relations after the War. At one point, Eisenhower had to remind Churchill that only the previous year he had endorsed full-scale bombing of German U-boat facilities in French ports without expressing undue concern for civilians. Finally, Churchill gave up his opposition to the Transportation Plan—but only after President Roosevelt refused his appeal to intervene.

Though Harris and Spaatz were unhappy about the plan's adoption, not all of their air crews agreed. For British fliers, the attacks on railways and repair shops turned out to be a welcome respite from the costly raids on Berlin, Nuremberg and other German cities. Moreover, the focus on smaller targets proved that Bomber Command was capable of far more accuracy at night than Harris had thought possible.

Much of this accuracy was attributable to a new way of marking and illuminating the target. In past raids a "master bomber" would circle the target during an attack, assessing the accuracy of the marking and broadcasting advice to the other bomber crews. The new tactic called for the master bomber, flying a Mosquito, to swoop earthward, sight the target visually and drop the markers himself.

The change in technique was pioneered by Squadron 617, the elite "dam busters" who had breached the Ruhr dams in the spring of 1943. The squadron was now under the command of Leonard Cheshire, at 25 the youngest group captain in the RAF. In his role as master bomber, Cheshire liked to swoop down to 700 feet, then race along over the streets of the target area, dropping his marker bombs. The accuracy of the low-level marking by the diving dam busters was demonstrated by a Lancaster attack on the rail yards at

On the morning of a combat mission, pilots of the all-black 332nd Fighter Group receive a briefing at their base near Ramitelli, Italy. Arriving in Italy in early 1944, the pilots of the 332nd flew P-47s until the middle of the year, when they were transferred from the Twelfth to the Fifteenth Air Force and reequipped with P-51 Mustangs. Within two weeks of switching over to the new planes, they scored more than a dozen kills. The 332nd was later awarded a Distinguished Unit Citation for defending bombers during a 1,600-mile round-trip raid against a Berlin tank factory— the longest mission ever flown by the Fifteenth Air Force.

Juvisy-sur-Orge, 11 miles south of Paris. Aiming at the master bombers' marks, the Lancasters dropped 1,000 bombs in such tight clusters that many craters overlapped.

The American bombers were permitted to vary their missions in France with occasional returns to Germany—thanks to the stubborn belief of General Spaatz that the real key to Allied victory in Europe lay in destroying Germany's oil installations. Eisenhower approved of a limited offensive against the installations whenever Eighth Air Force bombers could be spared from the campaign against the railways.

Spaatz, however, had another source he could tap without any hampering restraints: the Italian-based Fifteenth Air Force, which was not involved in the Transportation Plan. In the month or so since February's Big Week—the joint venture to Germany with the Eighth Air Force—the Fifteenth had mounted a score of missions ranging from the German submarine base at Toulon to the rail yards of Budapest and Bucharest and including repeated forays over enemy strongholds in Italy itself. The men of the Fifteenth were ready to take on the series of 20 missions—all to the same place—that would represent their most memorable contribution to the Allied cause.

The target was Ploesti, where Africa-based bombers of the Ninth Air Force and others on loan from the Eighth had met with disaster in August of 1943. The fields and refineries of the sprawling Rumanian oil center, once again operating at full tilt, were still Germany's biggest supplier of fuel. On April 5, the Fifteenth was dispatched to hit Ploesti's rail yards, where the oil was loaded for shipment to Germany. Enough of the U.S. bombs fell on the refinery district to cause substantial havoc. The success of the attack spurred others; the Fifteenth continued visiting Ploesti until mid-August, pounding it to a virtual standstill. The Fifteenth's own cost was high: 223 of its planes were lost.

Spaatz meanwhile was pressing his oil campaign in Germany itself as well. Beginning in May he sent planes of the Eighth Air Force, whenever they could be diverted from their primary tasks under the Transportation Plan, to bomb synthetic-fuel plants in the Reich. Spaatz was to be proved right in his insistence on the vulnerability of German oil, though the effects of the U.S. attacks were not fully evident until several months after D-Day.

Altogether, the Allied strategic and tactical air forces, including the medium bombers and fighter-bombers of the American tactical Ninth Air Force, newly based in England, flew some 200,000 sorties in direct support of the impending invasion. They severed France's railway lines at numerous points, destroyed 1,500 locomotives and cut all 24 bridges over the Seine between Paris and the sea. By the beginning of June, rail traffic in France was near chaos.

In addition to smashing the targets designated by the Transportation Plan, the American and British bombers and fighters destroyed 36 airfields, 41 radar installations and 45 gun batteries in the area. All of the raids were carefully calculated to mislead the Germans about the site of the Allied landings: for every target that was bombed in the Normandy area, two were attacked elsewhere.

A separate air campaign concentrated on German launching sites along France's west coast. These were the pads from which Hitler intended to fling his V-1 flying bombs against England. Destruction of the V-1 sites—whose existence had been shown by aerial reconnaissance photos as early as May 1943—was considered so crucial by the Allies that the Americans constructed full-scale replicas of them in Florida to perfect their low-level bombing techniques.

In all, in the six months before D-Day the Allies flew 25,150 sorties against the V-1 sites, knocking out 83 of them. Operation *Crossbow*, as the campaign was called, forced the Germans to abandon the sites and construct prefabricated launch pads. These pads could be assembled quickly and were small enough to be housed in ordinary farm or factory buildings, thus effectively concealing them from Allied aircraft. But the change-over delayed Hitler's plans for sending his *Vergeltungswaffe*—vengeance weapons—against England, and the Allies were ashore on the beaches of Normandy a week before the V-1s began flying.

On D-Day itself—June 6,1944—the Allied air forces put on a show that overshadowed all that had gone before in the skies over Europe. During the 24 hours of D-Day, more than 8,000 bombers and fighters—the smaller planes had their wings and fuselages painted with bold stripes for quick identification—flew nearly 14,700 individual sorties. The planes pounded coastal gun batteries, dropped airborne troops and towed glider-borne men into battle, flew protective cover for the seaborne invasion convoys, strafed German troop positions and patrolled over the Normandy beaches. They also completed the job of interdicting roads and railways. Their destructive work was so thorough that the German 2nd SS Panzer Division took 17 days to travel 450 miles from southern France to the fighting front, and many of the German troop reserves had to make their way to Normandy on foot.

The strangest Allied air mission on D-Day called for neither bombing nor strafing but for elaborate subterfuge. Long before dawn, two RAF bomber units—the Stirlings and Halifaxes of Squadron 218 and the Lancasters of dambusting Squadron 617 under Leonard Cheshire—headed across the Channel toward the Pas-de-Calais area on the northwest coast of France. Their purpose was to lead the Germans to believe that the Allied invasion force would land there instead of on the beaches at Normandy, some 150 miles to the southwest.

The scheme—the brainchild of British radar scientist Robert Cockburn—called for flooding German radar screens in the Pas-de-Calais area with bogus blips that indicated the advance of two huge armadas, one of aircraft and the other of ships. Though most of the German radar stations in the area had been knocked out by Allied planes before D-Day, some had been deliberately left untouched for the purposes of this deception.

To carry it out, Cockburn's team of mathematical wizards had worked out an incredibly complex series of calculations calling for the two RAF squadrons to fly a pattern of rectangular orbits each about eight miles long and two miles wide, moving one mile closer to the French coast as they completed each orbit. In the meantime, they dropped the metal-foil strips of Window at the rate of 12 bundles every minute. The wizards had even figured out the size of the strips needed to enhance the impression of the immensity of the invading air armada; the longest were nearly six feet long.

Below the RAF bombers, the "fleet" they were supposedly covering—18 small launches—churned along toward the Pas-de-Calais playing their own part in the deception. Each launch carried at least one 29-foot-long balloon with a radar reflector built into it. This device picked up the pulses of enemy radar, amplified them and sent them back, producing an echo equivalent to that of a 10,000-ton ship.

Cockburn's scheme, which had been rehearsed successfully with captured German radar in Scotland's Firth of Forth, worked equally well on the coast of France. The Germans were so convinced of what their radar screens showed that their coastal batteries actually began hurling 12-inch shells seaward. Inexplicably, not a single German night fighter flew out to reconnoiter the enemy armadas.

Indeed, so few German aircraft appeared at any time, anywhere, on D-Day that the commander in chief of the Allied air forces for the invasion, Air Chief Marshal Sir Trafford Leigh-Mallory, paced his office at headquarters outside London, asking over and over, "Where is the Luftwaffe?"

The answer was that virtually all of the Luftwaffe was in Germany. It had been forced there first by the need to defend the homeland against the massive U.S. bombing raids of previous months, then by preinvasion attacks that had made airfields in France and Belgium unusable. All told, the Luftwaffe only managed some 300 sorties over France on D-Day—one for every 50 by the Allies.

Two of the day's bravest and most futile Luftwaffe sorties were flown by Major Joseph Priller, a fighter-wing commander, and his wingman, Flight Sergeant Heinz Wodarczyk. The pair were alone that morning at the unit's former base near Lille. Under orders from higher up, the rest of Priller's day fighters had recently been scattered to bases around inland France, away from the coastal areas where Priller was certain the invasion was imminent. Priller, an ace with more than 90 combat victories and a reputation for talking back to his superiors, had bitterly protested the dispersal of his unit and then, on the eve of the invasion, had gotten drunk with Wodarczyk.

Early on D-Day, Priller and his wingman, nursing hangovers, raced southwest to Normandy in their FW-190s. They swooped down scarcely 100 feet over the swarming British beachheads, shot up all their ammunition and scurried back to Lille—staggered by the enormity of what they had seen and astonished that they had flown unscathed through the gauntlet of Allied fighters and antiaircraft fire.

Priller and his wingman were among the few German pilots to brave the beaches of Normandy during the daylight hours of D-Day. After dark, a handful of Ju-88s also scattered bombs there. These were the only exceptions to the fulfillment of Eisenhower's confident prediction to his ground forces on the eve of the invasion: "If you see fighting aircraft over you, they will be ours."

AIR SUPPORT FOR THE ARMY

Flying at treetop level, a P-47 Thunderbolt returns after scouting the route ahead of three American tanks advancing along a country road in northern France.

THE ALLIES' WINNING AIR-GROUND TEAM

Tactical air power—the use of planes to support troops in the field rather than for the strategic purpose of undermining the enemy's overall warmaking ability—was pioneered with awesome effect by the Luftwaffe. Thousands of German planes, acting in close coordination with armored and infantry units, lent terrifying potency to the German juggernaut that rolled across Europe in 1939 and 1940. But by mid-1943, the British and Americans had seized the lead in developing tactical air techniques, and their hard-hitting sorties ultimately helped tip the balance in their favor on the battlefields of Western Europe.

The Allies employed tactical air power in a deadly three-stage pattern, throwing into the fray planes of all types—even heavy bombers normally used on strategic missions. First, planes of all sorts ranged well ahead of the ground assault forces, attacking any Luftwaffe planes and bases in the chosen zone to achieve local air superiority—if not total mastery. Then, to isolate the enemy forces in the battle area, bombers and fighters plastered rail lines, highway junctions, truck convoys and trains. Finally, as Allied ground forces moved forward, fighter-bombers hit enemy troops and strong points that stood in the way of the advance. These dangerous operations were executed primarily by airmen of the British Second Tactical Air Force, the U.S. Ninth Air Force and the U.S. First Tactical Air Force, who had received months of special training for the job.

The mightiest—and most successful—tactical air operation supported the Allied invasion of Normandy in June 1944. Tactical air forces operated from England until the beachhead was secured, then moved to hastily built airstrips in Normandy. Thereafter, tactical units were constantly on the move, not only flying several sorties a day but also relocating their makeshift bases to keep up with ground advances. The pace was exhausting, but the pilots thrived on combat. "Our eyes sharpened with each mission," said Lieut. Colonel Norman Holt, commander of the 366th Fighter Group. After a sortie, said Holt, "all of us wanted to get back, refuel, re-arm and get in another sock at the Nazis."

In a sod-floor operations hut in Normandy, P-47 pilots study tactical targets pointed out by their commander, Lieut. Colonel Norman Holt.

Paving the way for a ground attack, two B-26 Marauders leave ruins behind them after a bombing raid on a rail yard and power station at Charleroi, Belgium.

Climbing for another pass, a P-38 Lightning flies over a smouldering locomotive. Some German trains carried guns for defense.

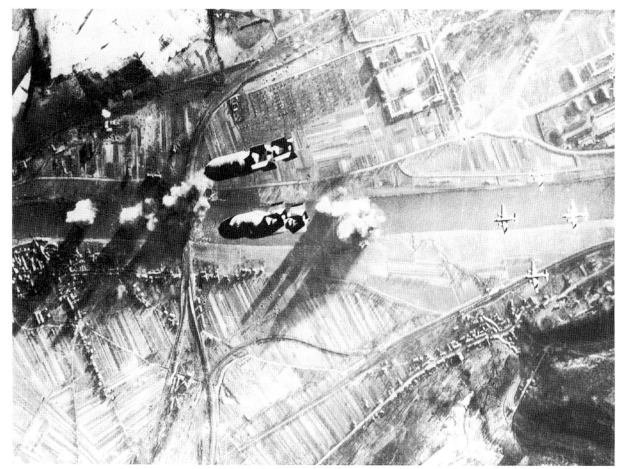

Bombs fall on a vital bridge across the Moselle River north of Trier, Germany, as four B-26s prepare to add their load to the assault.

Entangled track and

demolished trains litter the railway marshaling yard near Limburg, Germany. The yard was struck by medium and light bombers of the U.S. Ninth Air Force.

CUTTING OFF AND CUTTING UP THE COMBAT ZONE

After minimizing the Luftwaffe's ability to interfere with ground operations, Allied air units drew a broad circle of destruction around the combat zone. Roads and rail lines were cut, bridges were bombed and enemy shipping disrupted. This prevented supplies and reinforcements from reaching the front—and it also obstructed the German troops who were trying to leave the combat zone and establish new defense lines elsewhere.

The objectives that offered the biggest dividends were railway marshaling yards, where tracks converged and trains were loaded. By knocking out one such clearing point (about 500 tons of bombs would do the job, the Allies calculated), bombers could stop rail traffic over a vast area.

Meanwhile, other aircraft flew tactical missions against enemy transport within the battle zone. Many trains, immobilized by bombed-out rails to the front and rear, were blown to bits by low-flying fighter-bombers. "I had to fly through one of the explosions," an American pilot said. "I saw a box car wheel go up by my wing."

A British Beaufighter (top) fires its rockets at a ship in the North Sea. Such tactical strikes claimed uncounted victims, among them the minesweeper M-37 (bottom), which burned and sank in the Bay of Biscay in August 1944.

A German truck convoy carrying ammunition and fuel blows up, ignited by .50-caliber tracer bullets fired from the P-47 that took this photograph. The explosion of one truck started a lethal chain reaction that destroyed approximately 90 per cent of the convoy.

A P-47 escapes the inferno of an ammunition truck it has just hit. Many low-flying planes were destroyed when their targets exploded.

175

Scanning the sky from the hatch of a Sherman tank, a fighter pilot serving as air liaison officer directs support planes to their target by radio. Liaison duty was highly unpopular with most pilots; they were eager to return to their P-47s and P-51s, which they considered safer than tanks.

A P-47 Thunderbolt (upper right) dives and strafes a smoke-shrouded German position outside Couptrain, France, in August 1944. U.S. armored troops watch the action while awaiting orders to proceed toward town. Often, supporting fighters made tactical attacks with surgical precision on enemy strong points only a few hundred yards from Allied ground units.

THE "GUARDIAN ANGELS" OF ALLIED ARMOR

Tactical air units were a natural partner and complement to the fast-moving tank columns that ranged ahead of the infantry. Because success depended on a knowledgeable dialogue between the men in the planes and those on the ground, fighter pilots, thoroughly familiar with the capabilities of close-support aircraft, were assigned to ride as air liaison officers in tank units rigged with aircraft radios. The pilots of the covering planes—usually flights of four P-47s—hit close-in targets at the request of the liaison officer or, free-lancing ahead, struck danger spots and warned the advancing tanks of what to expect.

Tankmen were duly grateful to the fliers, whom they called their "guardian angels." After P-47s had demolished a German position that was holding up an armored unit near Liege, Belgium, in 1944, the exuberant column commander radioed his flight leader: "Great! With support like that we can go all the way to Berlin."

6

In the summer of 1944, the German soldiers fighting the Allied invaders of Normandy got a bitter foretaste of what would befall their own homeland during the final phases of the air war. Armadas of as many as 2,000 enemy bombers roared over them, disgorging explosives in such enormous quantities that the terrified troops below called them *Bombenteppich*—"carpets of bombs."

For the Allies, carpet bombing had a particular purpose: to help their ground forces break out of Normandy by obliterating certain German strong points that blocked the paths of advance. When artillery alone did not suffice, carpet bombing—concentrated on a few square miles of battleground—reduced the German positions to corpse-strewn debris, literally clearing the way for the Allied soldiers to move on.

Since the opposing forces were sometimes separated by a distance of as little as 1,000 yards, carpet bombing required the utmost precision to avoid Allied casualties. Close coordination with the Allied ground commanders was also essential. Their troops had to be ready to move as soon as the target area was laid waste; otherwise, those Germans who had survived the saturation attack would have time to regroup or call in reinforcements.

The carpet-bombing tactic turned out to be sounder in theory than in practice. On July 7,1944, when 457 RAF bombers came to the aid of British and Canadian infantry stalled outside Caen by dropping some 2,300 tons of bombs on the northern sector of the city, the infantrymen were able to advance—but the tanks and supply columns were not. The carpet bombing had cratered Caen's streets and blocked them with rubble, making it impossible for any sort of vehicle to get through.

A more serious concern was the bombers' accidental toll of the men they were supposed to be supporting. Allied ground commanders had vigorously expressed their fear of this possibility, insisting that the bombline be no closer to their troops than 1,200 yards. Still, a number of bombs fell short of their intended mark, most notoriously on the 24th and 25th of July, when planes of the United States Eighth and Ninth Air Forces targeted the area around a key highway between Saint-Lô and Périers. The Germans' elite Panzer Lehr Division held one side of the road, and troops of the American First Army held the other side.

THE FINAL ONSLAUGHT

The attack on July 25 employed 1,900 bombers carrying a total of 3,950 tons of bombs. From his side of the road, the panzer commander, Major General Fritz Bayerlein, watched in stupefaction as the monster armada appeared. "The planes kept coming over as if on a conveyor belt, and the bomb carpets unrolled in great rectangles," he recalled. "My flak had hardly opened its mouth when the batteries received direct hits which knocked out half the guns and silenced the rest. After an hour I had no communication with anybody, even by radio. By noon nothing was visible but dust and smoke." Surveying the scene around him, Bayerlein was reminded of a lunar landscape. About 1,000 of his men lost their lives in this carpet bombing; so many others were wounded or numb with shock or babbling insanely that for all practical purposes the Panzer Lehr Division was out of action.

On the other side of the highway, the Americans were also counting their losses: errant bombs had killed 111 men and wounded 490 others. Two days later the U.S. breakout near Saint-Lô took place, creating an opening for the Allied sweep across the rest of France. But the grief visited upon American troops by American planes brought a swift response from Supreme Allied Command headquarters. General Eisenhower, who had previously approved of carpet bombing because of its "most heartening effect upon our own men," now ruled that heavy bombers were no longer to be used for close ground support.

The power of the bombers was brought to bear for another special purpose: the destruction of German installations that were suspected of housing the launching pads and the storage depots for Hitler's "vengeance" weapons. Scores of such sites had been destroyed along France's west coast before the invasion; now the operation was focused mainly on those in northern France. From this area the V-weapons not only had a lesser distance to travel to their projected primary target, London, but also posed a threat to the Allies' newly won positions in Normandy.

To smash the German installations, which were protected by iron-and-concrete domes as thick as 30 feet, required explosives in extraordinary quantities. The British and the Americans came up with separate answers to the problem. The RAF bombers carried a six-ton blockbuster designed by Barnes Wallis, who had devised the huge, spinning bombs used against the Ruhr dams in 1943. The new bomb, 21 feet long, was appropriately dubbed Tallboy. Streamlined to achieve a speed of about 750 miles per hour as it hit the ground, it was capable of boring through dozens of feet of concrete or rock before it was detonated by a delayed-action fuse deep inside the bomb.

The Americans experimented with a different sort of firepower. Expendable battle-worn Flying Fortresses and Liberators were packed with 20,000 pounds of high explosives; then, manned by a pilot and copilot, they were flown toward France. At a point on the English coast, just before the Channel was to be crossed, a fuse would be set and the two men aboard would bail out; a reconnaissance plane overhead would note their landing place so that they could be picked up. Meanwhile, their lethal aircraft roared on toward the target, remotely controlled by radio equipment contained in a conventional "mother" plane that guided the drone into the target.

Seven such missions, given the code name *Aphrodite*, were mounted in August of 1944, some with unhappy results. Several of the drone planes blew up prematurely, killing their pilots. Among the victims was a U.S. Navy lieutenant on loan to *Aphrodite*, Joseph Kennedy Jr., the older brother of a future U.S. President.

The bombing of the V-weapon sites turned out to be a case of too much, too late. The four main targets, all in the Pas-de-Calais area, were quickly overrun by Allied troops, and showed no signs of occupancy except by rats and cockroaches. At Hitler's order, the installations had been moved farther eastward.

One of the abandoned sites—at a hamlet named Mimoyecques, near the port of Calais—was found to contain a partially assembled V-weapon previously unknown to Allied intelligence and completely different from the V-1 flying bomb and the V-2 rocket. The V-3 was an enormous gun designed to have 50 barrels, each 416 feet long; one Allied expert described it as "perhaps the most extraordinary weapon of the Second World War, excluding the atomic bomb." The gun was intended to shower London with 300-pound shells hurled at the rate of one every six seconds. Though London was 95 miles away, the V-3's potential range was 100 miles; this remarkable range was to be achieved by the ignition of explosive charges placed at intervals along each barrel. Fortunately for the Londoners, who were already having to cope with the V-1s, the V-3's projectiles had proved unstable in flight. Despite their tremendous velocity inside the barrel, they tended to wobble after leaving the gun, and the increased air resistance reduced the range.

Together, the campaign against the V-weapons and the carpet-bombing missions represented but a fraction of the effort expended by the Allied air forces in aid of the invasion of the Continent. During the summer of 1944, the bombers of the U.S. Eighth Air Force and RAF Bomber Command, in concert with the medium and light bombers and fighter-bombers of the U.S. Ninth Air Force and the RAF's Second Tactical Air Force, supported the advancing troops by flying nearly half a million sorties—pounding rail lines, road junctions, bridges, barges, airfields, supply depots and enemy troops on the run. The flights were not only shorter but far less hazardous than the previous operations over Germany itself had been; on the Western Front, the Allied planes outnumbered the Luftwaffe by about 8 to 1. Predictably, the Allied pilots came to look upon their sorties as mere "milk runs."

As they fled from Normandy, the German troops tried desperately to elude attack from the air by taking advantage of the peculiarities of the local terrain. Carefully avoiding the major roadways, they traveled along lanes lined with ditches, thick hedges and tall, overarching beeches and hornbeam trees that formed natural tunnels; as an added attempt at cover, they stacked the roofs of their vehicles with fresh-cut branches.

But concealment from the sky was not always possible. In mid-August, after the rout of the Germans at Falaise, a British ground observer inspected a one-mile stretch of a lane along which a fleeing enemy column had come under rocket and cannon fire from Typhoons of the RAF Second Tactical Air Force, fighter planes that were especially effective in low-flying attacks. The observer reported:

"Where the retreating Germans had been caught in the open, they lay in irregular swathes mostly in the shallow ditches. Their transport was mixed. Cars of every description, many of them Citroens, Renaults and other French makes, strewed the fields, mingled with horses dead in the shafts of stolen carts and even old-fashioned traps of two generations ago. I noticed one up-to-date limousine painted with the stippled green and brown camouflage affected by the Germans. It contained on the back seat a colonel and his smartly dressed mistress. Each had been shot through the chest with cannon shells. The driver, who had quitted the wheel, lay a yard or two further on in the ditch with a very dead cow for company. At the entrance to the next section of leafy lane a tank, its gun pointing skywards, straddled the road. From the turret hung a German, his bloated face black with flies. . . . In the sunken lane under the semi-darkness of the arching trees in full August leaf the picture of destruction was complete and terrible to the last detail."

In the view of the British and American bomber bosses, Air Chief Marshal Harris and General Spaatz, these missions were diversions from their principal strategic objective— the extinction of Germany's capacity to make war. Harris and Spaatz were impatient to get on with the job. For the first time since the start of the air war, their forces possessed sufficient numbers of heavy bombers—almost 5,000—and the requisite air superiority to strike decisive blows against the German homeland.

Both men thought it might "still be possible," as Spaatz put it, "to beat up the insides of Germany enough by air action to cause her to collapse" by the spring of 1945. But they had sharply differing opinions as to the surest way to bring on the collapse. Spaatz remained wedded to the idea that wrecking Germany's oil industry would speed the end. In pursuit of this unshakable belief, he had already taken advantage of Eisenhower's agreement to let him conduct a limited offensive against the enemy's oil resources, both natural and synthetic, whenever his planes could be spared from missions in Normandy. By summer's end, Rumania's Ploesti oil fields and other German suppliers in Eastern Europe, as well as synthetic-fuel plants in Germany itself, had been hit by Spaatz's airmen.

Harris had grudgingly allotted RAF bombers to join in some of these strikes, but his own idea of how to knock out Germany was the same as it had been in 1942, and no less adamant. He continued to insist that the Reich would collapse when enough of its cities lay in ruins. Harris was certain his bombers could finish the job they had started

NEW PLANES, VAIN HOPES

Toward the end of the War, German engineers produced an assortment of seemingly farfetched military aircraft. Though all of them had technical problems, one epoch-making creation regularly outperformed the Allies' best planes in combat. Following a losing encounter with a jet-powered Messerschmitt-262, a Spitfire pilot worried: "Should the enemy possess reasonable numbers of these remarkable aircraft, it would not be long before we lost the air superiority for which we had struggled." But Germany's bold aeronautical initiatives came too late to do much more than stir the Luftwaffe's yearning for what might have been.

The Me-262, introduced in July 1944, was the first jet plane to fly combat. The 540-mph planes claimed more than 500 Allied aircraft.

The Messerschmitt-163 Komet was propelled by a rocket engine that took off at full throttle, burning up its entire fuel supply in minutes.

The composite Mistel consisted of an FW-190 mounted on an unpiloted, bomb-laden Ju-88 that was guided to the target by radio.

The Dornier-335 was powered by two engines, one pulling from the front, the other set in the tail and pushing from the rear.

The Heinkel-162 jet was simply designed and built of inexpensive materials, but its mass-production potential failed for lack of time.

two years earlier. He had more planes than ever at his disposal; though the U.S. planes outnumbered the British planes by more than 2 to 1, Bomber Command now had round-the-clock capability on its own. Beginning in September the RAF planes could fly missions by day, escorted by U.S. fighters or shorter-range British Spitfires operating from forward bases in liberated sections of France. And at night, Harris' bombers at last had the superiority over the Luftwaffe that had eluded them for so long.

In part, this newly acquired advantage was due to the hard-won advance of the Allied ground forces through France and Belgium. By overrunning German night-fighter bases and ground control stations, the troops knocked out the cornerstones of the Luftwaffe's early-warning network. German night fighters no longer would be able to receive the signals that had alerted them to intercept the British bombers 100 or so miles from their targets, as had been the case during the disastrous RAF mission to Nuremberg in March of 1944.

The RAF's night fliers also benefited from a lucky fluke. In July, a rookie Luftwaffe pilot, thinking he was over a German-held base in Holland, landed his night fighter at an English airfield. Apparently he had been attracted by the glare of oil burners placed on the field to heat the air and disperse the fog over the runways.

The German plane, a Junkers-88 of the latest type, carried two electronic devices, previously unknown to the British, that had enabled the Luftwaffe's night fighters to detect aircraft in the dark. One was the SN-2 airborne radar, which used a long wavelength that could not be jammed by the metal strips of Window; the Germans had made good use of SN-2 against the Nuremberg-bound RAF bombers. The second instrument, which was code-named Flensburg, enabled the Luftwaffe's night fighters to track down enemy bombers by homing in on transmissions from a special radar device aboard the RAF planes. This device, code-named Monica and installed in the tail of a bomber, gave warning of a German fighter's approach from the rear.

By careful study and testing of these unexpected gifts from the rookie German pilot, the British came up with a couple of effective countermeasures. A new type of Window strip, matched to the SN-2's wavelength, made the night fighters' radar susceptible to jamming. And the threat presented by the Flensburg homing device was dealt with simply by removing Monica from the RAF bombers. The Luftwaffe's only technological advantages in the night skies were thus neutralized.

On September 14, 1944, Harris and Spaatz got the go-ahead they had restlessly awaited. Authority over the bombers formally reverted to them under a directive issued by the Combined Chiefs of Staff. Supreme Allied Commander Eisenhower, who had held control over the bombers for the past six months, retained first call on them for emergency tactical missions. But Harris and Spaatz were now free to resume a full-scale bomber offensive against the German homeland. The Combined Chiefs of Staff designated Germany's oil industry as the top-priority target and its lines of communication as the second most important. Without canals and railways and highways to transport fuel and other essential supplies, the German war machine would be stopped dead in its tracks.

In the next seven months, Allied planes were to ravage Germany with more than 800,000 tons of bombs—some 60 per cent of all the tonnage dropped on the Reich in nearly five years of war. Oil targets alone were hit with 220,000 tons, finally reducing the Reich's production to a mere 5 per cent of what it had been before the concentrated attacks began. Raids of 1,000 planes—the number Harris had barely scraped together for his epic mission against Cologne in 1942—became commonplace.

The process of assembling these gigantic armadas had by now been refined virtually to an exact science. Spaatz's Eighth Air Force bombers would take off from their bases in southeastern England at intervals of about 30 seconds. Each plane would fly out to sea on a predetermined heading and for a predetermined length of time. It would then double back toward the English coast to an assigned radio beacon, approach at an assigned altitude and look for its own group. To make the search easier as the sky filled with incoming bombers, each group had a so-called assembly plane, a battle-worn castoff painted with polka dots, zebra stripes or other distinctive markings; some planes had the group letter blazoned 10 feet high on the side and outlined in flashing lights.

Human skill took over from science once the bomber

A B-24 assembly plane, painted with red, yellow and black polka dots to offer maximum visibility, stands ready to serve as an aerial rallying point for bombers forming up prior to a mission over Germany. Bombers used as assembly planes were usually older models no longer fit for combat; after the formation was complete, they retired to home base.

located its group and moved to get into the formation, a maneuver much like hopping aboard a speeding carrousel. An experienced pilot learned how to time his bomber's turn—its turning radius was about five miles—to meet the group formation as it came around on its next circle. Collisions with other planes trying to join the formation were frequent, and even more so on days when vapor contrails hampered visibility.

At a certain time, exact to the minute, the command pilot leading the group would leave the beacon on a given heading and begin to work his way into the main bomber stream. Very gingerly, 1,000 planes would edge into formation and head toward Europe, rising, lowering, tipping, skidding and rocking to stay in position. The strain of the entire exercise showed in odd ways. One copilot of a B-24 recalled: "I've seen the steam rising from the throttle hand of my pilot with the temperature in the cockpit around 50 below."

By October of 1944, General Spaatz's oil campaign was in full swing. He no longer had to concern himself about the Germans' major outside source of oil, Ploesti. The Rumanian oil fields, heavily damaged by his Fifteenth Air Force bombers striking from Italy, had been captured in late summer by the resurgent Russian armies; in their sweep into Eastern Europe, the Russians had also overrun a number of refineries in Poland. The Reich's chief remaining outside supplier was Hungary. While the Fifteenth's bombers raided the oil-rich area around Budapest, Spaatz's Eighth Air Force bombers, flying from England, pounded the Germans' last bastions of oil production—some two dozen synthetic-fuel plants situated inside Germany itself.

Air Chief Marshal Harris, despite his unconcealed preference for bombing the enemy's cities, threw the weight of RAF Bomber Command into the oil campaign. The British planes possessed advantages the American planes lacked: the capacity for carrying bigger bombs, and an improved radar device called GH, which permitted blind bombing of the target through cloud cover and smoke when visual sighting proved futile. But most important, the joint efforts of the bombers of the RAF and the U.S. Eighth and Fifteenth Air Forces made it possible to carry out a systematic attack on the oil installations.

The prospect of just such an attack "had been a nightmare to us for more than two years," Albert Speer later revealed. The Allied raiders were no longer switching from target to target and paying their visits irregularly. Speer, now presiding over all of Germany's war production, knew that it faced strangulation.

He launched an all-out effort to save the oil. Workers—largely slave laborers—ringed the most important parts of the plants with blast walls of thick concrete. They built air-raid shelters inside the plants so that oil crews would lose no time returning to their jobs when the Allied bombers left. After a raid, the workmen toiled to repair and piece together the wreckage so that plants could resume operating as quickly as possible. But the workers were not always cooperative; during one Allied raid, an Italian conscript was caught surreptitiously spreading the fire started by the Allied bombs.

Speer was banking on the usual bad weather of late autumn to slow down the Allied campaign and permit at least partial restoration of production. He was also counting on enemy strategists to display some of their earlier incon-

sistency. "Our one hope," he once remarked to Hitler, "is that the other side has an air force General Staff as scatter-brained as ours."

But throughout the fall and winter of 1944, the Allied air strategists had the right targets in mind, the weather turned out better than Speer had anticipated and the Allied resources were so great that there was no question about follow-up. The bombers were able to return again and again, repeating their attacks until repair efforts became more and more futile.

The most dramatic demonstration of the Allies' new staying power was directed at the giant Leuna chemical-fuel works 100 miles southwest of Berlin, not only the largest producer of synthetic fuel in Germany but also the most heavily defended. It was guarded by the biggest concentration of gun batteries the Germans had yet assembled, and it could be further shielded during a raid by a dense smoke screen produced by the fumes of an acid solution sprayed into the air. In all, the Allies mounted 22 missions against Leuna, 20 by the Eighth Air Force and two by the RAF, reducing its output to a monthly average of 9 per cent of its normal capacity.

By the end of 1944, the Allies' destructive attacks were clearly outstripping Speer's herculean efforts at restoration. On December 16, when Hitler began a last-ditch counter-offensive against the Allies in the Ardennes region of Belgium, his tanks started out with only a five-day fuel supply—and the offensive was literally to run out of gas.

For the Luftwaffe, the oil campaign packed a double punch. As supplies of aviation gasoline dwindled, the interceptors had to be grounded for days at a time. And when they did go up to do combat, they faced unbeatable odds. German fighter-pilot losses were so high that Heinz Knoke, a young commander whose unit of Messerschmitt-109s was sometimes outnumbered by as much as 40 to 1, wrote in his diary: "Every time I close the canopy before taking off, I feel that I am closing the lid of my own coffin."

The Luftwaffe's last great hope—and the Allied air strategists' chief worry—during the closing months of 1944 centered on two new German fighter planes that did not need conventional high-octane fuel. There was, in fact, little that was conventional about either plane. One was powered by a rocket motor; the other was a jet. Both could outspeed and outclimb any plane in the world.

The rocket-powered fighter, the Me-163 Komet, had a short, squat shape, and was dubbed the "powered egg" by the hand-picked pilots who flew it. The Komet had plenty of power. Its top speed was about 590 miles per hour, 100 miles per hour faster than the U.S. Mustang, and it could climb straight up at the rate of 11,500 feet per minute. In one of the plane's first combat trials, during an American raid on Magdeburg in August of 1944, a trio of Komets had easily overwhelmed a formation of Mustang escorts. The German fighters climbed high above the formation, looped and suddenly zoomed down on the Mustangs, scoring three quick hits.

But the Komet also had problems. One was landing. The Komet took off on wheels, but these were jettisoned in flight and the plane had to land—at 120 miles per hour —on a skid fastened to its undercarriage. A more serious problem was the Komet's lack of endurance. The fighter exhausted its 437-gallon fuel supply in four to seven minutes; even if the enemy could be engaged in that short period of time, the pilot would have to cut off combat and glide back to base. This limited the Komet's radius of action to about 25 miles from home.

The worst problem lay in the fuel itself—actually two distinct fuels that burned when they were mixed in the engine. The mixture consisted of a catalyst called C-Stoff, mainly methyl alcohol, and T-Stoff, concentrated hydrogen peroxide. Both were so corrosive that they could dissolve flesh, and the mixture itself was so volatile that a number of Komets simply exploded on the runway.

Only 279 Komets came off the German assembly lines, and perhaps a quarter of them saw combat. Though Komet pilots claimed a total of nine Allied bombers and fighters, the troublesome plane took a much larger toll of the Germans who tried to fly it.

If the Komet proved to be no more than a historical oddity, the Luftwaffe's other new fighter, the jet-powered Messerschmitt-262, represented the wave of the future. It was a bit slower than the Komet, with a top speed of 540 miles per hour, but it could stay aloft for well over an hour. Moreover, the Me-262's twin engines consumed common diesel fuel, which posed none of the dangers of the volatile rocket fuels and which was easier to come by than high-octane aviation fuel.

A few of the Me-262s were sent into combat during the summer of 1944 and quickly took the measure of some of Britain's fast-flying Mosquito reconnaissance planes. At first, the German jets avoided the enemy bomber formations and their fighter escorts. But the very presence of such a formidable new weapon alarmed the Allied air commanders; they were aware that sufficient numbers of jets might well jeopardize their entire bomber offensive. The British had a jet interceptor, the Gloster Meteor, but its range was too short to get it to Germany, and an experimental American jet was more than a year from combat readiness.

Fortunately for the Allies, the Luftwaffe as yet had only a few Me-262s. Hitler had dallied too long in developing the jet. When Germany's aeronautical experts unveiled the world's first model in August of 1939, four days before the start of the War, the Führer was so confident of an early victory in the coming conflict that he paid little attention to the enormous military potential of the jet. By November of 1943, when the Me-262 reached the stage when it could be mass produced and employed as a fighter, Hitler was so obsessed with pressing offensive action against the Allies that he had only one question to ask about the plane: "Can this aircraft carry bombs?" And when his compliant Luftwaffe chief, Göring, answered, "Yes, my Führer, theoretically yes," Hitler ordered the Me-262 put into production—but as a fighter-bomber.

At the time, however, the Me-262 had no fixtures for releasing bombs, and modifying it would have critically delayed deliveries. Hitler's order was quietly disobeyed by Göring's top deputy, Field Marshal Milch. As Director of Air Armament for the Luftwaffe, Milch knew that the jet was desperately needed to fend off the Allied bombers, and he put the plane into production as a fighter. But in May of 1944 the Führer learned that his order had been flouted. Furiously he halted production, called in Milch and demanded an explanation.

Milch compounded his dilemma. "My Führer," he burst out, "the smallest infant can see that this is a fighter, not a bomber aircraft!" A shocked silence filled the room; no one talked to Hitler that way. *"Aufschlagbrand"* (crashed in flames), one awed witness whispered. Within the month Milch was out of a job, consigned to less prestigious duties within the Luftwaffe.

Hitler thereafter forbade mention of the Me-262 as anything but a "blitz bomber." But some of the men around him, including Speer, dared to keep up the pressure for its full-scale production as a fighter. The most vociferous advocate was Adolf Galland, the Luftwaffe's outspoken fighter chief. Galland had test-flown the Me-262 in 1943 and had found the experience "like flying on the wings of an angel." He declared that he would rather have one jet than five conventional fighters.

In late September of 1944, Hitler finally relented. A second jet plane, the Arado 234, which had been intended from the beginning as a light bomber and reconnaissance plane, was now slowly coming off the assembly lines. Hitler grudgingly made a deal with Galland and the other jet-fighter proponents: for every Arado bomber produced, he would permit one Me-262 to go into action as a fighter.

A week later, on October 3, the Luftwaffe's first jet-fighter unit became operational at two bases near Osnabrück, not far from the border with Holland athwart the main U.S. bomber route to Germany. The unit consisted of about 30 Me-262s commanded by Major Walter Nowotny, an Austrian-born pilot who, at the age of 23, had become the first Luftwaffe ace to be credited with 250 aerial victories. His remarkable total was run up mainly against easier opposition on the Eastern Front, and it also reflected the German practice of giving credit for kills even though the enemy was not seen to crash or bail out (the Allies would list such victories as "probables").

Under Nowotny's enthusiastic leadership, the new unit tackled American bomber formations on the way to their targets in Germany—and the Mustang escorts were soon forced to revise their tactics. Instead of ranging ahead of the bomber formations to seek out the Germans, they had to stick close to their Big Friends to screen off the swiftly darting Me-262s. During the first month of operations, Nowotny's jets shot down 22 enemy bombers and fighters.

But technical troubles and inadequate pilot training in the tactical uses of the Me-262—as well as the overwhelming numbers of American fighters—soon took their toll. Since the jet engines required a complete overhaul after every dozen hours of use, Nowotny could seldom put up more than three or four planes on a given day. Moreover, the takeoffs and landings of the Me-262s—their toughest maneuvers—had to be made through a gauntlet of Mustangs and Thunderbolts patrolling above the jet bases.

On the morning of November 8, Nowotny led a flight of five jets against an American bomber formation. Three Me-262s went down, but Nowotny radioed back to base that he had just claimed his 258th kill. Then one of his engines died. Nowotny was attempting to make a landing with a swarm of Mustangs on his tail when the plane suddenly plunged to earth and exploded.

Among those witnessing the crash was General Galland, who was at the base waiting for Nowotny's return. Galland withdrew the unit from operations; the day's losses had left it with only four serviceable jets. While a new unit was being formed with Nowotny's surviving pilots as the nucleus, Galland fell back on his one remaining hope for a Luftwaffe triumph—a plan that would make use of his conventional fighters.

The scheme called for assembling an armada of 3,000 fighters, then flinging them—all in one day—against a big American bomber mission. All through the autumn Galland had been husbanding his Me-109s and FW-190s. He was prepared to lose as many as 500 fighters if he could bring down as many enemy bombers in one powerful stroke. He called his plan *Der Grosse Schlag*—The Great Blow. Galland believed that if the bombers could be dealt such a blow in one day they would be forced to suspend their campaign against Germany's oil.

However, circumstances chipped away at Galland's plan. The enemy bombers appeared a total of 13 days that November, unloading their highest tonnage ever on the oil targets. The Luftwaffe had to commit reserve planes to fend off the raiders, and in just four days of fierce combat the Germans lost a total of nearly 300 pilots killed or wounded. Then, in mid-November, Hitler took away the remaining fighters Galland had assembled for his Great Blow and sent them to the Western Front in preparation for the big counteroffensive in the Ardennes.

Hitler wanted the fighters to stage a massive surprise strafing attack on Allied forward airfields in Holland, Belgium and France, then provide air cover for his panzers' advance. The panzers moved on December 16, but thick winter fog delayed the Luftwaffe's assault on the Allied air bases. By the time it was launched on the morning of New Year's Day, 1945, the huge German fighter force had been whittled to less than half by Allied strafing and by combat in the skies over the front lines.

The New Year's strike force consisted of nearly 900 Messerschmitts and Focke-Wulfs, practically the entire available strength of the Luftwaffe's fighter arm. Many of the pilots were ill-trained novices, and some of the older hands were hung over after a celebration of what they believed would be their last New Year's Eve. As a result, many pilots never found the Allied bases. But others did, and they caught several of the bases by complete surprise. They destroyed or severely damaged 206 enemy planes, most of them still parked on the ground.

Elsewhere, U.S. and British fighters quickly rose to the defense, and furious aerial combat ensued. At the U.S. base at Asch, in Belgium, a dozen Mustangs were taking off shortly before 10 a.m. when 50 German raiders swooped down. The Mustangs were led by Lieut. Colonel John C. Meyer, deputy commander of the 352nd Group and a fighter ace. Had Meyer followed the official orders for the day, his pilots would have been in their snow-covered tents preparing for a bomber-escort mission to Germany. But earlier that morning, on a hunch that the Luftwaffe might show up over the Ardennes front, Meyer had talked his commanding general into permitting part of his group to remain behind to fly a tactical patrol.

Meyer was leading his Mustangs off the runway when he suddenly looked up and saw an FW-190 coming straight at a nearby transport plane on the field. He quickly pulled up his landing gear, gave the Mustang full throttle and gunned down the intruder. For the next hour, Meyer and his pilots tangled with the Germans while frantically dodging barrages of antiaircraft fire from American gunners around the base. Though Meyer lost a chunk of his wing to his own ground gunners and almost ran out of ammunition, he survived both the flak and the enemy fighters. His Mustangs destroyed nearly half of the 50 raiding planes.

Meyer was credited with two Focke-Wulfs shot down that morning, giving him a total of 24 aerial victories for the War.

A group of three Spitfires, piloted by French exiles serving with the RAF, prepares to make a landing near others on a recaptured airfield at Luxeuil-les-Bains, France, in September 1944. American bombers demolished the hangars and the Luftwaffe plane at left before the Germans retreated.

These kills made him one of the highest-scoring American aces in Europe. That afternoon, Meyer safely flew a tactical patrol mission. Soon afterward, he was grounded for the duration of the War—by injuries suffered in an automobile accident.

Asch was only one of the bases over which the German raiders incurred heavy losses. Of the nearly 900 pilots involved in the New Year's mission, 253 were killed, wounded or taken prisoner. This represented the Luftwaffe's largest loss in a single day of the War, and one the Germans could no longer afford. What had begun as Galland's Great Blow had been transformed—by Allied fighter power and by Hitler's meddling—into the Luftwaffe's last gasp.

Early in 1945, the Allied bombers turned their full fury upon the Reich, now virtually defenseless. Vast carpets of bombs unrolled across its cities, leveling those that had escaped Allied attention and piling rubble upon ashes in those that had not. By then, large parts of most big German cities—those with populations of more than 100,000—lay in ruins.

The champion of the area-bombing policy, Air Chief Marshal Harris, had started in early 1943 with a list of 60 cities he intended to destroy, and he kept ticking them off one by one. He persisted despite intense pressure from his boss, Chief of the Air Staff Portal, to concentrate on the top Allied bombing priorities, oil and communications—targets whose destruction was paying far greater dividends to the Allied cause than were being gained by the wholesale onslaught on the cities.

Portal and his superiors questioned only the effectiveness of the area bombing, not its morality. Portal himself had recently put forward a proposal to stage a massive attack on Berlin, calling for round-the-clock punishment by British and U.S. bombers. The purpose of the operation, code-named *Thunderclap*, was to shatter popular morale so that the Germans would give up and sue for peace. However, the operation had been shelved because the Americans could not provide sufficient fighter escort for all the bombers the plan required.

In any case, General Spaatz opposed *Thunderclap* and,

indeed, the entire concept of bombing cities. The U.S. bomber boss said he did not want to be "tarred" with the aftermath—the recriminations that would surely follow after the War. Despite Spaatz's intentions, however, the distinction between British area bombing and U.S. precision attacks was not all that clear. When bad weather prevented the sighting of a target, the American bombardiers resorted to blind bombing, using newly developed radar devices like those employed at night by the British. Bombs dropped by radar—a method exploited at least in part during about 80 per cent of the American raids in the last three months of 1944—sprayed all over the area, spreading destruction far from the refinery or railway marshaling yard that was the specific target. On the average, fewer than one third of the bombs fell within 1,000 feet of the target.

Moreover, early in 1945, after Hitler's Ardennes offensive had shaken Allied confidence in the likelihood of an early end to the War, there was increasing pressure on Spaatz to come up with some decisive, *Thunderclap*-like blow from the air. In this atmosphere of impatience and frustration, Spaatz abandoned his usual stance. On February 3, 1945, he sent nearly 1,000 bombers against Berlin. The raid was directed at rail yards and other transportation targets, but many of the bombs fell on government buildings at the center of the city. Later, Spaatz admitted that his Fortresses had bombed indiscriminately, "making no effort to confine ourselves to military targets." Perhaps 25,000 Berliners died in that raid.

An even deadlier attack on another city soon followed. On February 13 and 14, British and American bombers raided Dresden, 100 miles south of Berlin. The destruction of Dresden became the symbol of the air war's final months of terror from the sky.

On the hit list kept by Air Chief Marshal Harris, Dresden ranked near the bottom; it was, in fact, the largest German city to have escaped full-scale bombing thus far. It had been touched by bombs just twice—in both instances by American planes that were diverted to Dresden's rail yards after clouds obscured their primary targets, oil installations. Dresden had little else of importance to the Allied strategists. Throughout Germany, it was known for its cultural and historical amenities—parks, museums, an opera house and buildings, some of which dated back to the 13th Century. The world beyond Germany identified Dresden with the delicate porcelain that was actually produced in a village about 12 miles away.

The initiative for the attack on Dresden came from Prime Minister Churchill, as part of a larger plan to bomb a number of cities in eastern Germany. Churchill's motive was essentially political. He and President Roosevelt were soon to meet with Stalin at Yalta, and neither Western leader had much to show the Soviet dictator in the way of recent Anglo-American ground successes. The British and U.S. armies were stalled at the western approaches to Germany while a massive Russian Army offensive was in progress along the Reich's eastern borders.

Blasting Dresden and other cities in eastern Germany from the air would give Stalin tangible proof of the efforts of the British and the Americans on Russia's behalf. The raids would not only sow confusion among the hundreds of thousands of Germans fleeing the Red Army offensive, but would also hamper the movement of German troops to the Eastern Front. Not incidentally, the raids would also remind Stalin of the awesome air power possessed by Britain and the United States.

The staff planners at RAF Bomber Command showed no great enthusiasm for hitting Dresden. They knew little about the city's defenses and even lacked a standard target map of the area. Harris himself seemed surprised at his new orders. Some of his squadrons expressed their disapproval of the assignment by voting to forgo a customary ritual—the dropping of bottles, bits of concrete and other junk intended as an insult to the Germans.

Otherwise, the manner in which the attack on Dresden was delivered was, by this late stage of the air war, distinctly routine. On the night of February 13, the British sent two separate waves of Lancasters. The first wave, 234 planes, bombed for 17 minutes. The second wave, 538 planes, arrived three hours later and aimed at the fringes of the spreading flames below. Altogether, the British dropped 2,656 tons of bombs, a load by now regarded as unexceptional. About 75 per cent of the bombs were incendiaries, standard procedure for an old city whose wooden dwellings were so flammable. Some 10 hours after the last British bombs fell, the Americans arrived. It was Ash Wednesday,

Atop Dresden's town hall, a sandstone figure gestures with eerie serenity toward the ruins of the city's old quarter, ravaged in a fire storm set off by Allied bombing in February 1945. A British pilot wrote: "For the first time in many operations I felt sorry for the population below."

and shortly after noon the 311 Flying Fortresses bombed by radar, aiming 771 tons at the city's railway stations and marshaling yards.

What made the Dresden attack so extraordinarily destructive was an unusual combination of circumstances. There was virtually no opposition; the city's antiaircraft guns had been removed the previous month and sent to the Russian front, and though a unit of Me-110 night fighters was based only five miles away, the fuel shortage was now so acute that the pilots were forbidden to take off without authorization from division headquarters. The authorization came too late, and the pilots had to sit in their planes on the runway and watch Dresden burn.

Moreover, the weather over Dresden was unusually clear during the night. The clouds covering Germany broke for a few hours, allowing the RAF's Lancasters to concentrate their bombs with an aiming accuracy that had been perfected after five years of trial and error. Most important, Dresden was woefully unprepared for an attack of such dimensions. In all the city there was but one concrete bunker suitable for a bomb shelter—and it was reserved for the local gauleiter. Neither Dresden's officials nor its citizens had wanted to believe that their city would be bombed. Local rumor had it that Dresden would be spared because the Allies intended to relocate Germany's capital there after the War—or because relatives of Churchill's supposedly resided in the city. The lack of preparedness was compounded by the presence of refugees from the Eastern Front, who had swollen the city's population of 630,000 to well over a million. Many of the refugees came from remote country areas and had never heard an air-raid siren.

Dresden burned for a week. The worst fire came within an hour after the British attack, when thousands of separate blazes merged into a howling fire storm of the type created by the RAF at Hamburg in July of 1943. It engulfed some 1,600 acres, practically the whole of old Dresden, generating winds of tornado force, incinerating everything and everyone in its path, and sucking the life out of those who had attempted to seek refuge in the cellars of the city. A Dresden schoolmaster named Hanns Voigt, who was pressed into service as chief of an emergency agency called the *Abteilung Tote*, or dead-persons department, later described the horror. "Never would I have thought that death could come to so many people in so many different ways," he recalled. "Never had I expected to see people interred in that state: burnt, cremated, torn and crushed to death; sometimes the victims looked like ordinary people apparently peacefully sleeping; the faces of others were racked with pain, the bodies stripped almost naked by the tornado; there were wretched refugees from the East clad only in rags, and people from the Opera in all their finery; here the victim was a shapeless slab, there a layer of ashes shoveled into a zinc tub."

The task of identifying and removing the dead proved so difficult that, to prevent typhus and other epidemics, Dresden's authorities finally cordoned off the center of the city and set up 25-foot-long grills where thousands of the victims were cremated.

Initial estimates of the death toll, ranging as high as 135,000, were later revised downward to 35,000—less than the number of people who had perished at Hamburg in 1943. But the earlier estimates—and an unprecedented barrage of German radio propaganda—served to perpetuate Dresden's tragedy as a symbol of air power gone amok. In the days immediately following the attack, many Americans and Britons became aware for the first time that Allied bombing was not always directed at military and industrial targets—as their governments had led them to believe. On February 17, 1945, an Associated Press dispatch reported that the Allied air chiefs had made the "long-awaited decision to adopt deliberate terror bombing of the great German population centers as a ruthless expedient to hasten Hitler's doom." The dispatch was incorrect in suggesting that the decision was a new one; actually, indiscriminate bombing was by this time an old story—although the Allied chiefs balked at the use of the term "terror bombing."

The Associated Press dispatch was widely published in American newspapers but was suppressed by the British government. Nonetheless, questions about Dresden and area bombing were raised in the House of Commons on March 6. Even Churchill had second thoughts, although he seemed to be less concerned about morality than about Britain's own self-interest.

On March 28, Churchill stated his view in an infelicitously worded memorandum to Chief of the Air Staff Portal. "It seems to me," the Prime Minister wrote, "that the moment has come when the question of bombing German cities simply for the sake of increasing the terror, though under other pretexts, should be reviewed. Otherwise we shall come into control of an utterly ruined land. We shall not, for instance, be able to get housing material out of Germany for our own needs because some temporary provision would have to be made for the Germans themselves."

The reference to "terror" bombing so incensed Portal that Churchill reworded the memorandum. However, indiscriminate bombing was now clearly out of favor with Churchill, Portal and other officials who had originated the policy even before Air Chief Marshal Harris took over its implementation in 1942. When the British Government showered formal honors on its fighting men at the end of the War, Harris and RAF Bomber Command were to be conspicuously ignored. On the first anniversary of the Dresden raid, Harris retired to Rhodesia.

Despite its powerlessness at Dresden, the Luftwaffe fought on. In March of 1945 it managed to send up 40 or 50 jet fighters at a time to try to fend off new attacks by the Allied bombers. One of the new jet units was led by Adolf Galland, who had begun the War as a squadron commander and wanted to end it in the same capacity. Göring, with Hitler's approval, had finally ousted Galland as the Luftwaffe's fighter chief after he had openly ridiculed the Führer's newest pet scheme for winning the air war. This scheme involved a wonder weapon, not yet operational,

known as the *Volksjäger*—People's Fighter. It was a small, single-engined jet that, as Hitler envisioned it, would be flown by fanatical 16- to 18-year-old boys after a brief period of training in gliders.

To Galland's new unit flocked the Luftwaffe's last surviving aces. So eager were they to serve under him—and to end the War with honor by flying the world's fastest fighter—that several pilots left their hospital beds to join up. Göring himself told Galland that he would have been happy to serve if "I were a few years younger and less bulky."

Galland and his aces, sometimes taking off from bomb-cratered runways and flying against insuperable odds, succeeded in shooting down nearly 50 Allied planes. Then, one April day, Galland's own jet was badly shot up. He skillfully crash-landed it at 150 miles per hour and was taken to the hospital with shell fragments in his knee.

On the previous day, 318 RAF Lancasters had gone after Hitler himself, bombing the Führer's mountain retreat at Berchtesgaden. Hitler was not there. He was 300 miles away in Berlin, holed up in the bombproof bunker where, five days later, he would take his own life.

The mission to Berchtesgaden was one of the last to be flown by the Allied bombers. By April, they had simply run out of targets. On April 16, with the U.S. and Russian ground forces converging in the heart of Germany, the Anglo-American strategic air offensive was officially ended.

The offensive had been waged at a cost of nearly 160,000 Allied airmen—79,265 American, 79,281 British—and an undetermined number of German fliers. The effectiveness of the bombing, as well as the morality of killing an estimated 305,000 German civilians, would be the subject of endless postwar debate. The bombers did not fulfill the dreams of the early prophets who had predicted that air power alone could win a war. Nor did bombing crack the German will to resist. But the Allied ground armies that were now overrunning the Reich were there in large part because of the devastation that had been wrought at such cost by the bomber offensive.

THE AIRMEN'S ARSENAL

BOEING B-17G FLYING FORTRESS

Power plant: Four 1,200-hp Wright Cyclone radial engines
Wing span: 103 ft. 9 in.
Length: 74 ft. 9 in.
Gross weight: 65,000 lbs.
Range: 1,850 miles with 4,000-lb. bombload
Maximum speed: 302 mph at 25,000 ft.
Armament: Thirteen .50-caliber Browning machine guns; standard bombload, 6,000 lbs.; maximum, 12,800 lbs.
Crew: 10

A B-17G, the most numerous of the six operational Flying Fortress models, bears the red and yellow markings of the Eighth Air Force's 487th Bomber Group.

LEAPFROGGING GAINS IN PLANE MAKING

Throughout the War, Britain, the U.S. and Germany engaged in a technological race to equip their air forces with bombers and fighters that could outfly, outshoot and outlast the enemy's planes. Between them, the aviation industries of the combatants built hundreds of thousands of aircraft in hundreds of different models. Some of the most effective and widely used planes are shown on these pages, along with average specifications for the craft.

The balance of power in the air war shifted repeatedly as one side, then the other, produced new planes—or new models of old ones—that had an edge over enemy aircraft. At the outset of the War, Germany possessed thousands of superior Heinkel-111 medium bombers and Messerschmitt-109 fighters; they spearheaded the swift conquest of Poland, France and the Netherlands, and the subsequent assault on Britain. The British, however, countered with the nimble Supermarine Spitfire, which was instrumental in thwarting the Luftwaffe onslaught. When Britain switched to the offensive, their strategic bombers at first were inadequate. But the advent of the heavy, long-range Lancaster, and later American B-17s and B-24s, gave the Allies the most potent bombing trio of the War. The Luftwaffe took a heavy toll of Allied bombers with its relatively new, deadly Focke-Wulf 190s. But the U.S. quashed this threat by producing the P-47 and P-51, brilliant counterfighter fighters with sufficient range to protect bombers on raids far into Germany.

A few great planes—such as the Me-109 or the sleek Boeing B-17—were admired by friend and foe alike. Several important aircraft had equivocal reputations: for example, the hard-to-handle B-26 Marauder, built at Martin's Maryland aircraft plant, was nicknamed the "Baltimore Whore" because its short, stubby wings gave it "no visible means of support." Yet nearly all of the planes were loved by the men who flew them. "To most pilots," said RAF Group Captain Leonard Cheshire, "the aircraft ceased to be just a machine and became almost another person . . . a being to be cherished and looked after, who in turn would respond to one's own demands to an almost superhuman degree."

FOCKE-WULF 190A-8

Power plant: One 1,700-hp BMW radial engine
Wing span: 34 ft. 5½ in.
Length: 29 ft. 4¼ in.
Gross weight: 10,800 lbs.
Effective operating radius: 942 miles with extra fuel tanks
Maximum speed: 408 mph at 20,670 ft.
Armament: Two 13mm MG 131 machine guns and up to four 20mm MG 151 cannon
Crew: One

Powerful and versatile, the Focke-Wulf 190 was considered Germany's best all-

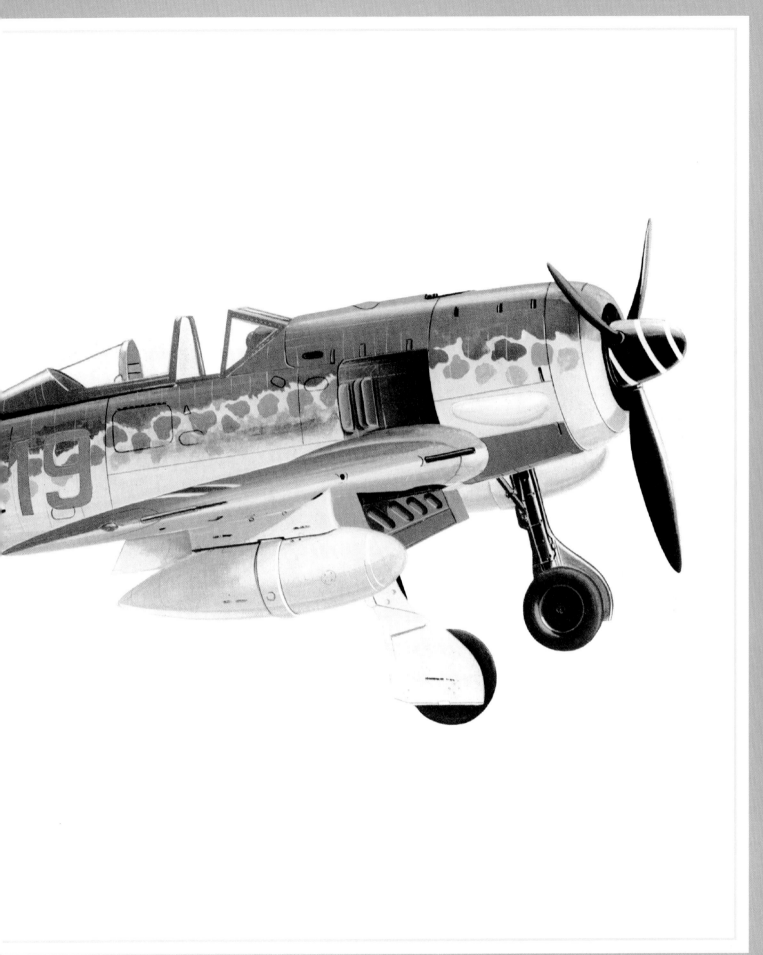

around fighter. Later models, like this camouflaged FW-190A-8, introduced in 1943, were used primarily to intercept enemy bomber formations over the Reich.

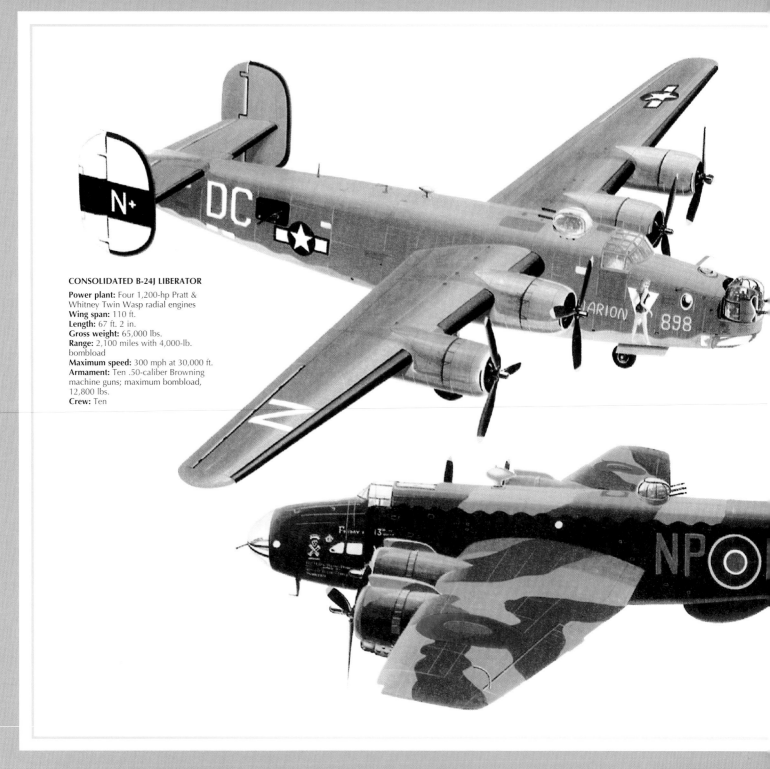

CONSOLIDATED B-24J LIBERATOR

Power plant: Four 1,200-hp Pratt & Whitney Twin Wasp radial engines
Wing span: 110 ft.
Length: 67 ft. 2 in.
Gross weight: 65,000 lbs.
Range: 2,100 miles with 4,000-lb. bombload
Maximum speed: 300 mph at 30,000 ft.
Armament: Ten .50-caliber Browning machine guns; maximum bombload, 12,800 lbs.
Crew: Ten

THE HEAVYWEIGHTS

To hit targets far inside Germany, Britain and the U.S. built several types of long-range, high-altitude heavy bombers. One of the two best British heavyweights was the Handley-Page Halifax, first produced in 1940 and improved steadily in nine subsequent models. The Halifax Mark III, which could carry 13,000 pounds of bombs, was versatile enough to serve as a troop transport, cargo plane, glider tug and antisubmarine patroller.

Overshadowing the Halifax in numbers and performance was the Avro Lancaster, the work horse of RAF Bomber Command. By the War's end, 7,378 Lancasters had flown more than 156,000 sorties to drop 608,612 tons of bombs, more than twice the total load delivered by the Halifaxes.

Of the two U.S. heavy bombers used in Europe, the Boeing B-17 Flying Fortress was more effective, on balance, than the Consolidated B-24 Liberator. But Liberators outnumbered B-17 Flying Fortresses because they were easier to mass produce.

AVRO LANCASTER B. MARK I
Power plant: Four 1,460-hp Rolls-Royce Merlin engines
Wing span: 102 ft.
Length: 69 ft. 6 in.
Gross weight: 68,000 lbs.
Range: 2,530 miles with 7,000-lb. bombload
Maximum speed: 275 mph at 15,000 ft.
Armament: Ten .303-in Browning machine guns; maximum bombload, 14,000 lbs.
Crew: Seven

HANDLEY-PAGE HALIFAX B. MARK III
Power plant: Four 1,615-hp Bristol Hercules radial engines
Wing span: 98 ft. 10 in.
Length: 71 ft. 7 in.
Gross weight: 65,000 lbs.
Range: 1,985 miles with 7,000-lb. bombload
Maximum speed: 282 mph at 13,500 ft.
Armament: One .303-in. Vickers "K" machine gun and four .303-in. Browning machine guns; maximum bombload, 13,000 lbs.
Crew: Seven

From 1941 to the end of the War, some 18,400 B-24s were built by five factories in the U.S.; at Ford Motor Company's half-mile-long aircraft assembly line at Willow Run, Michigan, a Liberator could be produced every 50 minutes. Big and boxy, the B-24 had very long, tapered wings that made for excellent load capacity, and rate of climb and range. But Liberator pilots complained about the bomber's difficult handling above 20,000 feet. Said one, "In the air it was like a fat lady doing a ballet."

These three heavy bombers were improved models of old stand-bys. The B-24J had a new nose turret, revamped fuel lines and a better bomb-sighting system. The Halifax Mark III, shown here with its nose emblazoned with bad-luck signs to ward off evil spirits, had more powerful engines than earlier models. The Lancaster B. Mark I, sporting a painted bomb for each mission, was a four-engined descendant of the Manchester bomber.

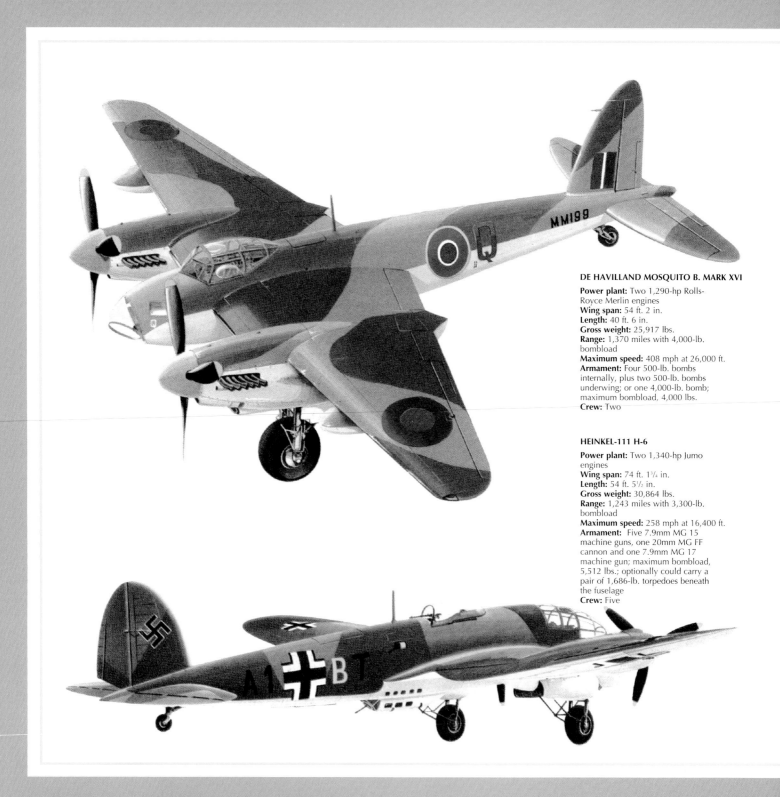

DE HAVILLAND MOSQUITO B. MARK XVI
Power plant: Two 1,290-hp Rolls-Royce Merlin engines
Wing span: 54 ft. 2 in.
Length: 40 ft. 6 in.
Gross weight: 25,917 lbs.
Range: 1,370 miles with 4,000-lb. bombload
Maximum speed: 408 mph at 26,000 ft.
Armament: Four 500-lb. bombs internally, plus two 500-lb. bombs underwing; or one 4,000-lb. bomb; maximum bombload, 4,000 lbs.
Crew: Two

HEINKEL-111 H-6
Power plant: Two 1,340-hp Jumo engines
Wing span: 74 ft. 1¼ in.
Length: 54 ft. 5½ in.
Gross weight: 30,864 lbs.
Range: 1,243 miles with 3,300-lb. bombload
Maximum speed: 258 mph at 16,400 ft.
Armament: Five 7.9mm MG 15 machine guns, one 20mm MG FF cannon and one 7.9mm MG 17 machine gun; maximum bombload, 5,512 lbs.; optionally could carry a pair of 1,686-lb. torpedoes beneath the fuselage
Crew: Five

FOUR FAST BOMBERS

Swifter but smaller than the heavy bombers, with only modest armament and bomb capacity, the medium and light bombers were best suited for short-range tactical air strikes in support of ground troops.

The Germans, who built no successful heavy bombers, believed that large numbers of these fast, agile bombers could do the work of heavyweights, and the Luftwaffe ordered more than 7,000 Heinkel-111s. But the plane, miscast in a strategic

role, lacked adequate firepower and armor and proved vulnerable to British fighters. Along with other Luftwaffe light and medium bombers, it failed to do the damage expected of it.

The Allies used their fast bombers in tactical operations and were more successful. The smooth-flying, dependable Douglas A-20G packed six .50-caliber machine guns in its nose, carried 2,000 pounds of bombs and was deadly in ground attacks

MARTIN B-26C-25 MARAUDER

Power plant: Two 2,000-hp Pratt & Whitney engines
Wing span: 71 ft.
Length: 58 ft. 3 in.
Gross weight: 37,000 lbs.
Range: 1,150 miles with 4,000-lb. bombload
Maximum speed: 317 mph at 14,500 ft.
Armament: Twelve .50-caliber Browning machine guns; maximum bombload, 4,000 lbs.
Crew: Seven

DOUGLAS A-20G HAVOC

Power plant: Two 1,600-hp Wright Double Cyclone radial engines
Wing span: 61 ft. 4 in.
Length: 48 ft.
Gross weight: 24,000 lbs.
Range: 1,025 miles with 2,000-lb. bombload
Maximum speed: 339 mph at 12,400 ft.
Armament: Nine .50-caliber Browning machine guns; maximum bombload, 4,000 lbs.
Crew: Three

and light bombing. The Martin B-26 Marauder was an excellent "medium," but the plane was hampered by temperamental flying characteristics. Pilots joked that the Marauder was a "beautiful piece of machinery, but it will never take the place of the airplane."

Of all the medium and light bombers, the most admired was Britain's wooden De Havilland Mosquito; it was so sturdy, versatile and fast—faster than most fighter planes—that Hermann Göring declared, "I wish someone had brought out a wooden aircraft for me." The Mosquito—"Mossie," the British called it—performed best on low-level, high-speed bombing and target-marking runs. Raids by Mosquitoes inevitably came to be known as "Mosquito bites" and, said Adolf Galland, the fighter chief of the Luftwaffe, "like their namesake they became a plague to our command and the population."

Medium and light bombers, such as the Mosquito B. Mark XVI, Heinkel-111 H-6, B-26B and A-20G, were most effective in attacks on troop concentrations, fuel and ammunition dumps, airfields, ships, railroads and bridges.

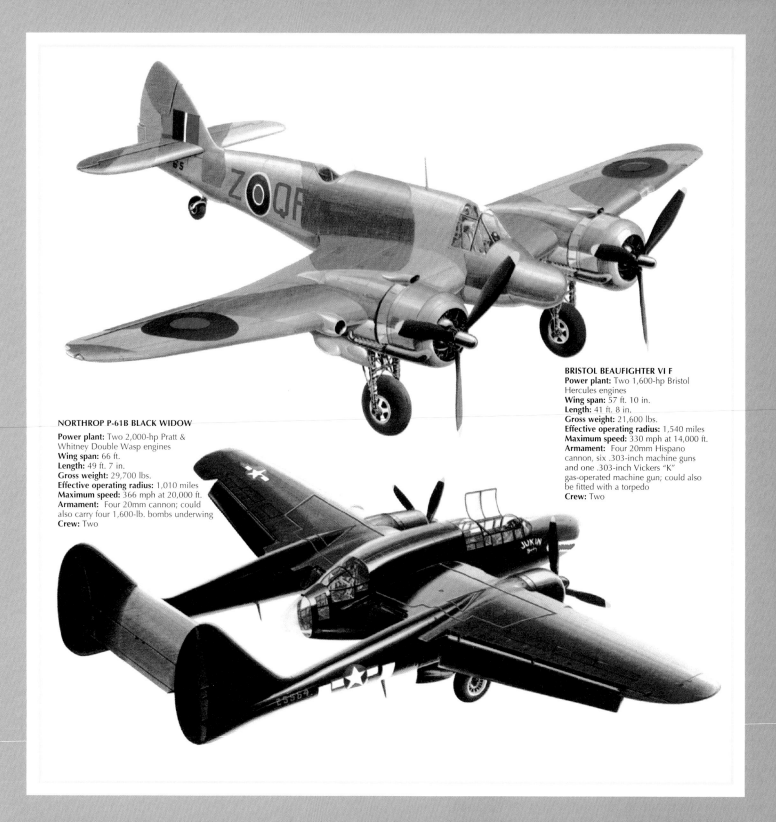

BRISTOL BEAUFIGHTER VI F
Power plant: Two 1,600-hp Bristol Hercules engines
Wing span: 57 ft. 10 in.
Length: 41 ft. 8 in.
Gross weight: 21,600 lbs.
Effective operating radius: 1,540 miles
Maximum speed: 330 mph at 14,000 ft.
Armament: Four 20mm Hispano cannon, six .303-inch machine guns and one .303-inch Vickers "K" gas-operated machine gun; could also be fitted with a torpedo
Crew: Two

NORTHROP P-61B BLACK WIDOW
Power plant: Two 2,000-hp Pratt & Whitney Double Wasp engines
Wing span: 66 ft.
Length: 49 ft. 7 in.
Gross weight: 29,700 lbs.
Effective operating radius: 1,010 miles
Maximum speed: 366 mph at 20,000 ft.
Armament: Four 20mm cannon; could also carry four 1,600-lb. bombs underwing
Crew: Two

SCOURGES OF THE NIGHT

Jolted by the German night blitz of 1940, Britain countered with its radar-equipped night-fighting Bristol Beaufighter. At the time of its debut late that year, the rugged, twin-engined "Beau" was the RAF's only fighter that had the size and power to fly effectively with the bulky Airborne Interception (AI) Mark IV radar gear. The plane was to be a notable success—neutralizing the Luftwaffe's advantage in night attacks.

When the RAF retaliated with strategic bombing of its own, The Luftwaffe hastily modified two of its mainstays, the Junkers-88C and Messerschmitt-110, to serve as night fighters. Both planes were outfitted with primitive radar, whose cumbersome antenna array cut their top speed by 25 miles per hour and significantly reduced their climbing rate and ceiling.

The United States was a late entrant in

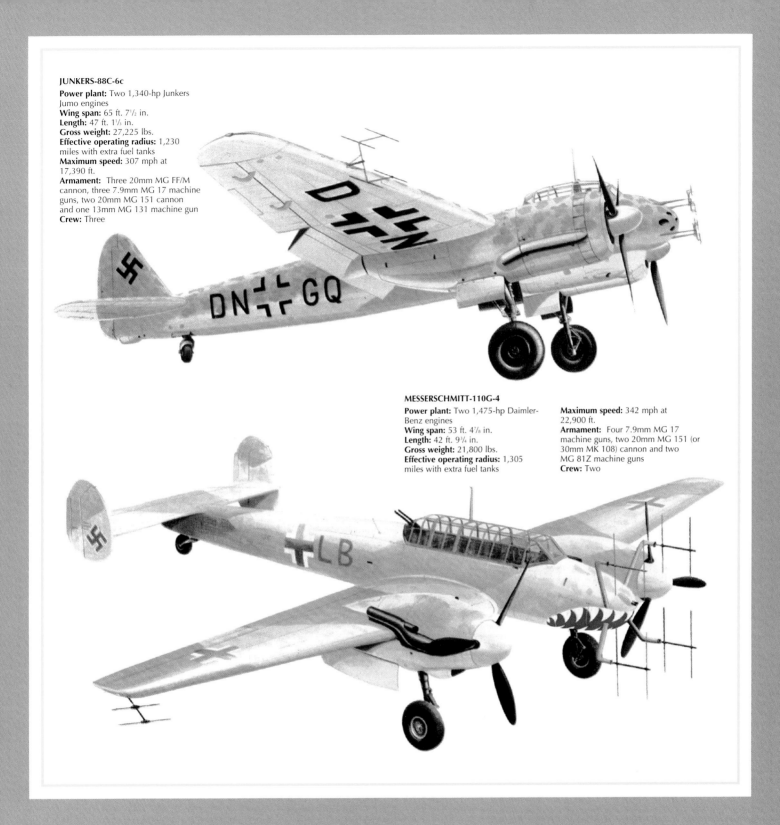

JUNKERS-88C-6c

Power plant: Two 1,340-hp Junkers Jumo engines
Wing span: 65 ft. 7½ in.
Length: 47 ft. 1⅓ in.
Gross weight: 27,225 lbs.
Effective operating radius: 1,230 miles with extra fuel tanks
Maximum speed: 307 mph at 17,390 ft.
Armament: Three 20mm MG FF/M cannon, three 7.9mm MG 17 machine guns, two 20mm MG 151 cannon and one 13mm MG 131 machine gun
Crew: Three

MESSERSCHMITT-110G-4

Power plant: Two 1,475-hp Daimler-Benz engines
Wing span: 53 ft. 4⅞ in.
Length: 42 ft. 9¾ in.
Gross weight: 21,800 lbs.
Effective operating radius: 1,305 miles with extra fuel tanks

Maximum speed: 342 mph at 22,900 ft.
Armament: Four 7.9mm MG 17 machine guns, two 20mm MG 151 (or 30mm MK 108) cannon and two MG 81Z machine guns
Crew: Two

the night-fighter race. However, the twin-fuselage Northrop P-61 Black Widow that was introduced in 1944 was the first airplane designed expressly for night fighting, and it caused a sensation. Two Pratt & Whitney Double Wasp engines, the most powerful motors available, were needed to drive the P-61, whose combat weight of 28,000 pounds made it the heaviest fighter of the War.

Night fighters equipped with radar gear were used almost exclusively as interceptors. The Junkers-88C-6c was the Luftwaffe's most potent night aircraft, while the American P-61B was the Allies' most advanced model.

THE FIGHTERS: DAZZLING AERIAL ACROBATS

The most glamorous performers of the air war were the swift, acrobatic fighters that flew escort and intercepted bombers and staged low-level attacks. The pacesetting early fighters were the RAF's Supermarine Spitfire and the Luftwaffe's Messerschmitt-

109. The two remained archrivals throughout the War—the Spitfire relying on unmatched maneuverability, the Me-109 on its superior climbing rate and its performance at high altitudes.

The outstanding American fighters were the heavily armed Republic P-47 Thunderbolt—nicknamed "The Jug" because of its bulky body—and the North American P-51 Mustang, a favorite of pilots. The Mustang's sleek airframe, large fuel capacity and powerful Rolls-Royce Merlin engines combined to produce the high speed, long range and maneuverability that made the P-51 the War's best all-around fighter.

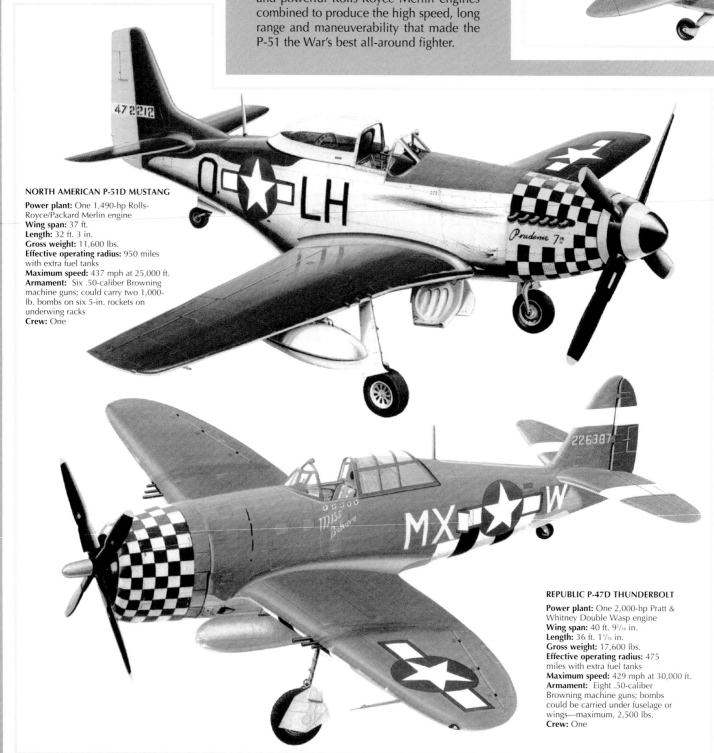

NORTH AMERICAN P-51D MUSTANG
Power plant: One 1,490-hp Rolls-Royce/Packard Merlin engine
Wing span: 37 ft.
Length: 32 ft. 3 in.
Gross weight: 11,600 lbs.
Effective operating radius: 950 miles with extra fuel tanks
Maximum speed: 437 mph at 25,000 ft.
Armament: Six .50-caliber Browning machine guns; could carry two 1,000-lb. bombs on six 5-in. rockets on underwing racks
Crew: One

REPUBLIC P-47D THUNDERBOLT
Power plant: One 2,000-hp Pratt & Whitney Double Wasp engine
Wing span: 40 ft. 9⁵⁄₁₆ in.
Length: 36 ft. 1¹⁄₁₆ in.
Gross weight: 17,600 lbs.
Effective operating radius: 475 miles with extra fuel tanks
Maximum speed: 429 mph at 30,000 ft.
Armament: Eight .50-caliber Browning machine guns; bombs could be carried under fuselage or wings—maximum, 2,500 lbs.
Crew: One

A P-51D and a P-47D bear checkerboard markings on their noses so that American pilots would not mistake them for the enemy in the heat of battle.

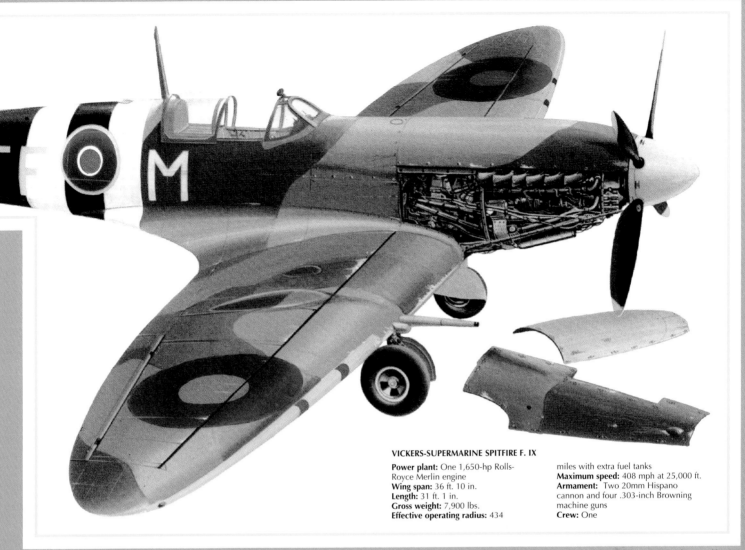

VICKERS-SUPERMARINE SPITFIRE F. IX

Power plant: One 1,650-hp Rolls-Royce Merlin engine
Wing span: 36 ft. 10 in.
Length: 31 ft. 1 in.
Gross weight: 7,900 lbs.
Effective operating radius: 434

miles with extra fuel tanks
Maximum speed: 408 mph at 25,000 ft.
Armament: Two 20mm Hispano cannon and four .303-inch Browning machine guns
Crew: One

Its cowling removed, the Supermarine Spitfire F. IX shows its powerful new engine, which enabled it to compete with the swift and evasive Focke-Wulf 190.

MESSERSCHMITT-109G-6/R6

Power plant: One 1,475-hp Daimler-Benz engine
Wing span: 32 ft. 6½ in.
Length: 29 ft. 8 in.
Gross weight: 7,491 lbs.
Effective operating radius: 650

miles with extra fuel tanks
Maximum speed: 386 mph at 22,640 ft.
Armament: Three 20mm MG 151 cannon and two 13mm MG 131 machine guns
Crew: One

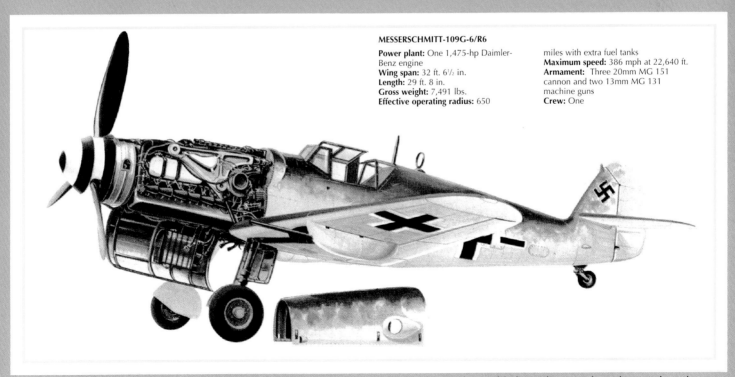

The Me-109G-6, a late model of the original plane, was equipped with a fuel-injection system that enabled it to dive steeply—a key combat advantage.

BIBLIOGRAPHY

Anderson, Wing Commander William, *Pathfinders*. Jarrolds Ltd., 1946.

Andrews, Allen, *The Air Marshals*. William Morrow & Co., Inc., 1970.

Angelucci, Enzo, and Paolo Matricardi, *World War II Airplanes*, Vols. I, II. Rand McNally & Co., 1978.

Arnold, H. H., *Global Mission*. Harper & Bros., 1949.

Barker, Ralph, *The Thousand Plane Raid*. Ballantine Books, Inc., 1965.

Beauman, Wing Commander Bentley, *The Airmen Speak*. Doubleday, Doran & Co., Inc., 1941.

Bekker, Cajus, *The Luftwaffe War Diaries*. Ballantine Books, Inc., 1969.

Bishop, Edward, *The Wooden Wonder*. Max Parrish & Co. Ltd., 1959.

Bombers' Battle: Bomber Command's Three Years of War. Duckworth, 1943.

Bowyer, Chaz, *History of the RAF*. Bison Books Ltd., 1977.

Boyle, Andrew, *Trenchard*. W. W. Norton & Co., Inc., 1962.

Braddon, Russell, *Cheshire V.C.* Arrow Books Ltd., 1966.

Brereton, Lieut. General Lewis H., *The Brereton Diaries*. William Morrow and Co., 1946.

Bridgman, Leonard, ed., *Jane's All the World's Aircraft 1945/6*. David and Charles, Ltd., 1970.

Brookes, Andrew J., *Photo Reconnaissance*. Ian Allan Ltd., 1975.

Brown, Anthony Cave, *Bodyguard of Lies*. Bantam Books, Inc., 1976.

Caidin, Martin:
 Flying Forts. Meredith Press, 1968.
 Me 109: Willy Messerschmitt's Peerless Fighter. Ballantine Books, Inc., 1968.

Campbell, James, *The Bombing of Nuremberg*. Doubleday & Co., Inc., 1974.

Carter, Kit C., and Robert Mueller, *The Army Air Forces in World War II: Combat Chronology 1941-1945*. Office of Air Force History, 1973.

Carver, Field Marshal Sir Michael, *The War Lords*. Little, Brown and Co., 1976.

Cheshire, Squadron-Leader Leonard, *Bomber Pilot*. Hutchinson & Co. Ltd., no date.

Churchill, Winston S.:
 The Second World War. Houghton Mifflin Company.
 Vol. II, *Their Finest Hour*. 1949.
 Vol. III, *The Grand Alliance*. 1950.
 Vol. IV, *The Hinge of Fate*. 1962.

Coffey, Thomas M., *Decision over Schweinfurt*. David McKay Co., Inc., 1977.

Cole, Hugh M., *United States Army in World War II*. Office of the Chief of Military History, 1965.

Craven, Wesley Frank, and James Lea Cate, eds.:
 The Army Air Forces in World War II. The Univ. of Chicago Press.
 Vol. I, *Plans and Early Operations, January 1939 to August 1942*. 1948.
 Vol. II, *Europe: Torch to Pointblank, August 1942 to December 1943*. 1949.
 Vol. III, *Europe: Argument to V-E Day, January 1944 to May 1945*. 1951.
 Vol. VI, *Men and Planes*. 1955.

Divine, David, *The Broken Wing*. Hutchinson & Co. Ltd., 1966.

Dugan, James, and Carroll Stewart, *Ploesti*. Random House, Inc., 1962.

Earle, Edward Mead, ed., *Makers of Modern Strategy*. Princeton Univ. Press, 1944.

Ford, Brian:
 Allied Secret Weapons: The War of Science. Ballantine Books, Inc., 1971.
 German Secret Weapons: Blueprint for Mars. Ballantine Books, Inc., 1969.

Frank, Howard, *The Conquest of the Air*. Random House, Inc., 1972.

Frankland, Noble, *Bomber Offensive: The Devastation of Europe*. Ballantine Books, Inc., 1970.

Freeman, Roger A.:
 The Mighty Eighth. Doubleday and Co., Inc., 1970.
 The U.S. Strategic Bomber. Macdonald and Jane's, 1975.

Galland, Adolf, *The First and the Last*. Henry Holt and Co., 1954.

Gibson, Wing Commander Guy, E*nemy Coast Ahead*. Michael Joseph Ltd., 1953.

Gilbert, James, *The World's Worst Aircraft*. M. & J. Hobbs Ltd. and Michael Joseph Ltd., 1975.

Goddard, Brigadier General George W., USAF (Ret.), *Overview*. Doubleday & Co., Inc., 1969.

Godfrey, John T., *The Look of Eagles*. Random House, Inc., 1958.

Goldberg, Alfred, ed., *A History of the United States Air Force*. Arno Press, 1974.

Green, William:
 Famous Bombers of the Second World War. Doubleday and Co., Inc., 1959.
 Famous Fighters of the Second World War. Hanover House, 1960.
 Warplanes of the Third Reich. Doubleday and Co., Inc., 1970.

Gunston, Bill, *Night Fighters*. Charles Scribner's Sons, 1976.

Hall, Grover C., Jr., *1,000 Destroyed*. Brown Printing Co., 1946.

Hallion, Richard P., *Legacy of Flight*. Univ. of Washington Press, 1977.

Harris, Marshal of the R.A.F. Sir Arthur, *Bomber Offensive*. Collins, 1947.

Hess, William N., *Fighting Mustang*. Doubleday and Co., Inc., 1970.

Higham, Robin, and Abigail T. Siddall, *Flying Combat Aircraft of the USAAF-USAF*. Iowa State Univ. Press, 1975.

IMPACT, Vol. 1, 1943; Vol. II, 1944; Vol. III, 1945. United States Air Force.

Infield, Glenn B., *Unarmed and Unafraid*. The Macmillan Co., 1970.

Irving, David:
 The Destruction of Dresden. Holt, Rinehart and Winston, 1963.
 The Rise and Fall of the Luftwaffe. Little, Brown and Co., 1973.

Jablonski, Edward, *Airwar*, Vols. I, II, III, IV. Doubleday & Co., Inc., 1971.

Jones, R. V., *The Wizard War*. Coward, McCann & Geoghegan, Inc., 1978.

Kirk, John, and Robert Young Jr., *Great Weapons of World War II*. Walker and Co., 1961.

Lawrence, W. J., *No. 5 Bomber Group R.A.F.* Faber and Faber Ltd., 1951.

LeMay, General Curtis E., and MacKinlay Kantor, *Mission with LeMay*. Doubleday & Co., Inc., 1965.

Longmate, Norman, *The G.I.'s: The Americans in Britain 1942-1945*. Hutchinson of London, 1975.

Lyall, Gavin, ed., *The War in the Air*. William Morrow & Co., Inc., 1968.

McCrary, Captain John R., and David E. Scherman, *First of the Many*. Simon and Schuster, 1944.

Maurer, Maurer, ed.:
 Air Force Combat Units of World War II. USAF Historical Div., 1960.
 Combat Squadrons of the Air Force, World War II. USAF Historical Div., 1969.

Michie, Allan A., *The Air Offensive against Germany*. Henry Holt and Co., 1943.

Middlebrook, Martin, *The Nuremberg Raid*. William Morrow & Co., Inc., 1973.

Moyes, Philip J. R., *Royal Air Force Bombers of World War II*. Doubleday & Co., Inc., 1968.

Obermeier, Ernst, *Die Ritterkreuzträger der Luftwaffe*. Verlag Dieter Hoffmann, Mainz, 1966.

Olsen, Jack, *Aphrodite: Desperate Mission*. G. P. Putnam's Sons, 1970.

Price, Alfred:
 Battle over the Reich. Charles Scribner's Sons, 1973.
 Instruments of Darkness. Macdonald and Jane's, 1977.
 Luftwaffe: Birth, Life and Death of an Air Force. Ballantine Books Inc., 1971.

Redding, Major John M., and Captain Harold I. Leyshon, *Skyways to Berlin*. Bobbs-Merrill Co., 1943.

Reit, Seymour, *Masquerade: The Amazing Camouflage Deceptions of World War II*. Hawthorn Books, Inc., 1978.

Revie, Alastair, *The Lost Command*. Corgi Books, 1972.

Richards, Denis:
 Royal Air Force 1939-1945. Her Majesty's Stationery Office.
 Vol. I, *The Fight at Odds*. 1974.
 Vol. II, *The Fight Avails*. 1954.

Roseberry, C. R., *The Challenging Skies*. Doubleday & Co., Inc., 1966.

Rumpf, Hans, *The Bombing of Germany*. Holt, Rinehart and Winston, 1961.

Rust, Kenn C.:
 Fifteenth Air Force Story. Historical Aviation Album, 1976.
 The 9th Air Force in World War II. Aero Publishers, Inc., 1970.

Saundby, Air Marshal Sir Robert, *Air Bombardment*. Chatto & Windus Ltd., 1961.

Saunders, Hilary St. George, *Royal Air Force 1939-1945*, Vol. III, *The Fight is Won*. Her Majesty's Stationery Office, 1975.

Saward, Group Captain Dudley, *The Bomber's Eye*. Cassel and Co., Ltd., 1959.

Shepherd, Christopher, *German Aircraft of World War II*. Stein and Day, 1976.

Shores, Christopher, and Clive Williams, *Aces High*. Neville Spearman Ltd., 1966.

Sims, Edward H.:
 American Aces. Harper & Bros., 1968.
 The Greatest Aces. Harper & Row, 1967.

Smith, Constance Babington, *Evidence in Camera*. David & Charles Ltd., 1974.

Smith, Melden E., Jr., *The Bombing of Dresden Reconsidered*. Unpublished manuscript, 1971.

Speer, Albert, *Inside the Third Reich*. The Macmillan Co., 1970.

Tantum, W. H. IV., and E. J. Hoffschmidt, eds., *The Rise and Fall of the German Air Force (1933 to 1945)*. WE Inc., 1969.

Target: Germany—The Army Air Forces' Official Story of the VIII Bomber Command's First Year over Europe. Simon and Schuster, 1943.

Taylor, John W. R., *A History of Aerial Warfare*. Hamlyn Publishing Group Ltd., 1974.

Taylor, John W. R., and Kenneth Munson, *History of Aviation*. Crown Publishers, Inc., 1977.

Tedder, Marshal of the Royal Air Force Lord, *With Prejudice*. Little, Brown and Co., 1966.

Toliver, Colonel Raymond F., USAF (Ret.), and Trevor J. Constable, *Fighter Aces of the Luftwaffe*. Aero Publishers, Inc., 1977.

Tubbs, D. B., *Lancaster Bomber*. Ballantine Books Inc., 1972.

Turner, Lieut. Colonel Richard E., USAF (Ret.), *Big Friend, Little Friend*. Doubleday & Co., Inc., 1969.

United States Army Air Forces, *The United States Strategic Bombing Survey*. 1945.

Vader, John, *Spitfire*. Ballantine Books Inc., 1969.

Verrier, Anthony, *The Bomber Offensive*. The Macmillan Co., 1968.

Weal, Elke Co., compiler, *Combat Aircraft of World War II*. Macmillan Publishing Co., Inc., 1977.

Webster, Sir Charles, and Noble Frankland, *The Strategic Air Offensive Against Germany 1939-1945*, Vols. I, II, III, IV. Her Majesty's Stationery Office, 1961.

Whitehouse, Arch, *The Years of the War Birds*. Doubleday & Co., Inc., 1960.

Wilmot, Chester, *The Struggle for Europe*. Collins, 1952.

Wolff, Leon, *Low Level Mission*. Doubleday & Co., Inc., 1957.

Zuckerman, Solly, *From Apes to Warlords*. Harper & Row, 1978.

PICTURE CREDITS
Credits from left to right are separated by semicolons, from top to bottom by dashes.

DUST JACKET, COVER, and page 1: U.S. Air Force. 2, 3: Map and legend by Elie Sabban.

FORGING A MIGHTY WEAPON—8, 9: Radio Times Hulton Picture Library, London. 10: Flight International, London. 11: U.S. Air Force. 12: National Air and Space Museum, Smithsonian Institution. 13: National Air and Space Museum, Smithsonian Institution, copied by Charlie Brown; U.S. Air Force—Lockheed-California Company, inset, Wide World. 14, 15: U.S. Air Force; Bildarchiv Preussischer Kulturbesitz, Berlin—John W. R. Taylor, Sorbiton, Surrey; National Air and Space Museum, Smithsonian Institution, copied by Charlie Brown. 16, 17: Radio Times Hulton Picture Library, London; U.S. Air Force—National Air and Space Museum, Smithsonian Institution; Pilot Press Ltd., Bromley, Kent. 18, 19: U.S. Navy, National Archives; British Airways—Douglas Aircraft Company; U.S. Navy, National Archives. 20, 21: Flight International, London—United Press International; United Press International—Flight International, London. 22, 23: National Air and Space Museum, Smithsonian Institution, copied by Charlie Brown—courtesy Pan American Airways; U.S. Air Force.

BRITAIN GOES IT ALONE—26: Imperial War Museum, London. 27: Stato Maggiore Aeronautica, Rome. 28: Bruce Robertson, London. 30: Imperial War Museum, London; The Auckland Collection, St. Albans, Herts. 32: Radio Times Hulton Picture Library, London. 34: Flight International, London. 37: Ullstein Bilderdienst, Berlin. 38: Imperial War Museum, London.

HARD TIMES FOR THE RAF—40, 41: Painting by Frank Wootton, courtesy RAF Strike Command Headquarters, High Wycombe. 42: Radio Times Hulton Picture Library, London. 43: Painting by Frank Wootton, courtesy M. Mandall. 44, 45: Painting by Frank Wootton, courtesy RAF Strike Command, 11 Group, Bentley Priory, Stanmore; painting by Frank Wootton—United Press International. 46, 47: Painting by Frank Wootton, owned by the artist and on loan to the National Air and Space Museum, Smithsonian Institution; Imperial War Museum, London—Painting by Frank Wootton, courtesy RAF Strike Command, 11 Group, Bentley Priory, Stanmore. 48, 49: Painting by Frank Wootton, courtesy RAF, Waddington, Lincolnshire—Radio Times Hulton Picture Library, London; painting by Frank Wootton, courtesy RAF Strike Command Headquarters, High Wycombe. 50, 51: Painting by Frank Wootton, courtesy RAF Staff College, Bracknell.

"BOMBER" HARRIS TAKES OVER—54: Imperial War Museum, London. 56: Bob Landry for LIFE. 57: Imperial War Museum, London. 61: Map by Elie Sabban.

ALL-SEEING EYES IN THE SKY—66, 67: Radio Times Hulton Picture Library, London. 69: British Official. 70, 71: U.S. Air Force—Andreas Feininger for LIFE; Radio Times Hulton Picture Library, London. 72, 73: U.S. Air Force, except top right, British Official. 74: Radio Times Hulton Picture Library, London—Imperial War Museum, London. 75-79: U.S. Air Force.

BOMBING ROUND THE CLOCK—82: U.S. Air Force. 84: Courtesy Chaz Bowyer, Norfolk, England. 87: U.S. Air Force. 88: United Press International; U.S. Air Force. 89: Illustration by Martin Caidin from the book *Flying Forts* by Martin Caidin. 91: Imperial War Museum, London. 92: Diagram adapted by John Batchelor from *Allied Secret Weapons: The War of Science*, by Brian J. Ford, © 1971 by Brian J. Ford. Reprinted by permission of Ballantine Books, a division of Random House, Inc. 94: Imperial War Museum, London.

ANATOMY OF A MISSION—96, 97: U.S. Air Force. 98: David E. Scherman for LIFE. 99-103: U.S. Air Force. 104, 105: United Press International, except top left, U.S. Air Force. 106, 107: U.S. Air Force. 108,109: U.S. Air Force, except top left, David E. Scherman for LIFE. 110, 111: Imperial War Museum, London, inset, U.S. Air Force.

A HAZARDOUS CALLING—112,113: U.S. Air Force. 114: Wide World. 115: U.S. Air Force. 116: ADN-Zentralbild, Berlin, DDR. 117: U.S. Air Force. 118,119: U.S. Air Force, except bottom right, Wide World. 120-123: U.S. Air Force. 124: Imperial War Museum, London, except center, U.S. Air Force (2). 125: U.S. Air Force, courtesy United Press International; U.S. Air Force (2)—Imperial War Museum, London (2). 126, 127: Ullstein Bilderdienst, Berlin.

THE LUFTWAFFE FIGHTS BACK—131: Ullstein Bilderdienst, Berlin. 133: U.S. Air Force. 136, 138: Ullstein Bilderdienst, Berlin.

THE LUFTWAFFE'S ELITE—140, 141: Bundesarchiv, Koblenz. 142: Ullstein Bilderdienst, Berlin. 143, 144: Bundesarchiv, Koblenz. 145: Ullstein Bilderdienst, Berlin, except top right, Süddeutscher Verlag Bilderdienst, Munich. 146, 147: Bundesarchiv, Koblenz, except bottom left, Süddeutscher Verlag Bilderdienst, Munich. 148: Bundesarchiv, Koblenz. 149: Bundesarchiv, Koblenz—Ullstein Bilderdienst, Berlin. 150, 151: Bundesarchiv, Koblenz.

SUPREMACY IN THE SKY—154, 156: U.S. Air Force. 159: Courtesy Ernst Obermeier, Munich; Ullstein Bilderdienst, Berlin (2)—Imperial War Museum, London (3)—U.S. Air Force (3). 161, 163: U.S. Air Force.

AIR SUPPORT FOR THE ARMY—166, 167: U.S. Air Force. 168: Radio Times Hulton Picture Library, London. 169-171: U.S. Air Force. 172,173: U.S. Air Force (2); U.S. Army. 174: Imperial War Museum, London—Crown Copyright. 175: U.S. Air Force—United Press International. 176, 177: U.S. Air Force; U.S. Army.

THE FINAL ONSLAUGHT—181, 183: U.S. Air Force. 187: U.S. Army. 189: Ullstein Bilderdienst, Berlin.

THE AIRMEN'S ARSENAL—192-203: Illustrations by John Batchelor, London.

ACKNOWLEDGMENTS

For help given in preparing this book the editors are especially grateful to Dana Bell, Archives Technician, U.S. Air Force Still Photo Depository, Arlington, Va., and Donald S. Lopez, Assistant Director for Aeronautics, National Air and Space Museum, Washington, D.C. The editors also wish to express their gratitude to Virginia Bader, Virginia Bader Fine Arts, Washington, D.C.; Ian Ballantine, Bantam Books Inc., New York; Denis Bateman, Air Historical Branch, London; Hans Becker, ADN-Zentralbild, Berlin, German Democratic Republic; Carole Boutté, Senior Researcher, U.S. Army Audio-Visual Activity, Pentagon, Arlington, Va.; Chaz Bowyer, Norwich, England; Walter J. Boyne, Curator of Aeronautics, National Air and Space Museum, Washington, D.C.; Jack Bruce, RAF Museum, Hendon, England; Harry E. Calkins, Manager, Editorial Services, Douglas Aircraft Company, Long Beach, Calif.; Contessa Maria Fede Caproni, Museo Aeronautica Caproni di Taliedo, Rome; Alan Cooper, Kent, England; V. M. Destefano, Chief of Research Library, U.S. Army Audio-Visual Activity, Pentagon, Arlington, Va.; Ensign Robert C. Dobson, USN, Naval Air Station, Whiting Field, Milton, Fla.; James N. Eastman Jr., Chief, Research Branch, Albert F. Simpson Historical Research Center, USAF, Maxwell Air Force Base, Montgomery, Ala.; HansJoachim Ebert, Messerschmitt-Bölkow-Blohm, Munich; Robert C. Ferguson, Public Relations Photo Coordinator, Lockheed-California Company, Burbank, Calif.; Virginia Fincik, Chief, Research Unit, U.S. Air Force Still Photo Deposi-tory, Arlington, Va.; Frederic G. Fleming, Port Washington, N.Y.; Ulrich Frodien, Süddeutscher Verlag, Munich; Adolf Galland, General (Ret.), Bonn-Bad Godesberg, Germany; Amy Geoghegan, Archives Technician, U.S. Air Force Still Photo Depository, Arlington, Va.; Marylou Gjernes, Curator, Center of Military History, Department of the Army, Alexandria, Va.; Robert L. Griffin, Colonel, CAF, Director of Operations, Confederate Air Force, Harlingen, Tex.; David O. Hale, Woodbridge, Va.; Gerard E. Hasselwander, Historian, Albert F. Simpson Historical Research Center, USAF, Maxwell Air Force Base, Montgomery, Ala.; Dr. Matthias Haupt, Bundesarchiv, Koblenz, Germany; WernerHaupt, Bibliothek für Zeitgeschichte, Stuttgart; William Holland, Meridale, N.Y.; Colonel Peter Jungmichel, Air Attaché, Embassy of the Federal Republic of Germany, Washington, D.C.; Dr. Roland Klemig, Bildarchiv Preussischer Kulturbesitz, Berlin; William H. Leary, Archivist, National Archives, Still Photo Branch, Washington, D.C.; Rolf-Ole Lehmann, Lütjenburg, Germany; Library of the New York State University Agricultural and Technical College at Delhi, N.Y.; Margaret B. Livesay, Chief, U.S. Air Force Still Photo Depository, Arlington, Va.; Robert B. Meyer Jr., Curator of Aero-Propulsion, National Air and Space Museum, Washington, D.C.; Ernst Obermeier, Munich; Janusz Piekalkiewicz, Rösrath-Hoffnungsthal, Germany; Dominick A. Pisano, Reference Librarian, National Air and Space Museum, Washington, D.C.; Mrs. Alice Price, Administrator, Air Force Art Program, U.S. Pentagon, Washington, D.C.; Hans Ring, Ubersee-München, Germany; David Schoem, Chief, Support Division, Headquarters USAF, Office of Air Force History, Washington, D.C.; Axel Schulz, Ullstein Bilderdienst, Berlin; Mindy K. Small, Archives Technician, U.S. Air Force Still Photo Depository, Arlington, Va.; Melden E. Smith Jr., Boston State College, Boston; Virginia Smith, Archives Technician, U.S. Air Force Still Photo Depository, Arlington, Va.; Jay P. Spenser, Research Assistant, National Air and Space Museum, Washington, D.C.; Lieut. Colonel Roy M. Stanley II, USAF, Fairfax, Va.; Stato Maggiore Aeronautica, Rome; James Stewart, Dayton, Ohio; Richard L. Thurm, Archivist, National Archives Still Photo Branch, Washington, D.C.; James H. Trimble, Archivist, National Archives Still Photo Branch, Washington, D.C.; Alison Uppard, RAF Museum, Hendon, England; Ann White, Public Relations, Pan American Airways, N.Y.; Paul L. White, Archivist, National Archives Still Photo Branch, Washington, D.C.; Alan Williams, Imperial War Museum, London; Marjorie Willis, Radio Times Hulton Picture Library, London.

The index for this book was prepared by Nicholas J. Anthony.

205

INDEX

Numerals in italics indicate an illustration of the subject mentioned.

Printed in U.S.A.